imagining the Turkish House

A

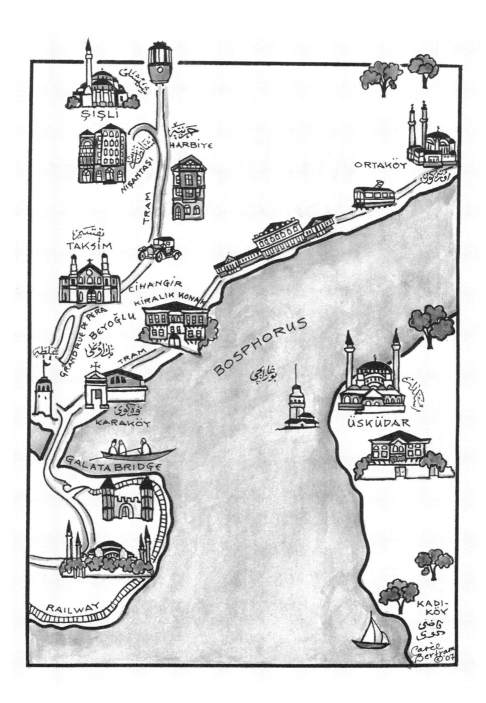

IMAGINING
the
Turkish
House

*Collective Visions
of Home*

CAREL BERTRAM

University of Texas Press　Austin

COPYRIGHT © 2008 BY THE UNIVERSITY OF TEXAS PRESS
All rights reserved
Printed in the United States of America
First edition, 2008

Requests for permission to reproduce material from this work
should be sent to:
  Permissions
  University of Texas Press
  P.O. Box 7819
  Austin, TX 78713-7819
  www.utexas.edu/utpress/about/bpermission.html

♾ The paper used in this book meets the minimum requirements
of ANSI/NISO Z39.48-1992 (R1997) (Permanence of Paper).

LIBRARY OF CONGRESS CATALOGING-IN-PUBLICATION DATA

Bertram, Carel
Imagining the Turkish house : collective visions of home /
Carel Bertram.
    p.   cm.
Includes bibliographical references and index.
    ISBN 978-0-292-71825-8 (cloth : alk. paper) —
    ISBN 978-0-292-71826-5 (pbk. : alk. paper)
1. Architecture, Domestic—Turkey. 2. Architecture, Turkish.
3. Architecture and society—Turkey. I. Title.
    NA7394.B47 2007
    728.094961—dc22   2007042907

To my parents,
Manya and Barry Bertram,
whose love never stopped flowing,
and to Tracy Lord and
Ahmet Turhan Altıner,
who shared the sparkle
of their intelligence and wit.

contents

acknowledgments

No one told me how much I was going to enjoy the research and writing of this book. It was not merely that the topic was endlessly intriguing but that I met and came to know inspiring colleagues who shared my interests or supported my work, and I made friends for life. These people grace the pages of this book, and you will meet many of them in the footnotes. But I want to thank as many as I can here, for without them this book could not resonate, as I hope it does, with so many ideas and so much joy.

I begin with those who contributed to my ability to envision, grasp, play with, and refine my topic and make it into a dissertation. Irene Bierman, my diva graduate advisor, brought me from Berkeley to UCLA to study Islamic art, and then seditiously changed my interests from illustrated manuscripts to architecture and the city. Spiro Kostof, at the end of his life, then welcomed me into the study of the city and spoke with me at length about how to picture the urban. As I was writing my first draft in Turkey, Tracy Lord, with whom I had worked on other Turkish topics, joined my mental conversation, sparking ideas, tossing about concerns, and making the project feel globally important. Ahmet Altıner, architect and lover of the Turkish house, opened a thousand doors and even read aloud from *Kiralık Konak*, becoming Naim Efendi for me. Writing at home, Hasmig Cingöz helped me read between the lines of Nono Bey and other stories of life on the Bosphorus. Research quagmires? My dear Jean Davison, whom I met years ago in Yugoslavia, en route to Turkey, solved them. She even found Turkish sources in London and brought them to Istanbul, along with birthday cake and candles. How can I praise you all enough?

Others who helped as I worked my way into the past were my Turkish teachers, Ralph Jaekel at UCLA and Yildiray Erdener and Sabahat Sansa at UC Berkeley. Sabahat then became a dear friend and muse. Also: Gary

Leiser, who translated the most inscrutable Ottoman texts, Bilge Erengül, who offered cultural translations and good conversation, and the Istanbul *Karagöz* master, Emin Şenyer, who explained how the stage operates and allowed some of his own creations to be used as examples. Also the architect Ali Kamil Yalçın, who walked me through the old houses of Amasya, the Amasyalı Muammer Ülker at the Süleymaniye Library, who let me read anything I wanted, and my talented, devoted, and beloved Amasya sidekick, the internship student Cennet Yumlu, who went on to become a city planner.

On the practical side, Tony Greenwood at the American Research Institute in Turkey lent me his computer every night for months after Fred (all my computers have always been called Fred) had a permanent out-of-body experience. ARIT was one of my financial supporters as well, along with Fulbright Hays, the Council of American Overseas Research Centers, the American Association of University Women, and my parents, Manya and Barry Bertram.

Without Ann Bertram, who read my dissertation through and through, addressing issues, strengths, and weaknesses, this work would never have left the bottom drawer to become a book. What angel made this talented and sensitive thinker move to our street when I was a kid, marry my brother, and then become a crack editor? A final reading was done by Martin Turner, writer and musician, now known as Dr. Comma. The poetic part is that I met him in Amasya when I first began this project, and then he offered to help me tie it up.

My friends were my village: my special Donna Osman Larsen, who has joined me in all my Turkish and other artistic and intellectual meanderings, nursed my soul, and then worked her PhotoShop magic on every single image in this book. Others include Jere Bacharach, Hülya Birtek (who made me endless cups of morning tea in Istanbul), Faruk Birtek, Jane and Bernie Brenner, Pelin and Gülgün Derviş, Michael Esposito, Laurie Firestone, Foster Foreman, Dee Goluba, Dorothé Gould-Pratt (who tried to live long enough to see this in print, but that was asking too much, alas), Aleksandar Ignjatović, Deborah Loft, Amy Mills, Leslie Peirce, Alison Snyder, Denise Spellberg, David Stronach, Paul Young, and the precious Dehen Altıner. Dehen and Ahmet Altıner led me to Elçin Gürkan, who graciously allowed Faiz Bey and Neriman to come to life through her own mother and grandfather's photograph, and to Necdet Sakaoğlu, who kindly allowed his own grandfather to stand in for Naim Efendi. But perhaps most of all, I bless Walter Denny, who gave me my love of Turkey in the first place and then walked with me through Istanbul, semt semt.

By the time this book was ready for a press, the University of Texas Press was ready for me, and I fell into the lap of two warm-hearted editors, Wendy Moore and Jim Burr. They treated me and my manuscript with such care and respect that you might have thought there was going to be money in it. Wendy shepherded it through to the final acceptance by the press; Jim (affectionately called James Dean) got it the stamp of approval and worked it through its kinks to publication, aided by the careful work of Megan Giller and Marjorie Pannell, as well as Derek George, who designed the cover and the book itself. Actually, I didn't fall into their lap: Annes McCann Baker, then editor of the Center for Middle Eastern Studies publications at the University of Texas at Austin, had read my work and introduced me to them. All of these people have helped me find my conceptual and grammatical errors. I leave it to my readers and reviewers to point out any that remain.

Last and lastingly, my family: my parents, Manya and Barry Bertram; my brother Neal; my older daughter Alanya Snyder Jones (and her brood, Mike, Selim, and Naveed, who joined in one by one), my younger daughter Rumeli Snyder, and their father, Neal Snyder, and his talented wife, Yvonne García; and my so close relative, Suat Çapas, who holds all of Turkey together for me: thank you for your comments, interventions, errands, and strength; you were with me every single step of the way. And thank you to my dear Fred Donner, who was always with me, too. To all of you who joined in this venture of intellectual curiosity about the past, let me repeat an Ottoman expression that I think I once heard: "Blessings on your eyelids."

ımagining the ᴛurkish ʜouse

A house in Istanbul, Zeyrek Mahallesi. Courtesy of Walter B. Denny, 1990.

introduction

*Welcome to
the House*

There is a distinctive type of house that once was found wherever the Ottomans lived. From the seventeenth century up until the first days of the twentieth century, when regions like Bulgaria, Greece, Bosnia, and Turkey were claiming a private title to their own part of this once great empire, timber-framed houses with protruding upper stories characterized a wide landscape, giving it a distinctive Ottoman stamp. Although these houses shared a common style, this book is not about their architectural vocabulary but about the way this type of house came to be imagined poetically at a turning point in Turkish history, and about the people who created and understood its poetic impact. At a higher level, this book addresses the powerful way in which the concept of home inhabits our memory and our imagination, and in so doing how it becomes a muse that can shape our personal and shared identities.

The project for this book began when I was a Fulbright Scholar in Turkey in 1993, investigating, as an Islamic art historian, the architecture of what by then was known as "the Turkish house." People were forever asking what a foreigner like me was doing in Turkey, and my simple answer was that I had come to do research on the Turkish house. What I found, to my surprise, was that I had only to utter those three words to have my interlocutors' faces become positively beatific. In fact, I came to expect a glow, as they repeated the words with a reverent love: "the Turkish house. . . ." After the glow, and a pause, would come stories about a specific house they knew, or one they had missed knowing: their grandfather's house, their great-grandfather's house, their uncle's house that had been torn down or that was in a village they had not visited, or they had visited it, and how they wished to live in one.

During that Fulbright year I began to collect those stories until I finally realized that my research question, which once asked why and how the architecture of this house changed over time, itself changed: How did this house come to evoke such strong emotions and memories of the past in the Turkish imagination? And what exactly do these emotions and memories express?

In Turkey, representations of the Ottoman house, with its recognizable profile, began to take on this larger-than-life power at a crucial time of transition: between the beginning of the early twentieth century and the late 1930s, as a young Turkey struggled to release itself from its Ottoman past and take its place in the world family of nations. With the establishment of the state of Turkey in 1923, this transition took on an increasingly Westernizing trajectory: not only was the Ottoman political system of the sultan and his realm replaced by that of a Turkish republic and its citizens, but language, literature, music, script, dress, codes of behavior, and almost every other area of cultural production were regulated and revised in such a way that the Ottoman past was defamed or erased.

Yet as these former Ottoman citizens became Turkish citizens, these men, women, and children, these imams and schoolteachers, these bureaucrats, shopkeepers, and housewives brought images and memories of an Ottoman house with them, and as they reconceptualized themselves as Turkish, they reconceptualized this house, making it Turkish, too.

In *Imagining the Turkish House*, then, you will meet these people, especially the Ottoman citizens who became Turkish ones, and see how their values, their uncertainties, their spiritual longings, and their political strategies contributed to transforming the old Ottoman house into a Turkish emotive image, and how it became lodged in the Turkish imagination. You will meet Naim Efendi, the Ottoman patriarch who, as a character in the novel *Mansion for Rent* (*Kiralık Konak*, 1922), wrestles with a new Turkish world. In his old wooden house, he picks up a novel left by his son-in-law, but he cannot read it. It is in a new script, with a new vocabulary; even the genre of the novel itself is new. The educated Naim Efendi had never read a novel in his life! You will meet another old man, too, connected emotionally to another old wooden house, but he is a character in a 1996 cartoon. This old man has located his childhood house in a run-down neighborhood in Istanbul and, while looking at it, imagines that all the refinements of a lost Ottoman era are still alive inside. I will also introduce you to Hodja (teacher) Ali Rıza Bey, the Ottoman painter who, by the beginning of the twentieth century, had already captured many Ottoman houses on canvas, and who conveyed his love for them to his many students.

You will also encounter Arif Hikmet Koyunoğlu, one of the architects who hoped that the Turkish house would become an inspiration for a new national architecture. In 1928, he designed and finished at his own expense a model Turkish room in the Turkish Hearth Association Building in the new capital of Ankara. And do not forget the hostess named Ay Hanım Efendi, famous for her weekly evenings of tea and conversation and very proud of the "Turkish room" that she designed in her 1931-modern apartment.

Except for our cartoon character, all of these people are the cohort who lived in or came to life during this important period when modern Turkey struggled to come into being and its former Ottoman citizens were coming to terms with a cataclysmic rupture with their past. It is this cohort that helped to redefine the Ottoman house as Turkish and to invest it with a very specific aspect of Turkish identity. This identity was not without its raw edges and contradictions, and I trace these too. Yet the durability of the emotional meanings that they helped assign to this house can be seen when its image is examined at the end of the twentieth century, for example, in the thoughts of our cartoon character, or in the idyllic drawing of Turkish houses by a 1990 middle school girl in Istanbul who, when asked to draw a perfect future, drew a landscape of houses from the Ottoman past.

The primacy of the old Ottoman house as a space of meaning in the Turkish collective imagination is especially interesting because hardly a Turkish house remains in Turkey today, and their position on the Turkish landscape was already waning by the end of the nineteenth century. These wooden houses that once covered Istanbul, Anatolia, and the Balkans were ravaged by serial fires and replaced by serial rebuildings until the turn of the twentieth century, when they were no longer suited to the new demographics, economics, and lifestyle needs of a growing and modernizing nation. Thus, what we today call the Turkish house is actually a house that characterized Ottoman urban space but did not survive as a viable built form into the Turkish republican period. At some time around the turn of the twentieth century they stopped being built forever, so that our real and fictional protagonists never knew them in their original state. *Imagining the Turkish House*, then, investigates how this Ottoman house took on a second life, and how it still lives on as a visual and textual memory image that does serious cultural work.

Aristotle, and many philosophers following him, believed that memory was always stored in images. Theorists like Richard Terdiman,[1] paralleling

A street in Istanbul, eighteenth century.

Aristotle to some degree, consider memory almost coincident with images or representation, suggesting, in fact, that memory cannot exist *without* its representation. Following these ideas, I suggest that representations of the Turkish house as they are found in art, in descriptions, or in literary evocations came to function as symbols for ideas related to the past, such as spirituality, or as surrogates, such as when the image of the Turkish house became a code for an Ottoman life-world that could only be thought of in secret, a situation we encounter in Chapters 3 and 4. Terdiman suggests that a representation might even, following Jean Baudrillard, be a "simulacrum," an exact copy of something that never existed.[2] An example of this might be the construction of a replica Turkish house as a museum or even a

A house in Istanbul, Akbıyık Mahallesi. Photograph by Carel Bertram, 1990.

small hotel, combining idealized forms and furnishings from various periods or places.

What I show in *Imagining the Turkish House* is just how and when—and why—these symbols, surrogates, and simulacra were created, and how they took on meaning for a large cohort of people. In fact, the idea of memory that I am discussing and the type of memory that I am uncovering here is never an individual's memory at all but an example of what is called collective memory, as Halbwachs would have thought it, and this is a major theoretical underpinning of my work.

Maurice Halbwachs (1877–1945), a student of Emile Durkheim, who theorized the idea of social thought in *The Rules of Sociological Method* (1895), went on to theorize memory itself as "social historical thinking." This is a type of memory that exists independently from individual, autobiographical thoughts or memories, and it was he who first called this nonautobiographical thought collective memory. It is social because it is shared by a group in a specific group context; it is historical because it comprises shared notions about the past. It is collective memory, then, because it is composed of loosely focused thoughts (rather than remembered experiences) that are accumulated and combined into an overlapping set of ideas about the past.

But if this memory is not individual and autobiographical, where does it come from? It comes from group-owned ideas about the past that are shared in myths, stories, images, rituals, and traditions, all of which have their own ways of representing group history. The representations stored in collective memory may be topically specific, for example, a Jewish collective memory of the Exodus from Egypt, or a second- or third-generation Palestinian's memory of exile, but they are always generalized or generic, and in no case are they memories of events that have been experienced directly. Those memories would be part of a different genre entirely. (A collective imagination is a similar notion, and I use that term as well, although it often refers to image-based thoughts rather than event-based ones.)

Imagining the Turkish House shows how the concept of the Ottoman (and then Turkish) house became a collectively held memory about the Ottoman past.[3] It could not be autobiographical memory because, by the time of our period of study, although old houses were still visible and even inhabited, the lifestyle of that house had disappeared. (In the United States today, people who live in old Victorian houses, for example, are not Victorians.) For the citizens of the emerging Turkish Republic, then, a meaning for the old Ottoman house could only be imagined through representations of it.

It is these representations that I investigate, as they entered the collective imagination, becoming the places where the past was collectively remembered, and took on the ability to trigger, rehearse, repeat, contest, or change important ideas about the Turkish self. In fact, it is because images in the mind change over time that they can be historicized: memory images emerge and transform, and sometimes disappear. For this reason, we can use images and representations to talk about "the history of memory." On occasion I refer to this group of images, ideas, and representations as the Turkish imaginary.

By focusing on collective memory as an interpretation of the past in the present, a second theory is also implicit in this work, one that has variously been called reception theory or reader-response theory—or, by logical extension, viewer-response theory. Here, when studying a text or an artistic piece, a building or an artifact, the emphasis is shifted from what the author intended, or even from the author's discourse or experience, to what the reader or viewer (that is, the audience) might have understood or misunderstood, and especially to what the reader might have felt, and thus to the ideas and feelings created in their minds in response. In reception theory, "the meaning of a text is literally *created* in the act of its being read."[4]

In *Imagining the Turkish House*, I read a variety of "texts" both chronologically—that is, as they entered the social arena over time—and in combination, accumulation and association—that is, with the hope of entering the larger imaginative world of the citizens of this era as they created a collective idea. In Chapter 1 I refer to this constructed and accumulated meaning as "the mysterious plus." I hope to convince you that this focus on the point of view of the reader, in his or her social-historical context, allows us to recapture new meanings as they became a part of historical consciousness.

When I follow the reader into the world of memory, I am not alone. Today, literary studies have begun to embrace the interplay of memory and place. At the top of this list is the work done on Diaspora studies, and the prime example is how literary expressions and metaphors have connected Palestinian self-conceptions to an internalization of spaces of loss and longing.[5] There are also the "literary memory spaces" of South Asian memoirs and Greek novels investigated in Eleni Bastea's *Memory and Architecture*.[6] In the realm of "historical memory," Turkish and Ottoman studies have contributed as well, for example, Ahmet Evin's work on the literary and aesthetic history of the Ottoman and Turkish novel, Emel Sönmez's study of women in nineteenth-century Turkish novels, and Jale Parla's use of novels to investigate the ambivalent feelings about the role of the patriarch/father and changing domestic visions at the close of the Ottoman Empire.[7] (I refer to many of these types of works in subsequent chapters.)

Literature, one might say, is the obvious container and shaper of memory. Renate Lachmann's comprehensive review of literary theorists and her close readings of Russian texts suggest how "literature supplies the memory for a culture and records such a memory. It is itself an act of memory."[8] Lachmann's readings also show the importance of reading intertextually, which is simply reading texts in relation to other texts.

Yet much of the work that relates specifically to the house (and household) in Turkey has not been in the field of literary studies but has been guided by the disciplines of sociology or art and architectural history. Alan Duben's and Cem Behar's studies of the sociological construction of the Ottoman Turkish family counter stereotypes of extended families and multiple wives,[9] Deniz

Kandioti's work shows how the real—and the iconic—roles of fathers, sons, and daughters related to ideas of modernity at the time of the new republic,[10] and Fatma Müge Göçek's work on Turkish nationalism[11] widens our understanding of what nationalism means and meant for various groups.

The earliest works on the Turkish house itself are specifically architectural, especially the monumental and pivotal studies done by the architect and historian Sedad Hakkı Eldem,[12] who documented and typologized them. There are also many newer works, every one of them indebted to Eldem,[13] as well as the publications of the Turkish Association for the Preservation of Historical Houses.

Sibel Bozdoğan's work on Turkish architectural culture, however, is one that crosses disciplines, and in some ways it is the closest work to my own, yet she stands at the other end of the spectrum of research interests and strategies. In *Modernism and Nation Building: Turkish Architectural Culture in the Early Republic*,[14] Bozdoğan addresses, with depth and sensitivity, the complex and interwoven architectural culture of the new Turkish Republic, including its antecedents, by investigating the work, worldviews, discourses, and political philosophies of the architects, city planners, teachers, and nationalists who were working to define it. Unlike a traditional architectural historian, who might focus on form and style, Bozdoğan searches for the ideologies and utopias that informed the real—or hoped-for—built environment during what she refers to as "the long 1930s." But how what was built, and especially what was lost, might have taken on emotive power in the general urban population is not the thrust of her project. Although both her work and mine are concerned with the history of thought, my inquiry sources and inquiry questions hope to open a different door, one that exposes different historical knowledge and different historical meanings: ones that refer to the lived emotions of this period. That is, I give this period and these sources a poetic reading.

Whatever could this mean?

If we read our sources as if they were poetry, we read them quite differently than if we are looking for their literal meanings or even their distinct social purposes. We read a poem for abstract ideas, symbolic significances, and especially for our emotional reactions to what is described or evoked. With the introduction of the idea of a poetic reading of my sources, I also suggest that the places, novels, images, and popular texts that contain references to—or representations of—the old Ottoman house can be read poetically, and furthermore that they must be read as a poetic combination, as something larger: as a poetry that holds human meanings that can only be understood from their association with one another—a poetic reading of the mysterious plus.

My methodology, then, has been to search for representations of the old wooden house as they enter into the Turkish imaginary, there to evolve as part of a collective repertoire of images, and to read or see them as the contemporary viewer might have done, with his or her social knowledge and understanding of a related world of emotionally heavy symbols. I rely particularly on novels, which with their conscious verbal depictions of places are a perfect site of collective memory. It was in these literary renderings and artistic depictions, as well as in the political rhetoric and even the built environment—namely, in the space of the imagined and imaged—that I discovered just how—and to what depth—houses can became poetic expressions of longing for a lost past, voices of a lived present, and dreams of an ideal future. It is in a poetic reading that the Turkish imaginary becomes a Turkish symbolic universe.

My interest, then, is not in the specific architectures of the house or in the house as a built fact, and my work is not a traditional, art historical analysis of buildings, their style, their patrons, their architects, or even the social and historical forces or discourses that brought them into being. Rather, I consider the house as a poetic abstraction, with the particular validity that only poetic abstractions can have, and the meaning of which can only be fully realized in this larger poem. Thus, the subject here is the emergence and transformation of this abstract poetic image—the imaged and imagined Turkish house—and the imagining minds that gave it meaning at a critical moment of social change, when the Ottoman centuries were slipping away.

THE CHRONOLOGY OF THIS BOOK

I begin this poetic reading by asking how and when the Ottoman house first became a representation. Throughout the Ottoman period this house was not idealized, and it had no architectural name or studies done about it. For those who lived in them, they were just a place to hang your fez. In Chapter 1, we see that the Ottoman house was first "pictured" as a stage prop in the Turkish shadow theater productions of the seventeenth through nineteenth centuries. This stage prop established a visual image that would be repeated over time, with particular emphasis on the cantilevered upper floor. By capturing a real feature of a widely recognizable architectural type, the stage prop established a generic image that could easily be disseminated with a larger meaning. In Chapter 1, I argue that the meaning that this first image carried was that of the life-world of a timeless Ottoman neighborhood.

In Chapter 2, I show how the Ottoman house began to lose this association with time immemorial and took on a clear association with a past that was over. This change occurred in the period when the Turkish Republic was being envisioned, and significantly, this is when the Ottoman house began to be called "Turkish," making it available as a player in the creation of a new Turkish self. It is in this transitional period that the beloved Hodja Ali Riza Bey began to record the national heritage in pen and watercolors, images that might well have been illustrations for the political rhetoric of Hamdullah Suphi, who, as president of the Turkish Hearth Association, was defining and promoting a Turkish national consciousness.

We meet Hamdullah Suphi as he is describing a coffee ceremony inside "an old Turkish house" as a way to evoke a shared past that was authentically local. Hamdullah Suphi is an important character in our cohort of transition and one who epitomizes the complexity of the period. For example, with his nationalist valorization of Westernization and secularism, Hamdullah Suphi actively supported equality for women. In 1921, he was forced to resign as minister of education because he had supported a co-ed teachers' conference. But the idea of the equality of all Turks was also one that would erase very real ethnic, confessional, and regional differences. The image of the Turkish house thus began its history as a *lieu de mémoire*,[15] a site of memory that bound all Turks together by a common memorial heritage in spite of demographic data to the contrary and in spite of the complexity of what constitutes a real Turkish heritage.

In Chapter 2, we reevaluate Koyunoğlu's museumized room, Rıza Bey's nostalgic paintings, and Suphi's "house of shared origins" as places that were also valorized as intrinsically modern. In the early republican period, for example, the house was being discussed in the vocabulary of Le Corbusier—that is, as both hygienic and light. With such intrinsically avant-garde design characteristics, it could then be imagined to have housed a Turkish self that was modern at its core. This was a memory that privileged the house for the way that it looked: an exteriorized house, a house that deferred to an Orientalist-Westernist authority that was defining Turkish identity from the outside.

But in Chapter 2, we find another concept of the house that contested this view. This is the image of the house as it was understood affectively, in which the Turkish self was presented from a spiritual, emotional, and psychological viewpoint. This image self-consciously represents the Turkish house at its most authentic, that is, from the inside. But this image of the house often existed secretly or in code, as it represented an attachment to a way of life that was strongly sanctioned by a secular, republican Turkey. *Imagining the Turkish House* investigates this interiorized space as it makes its appearance in contemporary novels that take place inside the old, wooden Ottoman house. At all levels of Ottoman society, the house had embedded within it an important element of privacy, but the novel invites us to enter, and even allows us to enter the most protected of its interior spaces, the emotional life of the people inside.

In Chapter 3 we meet Naim Efendi, of *Mansion for Rent* (*Kiralık Konak*), and find out why he had never read a novel in his life: the novel had only recently arrived in the Ottoman Empire, just as that world was about to end. In this chapter we look at these pre- and early republican novels and the people in them to see just how the Turkish house became a major marker of the past. But because these novels were set in the early republican present, at the time of transition and rupture, it also became the place for the characters and the reader to work out feelings about what was fading away—to hold on to important values and to mourn the loss of others, or to let them go with relief. We see this with a young married couple in the story *Harem* (1918) who use an image of the old Turkish house to help them define who they are in their new apartment. (All of these important players, fictional and real, are listed by their dates at the end of this book.)

Chapter 4 moves to the novels of the 1930s, a time when Westernization of the Turkish Republic was at its most strident. By this time, the concept of Westernization was firmly associated with progress and materiality. But for many, the issue was how to maintain what had come to represent its opposite: something that was at once Eastern, authentic, spiritual, and Turkish. I show how novels of this period confronted these issues from inside the old Turkish house. For example, what is Neriman, a seventeen-year-old woman, to do when she first sees the café life of the most Westernized neighborhood of Istanbul? And how does her father react when he understands that when she boards the tram to go there, it could be a one-way trip? How they confront and negotiate this situation may surprise the reader, but it is clear that the old Turkish house, where their conversations take place, is a protagonist in their story.

I believe that the elements of these Turkish house novels and stories— the narrative, the characters, the plot, the poetic imagery, and the emotions these conjure up in the reader—become players in the Turkish collective memory. But because these stories take place in a time when the real Ottoman house is obsolete, the memories inside them are of a past that was not experienced directly by the reader. The stories are in no way autobiographical; rather, they are incipient players, just as Halbwachs suggests, in the construction of a collective memory of the past. They are in no way autobiographical, and yet, because they describe contemporary emotional truths, they ring true. It is this sense of a "felt real" that made these novels important at the time as well as important historically, for in them the image of the Turkish house became the sign of continuity, which is essential if one is to identify with one's origins.

While the Turkish collective memory was developing inside the historical novel, real architecture was being designed for the new Turkey. In order to contextualize contemporary images of the Turkish house, we meet Turkey's most famous architect, Sedad Hakkı Eldem, who might have restored or revived the Turkish house on the ground, although his project was actually to revive some of its parts for a new, historically referent architecture. If this had happened, the real architecture of the 1930s and early 1940s might have had a different place on the trajectory of memory about the Turkish house. But it did not happen. Yet at this time, Eldem began to clarify how the Turkish house operated as an architectural typology: how its cantilevers captured breezes and vistas and how its elements were modular. This work inaugurated a period of intense memory collection that would be seen in the encyclopedias of the 1940s through the coffee-table books of the later twentieth century. We can credit Eldem with disseminating the idea that to catalogue Turkey's urban past is to catalogue its wooden houses. In Chapter 5, then, we return to the built house as it becomes an object of study that will lead to the simulacra of the museumized house or to a themed, gated community, as well as to an interest in historical preservation.

Chapter 5 also brings the reader closer to the present with a continued look at how the house survives as a literary image. Mid-twentieth-century authors were still writing from inside the old house, but there was a shift in interest: characters began to replace questions about who they were with questions about what they had become. The long string of memory images now approached the present through the stories, cartoons, and other representations that struggled to remember and preserve meaning for the Turkish house, delaying or softening its slip into nostalgia.

Imagining the Turkish House, then, has three main thrusts. The first is to participate with you, the reader, in the drastically new life-world that citizens of the new Turkish Republic experienced as they crossed into it from the older Ottoman Empire. This explains my interest in accessing an aspect of the early twentieth century as a Turkish citizen might have known it, but at the same time in presenting human emotions that would have resonated in the reader's life-world. The second is, by using ideas of collective memory and reception theory, to introduce a theoretical understanding of the interaction between memory and representations, and also to show how a methodology that reads the images and poetic texts that the citizens would have known helps us approach and understand their world. The third step is to tie these two together to show that the mental image of the Turkish house as a poetic image was an important, even strategic player in this transitional period, becoming a bridge that brought the old into the new at a time when there was pressure to forget the old altogether.

As Walter Benjamin reminds us, "every image of the past that is not recognized by the present as one of its own concerns threatens to disappear irretrievably."[16] Clearly, the image of the Turkish house continues to "flash up" in the present because it provides a space of legitimacy for the present's concerns. This is corroborated by images of the Turkish house that stand for a nonautobiographical past while exhibiting surprising contemporary and autobiographical components. Thus, I suggest that there is a crossover between collective memory and individual meaning, for what a collectivity brings to the present as memory arrives there to serve something that is still experienced, felt, or valued by individuals. Investigating the private aspect of memory enriches our understanding of the meaning of historical consciousness, how it operates, and what it serves in the present and augers for the future.

Memory, as William James said, is "the association of a present image with others known to belong to the past."[17] But the Turkish house is also an image that creates the future, an image of expectation, which according to James "is the association of a present image with others known to belong to the future."[18] This, as James saw, is the other side of memory. Perhaps more than any other image in the Turkish imaginary, the Turkish house as Naim Bey or Neriman or Hamdullah Suphi knew it still stands at this crossroads, between memory and hope.

A street in Tokat. Photograph by Carel Bertram, 1993.

ONE

Bringing the Turkish House into Focus

Characteristics,
Representations,
Memories,
and Memory

Since the beginning of the Turkish Republic in the early twentieth century, the built landscape of Turkey has undergone dramatic changes. This is not a situation that is peculiar to Turkey but one that is mirrored in many countries that began their architectural modernization during the twentieth century or at the end of the nineteenth. What is interesting for Turkey is that as its landscape of distinctive Ottoman-period houses was replaced by one of concrete apartments, and as the urgency to live in modern housing was nourished, an image of the old, disappearing Ottoman house began to emerge and take on symbolic meaning and aesthetic value in the Turkish consciousness. The meaning that was given to the image of Ottoman-period wooden houses, however, did not develop in a consistent way; for example, it did not and does not always signal a sense of loss or a uniform desire for preservation and restoration. It is this nonlinear and nonuniform nature that makes the image of what has come to be called "the Turkish house" an example of how memory operates in society, as well as an important example of the complexity of Turkey's struggle to invent or synthesize itself by imagining its past in selective ways.

As the old Ottoman-period house entered the collective memory as an image or idea, it underwent a process that eventually led to a conceptual monumentalization—that is, it began to take on a larger-than-life meaning in Turkish collective thought, moving from obscurity and even derision. As a monument, it was removed conceptually and even physically from its natural setting in the neighborhood and revised as a didactic object, like a museum or pension or restaurant. This process could be called "monumentalizing the quotidian," and it is this process of monumentalization that places the house at the crossroads of history and ideology because it involves collectively held beliefs about the past. As Lefebvre said, "Ideology *per se* might well be said to consist primarily in a discourse upon social space."[1] But what is intriguing about this monumentalization process is not just its connection to ideology but that, unlike the process of building monuments, such as royal mosques or statues of great leaders, the process of making the house into a monument runs backward: instead of translating an abstract conception into visible form, it does the exact opposite.

THE EMERGENCE OF THE OLD WOODEN HOUSE IN THE TURKISH COLLECTIVE CONSCIOUSNESS

The 1970s in Turkey saw the formalization of an already developed interest in its own domestic architecture. In 1973, the first Antiquities Law, the Eski Eserler Kanunu No. 1710, was enacted,[2] which broadened the scope of conservation to include not only monuments such as mosques, caravansarays (merchant hostels), and public baths but also vernacular residences and "urban ensembles." In 1976, the Turkish Association for the Protection of Historic Houses (*Türkiye Tarihi Evleri Koruma Derneği*) was established with the intention of making the preservation of old houses and neighborhoods possible. Its goal was to show the general public that houses left from the Ottoman period in Turkey were part of a shared cultural heritage, and

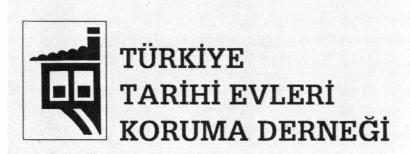

Logo, Turkish Association for the Protection of Historic Houses. Courtesy of the Türkiye Tarihi Evleri Koruma Derneği.

then to find financial support to help individual owners maintain their old homes.³ The institutionalization of these two protective measures for the historic house and its environment represented a formal social recognition that a valued cultural item was in danger and thus signaled that the Turkish house had become an important image in the Turkish memorial heritage. The logo designed by the Association for the Protection of Historic Houses is a silhouette of the cantilevered upper story of a typically Ottoman-period wooden frame house.

Although there are many styles of Ottoman-period houses in Turkey, including those made of stone rather than wood, it was felt that the wooden house with this shape had the power of universal recognition, as the image that best represented a "Turkish house" and the Turkish domestic past in the collective imagination.

By the late 1980s, not only was this wooden or sometimes half-timbered house with its projecting upper floor widely understood as a signifier of the lost beauty of the Turkish architectural past, its use as an icon of this past was encouraged and rewarded. For example, in a 1990 children's art competition in Istanbul, first place was given to Beren Tuncay, a schoolgirl who painted a romantic panorama of Istanbul filled with these wooden houses.

Thus, by the 1980s, domestic architecture from the Ottoman period had taken shape in the Turkish imagination, both in this literal sense of the logo of the Association for the Protection of Historic Houses and in the child's drawing of the past. Although these are literal drawings, they represent how Ottoman-period houses were imagined in a figurative sense, that is, they had taken on meaning through the research and writing that was done about them. In scholarly work especially, these everyday residences had become the subject of specific research, in the course of which they began to be referred to as "the Turkish house" or "the Anatolian house," that is, they acquired an identity of place or even the weight of nationalism.

The Ottoman-period house also took on value and meaning in the realm of literature, where it was imagined according to what was believed to have gone on inside it and how that lifestyle was interpreted. A book written during the 1980s depicts this nicely: its subject matter is the Istanbul lifestyles of the pashas, veziers, and ambassadors of the First and Second Constitutional Period in Turkey (1876 and 1908–1918), including their summerhouses (yalıs) and mansions (konaks) and their entertainment, music, and literature. The cover of this book, on page 20, shows the exterior of a wooden Istanbul konak with cantilevered "çıkmas" that frame an interior filled with a scene suggestive of sophisticated good times.

Child's drawing of Istanbul. From UNICEF, *1990, no. 16.*

Istanbul. The 1853 Ortaköy Mosque and the 1973 Bosphorus Bridge.
Photograph by Carel Bertram, 1996.

Istanbul. A street in Ortaköy. Photograph by Carel Bertram, 1996.

Cover, The Adventures of Nono Bey. *From Birsel, 1982.*

However, what had become known by the 1970s as the Turkish house did not always have this romantic aura, let alone this appellation, and what evokes a positive image in the mid- to late twentieth century often called forth an image of liability and disease for the nineteenth-century dwellers who lived in them. One can see this transition by observing how these common everyday houses of the late Ottoman period have been imagined over time. What we will see is that images of the house moved from representing the present to becoming an iconic visual or conceptual symbol of the past, with a highly charged and very specific meaning in the Turkish imagination.

CHARACTERISTICS OF THE TURKISH HOUSE

The Ottoman-period house that has come to be referred to as the Turkish house or the traditional Turkish house is a timber-framed house found mainly in Istanbul, Anatolia, Greece, and the Balkans. Although these houses varied according to local building materials, as well as according to the wealth and size of the families they housed, they all shared a basic architectural vocabulary.

Sarajevo, Bosnia, Alifaković Mahallesi. Postcard from around 1900. Reproduced courtesy of the Library of Congress, Prints and Photographs Division, Photochrome Collection, ppmsc-09311.

Urban houses and even many rural ones were almost invariably a minimum of two stories in height, with the ground floor acting as a service area for animals or for storage. The living rooms were situated above. In houses with more than two stories, the highest floor was often used for summer residence and the middle floors were used during the winter, as these best held the heat.

The Tahtani or Ground Floor, and the Taşlık

The ground floor was planned to adjust to the street and the topography of the land. The walls of the ground floor were made of stone or rubble and were windowless (or had ventilation windows) on the street side. In neighborhoods that were not overly dense, these walls extended to become a street-sided garden wall that gave complete privacy to the garden and also defined the urban plot. Usually a gate was cut into this wall, giving access to the garden or courtyard first, and then to the house. This lower floor area, windowless to the street, was often completely open to the garden, as a sheltered place either for animals or for household activities such as food preparation. Its floor was paved with polished river stones or pebbles and was therefore called the *taşlık* (stone floor area, pronounced *tashlik*). These shining stones could easily be cleaned with water, and during the hot months they held the moisture of water that was poured on them, cooling the breezes that passed over them. In many houses, especially those of Istanbul, this stone-floored taşlık area became an enclosed entry courtyard with a high ceiling and stairways leading to the rooms above.

In dense urban areas where there was no land for a garden, the tahtani might even be entered through a door to the street. But whether enclosed by four walls or open to the garden, the tahtani[4] entry area of large houses often had a room suspended within it and open to it, a type of mezzanine or large low loft called the *asma oda* (suspended room) that was used by the housekeeper or even the grandmother as a type of extra room during the day.

The Fevkani or Upper Floors[5]

The external facade was characterized by wide overhanging eaves or *saçak* (pronounced sajak), which protected the windows and the walls from the sun, but it is the upper floors of the Ottoman-period wooden house that give it its distinctive exterior appearance. Sitting on a stone base that was sited to the land, the upper floors were adjusted for privacy or for light, views, and

A street in Izmir. Drawing by T. Allom, 1838.

*A street in Antakya around 1900. Reproduced
courtesy of the Library of Congress, Prints and
Photographs Division, LC-M32- 1792[P&P].*

*A street in Safranbolu. Photograph by
Carel Bertram, 1990.*

ventilation. Thus, the upper floors might be positioned at a different angle than the ground floor. But the most characteristic approach was to have whole rooms protrude over the closed ground floor and into the street.

The general name for this protruding room, or entire floor if the house was small, was *çıkma* (prounced chickma). If the çıkma was made up of a projecting room, it was called a *cumba* (pronounced joomba). If the çıkma was made up of a protruding central communal area (a *sofa*), it was called a *şahnış* (pronounced shahneesh) or *şahnışan* (pronounced shahneeshan). A house would take its external character from its several çıkmas, an *eywan*, the small extension of a sofa, or its single, central şahnışan.

It is believed that in the sixteenth and seventeenth centuries the exterior wall that faced the interior garden or courtyard, in the houses of central Anatolia particularly, was open both at the ground or tahtani level with its open taşlık and on the first of the upper floors, which jutted over the garden in the form of a verandah, frequently called the *hayat*,[6] although its name changed from region to region. The hayat opened inward to the rooms, a separate door for each, and thus served as a type of external hallway and a

Safranbolu. A house with a protruding central room, or sofa, the şahniş.
Photograph by Carel Bertram, 1990.

Antalya. Interior of a sofa. Photograph by Carel Bertram, 1992.

Istanbul. The architect Ahmet Turhan Altıner on a sedir *in an* eywan, *an alcove that protrudes into the street. Photograph by Carel Bertram, 1998.*

A house in Muğla. The garden side of the house often had a verandah that opened to individual rooms. Note the remnants of the taşlık *in the foreground. Photograph by Carel Bertram, 1993.*

communal area. Because it faced the garden, this type of house plan has been called an extroverted plan.

It is suggested that in the dense capital of Istanbul, gardens and court-yards were diminished or abandoned, and the hayat was first enclosed and then moved completely indoors, becoming a central hall, which was also an interior gathering place called the sofa. Running from garden to street, it often protruded as the *şahnışan* on the street side. Individual rooms also opened to the sofa. This was the introverted plan, which became dominant in the eighteenth century.

The Oda *or Room*

The *oda* (room) of a traditional Ottoman-period house is theorized by most architectural historians as the original element of the house, once standing alone. It is often described as a sedentary or stationary version of the Central Asian tent.[7] In this capacity, each oda was designed as a complete family liv-ing unit that housed a nuclear family of parents and children. When several odas were combined to become a house, they maintained this isolated func-tion, each with a single door that would keep its own nuclear family separate from the communal spaces of the extended household, with its own door that opened to the sofa or to the hayat.

The historical connection of the oda to the Central Asian tent remains problematic, but it is true that each room was self-contained in that it served many functions, depending on its owners and the time of day or season. Thus, unlike Western rooms, which are differentiated by use, such as for dining, sleeping, socializing, and work, the oda served all these functions but at different times. Most rooms had a small *gusülhane* (bathing closet) next to the fireplace in order to heat the water and keep the space warm. Full bathing, however, was done at the neighborhood bathhouse (*hamam*) unless the house was large enough to have a hamam room of its own. Cooking was always done in a separate area, often the courtyard, and toilets were at the extreme edges of the garden.

The windowless wall (or walls) of the oda were lined with cabinets (*yüklük*), where bedding was stored during the day. At mealtimes, trays would be car-ried in from the kitchen areas and the room would be used as a dining area, with diners seated on the floor around it. Cleared of tables and mattresses, the room was without furniture except for permanent cushioned bench seat-ing (*sedir*) that lined the windowed walls. With no special furniture, the room became a sitting room suitable for entertaining guests.

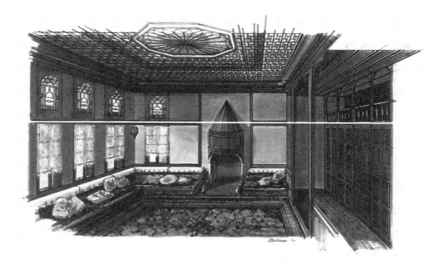

The organization of the oda, *or room. The line is the "upper limit of functional area with shelf," showing that the room is organized in human scale. From Küçükerman,* Turkish House in Search of Spatial Identity, *1978, p. 60. Reproduced courtesy of the Türkiye Turing ve Otomobil Kurumu.*

Safranbolu. The seventeenth-century Emirhocazade House. The windowless wall has a fireplace, cupboards, and niches framed by arabesque shapes. (Restored.) Photograph by Carel Bertam, 1992.

The finest room, with the finest views and light, was the *baş odası* (main or "head" room, pronounced bash odasuh), which could be used to entertain male guests by day but was the enclave of the house owner, the patriarch, and his family by night. The baş odası was given dignity by having the finest interior appointments that the inhabitants could afford; it was the largest room of the house and usually had the finest windows, and thus it was noticeable from the street. It would also have the finest wood carving on the walls and cabinets, and the most decorated wooden ceiling. Some grander houses in the Balkans would have a *divhane*, a room that was for socializing only; therefore the divhane would have no closets to store clothing and bedding, and could maximize wall and window seating.

The windows of the rooms were originally closed only by shutters. For this reason, nonopening windows with bottle glass, and later stained glass, were positioned above the shuttered windows to allow for light even when the windows had to be closed for reasons of weather or privacy. After the seventeenth century, shutters began to be replaced with glazed sash windows, after which the upper rows of windows sometimes disappeared. However, these glazed windows were protected on the street side by a lattice of wood, or *kafes* (cage), so that passersby could not see inside. Another latticed opening onto the street overlooked the door so that the residents could identify, without being seen, anyone who pulled the bell rope.

The Harem *and* Selamlık

Selamlık means greeting area and refers to the part of the house used by men for business and social relations with other men outside the family. In the Ottoman period, most government officials, such as judges, urban governors, and viziers, or the wealthiest members of urban neighborhoods carried on their work within the selamlıks of their large houses, or konaks. Because the selamlık served these needs, large konaks (mansions) had selamlıks without exception. A pasha of a konak, such as the one in the novel *Sinekli Bakkal*, would mediate neighborhood disputes or distribute largesse in this private section or suite of rooms. The selamlık might be entered through a common taşlık area that led to separate stairways (as was probably the case in Naim Efendi's house in the novel *Kiralık Konak*) or by a separate exterior door. In the konaks of provincial governors or viziers, the selamlık was often a separate building from the family section, or *harem*.

The harem was the area of the house restricted to the family. *Harem* means protected, and these rooms were protected from the public life of the street.

Here, women and children would live and eat together with the men of their family, but men past puberty would not be allowed in the harem section if there were women visitors from outside the family circle.[8] Thus, whether a separate house, as in the case of palaces, or a separate part of a large house or konak, or just rooms that were never used for official business or for entertaining male guests, the harem was always subject to the privacy rules of family life and gender relationships.

The Konak

Konak has been translated as mansion in most works, including my own, but it also encompasses a social system of extended family, including grandparents, grandchildren, brides, and sons-in-law, and an appropriate number of servants. A small konak might have ten rooms; a large konak could have over forty. Yet a konak is merely a wooden house on a grand scale and exhibits the full range of characteristics and architectural vocabulary of all Ottoman-Turkish wooden houses.

Although other types of houses than the ones I have just described also existed, built from local materials and with different plans, most shared the same characteristics of space division and room furnishings and arrange-

Amasya. The 1872 Hazeranlar konak beside the 1510 Bülbül Hatun Mosque. Photograph by Carel Bertram, 1993.

Istanbul. A yalı on the Bosphorus. Photograph by Carel Bertram, 1993.

ments. But these spatial divisions and decorative schemes reached their fullest development in the capital of Istanbul, and then spread to the provinces along with the princes and wealthy officials who were sent there.

The Köşk

When the term *köşk* (pronounced kushk; related to the English word kiosk) refers to a residence, it is a house intended as a summer residence of any size. However, since summer residences were the privilege of the wealthy, köşks were often merely suburban konaks. They differed from konaks, however, in that a köşk was always situated in a garden setting rather than on a street. A köşk can also be a single-room building within the confines of the Ottoman palace grounds, made special by having windows on every wall, and thus making it an enclosed but light-filled pavilion. Grand houses, too, might have a köşk attached, or an especially airy room on the facade or on the top floor, sometimes in the form of a belvedere or *cihannüme* (pronounced jihannuumeh). Houses with an open or extroverted plan might have a raised platform on one or both sides of the verandah or the hayat, and this too might be called a köşk.

The Yalı

A *yalı* is a house that faces the waterfront. Most often the term *yalı* refers to the summer residences along the Bosphorus in Istanbul, but there are also yalıs in river towns such as Amasya. The Bosphorus yalıs, because of their size and value, resemble konaks. Unlike urban dwellings with ground floors of windowless stone, these houses had windows that opened to the view at every level.

THE MEANING OF FORMS

Although it is imperative to understand the form of this Ottoman house, the larger question is one of meaning, and not merely what meaning load forms carry but just how these meanings came to be. For this, we will be looking at the important function of representations. Representations or images can refer to either visual depictions or textual descriptions of the house, including its psychological setting. For example, the textual descriptions of window grills are not very significant if they merely explain how the grills operate physically, but how these covered windows are represented in a story can be most telling.[9] These representations can only be developed, seen, used and understood within an accepted social framework and in a situation that rings true. It is exactly this shared social aspect of meaning, this shared understanding of forms, that permits the situating of the images we are investigating in the realm that we call collective memory or the collective imagination, terms that combine to make up a collective consciousness. It is for this reason that the images in texts that have a wide and public distribution are most valuable here. The methodology that I use, therefore, is one that considers representations both figuratively, as textual descriptions, and literally, as visual depictions, and one in which both scholarly and popular literature is essential. Both contribute to the collective imagination, and both play a cumulative part in the construction of meaning. By looking for the figure of the house in literature and scholarship and for the hidden text in figures and even in the forms of real buildings, we turn the literal and figurative on their heads. However, one is incomplete without the other, because the imagination blurs the lines between visual and textual representations, for texts conjure up visual images in the mind and artistic renderings recall or refer to contemporary ideas known from texts. This chapter and the following ones recount this process in detail.

Sign, Symbol, Karagöz, and "the Mysterious Plus"

The first literal, that is, clearly recognizable, visual representation of the Ottoman-period house is a type of puppet from the Turkish shadow theater, and it is a good example of how images also operate as signs and symbols. It is also an especially good introduction to the problem of how images signify geographic places, affective places (that is, places that resonate with meanings), and also time—all of which will become an essential part of our discussion of both memory and imagination. For the house in the Turkish puppet theater is both a sign for a specific type of building and a symbol for the activity in the places where these buildings are found, that is, the local neighborhoods, as well as a sign for a period of time that might be called time immemorial.

In defining a sign and symbol for these purposes, it is not necessary to involve a lengthy discussion of the scholarship of semiotics. Augustine is sufficiently clear: "A sign is a thing, which, over and above the impression it makes on the senses, causes something else to come into mind as a consequence of itself."[10] In the simplest cases, such as in a puppet theater, the representation of the house reproduces or re-presents sensory material, or some-

Karagöz and Hacivat on stage. From And, Karagöz: Turkish Shadow Theatre. *Reproduced by permission.*

thing that has at one point or another been seen or experienced by the viewer. That is, the viewer sees a depiction of a house exterior, but what comes to mind is something more complex, such as what the interior might look like, or the idea of an entire neighborhood made up of similar houses. In this case, the depiction stands for the generic. A sign can also take on the function of a symbol: a representation of a house becomes a symbol when it stands for the social relations or affectivity of the place.[11] Nonetheless, when sign and symbol are used interchangeably, as often happens, there is rarely a loss of understanding. Rather, what is really interesting is just how a representation (as a sign) gets its meaning or becomes symbolic. This process operates through a system of association with other signs, and also in the way that representations are used; in short, this is a process of "value added" that William James referred to as "the mysterious plus."[12]

The House-Tasvir and the Idea of Generic

The genre of the Turkish shadow theater, generally referred to as "*Hacivat* (pronounced Hadji-vat) and *Karagöz*," its two principal characters, or simply as Karagöz, is aptly named, because its origins are lost in the shadows of Indonesia or Central Asia. But records show that Karagöz shadow theater was alive in Ottoman Turkey in the sixteenth century, that it was deeply embedded by the seventeenth, and that by the late Ottoman period it was entirely domesticated, with indigenous characters, stock stories and dialogues (now referred to as "classic" stories), and an entirely Ottoman-Turkish visual repertoire.[13] In the nineteenth century, Karagöz plays were viewed by all social classes and by adults and children alike, and were a cherished part of the evening entertainments during the entire holy month of Ramazan.[14]

Turkish shadow theater uses a large cast of puppets that are backlit as they are placed against a linen screen and moved by puppeteers using sticks. The images (tasvirs) that depict houses in the Karagöz plays are stage scenery

Karagöz's house. Reproduced courtesy of the puppetmaker Emin Şenyer.

or props. There are two tasvirs that depict residences: the house of Shirin from the story of Ferhat and Shirin and an everyday house for the average Karagöz story.[15]

The house of Shirin (*Kasr-i Şirin* or *Şirin'in Köşkü*) is a particular form of house that is most often used in the Ferhad and Shirin love story. It is a narrow tower house with a balconied room at the top that looks out in all directions (this is a *cihannüme*). The distinctive shape of this house form derives from Turkish miniatures that in turn derive from Persian models.[16]

But it is the second scenery image, the house-tasvir, used to portray the houses of everyday characters, that is of interest to us. This house is usually depicted in profile so that its cantilevered upper floor room (çıkma/cumba) is prominent; in fact, it looks not unlike the stylized logo used by the Turkish Association for the Protection of Historic Houses. Although this house-tasvir is used to introduce a variety of plays

Shirin's house. Reproduced courtesy of the puppetmaker Emin Şenyer.

that take place in or near houses, the same tasvir is used regardless of the owner of the house, making it a generic type.[17] It is generic because it represents a class of houses by depicting what is common to all of them. As George Berkeley said, something—such as a word—becomes generic "by being made the sign, not of an abstract general idea but of several particular ideas, *any one of which* it indifferently suggests to the mind."[18]

At the time when the Karagöz plays were a part of everyday life rather than nostalgic or historic revival pieces, there was indeed a specific type of house "any one of which [the house-tasvir might] indifferently suggest to the mind," for it was to be found throughout the Ottoman Empire.

A great deal of research has been done on the Ottoman-period house, especially by the architect Sedad Hakkı Eldem and his students, who documented its structural and design characteristics.[19] This Ottoman-period house has a long pedigree on the ground as well as in the imagination. The lithographs of Antoine-Ignace Melling at the end of the eighteenth century and beginning of the nineteenth century show an Istanbul crowded with these houses, as do many artists' renditions.

Eldem, who documented how the finest and most typical of historic houses were those of Istanbul, was the first to point out that it was exactly this Istanbul-style house that spread to the provinces, eventually replacing most of the local styles.[20] Before the nineteenth century, Ottoman towns in Anatolia and the Balkans were characterized by a variety of local styles and materials, and although certain of these local styles, such as those found in the towns of Mardin and Diyarbekir, have survived with vigorous tenacity into the present, the late eighteenth century saw the beginning of a homogenization in housing types for most of the empire. At this time, mud-brick housing in most of Anatolia and the Balkans was replaced by timber-framed houses, and even more pervasively the spatial organization of the Ottoman room, with its windows, fireplace, built-in bench seating, and decorative wooden ceilings, was exported from the capital to become the standard for the provinces. As Tanyeli wrote in 1996,

> It may be said that an identical physiognomy is encountered from Trebin on the Adriatic coast to Plovdiv and from there to Kastamonu all the way to Kutahya. The unrivaled cultural stamp of Istanbul, the shedding of traditional introversion in the national economy and the ensuing new transport-communication facilities ushered in by the industrial age, here as elsewhere, have done away with local features.[21]

This makes our work easy in many ways, because it is not necessary to consider all the types of houses that the Ottoman period produced. Neither is it necessary to investigate the housing of the various ethnic groups, for they also shared a common visual style, the major variations being attributable to region rather than to religion or ethnicity. Furthermore, Eldem's work suggests that the homogeneity of domestic architecture had a design consistency that was found not only in everyday houses but also in the konaks or mansions of the wealthy and in the yalıs or summerhouses that lined the Bosphorus. According to Eldem, "A yalı was not very different from a house [ev] or a konak in plan, the main difference being that it was built over the sea on a man-made jetty [leb-i derya, lip of the sea] or over the shore with its own jetty jutting out into the water."[22]

Perhaps most important, these dwellings were highly visible. Although Ottoman domestic life was extremely private, and suburban mansions (köşks) were often hidden in large garden enclosures, the facades of everyday houses spilled over their foundation or over garden walls to define the street. Even the yalıs were visible because they faced the Bosphorus in Istanbul, or other river fronts, such as the Yeşil Irmak in Amasya, making these water-courses just another type of public thoroughfare.

Thus the representation of the house-tasvir seems to us today to be an appropriate representation of its own long nineteenth century, because it is designed to capture all the salient characteristics of the Istanbul house form that had spread to most provincial towns as well. The house-tasvir is most frequently, but not always, portrayed in profile to highlight its cantilevered upper floor, the çıkma, with a decorative but clearly visible supportive strut (*payanda*). As a house-tasvir, it is depicted with a wooden upper floor on a stone foundation floor and is often painted as many wooden houses were, with either a red or yellow ochre, blue, or green.[23] The upper floor windows are prominent and covered with a wooden grill (*kafes*). The distinctive upper row of stained glass windows, or the shutters of the lower ones, both essential to seventeenth- and eighteenth-century houses, are missing, suggesting either that the simplest type was chosen as the most appropriate or that this is a late-version piece.

This generic image of the house is an example of what is called "the mysterious plus" because meaning is added to the image by its mental association with a range of known images that are held in the collective imagination. In the case of the house-tasvir, meaning is also added by the way it is used:

Amasya, Savadiye Mahallesi. House with garden. Photograph by Carel Bertram, 1993.

Sivas. House with garden. Photograph by Carel Bertram, 1993.

as everyone's or anyone's dwelling.[24] William James said, when speaking on the sign value of sharp versus blurred images, "a blurred thing is just as particular as a sharp thing, and the generic character of either a sharp image or a blurred image depends on its being felt with its representative function." This function is the mysterious plus, or the understood meaning.[25]

In this way the house-tasvir becomes like an abstract idea that corresponds to the whole class of houses that any viewer was familiar with and most probably lived in. The represented house also becomes a fact in its own right, an abstract idea that is perfectly clear; and once one possesses it, one will never fail to recognize a Turkish house among other houses.

But the house-tasvir has yet another "plus" beyond being a generic house type, or a sign of a whole class of houses, and that is that it becomes symbolic of the neighborhood (*mahalle*). It takes on the meaning of "neighborhood" because of the way that it is used. Sabri Siyavuşgil, in fact, has suggested that the entire Karagöz play screen or "stage" represents the typical and thus generic mahalle of Ottoman Istanbul as it existed until 1908 (he gives it a cut-off date of the Young Turk Revolution)[26] and that the characters in these plays are a careful distillation of typical Ottoman mahalle types.[27] Yet he also suggests that the stories that these traditional plays depict do not derive from "typical" mahalle life at all but represent real newsmaking events of var-

ious periods, such as the wild drinking on the part of the Janissaries (Otto-man military elite guard) when they would break into the women's bath-houses, which was made into the play *Hamam* (*The Bathhouse*). A scandalous event in the sixteenth century, when the wife of a prominent man threw blas-phemous insults at an entire mahalle, was made into the play called *Kanlı Nigar* (*The Bloodthirsty Beauty*). In this play, all the men are thrown naked into the street by two women of loose morals. His suggestion is that current events were domesticated into local neighborhood stories and recast with local heroes so that they could continue to be played as placeless pieces.

In other words, what happened in one neighborhood might have happened in any neighborhood. One of the protagonists in Halide Edib's novel *Sinekli Bakkal*, which takes place during what is characterized as the oppressive reign of Abdülhamid II (1876–1909), is a Karagöz puppeteer who is exiled for using his art to ridicule a high government official, and thus to address the real fear and loathing that the official represented in every neighborhood.[28] If this is true, we can understand that the image of the wooden cantilevered house might well have been imagined as a symbol of the typical neighborhood of any viewer rather than as the house of a specific protagonist. That is, with the house-tasvir, this particular type of house has already become more than just a sign of an area populated by many houses of the same style; it has become symbolic of the types of people and relationships that one might find there.

Further corroborating this idea is that the cast of a Karagöz play con-sists of stereotypes of every character to be found in the typical Ottoman mahalle, such as the Gentleman (Çelebi) and the Lady (Zenne), the Hunch-back (Baba Ruhi), the Albanian (Arnavut), the Armenian (Ermeni), the Greek (Rum), and the Jew (Yahudi). The interactions of these characters are always stereotyped and, if they take place in the neighborhood, are set off by the generic house-tasvir, suggesting that the house had taken on this added plus of meaning in the collective imagination.

THE HOUSE-TASVIR, TIME, AND THE CONTINUAL PRESENT

We have found a representation of a generic place. Could there also be such an idea as generic time? If so, the house-tasvir would also qualify as a sign of it. The house-tasvir, although clearly symbolic of a shared present, was also understood to have a historical dimension in that it stretched the present seamlessly into the past to signify a shared history. As we are continuously and poignantly reminded, the present is continually becoming the past, which makes it difficult for us to establish which images, whether written or graphic, represent "today" and which represent a real memory of what "used to be" (not to mention which are a cumulative or an inherited memory of yesterday).

Yet it is clear that this first image we have of the Ottoman-period house represented neither the present nor the past. Rather, it represented what might be called the continual present, for it was an image meant to evoke the house "as it is today and has always been." This becomes clear when we look at how the costuming of various Karagöz characters changed to suit various periods. For example, the Çelebi or Gentleman can appear in either eighteenth-century or mid-nineteenth-century Tanzimat-era garb, and the Zenne or Lady can appear in eighteenth-century dress or with a nineteenth-century *ferece* and *yaşmak* (cloak and veil). But the symbol of the neighborhood, the cantilevered house, does not change, suggesting that the house and the neighborhood were believed to have a timeless visual stability. The house-tasvir, then, represented time immemorial.

The period that was considered time immemorial in the Turkish shadow theater, a time in which this generic type of house predominated in some form or other, later became known as "traditional time," clearly a notion that the Karagöz house-tasvir did not signify. For what traditional time always refers to is a time that is now over. Furthermore, traditional time is generally conceived of as containing the roots of one's heritage, or *le patrimoine*,[29] and thus a time imagined to have been more discrete, definable, simpler, and perhaps with clearer and more acceptable morals—in any event, a different sort of time than "now." Nonetheless, the convergence of the one hundred-plus-year period in which these houses were the visually dominant type throughout the empire offers the rare possibility of giving a date to an era that was once imagined as "the continual present" and that later became "traditional time"—that is, the long nineteenth century.

The image of the house-tasvir qualifies as generic because it abstracts the shared characteristics of its type. Additional meanings of "Ottoman neighborhood" and "time immemorial" were an added plus that came from the way it was used, and thus associated it with other ideas held in common to those who saw it. Although it was not a copy of any particular house, it was a house reminiscent of known houses: it was a "possible house" in the collective imagination, and therefore not an imaginary one.

DEPICTING THE IMAGINARY HOUSE

The house-tasvir may be a generic, almost documentary representation of the most common type of dwelling, yet it is an unusual image for its time. For although representations of houses existed in illustrated books and in paintings on walls throughout the Ottoman period, the wooden or half-timbered house with its cantilevers was rarely, if ever, the house chosen to be depicted by Ottoman artists. Instead, until the very end of the nineteenth century, what was being represented was neither documentary nor generic.

Beginning in the eighteenth century, houses were often part of decorative tableaus painted on the interiors of Ottoman private homes and public buildings: they are found in the interiors of konaks and even mosques, but more frequently in mosque outbuildings such as *Muvakitthanes* (Office of the Time Keeper, who made certain that the call to prayer was given at the right time) and in the inner domes covering *Şadirvans* (mosque ablution fountains). Just as house styles moved from the capital to the provinces, so did the convention of decorating walls with urban scenes. Research suggests that the first of these scenes can be found in the Topkapı Palace in the seventeenth century, and they have been traced thereafter as they spread to the wealthy homes of Istanbul and then to the provinces, where they were finally commissioned for public buildings as well.[30]

Most wall paintings of urban scenes, whether in the provinces or in Istanbul, have the capital city as their subject, and most are attributed to Western artists working in Istanbul or to Turkish artists copying Western depictions of Turkish scenes.[31] These scenes can be considered realistic or at least evocative in that they include recognizable urban elements, such as the Bosphorus or the Süleymaniye Mosque in Istanbul, but because they are not topographically or architecturally accurate, they could also be considered imaginary urban scenes.

It is possible that the artists who painted representations of Istanbul in the provinces based their paintings on other artwork they had seen in the capital or elsewhere, although this influence has yet to be traced. However, the scenes of the capital that we see in the provinces are most certainly a type of imaginary art to the viewer, for they depict scenes that are not based on what has actually been seen. People in the provinces knew about the Bosphorus and the Golden Horn, or the Süleymaniye Mosque and Bayezit Tower, but they did not have, in their personal knowledge, firsthand images to represent them. Rather, there was a collective repertoire of understood images, such as "the largest tower in Istanbul," understood because of their descriptive power, which were either imagined by local artists or imported, pre-made, from other media, but these were never attempts at representational accuracy. This can be seen in the depiction of Istanbul that was painted in about 1875 in the Şadırvan canopy in the courtyard of the Bayezid II mosque in Amasya.

In this image we see the Bayezid tower of Istanbul disproportionately dominating the skyline; it even outshines a very diagrammatic version of the Süleymaniye Mosque (understood only by the placement of its four courtyard minarets). Perhaps this dominance of the Bayezid tower is meant to emphasize the connection with the Amasya Bayezid II Mosque, but it is more likely that the whole ensemble was based on paintings that were circulating in Istanbul itself.[32] Nonetheless, although these paintings depict real places, their method of depiction is neither generic nor documentary but imaginary.

Likewise, provincial depictions of houses, whether freestanding or in urban ensembles, are never portraits of real houses but follow in the miniaturist tradition of painting that depicts houses in a block style with pointed roofs.[33] This artistic choice can be seen in the houses that surround the Bayezit tower in the Amasya Şadırvan. Even if these houses refer to those in the town in which they were painted, such as the scene in Yozgat of a local fire, or a representation of the finest house of Amasya that is painted inside the Amasya Gümüşlüzade Mosque, they remain highly stylized.

Houses such as these are referred to by Uğur Tanyeli as imaginary houses because they are hardly related to reality at all.[34] Nonetheless, these houses must have been firmly entrenched in the collective imagination as conventions, understood from other depictions to refer to real neighborhoods. In the same way, Tanyeli might consider the house-tasvir of Şirin as an imaginary house, not because it never existed in reality (it may well have done so) but because it came from an architectural tradition outside the Ottoman milieu and thus from outside the knowledge repertoire of the people who were viewing it.

However, in Istanbul and in a few fine konaks of courtiers in the provinces, there are realistic paintings of the mansions lining the Bosphorus (that is, of yalıs). For example, the scenes that were painted on the walls of the Şadrullah Pasha Yalı in Cengelköy (today's greater Istanbul) or on the Abutlar Yalısı are rich in realistic architectural detail.

Tanyeli calls these houses imaginary architecture too, because many of these mansions may not be real places, although some certainly were.[35] Yet the paintings often operate in a way similar to the purely diagrammatic houses that were drawn in the miniaturist tradition. That is, they are recognizable because they refer to a stock of known forms that existed in contemporary architecture, such as Mullah Uryanizade Cemil's nineteenth-century yalı in Kuzguncuk.

Until an argument is made that these wall paintings are portraits of real places, they, like the houses that refer to the miniaturist tradition, remain

Amasya. Istanbul depicted under the Şadırvan *(fountain) canopy, Bayezid II Mosque courtyard in 1874. From Arık,* Batılılaşma Dönemi Anadolu Tasvir Sanati, *Fig. 11.*

Yozgat. Wall painting in Nizamoğlu house of local fire. From Arık, Batılılaşma Dönemi Anadolu Tasvir Sanati, *p. 61.*

Istanbul, Cengelköy. The Sadrullah Pasha Yalısı. From Renda, A History of Turkish Painting, *p. 84.*

imaginary, and perhaps because of this they produced no art historical future in that they did not become at a later date representative of the period in which they were produced (or used) and therefore held no affective resonance. They are therefore not like or comparable to the generic Karagöz tasvir image of the Ottoman house, which both distilled its real architectural vocabulary and was used repeatedly in a believable, though make-believe, setting and thus could begin to enter the Turkish imaginary in a way that might recur, with particular associations, in the mind of a high school girl in 1990. Here we begin to see how images operate in the creation of the future. The creation of the future involves expectation, which, according to William James, "is the association of a present image with others known to belong to the future." This, really, is but another side of memory, which he defines as "the association of a present image with others known to belong to the past."[36]

REPRESENTATIONS AND COLLECTIVE MEMORY

And so we are back to the issue of memory.

Shared images can include the generic, the possible, the imagined, and the expected. But when what is imagined is also a sign of something that is permanently absent, something that is not just out of sight at the moment but gone forever, it becomes part of the collective memory.[37]

The house-tasvir of the Karagöz play may have been the first time that the Ottoman house took on a visible form that could signal a shared meaning. But, as we have seen, during its years as living theater, before it became a revivalist genre, there was never a sense that it signaled the time of the past, a time that existed in a separate time from now. However, the child's representation of Istanbul as an ensemble of romanticized nineteenth-century Ottoman-period wooden houses, because it was drawn by a young student in 1989, meets the requirement of collective memory in full. It is a representation that is made at some distance in time from the appearance of the content of the representation, that is, the old wooden house. At the same time, this drawing, by a person who could never herself have seen an Istanbul landscape of pristine wooden houses,[38] shows how the history of collective memory is a chain of representations, of memory images, for the memory image of an Ottoman-period house will not be created by a person who saw the original or, perhaps more accurately, felt the original. It is more likely that she or he has read the novels we will read in the next chapters or has heard stories associated with these houses, and so, when she or he recreates them artistically, she (in the case of the student Beren Tuncay) may in fact believe she is participating in a chain of history, recreating an image of the future that replicates what she believes was the past.

What she is really participating in is the chain of imagination. As Boyer has pointed out,

> History . . . gives the appearance that memory persists in a uniform manner, being handed down from one period of time to another and passing successively from place to place. [But in fact] because it is disrupted from its original time and historic place, the past [actually] reappears as a historical theater, presenting its voice to the spectator through a series of images.[39]

These memory images, as Boyer suggests, give an illusion of a continuation of history. And because they only exist, in both texts and drawings, as representations of the past, representations are indeed the links in history's chain of memory. It is exactly because these representations are created and live in cultural productions such as published art and literature that we understand that they are what one must investigate to access collective memory.

In 1987, for example, Ahmet Hamdi Tanpınar's popular collection of short stories, *Five Cities* (*Beş Şehir*), first published in 1946, went into its seventh printing. His description of Istanbul represents what might well have contributed to the collective memory shared by the Istanbul schoolgirl:

> These Sultans' palaces, mansions, and wealthy homes spread from Divanyolu to Sultanahmed and Akbıyık and today's Sirkeci, to Kumkapı and Kadırga, to Süleymaniye and Şehzadebaşı, and from there to Fatih and Edirenekapı, and on in the direction of Aksaray as far as Koca Mustafa Pasha and Yedikule. . . . From the 17th century onward, [these] mansions [konaks] that used to be called "palaces" [Saray] . . . were found on both sides of the Golden Horn. . . . In the 17th century there were summer homes [yalı] in Kadırga and along the shores and on the hills of the Bosphorus; and on the Kadıköy side, in the area that stretches from today's Moda as far as Fenerbahçe, there were orchards and gardens with large pavilions [köşk] in them.[40]

Clearly, the image of the house had changed from representing the present to representing the past. With the house-tasvir, we saw the house as representing an image of the continual present. How and when did this change?

THE BEGINNING OF MEMORY IMAGES:
SEARCHING FOR RUPTURES

Any revolution, any rapid alteration of the givens of the present, places a society's connection with its history under pressure.[41]

Terdiman suggests that memory images will emerge whenever there is a painful "loss of a sense of time's continuous flow and of our unproblematic place within it,"[42] or, as David Lowenthal puts it, when the past begins to look like a foreign country.[43] That is, because of a startling realization that the past existed in a separate time from now, the process of cultural remembering begins, whether to make the distance greater, giving the past what Bakhtin called "epic distance,"[44] or to make it closer.[45]

Ahmet Hamdi's description of Istanbul's Ottoman-period houses is an example of a memory image in the form of a description written in 1946 of the nineteenth century or earlier, and the child's drawing suggests that these images may then take on a life of their own. Yet it would seem that their relevance must always point to a cultural need for stability or self-understanding. In fact, Terdiman alerts us that if we find a sudden concern with memory, as in Ahmet Hamdi, rather than with reality, as in the house-tasvir, we should suspect a time of rupture or upheaval.

Terdiman's ideas lead to two related questions: When did the building of Ottoman-period houses end, and was this followed by a period of social disquiet that made this now lost house a memory issue? Without considering replicas or romanticized versions of it, one might ask, if building the Ottoman-style house was part of a vernacular tradition that ended, exactly when did that happen?[46] How exciting it would be to find a record of that very last house somewhere in the Ottoman *tapu* (title) registers! We know that in the mid-nineteenth century, Ottoman-style houses began to be replaced by stone houses and apartment buildings in major cities. And although we may not be able to identify the last house to be built, we do know how they began to be destroyed, and that the destruction was by fire.

Reports of fires destroying entire neighborhoods appear in travelers' accounts, city histories, and personal memoirs,[47] and the wooden character of Ottoman neighborhoods meant that no Ottoman town was exempt. Official records of fires in Istanbul begin in the seventeenth century,[48] and information on fires in provincial neighborhoods can be found hidden in the endowment records of the repair of public buildings. The frequency and dimensions of urban fires can be seen by comparing the endowment records of the mosques, *mescits* (neighborhood mosques), hamams (baths), and *tekkes* (dervish lodges) that needed repair due to a fire in the same period. For example, this type of evidence suggests that in 1730 in Amasya, once a provincial capital, at least four mahalles were completely destroyed.[49] Also, a fire in Amasya in 1915, during the war of independence but of unknown cause, erupted as the last Armenians were fleeing for their lives, destroying most of the wooden houses in a contingent group of five Muslim neighborhoods. The residents of these neighborhoods moved to the now empty Armenian houses.[50] Because of the speed with which these fires burned and spread from wooden house to wooden house, the inhabitants were lucky to escape with their lives and possibly one or two possessions.[51]

Nonetheless, although houses were continually being lost to fire, it seems clear that the slow disappearance of these houses through the long nineteenth century did not trigger the alarm that set memory in motion. Despite the consistent and devastating outbreak of fires that destroyed entire neighborhoods, there is no evidence that anyone worried that these houses, as a type or as a lifestyle, might disappear altogether, or that this loss signaled a rupture with the past and that one's own heritage might be in jeopardy. Ahmet Hamdi Tanpınar makes this clear when he recalls how the nineteenth-century elite reacted to these fires:

> How strange it is that the fires that left our life so naked, spread a coarse type of pleasure among the city dwellers after the Tanzimat period in Istanbul. Red-jacketed, half naked, the fire fighters ran with canes in their hands as thin as lances, and as soon as their voices—with that terrifying cry "Fire!"—was heard, . . . the famous Beys and Pashas would come out to watch. Hurrying their horse carts, if it was the cold season, they took blankets as well as wearing fur coats in order not to catch a cold, and spirit lamps called "*kaminota*" in case they wanted to make coffee during the course of the fire. When I was a child, in Şehzadebaşı a highly esteemed pasha had been one of those who ran off to watch fires with his horse and cart. Only this Pasha didn't bring coffee because he loved tea, and so he brought along his Samovar [coal-burning tea pot].[52]

This sense of spectacle was reported by various nineteenth-century travelers and captured by Abdülhamid's court painter Zonaro in his painting "*Fire!*" An American observer in Istanbul who described these spectacles in 1902 wrote, "Sometimes I think the firemen are more interesting than the dogs."[53] (Stray dogs were so ubiquitous in Istanbul that they were a part of every traveler's report.)

Ahmet Hamdi was born in 1901, so his childhood recollections of the pasha and the samovar help us to understand that, at least until the Balkan War period, the Ottoman house was not considered anything more than a place where someone lived. If these houses were thought about at all, and we have little evidence that they were, it was only with the expectation that the burned house would be replaced by another just like it, or possibly better.

In fact, there was a growing belief that something better was at hand, and that the traditional house made of wood should be replaced with flame-retardant "*kârgir*" (cut stone or brick and mortar).[54] Fire was not seen as the enemy; *the enemy was the house itself* and its siting on narrow streets. Not only was wood easily ignited by sparks from cooking or lighting fuel but densely built neighborhoods meant that a fire in one house traveled easily to its neighbor, and narrow, crooked streets meant that firefighting equipment would arrive slowly, if at all.

Until the middle of the nineteenth century in Istanbul, and later in the provinces, burned houses and burned neighborhoods were rebuilt to resemble what had been lost to fire.[55] But well before the republican period, at the onset of the modernizing Tanzimat Reforms (1839–1879), the wooden house that had long been at the mercy of rampant fires now became vulnerable to new construction codes that outlawed building in wood.[56] At the very beginning of this period, in 1839, an "official document" (*Ilmuhaber*) suggested a law to protect cities against the age-old problem of destruction by fire by requiring that kârgir replace timber in all new constructions—at least for those who could afford it.[57] A series of laws followed, all referring only to Istanbul, until 1863, when the Road and Building Regulations Laws (*Turuk ve Ebniye Nizamnamesi*) enlarged government supervision of the urban structure to include all other cities and large towns. This regulation stated that a map was to be prepared for any area that had been devastated by fire and that a new plan for it must be made that would include a plan to regularize and widen the streets so that fire fighting equipment could enter the neighborhoods in time to have some effect.[58] A law the following year decreed that all new building in Istanbul must be in kârgir; however, those citizens who could not afford kârgir were permitted to rebuild in timber if they also built a firewall to protect their neighbors.[59]

The problem of the relative expense of kârgir or brick to wood was addressed after the great Hoca (Hodja) Pasha fire of 1865, in which "a vast area, defined by the Sea of Marmara in the south, the Golden Horn in the north, the Beyazit Külliye (Mosque Complex) in the west and the Hagia Sophia—Sultan Ahmet Mosque axis in the east, was burned to the ground in a period of thirty-two hours."[60] One-third of the historic peninsula burned.

In 1866, taxes on brick and cement were abolished, and the Commission for Road Improvement (*İslahat-ı Turuk Komisyonu*) established its own brick and cement factory to sell affordable materials to those rebuilding after fires.[61]

As the new road and construction laws and the new pricing policies took effect, stone began to replace wood; cul-de-sacs (*çıkmaz*) were eliminated; curving, narrow streets were straightened and widened; and the urban landscape of Istanbul and then Anatolia began, however slowly, to change irrevocably.[62]

In Istanbul, the transformation from timber to stone began after 1850, first by the people who could most afford it, owners of large summer villas along the Bosphorus, and then by state buildings such as the Dolma Bahçe Palace, which was built in 1853. Because of its great expense, kârgir for residential purposes was affordable mainly by government or community groups. Thus, housing clusters or row-style apartment buildings were built, such as the *"Akaretler,"* built in Beşiktaş in 1870 by Sultan Abdülaziz for Dolma Bahçe Palace personnel, or the *Taksim Surp Agop* houses of 1890, built by the Armenian community, or the houses in Fener built by the Bulgarian Community Endowment (*Bulgar Vakfı*).[63]

The style of these new stone buildings was influenced by the desire of a contemporary reforming spirit to Europeanize the city, but the materials used were chosen in response to the new protective laws. Mustafa Reşit Pasha, an author of the Tanzimat Charter, and Helmuth von Moltke, who had been brought by Abdülmecit to redesign Istanbul's street fabric, agreed that not only would fire-resistant kârgir serve "the public good" (*menfaat-ı umumiye*), it would also be aesthetically superior to a "shapeless timber construction" (*"resimsiz ahşap"*) whose image could only damage the glory of the capital.[64] It was Moltke who brought the wide, straight street, the *"cadde,"* to Turkey. A cadde was owned by the municipality, whereas the local street or *sokak*, faced with houses and garden walls, was conceptually and realistically a part of the mahalle. As Çelik observes, "The ultimate goal envisioned by post-Tanzimat regulations was a [European-style] city with straight and uniformly wide streets defining rectangular or square blocks composed of stone or brick buildings."[65]

Clearly, the family wooden house had entered the collective—as well as the official—imagination, but as an item that was inherently dangerous and to be replaced. In his memoirs about the Istanbul fires such as the Uzunçarşılı fire of 1911, Malik Aksel wrote:

> While one quarter of the city was burning, and being destroyed, on the other side of the city they went right on building more wooden houses; and not only that, they coated these houses in oil paint. Most of the wood was pine with resin, so in the summer they could burn like kindling.[66]

The residents of Istanbul may not have realized that remodeling their street system inevitably entailed the destruction of their well-known streetscapes, but that may not have bothered them anyway. The narrow, muddy streets of Istanbul had been an irritant for its residents throughout the nineteenth century. An 1874 cartoon shows two gentlemen walking on stilts while a poor *hammal* (porter) struggles thigh deep in mud. "My dear Karagöz," says one to the other, "there's no other way to keep clean and still walk in the streets of Istanbul."[67] By 1909, these gentlemen are ready to leave entirely: a cartoon in the biweekly magazine *Kalem* (The Pen) shows two men talking during the rainy season (indicated by their umbrellas). The first says, "I'm just praying that I'll be saved from this neighborhood! There's no street, no street lamps, and mud up to the knees." And the other replies, "Better pray that a politician moves to our neighborhood, then we'll be rescued from this filth."[68]

In the 1970s, Malik Aksel remembered the first part of the century like this:

> If you wanted to see what Hell looked like on earth, Istanbul was the place to do it. The houses were so close that neighbors could lean out their windows and shake hands across the street.... These houses couldn't stand without the support of each other, and most of them were out of plumb and leaning to one side.[69]

In fact, by 1909 the thought of these old houses on their dark, narrow streets had become a symbol of all that was wrong with the Ottoman Empire in its final days. A cartoon in a 1909 issue of *Kalem* depicts the wooden houses of Istanbul with their upper floors projecting over menacingly dark and dilapidated streets. The cartoon is addressed to the municipality with a caption that (cynically) quotes Victor Hugo: "The Orient! Gateway to Light!"[70]

In this period, at the end of the Ottoman era, what we today call the old Turkish house seemed to have had at least two, somewhat conflicting asso-

ciations: first, it appeared to be an architectural given, one that did not signal either a lost past or imminent change. On the other hand, the house was
in need of replacement: it was both a place that could go up in flames at any
moment, making the rich poor in a day and putting everyone in fear of their
lives, and a symbol of a society in need of renewal and reform. Thus, the standard Ottoman-style house at the start of the twentieth century, if not disre-
garded, had enough of a negative image that its replacement with houses of
different materials on different types of streets was certainly more of a cause
for celebration than alarm. As late as 1914, when commenting on the changes
made possible in spaces leveled by fires, the historian Osman Nuri Ergin
wrote, "The big fire of Hoca Pasha brought more happiness than disaster to
Istanbul."[71]

But this sentiment was not shared by all, and as we investigate the historic
Ottoman-period house as it appears in later memory, it is seen as untenable.
Such negative thoughts could just never have belonged to the past.

"The Orient! Gateway to Light!" From Kalem: Journal humoristique et satirique paraissant le Jeudi, *1909, 1–2.*

Aşkımız
Aksaray'ın En Büyük
Yangını

Güngör Dilmen

TÜRKİYE İŞ BANKASI Kultur Yayınları

Our Love was the most devastating fire of Aksaray *(book cover)*.
From Dilmen, Aşkımız Aksaray'ın En Büyük Yangını, 1989.

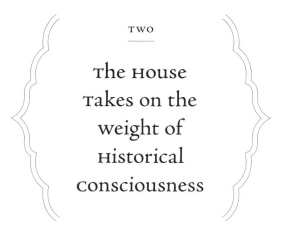

TWO

The House
Takes on the
weight of
Historical
consciousness

"Our Love was the most devastating fire of Aksaray," wrote a poet in 1992.[1] But the Aksaray fire was in 1911, and the poet Güngör Dilmen was not yet born when it lit the Istanbul skyline, making the residents of Aksaray and its environs run for their lives with their children to Bayezit Square's makeshift refugee encampment.[2]

By Dilmen's time the Aksaray fire had entered the collective memory, but in its own time it happened to real people. In the collective life of any country there are moments such as these that are felt to change both one's personal life and the collective life at the same time. That is, these events are autobiographical in nature, but they are also communally experienced and quickly become part of a shared memory. The double nature of this event serves to reinforce (as well as refine or revise) memory, giving it added weight. Adair Lara wrote about this phenomenon in our time, pondering why she could remember where she was when John F. Kennedy was shot, or how she felt during the 1989 San Francisco earthquake, or where she was when O. J. Simpson fled up the Los Angeles freeway in his Bronco. "Why should I remember that?" she asks. "I can't remember Patrick's first step, but I remember every detail of standing in that restaurant, watching that white Bronco, the other diners crowded around me." She concludes that "such events, those that happen to everybody, stick in the mind because they mark a moment when something changed—and changed for us all at the same time."[3] The Aksaray fire was a shared memory that was discussed in the newspapers for days, with bitter stories and humorous poems; in fact, many of the fire victims' only access to information about their own neighborhood was through the newspapers.[4]

Shared memory, then, is larger than autobiographical memory, but it is certainly rooted in the autobiographical and the contemporary in a way that collective memory, as Halbwachs imagined it and as we are using the term here, is not. Collective memory has no autobiographical component, for in collective or historical memory the person does not remember events directly; rather, memory is stimulated indirectly and inherited by way of memory images, such as the stories and songs that arose to recount the great Istanbul fires,[5] or the portrayals in contemporary novels, paintings, or pageantry, such as the Karagöz plays discussed in Chapter 1.

Collective memory, then, is a memory with a memory, or memory with a history. We could situate Dilmen's poem in this type of history by discussing how the memories of Istanbul's fires are kept alive in a variety of media such as songs and stories. Ultimately, however, we go back to a shared autobiographical moment.

Just as the old wooden houses of Turkey appear in the collective memory, they can also be traced back to a shared memory. Yet the literature that deals with old houses, even at the autobiographical level or a shared moment of remembering, records a historical consciousness that is not related to memory so much as to emotions and desire. As suggested by Dilmen's poem, it is only by looking at what appears to be memory that one can understand how the images that make up collective memory emerged and developed. It is for this reason, because we are always looking at what appears to be memory, that we must move backward in time.

The child's landscape painting of Ottoman-style houses, created in 1989, offers a useful way into the discussion. The prototypes for this painting were real houses in real places, but the painting was a memory image rooted in the collective imagination rather than an autobiographical memory of the Turkish cityscape. It marked, in fact, the central position of the Turkish house in the late twentieth-century Turkish collective imagination: the painting won first place in the 1991 Turkish UNICEF awards. Thus, the house was recognized in the real sense of the term, as an appropriate and emotionally believable representation of the past, as well as a hope for the future.

Likewise, in the 1998 celebration of Ramazan in Istanbul, the municipality of Eminönü sponsored a "traditional" celebration. The open area of the old hippodrome, now Sultanahmet Square, was made into a "traditional" neighborhood and lined with miniature facades of old wooden houses[6] of the type that once graced a city now almost fully composed of concrete apartments.

Istanbul. Celebration of Ramazan, Sultan Ahmet. Photograph by Carel Bertram, 1996.

Istanbul. Celebration of Ramazan, Sultan Ahmet. Photograph by Carel Bertram, 1996.

"*This is it . . . this is where my childhood lies.*" From Gülgeç, "Hikâye-i İstanbul,"
İstanbul Dergisi 17, 1996.

(from left to right) "*It's dying alone, with me.*" "*Do I have to take the past so hard? Am I so emotional
because there is no future?*" "*I'd carved my memories somewhere around here. . . .*" "GRRR" (*the sound
of a door squeaking open*). From Gülgeç, "Hikâye-i İstanbul," İstanbul Dergisi 17, 1996.

A banner across the hippodrome proclaimed, "This Ramazan, for the first time, experience a traditional Ramazan every night for one month in Sultanahmet Square. Brought to you by the Eminönü Municipality." Here, clearly, traditional means past, and it is equally clear that the old Ottoman-style house is the centerpiece of how this past is supposed to have looked. It is a memory image.

Another image that speaks to the Ottoman-style house as it is "remembered" and imagined in popular culture today is a cartoon story from an issue of *Istanbul Magazine* called "*Hikâye-i Istanbul*" (An Istanbul Romance).

In this cartoon, an old wooden Ottoman-style house appears against a hazy twentieth-century skyline. From the outside it is evident that it is uninhabited, for the walls have only enough timber to give the house a shape and the roof beams are mostly gone, making the interior open to the sky. An old man stands sadly in front of it, thinking that it is surely his childhood home.

When he walks up to the front door to see if his childish carving is still visible in the woodwork, the old man imagines that he is invited in by a beautiful young woman in Ottoman dress who sits him down while she goes to make coffee.

There is a moment when we share his hope that the past is not dead. But the artist makes it clear that this experience is a hallucination or a dream state

(from left to right) "Hello, [dear] old man." "You! Young lady!" "Yes, me, [dear] man."
From Gülgeç, "Hikâye-i İstanbul," İstanbul Dergisi *17, 1996.*

by making the rooms change from black and white to full color (and thus come alive in the old man's imagination) as the old man walks through them.

The past that is imagined for this old house is one from the mid- to late nineteenth century or earlier, as it admits of no Westernization at all in its furnishings or in the clothing of the young woman who lives there. This is unlike what we know from Turkish novels and paintings of Istanbul upper-class life at the turn of the twentieth century, when both dress and furnishing were somewhat if not completely Westernized. For example, beginning in the late nineteenth century, the centerpiece of most upper-class houses was a piano, which became the hallmark of an educated and modern family.[7]

It is true that much of this Western-oriented,[8] alafranga[9] life was concentrated in Beyoğlu, on the northern side of the Golden Horn, and not within what is now called the Historic Peninsula[10] where the cartoon house is depicted. Late Ottoman novels clearly differentiate between Beyoğlu and this "historic" area, which was characterized as almost immune to alafranga ways. Still, stories from the turn of the twentieth century suggest that even these were responsive to changes introduced in the nineteenth century. Nabizade Nazim's novel Zehra[11] shows how the tastes of the Westernized elites had filtered down to the middle class by 1890: the protagonist, Zehra, plays the piano and the dulcimer, and men and women share company in musical evenings and other social events.[12]

By the early twentieth century, this Westernization was even more widespread and more entrenched. In a charming story by Ömer Seyfeddin (1884–1920), "The Secret Temple" ("Gizli Mabet"), written sometime before 1920,[13] the author takes a European visitor to the old, "historic peninsula" section of Istanbul because the visitor badly wants to have an "Oriental experience" as he had come to expect it from the novels of Pierre Loti.[14] He loathes Turkey's "non-authentic" Westernized ways and longs to see a "real," that is, "un-Europeanized" Turkish home. The closest to it that the author can find is a place with a Victorian aura. Instead of light pouring into the guest room from a row of windows above the street, dark red curtains fall on dark red cushions in the "drawing room." Yet the author suggests that even this was hard to find; furthermore, the interior is portrayed as almost an anachronism, as it belongs to a very conservative old widow who refuses to let go of any of her mementos of the past.

The same sense is conveyed by Irfan Orga, who wrote of his childhood in Akbıyık, a neighborhood below Istanbul's Sultan Ahmet Mosque and the hippodrome. He wrote of his family's move in 1912 from their konak to a smaller house as the Balkan Wars approached:

The old man waits on the sedir *for his cup of Turkish coffee. From Gülgeç,*
"Hikâye-i İstanbul," İstanbul Dergisi 17, 1996.

"It's the human being, my dear old man, the human being. Anything with a human being living in it
will come to life and become beautiful." From Gülgeç, "Hikâye-i İstanbul," İstanbul Dergisi 17, 1996.

When we moved into our new house, the furniture was arranged, but to the satisfaction of no one, for the smaller, darker rooms looked unbearably over-crowded with my grandmother's unwieldy furniture.[15]

With this in mind, the cartoon image becomes problematic as a real, autobiographical memory of an old man taking a sentimental walk in 1996. How old would he have to be in 1996 if his boyhood memories are of the not-so-late nineteenth century? This cartoon, then, is not autobiographical but a memory image that gives the illusion of memory.[16] In fact, the memory it portrays is not the old man's at all but that of the cartoonist, İsmail Gülgeç. Clearly, the cartoonist, like the schoolgirl, is representing the house as it would be recognized as part of a contemporary collective memory. And this reminds us that when we are looking at memory, we are always already more in the present than we think.

How did this early to mid-nineteenth-century domestic image come, in the late twentieth century, to represent the remembered Ottoman past, and then some of its values? What visual images mediated between these images and others that preceded it? I suggest that one of the most important mediators is the Turkish house museum (ev müze). These museums are located in seventeenth- to late nineteenth-century houses, with rooms arranged to recall that magical era sought by Ömer Seyfettin's visitor, the era when "everything was Turkish," a designation that became an important attribute of the house as a nationalist memory image as early as 1912.

In Istanbul this phenomenon is visible at the Sadberk Hanım Museum, which was conceived in the 1960s but opened in 1980 to display the textiles and household items that Sadberk Hanım (Lady Sadberk or Ms. Sadberk) herself had collected, many from the Mahmut Pasha Bazaar behind Istanbul's Grand Bazaar.[17] The items displayed span a period from the seventeenth century to the early twentieth century, and the artifacts, including ones that the museum continues to acquire, are often arranged in dioramas that depict daily life and rituals in an Ottoman Turkish home, such as the serving of coffee to guests, the "henna night" (kına gecesi) before a wedding, or the celebration of a young boy's circumcision (sünnet). The coffee ritual dioramas are particularly striking because their setting and costumes so closely resemble those in the house depicted in the cartoon and show us dramatically how museums hold important images of the past for the present, making them available for appropriation.

The museum exhibit functions in a way similar to but more striking than the connection between the child's drawing and the writing of Ahmed

Ottoman dress of the wife of the Orientalist painter, Osmanhamdi Bey (1842–1910). Courtesy of the Sadberk Hanım Museum, Istanbul.

The Ottoman beauty at the Turkish door. "My God, what a beauty!" says the old man. From Gülgeç, "Hikâye-i İstanbul," İstanbul Dergisi 17, 1996.

Hamdi. It is important to remember, however, that the Sadberk Hanım House Museum is not a house that was "museumized" in the sense of being frozen in time; rather, it began as a place to store and display domestic mementos collected by Sadberk Hanım to preserve what she perceived as a rapidly disappearing past. It was never Sadberk Hanım's own home but was purchased after her death (in 1973), and then some of the rooms were "furnished" behind glass. For if this konak had been frozen in time—say, when it was built in 1870, or at any time afterward—it is unlikely that it would have been devoid of Western furnishings: it was far from the historic peninsula, in Büyükdere, near Sariyer, a wealthy area on the shore of the Bosphorus known for its yalıs and köşks and a prized residential property of foreign ambassadors.[18] Furthermore, this particular house had been the home of an Armenian civil servant who had been the Ottoman representative in Romania.[19] That is to say, it belonged to a member of the most Westernized element of the late Ottoman period.

What is important is not merely that the cartoon image of the house was not even the memory of the old man's but that the rooms we often find today in Ottoman house museums are not even their own rooms but have been made even older. Like the room in the cartoon, they are composite memories constructed from earlier images. Here, the museum is a site where memory can be dusted off and re-presented.

A HOUSE OF IDENTITY: THE *TÜRK SALONU* AND *TÜRK ODASI*

The memory embedded in the rooms of Turkish house museums is partly rooted in older museumized rooms, the most important of which was the *Türk Salonu* (Turkish Salon) that was built inside the Turkish Hearth Building in Ankara and officially opened in 1930.

This room, which was the centerpiece of the Turkish Hearth Society Headquarters in Ankara (today's State Fine Arts Museum), was in the style of, but not a replica of, a guest room of a seventeenth- or eighteenth-century konak. For example, it had an upper row of stained glass windows that are representative of the eighteenth century, but the windows below them are carried to the ground rather than ending at a banquette of interior win-

The Turkish Salon in the Turkish Hearth Building, Ankara.
From Suphi, "Türk Ocakları Merkez," Türk Yurdu, 1930.

The Turkish Hearth Building, Ankara. From Koyunoğlu, "Türk Mimari," 1929.

dow seating. The double row of windows, with the lower ones defining the view from the interior seating, characterized the exterior facade of seventeenth-century houses, and many in the following centuries as well.[20] In fact, it appears to be a meeting room that collected and displayed what were felt to be the finest examples of "Turkish" domestic architecture: a ceiling intricately decorated with wood inlay (*göbekli tavan*), recessed shelves and niches framed in arabesque (*hücre*), and a wall fireplace (*ocak*—here, not meant to be used) to rival that in any palace.

The Turkish Hearth Building was built to house the Turkish Hearth Society (*Türk Ocağı*), founded in 1911. The Türk Ocağı was the first organized Turkish response to the nationalist organizations that were forming all over the empire for everyone else, such as the Albanian *Başkim* and the Kurdish *Hoybon*.[21] In this way, the Turkish Hearth Society was institutionalizing for Turkish Ottomans the painful process of separating themselves from what had once been considered an Ottoman whole.

In 1926, Halide Edib, a leader in the women's emancipation movement, a novelist, a university lecturer and politician, and the cover girl of Turkish feminism of the pre- and early republican period,[22] wrote about this process of separation and reforming of identity:

The Ottoman Turk so far had been a composite being, an Ottoman citizen like any other, his greatest writers writing for all the educated men of the empire. . . . For the first time reduced to his elements and torn from the ensemble of races in Turkey, he vaguely faced the possibility of searching, analyzing, and discovering himself as something different from the rest. . . . Cast out or isolated in his own country, he not only saw himself different, but he also had the desire to find out wherein lay the difference. . . . The first separate organization formed by the Turkish youth in this sense was called the Turkish Hearth.[23]

The founding principles of the Turkish Hearth Society were nationalism (*Milliyetçilik*), populism (*Halkçılık*), and Westernism (*Garpçılık*), but along with these, a unifying interest in establishing Turkish solidarity through the principle of Turkism (*Türkçülük*). Turkism, in brief, was the awakening of a consciousness of a Turkish Muslim identity and its affiliation with a national homeland of other Turkish Muslims rather than with the eroded multiculturalism of the Ottoman Empire.[24] This identity of being a Turk rather than an Ottoman, along with a change in the concept of Turk from one of derision to one of pride and the fusion of Turk with Islam, had begun after the Greco-Turkish war of 1897, when the young poet Mehmet Emin wrote:

Ben bir Türküm
Dinim cinsim uludur.

I am a Turk,
My faith and my race are mighty.[25]

Turkism was elaborated as a coherent theory, or ideology, by Ziya Gökalp, who became the editor of *Türk Yurdu* (Turkish Homeland), the journal of the Türk Ocağı, in 1912. Mehmet Emin had been one of the journal's founders.[26] Thus, the Türk Ocağı was the institution of the "awakening" of the *hal-i bidar*, a term that was meant to describe this realization of difference and what it could mean to the people.[27] Its president, Hamdullah Suphi, wrote:

The Turkish Hearth was born during the time of the Ottoman Empire. It has a single intention: To spread solidarity among the Turks living in the environment of the Empire.[28]

Along with promoting Turkish nationalism, the Turkish Hearth Societies (there were chapters in all major cities and towns) were the first to have a cultural program in which women could perform on the stage, give speeches, and take courses along with men. Halide Edib, whom we have just met, made her first public appearances at the Turkish Hearth; it was the arena of her public inauguration as a female activist, and her classes for the Turkish Hearth members led to a later career teaching at the university.[29] Ziya Gökalp, the major political philosopher of the emerging Turkish Republic, also gave free lectures for the Türk Ocağı.

The Turkish Hearth Society was thus the natural choice to become the focus of culture at the beginning of the Turkish Republic, and it was a significant move to place the image of the Turkish house in its center.[30] Mustafa Kemal Atatürk, as president of the new Republic of Turkey,[31] was closely involved with the later activities of the Turkish Hearth, as he founded the Turkish Historical Society (*Türk Tarih Kurumu*) and Turkish Language Association (*Türk Dil Kurumu*) and planned to have these organizations housed in the Turkish Hearth Building. The Turkish Historical Society investigated or reconstructed the deep roots of Turkish culture, and the Turkish Language Association worked to reconstruct and disseminate a purely Turkish tongue. In other words, these organizations, like the Turkish Hearth Association, arose from an ideology of Turkism that sought historical and metaphorical spaces where "everything was Turkish."

But Atatürk also made this building the launching pad to disseminate aspects of European culture, such as the presentation of European operas. *Madame Butterfly* and *Tosca* were performed there in Turkish by an all-Turkish cast.[32] For this reason the building had a large auditorium, as well as lecture halls, seminar rooms, and a specialized library on Turkish history.

Atatürk was very involved in conceptualizing the building,[33] and it was he who suggested that it have a "Turkish Room" based on the old wooden house, thus aligning this house with a specifically Turkish identity. But the building itself was designed by the architect Arif Hikmet Koyunoğlu. Koyunoğlu was one of the architects who worked in the First National Style, a style of architecture that was the built counterpart of an ideology that attempted to maintain a national identity while assimilating Western civilization. Bozdoğan sums it up as "the recharging of Ottoman forms and details with 'Turkishness' . . . [that is] Elements derived from classical Ottoman Architecture (i.e., Turkish culture) were combined with European academic design principles and construction techniques (i.e., Western civilization)."[34] As an architectural style, the First National Style combined modern technology and materials with historicist decorative schemes that were meant to refer to an Ottoman heritage. That is, it had an eclectic approach that took ideas from monumental Ottoman architecture, ideas such as symmetry, arched windows and rich surface decorations, and then literally set them in concrete. The Turkish Hearth Building was perhaps the last public building to be built in the First National Style.

The Turkish Salon inside the Turkish Hearth Building was the last room to be finished. It was Arif Hikmet's personal project, for he had drawn the plan for the room based on his personal research on old houses, an interest perhaps stemming from his years as the art student of Hodja Ali Rıza Bey. He also used the research on Ankara houses that had been done by the Turkish Hearth Society under the supervision of its president, Hamdullah Suphi. But as the building neared completion, the money ran out, and Hamdullah Suphi came to him, sadly saying, "*Hikmet'ciğim*, my dear Hikmet, there is no money left, we have made a study for months of Ankara houses for you, and you made inspired drawings from them, what a shame that there is no more money left; we don't know what we are going to say to the Gazi." (By the Gazi—Commander—he means Atatürk, of course.) The unstoppable Hikmet replied that no more money was necessary, he would finish the room himself; and he went on to personally complete the ceiling with its plaster molding, and made the stained glass windows himself as well.

Arif Hikmet's own writings from this period suggest that his personal goals included a desire to provide local inspiration for a new national architecture[35] and to show that the classic Turkish room (which he contrasted with the rotting houses of the day) reflected a highly developed and deeply rooted Turkish standard and appreciation of beauty.[36] The room he chose to create was therefore from a period that predated any Western influence, at least in its surface decoration. Although it had no pianos, it was furnished with French antique chairs and tables, possibly because it was going to be used for meetings and gatherings of twentieth-century Turks and their guests.

This room should be seen as created rather than as replicating another room, for the Turkish Salon is more of a museum installation than a replica. Although Koyunoğlu was dedicated to the study of the Turkish house, with his own personal archive of photographs, and with an express directive by Atatürk to design decorative ceilings in the style of traditional Ankara houses, it appears that the room that he created was a type of historicist collage that "displayed" the main elements of the interior of a vernacular room:

the windows are not accurately positioned, the wall cupboards are not accurate, and the ceiling is not typical, being domed rather than flat. It seems that Koyunoğlu brought his penchant for monumentality and extravagant facades[37] to the interior, museumizing the domestic interior on a grand scale meant to be publicly celebrated. The opening celebration of the Turkish Hearth Building took place in this room, with speeches by the president, Hamdullah Suphi, and photographs in the Turkish Hearth journal.

The phrase "the Turkish house" in this chapter and the previous one should be understood as having invisible quotation marks around it, to call attention to the importance of the use of this term. The old wooden houses that had symbolized the Ottoman neighborhood in Karagöz theater and that housed the multiethnic and multireligious population of the Ottoman world had started to be called Turkish by 1928 within the confines of the Turkish Hearth Society and its ideology of Turkism and Turkish nationalism. Koyunoğlu was not the creator of this term, although he was among the first to use it. However, the Turkish Salon, by marking the interior of the old wooden house as Turkish, is the first example of physically visualizing the old wooden house within a memory of the past that was being created for the "new" Turkish people.

The salon was an example of the Turkish room of a Turkish house, reconstructed as a public symbol in a public space, but it was never meant to represent a desire to return to the past and certainly never to represent the slightest nostalgia for it; rather it claimed the Ottoman past for the new Turkish present. In Ankara, it was monumentalized in form in order to monumentalize this claim. As the new nation searched for its footing, Atatürk, and the architects of the new republic could now stand in solidarity inside a Turkish room, making clear how this place was to be understood as an appropriate symbol of this solidarity by members of an urban, educated elite who saw themselves in the service of what Atatürk represented.

A year later, however, in 1931, this now symbolic "Turkish Room" appeared in a private space, in a modernized konak or mansion in the upscale area of Şişli in Istanbul. We read of this "Turkish Room" (*Türk Odası*) in an issue of *Resimli Şark* (*The Illustrated Orient*), where it is the centerpiece of a three-page article that describes it as the pride of a hostess named Ay Hanım Efendi—famous for her weekly evenings of tea and conversation. The article emphasizes that the room that she has created and decorated is not merely an "Oriental Room" (*Şark Salonu*), which would associate it with the larger Middle Eastern or Islamic world, but a "Turkish Room," which spoke to a new Turkish present.

Ay Hanım Efendi's Turkish room, 1931. Razi, "Ay Hanımefendi."

In a large Oriental Room [*Şark Salonu*]—no, I used the term incorrectly . . . This salon is called a *Turkish Room* [*Türk Odası*] by Ay Hanım Efendi, . . . and all of her refined, hand-picked guests say *"Türk Odası"* when they speak of this salon.[38]

Oriental rooms were apparently known to the readership, perhaps because of Pierre Loti's Oriental rooms in his home in France, for anything that Pierre Loti did was always news in Turkey.[39] It appears, in fact, that others were including Oriental or Orientalist rooms or corners in their houses, for a 1923 article warns its readership that

The rooms that a great many of us believe we have furnished in the Oriental fashion, and which resemble shops in the Bedesten [Covered Market], do not interest us as meeting the description of Oriental. Many imitations and a number of boorish additions express this tastelessness, that is, [they are] nothing but a room that reveals a Western view and is furnished according to a Western taste.[40]

Clearly, in 1930, it was important to Ay Hanım Efendi that her room should not be confused with such a room. Yet unlike the Turkish Salon created in the Turkish Hearth Building, Ay Hanım Efendi's Turkish room is meant to be a real room in a real konak. It is furnished with traditional Turkish bench seating (*sedirs*) along the walls, although there are also some nineteenth-century chairs, and Turkish rugs and tiles on the floor.

But this room should not be mistaken for one merely left intact from the old days of the konak; it is as carefully a constructed marker of Ay Hanım Efendi's identification with Turkish nationalism, as was Koyunoğlu's Turkish Salon, and the name *Türk Odası* reinforces this. One wall is dominated by a large photo of Atatürk, another has photographs of the nationalist author Namık Kemal and the nationalist philosopher Ziya Gökalp. There are historical paintings as well that tie the room to the grandeur of a national past, such as one of "Budin Kale," reminding the viewer of the conquest of Budapest in the sixteenth century. This sense of identification is not lost on the reporter at all, for he says that in this room,

> Even the smallest detail that meets your eye brings your Turkishness to your memory; for this salon is *unmixedly Turkish* to that degree. The colors, the furnishings, the gracious and refined decoration of it all is entirely Turkish.[41]

This is, in fact, a "museum room" that depicts a Turkish national past. Ay Hanım Efendi has carefully positioned, for the purpose of display, a large turban on one of the embroidered sedirs. The reporter refers to Ay Hanım Efendi herself as a nationalist (*milliyetçi*). That this is a museum room rather than a real room in the house is also signaled to the readership by the imposition onto the photograph of the Turkish room of a cutout from what appears to be a Western magazine of the face of a "thoroughly modern Millie," a type well known to the readership from other articles and advertisements that have been taken directly from American or European sources. In a later photograph it is clear that this is not Ay Hanım Efendi herself. In fact, it is her daughter, Dr. Türkan Haşmet Hanım, who, like her mother, had a Western education. Its imposition here is meant to represent Ayhanım Efendi's modernness, to distance her from the lifestyle that the room is meant to recall to memory. The text makes clear that although Ay Hanım Efendi is from a family of viziers ("the honest ones"), or perhaps because of this, she was educated in European languages and culture. As an adult, she lived for many years in London with her husband, who was the ambassador there, and she later sent her older daughter to Cambridge, her younger daughter being at the American College in Istanbul's Bebek at the time the article was written.

But the coup de grâce that makes this room a museum room is the fact that the tea gathering (*Çay Söhbeti*) itself took place in another room altogether. Although this is not expressed in the text, a photograph shows Ay Hanım Efendi and her guests having their tea in a European-style library, complete with a European tea service. Furthermore, when the guests were ready, Ay Hanım Efendi would go to a piano in the corner, that ultimate marker of European refinement, and by hearing that "the first part of what is played is *entirely Turkish*," we also understand that most of what was played was not.

The Turkish room of the Turkish house had been brought into the service of Turkish nationalism and become a centerpiece of Turkish identity, whether in one's own home or known from articles about Ankara or about the homes of celebrities. It had become a way to organize space in order to "mediate the identity and heritage of people through time."[42] As "wholly Turkish," it positioned a diverse population in a common home whose ownership was clear; museumized, this common past could not interfere with the future. Ay Hanım Efendi's Turkish room and the Turkish Hearth Society's Turkish Salon are illustrations—or reifications—of this concept. But the concept itself predates them and can be found in textual form.

THE RHETORICAL HOUSE OF HAMDULLAH SUPHI

What memories do you have? Were these houses strongly attached to your childhood? Were you sad when you grew up and moved away?

Not surprisingly, the first clear and conscious association of the old wooden house with national identity arose within the Turkish Hearth Society, which was formed in 1911, twelve years before the Turkish Republic was proclaimed and almost twenty years before it was given a national headquarters in Ankara with the Turkish Salon in its center. The president of the Turkish Hearth Society during the time the Turkish Salon was being built was Hamdullah Suphi (Tanrıöver),[43] who had also been among its founders, and he had been entrusted with the task of overseeing the building process.[44]

It appears that it was Hamdullah Suphi who first gave voice to the idea of an "old Turkish house" as the marker of Turkish identity, and when Hamdullah Suphi spoke he was listened to, for he was famous for his oratorical abilities as well as his beautiful use of Turkish. In the closing years of the Ottoman Empire, which were the founding years of the Turkish Hearth Society, Hamdullah Suphi gave two public lectures titled "The Turkish House," which were also published in the organization's journal, *Türk Yurdu* (The Turkish Homeland). In one he posed the following questions, clearly intended to elicit the emotive aspects of the Turkish house:

> If we ask ourselves: what is it that binds our hearts to the places that we lived, if I ask this, certainly you will say it is memories that bind us to our surroundings. How did you feel when you left [your old houses]? What memories do you have? Were these houses strongly attached to your childhood? Were you sad when you grew up and moved away?[45]

Suphi answers for his audience by saying that each corner of their old houses was associated in memory with something: their mothers, their fathers, the things that they loved. After tying his audience emotionally to their houses, he reminds them that those houses are now gone because of the changes that have come to Turkey (emphasizing Istanbul). He goes on to discuss these changes, saying that they are not merely the result of the recent war but are due to a history of European influences that reach back to the Tanzimat Reforms.[46] The real or old Turkish house, then, is not merely a part of the past that is common to everyone's history (everyone in his audience), it also marks a specific type of Turkishness that is thrown into relief by being "not Western":

> If it were possible to raise our grandfathers from their graves and bring them back to our homes of today, as soon as they stepped across the threshold they would turn back with loathing and shout in our faces: "These are not Turkish houses! These are not Muslim houses! You have been invaded by the enemy to the extent that he has violated the sanctity of your houses!"[47]

It is only after these rousing words that Hamdullah Suphi begins his description of the Turkish house from the inside out. His description of the inside includes all the items that were found in the pre-Tanzimat house, such as *mangals* (braziers), carpets, embroidery, candles, Qur'ans, and Kütahya or İznik ceramic ware. His point is not that these items were beautiful but that they were Turkish, that virtually all of these things were produced in different parts of Turkey, and thus that the contents of the house, as well as the house itself, were representative of the nation. An argument could have been made, but pointedly was not, that Turkey did not exist at the time and that the house and the items in it characterized the Ottoman Empire, with its diverse geography and population. But with this speech we see how, in 1912, the concept of Turkish and the place of Turkey were well on their way to replacing and appropriating the Ottoman past, and this was the power driving the independence movement that culminated in the establishment of the Turkish Republic in 1923.

In the second half of his speech, Suphi does not describe the house at all. Instead he discusses Turkish history in terms of its production of goods, its skillful artisans and the guild system that stood behind them. His point is that when all of these Turkish goods that filled the Turkish house were being made, the Turkish nation was self-sufficient, independent, and not a beggar of Europe. Suphi reminds his audience of the gracious way of life inside the Turkish house by describing a coffee ceremony that would have delighted the old man in the cartoon, and described, too, the dress of the woman of the house in a way that would have been suitable to the old man's upper-class memory. His point, again, is to give his audience a sense of a specifically Turkish, non-Western pride, full of Ottoman amnesia:

How did women previously dress in our houses? In order to understand what changes have taken place in dress one only needs to read the report of Seyyid Ali Pasha Efendi. In his embassy to Paris he described the dress of the Parisian women. "Modern" Turkish fashion now sounds like his report from *Paris!*[48]

Although photographs of Istanbul up until the end of the 1940s show an urban fabric thick with wooden houses and konaks, clearly these were not the houses in which Hamdullah Suphi's audience now lived, or if they did live there, the interiors of these houses were much altered.[49] Tanyeli has shown that between the 1830s and the 1930s, Western artifacts, especially Western furniture, were accepted almost to the point of becoming a fetish, and that for the Ottoman Turk, modernity was often defined in terms of domestic objects.[50] Spiro Kostof succinctly described this phenomenon: "Every house is, for its occupants, a public stage and a private sanctuary."[51] By the time that Hamdullah Suphi spoke to the Turkish Hearth Society, most old wooden houses and konaks (in cities and towns, at least) had been partially or completely refurnished in a European manner, with beds replacing the mattresses that were once rolled into cupboards at night, with tables replacing trays that had been set up for diners who would sit around them on the floor, and with electrical appliances and pianos in the homes of the wealthy. This alteration in taste is clearly seen in the library of Ay Hanım Efendi's konak in Şişli.

But the transformation in housing was greater than merely one of decoration and use, for row houses and apartment buildings had begun to fill in areas lost to fire and to characterize the newly formed neighborhoods of an expanding Istanbul. Stone apartment buildings, which had once been relegated to the non-Muslim areas of Pera and Beyoğlu, now characterized the new Muslim neighborhoods to their north: Şişli, Nişantası, Beşiktaş, and Teşvikiye. These apartments might look like a huge stone konak on the outside, but the flats within them no longer had spacious rooms, walls with built-in niches, fireplaces, or washrooms hidden in the cupboard walls. Furthermore, the street patterns in the areas rebuilt after fires, and more specifically in the new areas on the Pera side of the Golden Horn, followed the modernization trends set in motion by Moltke. The street that once belonged legally and spiritually to the mahalle, the Ottoman sokak that had been defined by high garden walls that protected and defined houses and mansions, had been replaced by the cadde (pronounced jaddeh), or avenue. The cadde was straight and wide, regulated by the municipality, and lined with houses whose front doors opened to it, erasing the garden entrance and the privacy that it had afforded. The old wooden house, even if it remained, was thus resited and reconfigured externally as well as internally. But owing to the rising costs of land, as well as to new street laws and new tastes, most caddes were lined with apartments, which became the coveted homes of the new middle and upper classes, including the educated elite, who were taking it on themselves to spearhead the struggle for a new and modern Turkey.

Hamdullah Suphi did not wish to return to a premodern or even pre-Western past. He did not long to live again in the Turkish houses that he described, nor was he making a plea for their restoration. Rather, Suphi used the house rhetorically, as a device to persuade his audience that they shared a cultured, civilized, and aesthetic national past, and it was for this reason that the old wooden house was offered as the centerpiece of a specifically Turkish memory. By asking his audience to remember the moment when they left their own houses, and by telling them how they felt when that happened, he constructed a moment of shared memory that is as poignant and as communal as the Great Fire of Aksaray. That is, Suphi appealed to a memory that was at once autobiographical and communal, for although the event did not happen on the same day for each person, it was as if it had. When he crystallized memory around a Turkish house where "everything was Turkish," the house became a symbol of Turkish identity and, as we have begun to see, this Turkish house became available for a later collective memory, first as an icon of the lost Turkish past and then as an icon of an endangered future.

Hamdullah Suphi gave permanence to the anonymous wooden house of the Ottoman period by giving it a name, the Turkish house; the title of his lectures and speeches in 1912 was *Old Turkish Houses* (*Eski Türk Evleri*), and in these it was given textual depth. However, at the same time, the same house was being preserved by artists who were unaware of this name but who were giving it a picturesque form.

THE DEPICTED HOUSE OF HODJA ALI RIZA BEY AND RIFAT OSMAN

Let us not lose a single piece of the past, because it is the timber of the future.

In the nineteenth century, following the Tanzimat period, Ottoman painters began to work in a European style, many of them studying in Europe or in Turkey with European-trained teachers. Most of the early painters began their training in the military schools, where they produced idyllic landscapes of Istanbul's Imperial Palace grounds and buildings. The most famous Turkish artist of the late nineteenth century was Osman Hamdi Bey (1842–1910), who studied in Paris between 1860 and 1872. One of his teachers in Paris was the Orientalist Gérôme, and when Hamdi Bey returned to Turkey, he brought the Orientalist style, along with other modern French ideas, including realism in portraiture and landscapes. Although Osman Hamdi Bey remains one of the most respected artists in Turkish history, by the time of the republic he was considered an artist who saw Turkey with a European eye and thus a foreigner in his native milieu.[52]

Hodja Ali Rıza Bey (1864–1930), on the other hand, was the artist whom Turks viewed as one of their own. Although he adopted a Western realism, he was loved for painting the houses and neighborhoods of Istanbul and other nearby towns, crystallizing a real emotion in the Turkish imagination. There is no question that Ali Rıza Bey's painting style was European; by the time he painted there was no alternative. Thus there is no question as to whether or not his work was wholly derivative or at all innovative, although there was some question as to whether it was any good.[53] But there was never a question about its popularity or the popularity of Hodja Ali Rıza Bey himself.[54]

Ali Rıza Bey was born in Üsküdar, across the Bosphorus from Istanbul (and now a part of it). He was trained in the Military Academy (Mekteb-i

View from Üsküdar. Drawing by Hodja Ali Rıza Bey, 1897.
From Aydın and Uğurlu, p. 90.

Istanbul street scene by Hodja Ali Rıza Bey (watercolor, not completed). From Aydın and Uğurlu, p. 87.

Portrait of Hodja Ali Rıza Bey. From Erhan, Hoca Ali Rıza, *p. 80.*

Harbiye), where he became the assistant to the painting teacher, Osman Nuri Pasha. Later he too became an instructor there, continuing until 1908. He was also a painting instructor for a short time at the Darüşşafaka, a secondary school for the poor and orphans in Istanbul, and after retiring in 1911, he became the painting instructor at the Nümune-i Terakki Mektep, one of the model schools that were opened during the post-1908 Second Constitutional Period (II Meşrutiyet) to advance the teaching of foreign languages and professions, and at the Çamlıca Girls Lise. His students remember him as a man who awakened an appreciation of art in schoolchildren and military academy students both.[55] As a result of his sincere interest and devotion to his students, he was given the loving and respectful name of Hodja (teacher; Turkish spelling *hoca*).

Thus, even before Hamdullah Suphi began talking about the Turkish house, Hodja Ali Rıza Bey was painting them for an appreciative audience. He was also a founding member of the Ottoman Painters Group (*Osmanlı Ressamlar Cemiyeti*), which was organized in 1908, and a frequent contributor to its journal, the *Osmanlı Ressamlar Cemiyeti Gazetesi*, which was published between 1911 and 1914, with a break during the Balkan War. He was the subject of articles in that journal as well as in others, such as *Servet-i Funun*, and he also participated in many well-publicized art exhibitions.[56]

Hodja Ali Rıza Bey painted landscapes and portraits, but his most characteristic works were houses, which he painted in their natural setting in the neighborhood and in the condition in which he saw them (they were often in need of repair). He continued to paint after his retirement and until his death, so that the paintings and drawings that fill his notebooks span the years 1880–1930 and include studies of Turkish life and its house and streets.

By the 1940s, his students remembered Hodja Ali Rıza's work as a "memory of a past day,"[57] but it remains unclear whether he saw himself as chasing after a vanishing past, that is, whether he was involved with "memory." Clearly, however, he was part of the awakening of the Turkish public to the old wooden house, and he participated in bringing it out of its obscurity.

At the same moment, however, in Edirne, another artist, Rıfat Osman (1874–1933), was working to preserve the memory of the old house as part of a national treasury. "Let us not lose a single piece of the past," he said, "because it is the timber of the future."[58] Rıfat Osman used the word "*kereste*" for timber, a word that is often reserved for the framing wood, and his paintings of Edirne focus on these wood-framed houses that he painted between 1902 and 1927.

Rıfat Osman was a historian, a photographer, and a physician, as well as an artist. As an Ottoman military physician stationed in Edirne, he had experienced some of its destruction during the Balkan Wars, and as a historian he was well aware of the destruction that had occurred when Edirne was occupied by the Russians in 1829 and 1872. Although born in Üsküdar, he lived in Edirne from 1912 until his death in 1933. His interest in Edirne went beyond its buildings to include the social configuration of its 159 mahalles, whose demographic characteristics he charted over a thirty-year period, from 1889 to 1919.[59]

Hodja Ali Rıza Bey had learned to paint as part of his military training, Rıfat Osman learned to paint while studying medicine at the military academy, and both were influenced in their subject matter and style by European painters. Rıfat Osman, however, did not think of himself as an artist, and

House in Edirne. Painting by Rıfat Osman. From Ünver, Dr. Rıfat Osman: Edirne Sarayı, *cover.*

his paintings were never meant to be exhibited but were a private historical study of the old palaces and places of Edirne.[60] He filled his notebooks with historical notes and with paintings based on ruins or from old lithographs, although most of his neighborhood drawings were done from life.

The point can be made that both of these artists, when they were painting the houses and neighborhoods that existed around them, were not participating in memory at all but in documentation. However, both were interested in the aspects of their local urban environment that dealt with the past. And their work, particularly the work of Hodja Ali Rıza Bey, became the basis for the memory of later generations.

Hodja Ali Rıza's work concentrates on his own neighborhood of Üsküdar, and each of his paintings is conceptualized as a place that still existed as a continuation from the past. It was traditional in the sense that it was associated with former times and recognized with warmth, and this accounts in part for his great popularity. More important, there is never an imposition of the modern, whether of new building styles such as apartments or of roads or clothing. In fact, his interest was insistently on aspects of life that remained from his childhood, such as the coffee shops and their paraphernalia, making his work a type of visual memoir.

Rıfat Osman, on the other hand, was a historian who consciously documented the past. His paintings of Edirne, its houses and its *Saray* (palace), attempted to conflate what he saw with what he knew and felt about the past, culminating in many paintings that were "historical" in the same sense that historical novels are. For example, some of his paintings of Edirne's neighborhoods were based on old lithographs rather than on what he actually saw. Thus he, like Hodja Ali Rıza Bey, was making visible and visual a type of communally held autobiographical memory of the old wooden house when everything was Turkish, before the advent of apartment blocks and wide, straight, gardenless streets.

Without the benefit of text or titles other than *A Street in Üsküdar* or *Edirne*, we cannot know whether the artists were conceptualizing the Turkish house or merely the old and the not-Western. However, both artists were a product of the same military academy that produced the Young Turks[61] and the birth of Turkish nationalism, and their work and their personal histories secure each a major role in the positioning of the old wooden house in the Turkish imagination. Furthermore, both can be said to have been visualizing a shared memory, in that they were both cognizant, like Adair Lara, "that something was changing, and changing for us all at the same time."

Thus it was Hamdullah Suphi, in his 1912 speech to the Turkish Hearth Society, who gave the name "Turkish" to the old wooden house, but this sense of the localness of these houses had begun before him, particularly with Rıfat Osman and Hodja Ali Rıza Bey, who brought them into the imaginary as a romantic form.

There was also the work of Celal Esad Arseven, whose 1909 *Constantinople: De Byzance à Stamboul*, published in Paris, contained a section on domestic architecture. Celal Esad had, like just about every other educated man, it seems, studied painting with Hodja Ali Rıza Bey at the Istanbul Military Academy, where he was sent by his uncle in the hope that he would not fail the family by becoming a painter rather than a pasha.[62] Happily for the family, Celal Esad did not become a painter but an art and architectural historian. And happily for us, he began research on Istanbul, a project that was set in motion by a Mr. Pangalo, who suggested that he prepare an art historical work to accompany the Turkish Pavilion at the World's Fair in St. Louis in 1903. It was this work that would become *Constantinople: De Byzance à Stamboul*. This project included his work on the neighborhoods of Istanbul and on the Grand Bazaar, but also on residential architecture. Perhaps it was partly Hodja Ali Rıza who had directed his interest to houses; his drawings suggest that this might be the case. Or perhaps this came from his own childhood in a great konak in Beşiktaş. In any event, in *Constantinople* he describes both houses and konaks with a personal intimacy, and with a lament:

> Sadly, all these old houses are vanishing today, yielding room to unsightly and mis-shapen constructions, painted in loud colors in a banal taste. In all Constantinople, one does not find more than a score of these ancient houses, of which the oldest go back no further than the era of Mahmoud II [1808–1839]; the successive repairs have made them lose much of their primitive aspect.
>
> It is in the quarters of *Yuksek Kaldirim*, *Ak-Saraı* and *d'Eyoub* where one has the chance of finding the oldest of these houses. Among the suburbs which seem to keep more of their old houses, one can mention the villages of *Anadoli-Hisar*, *Arnaout-Keuy*, *Yeni-keuy*, *Tchenguelkeuy*, *Kousgoundjouk*, and above all *Scutari* that still have some of the ancient houses, sadly condemned to disappear from here in a dozen years.[63]

Arseven's familiarity and lament qualify as autobiographical memory, making his descriptions parallel the work of Rıfat Osman and Hodja Ali Rıza

Bey, who had been born or still lived in the Üsküdar that "still ha[d] some of the ancient houses, sadly condemned to disappear from here in a dozen years." But in spite of focusing both visually and textually on the old wooden house, he did not give it a national voice. In fact, Esad vacillates between describing these houses as Ottoman, Muslim, and Turkish, although when speaking of culture he refers to Turkish culture (e.g., "Women, and Turks in general, like to stay at home, and prefer wooden houses pierced with many windows").[64]

But it was in this climate that Hamdullah Suphi was able to give the old house its new name—"the Turkish house"—and to give it at the same time a national voice—to have it speak with the voice of the Turkish nation,[65] removing it from its Ottoman milieu, in which the same house forms were shared by all religions and ethnicities. Thus this was neither a coincidence nor a careless use of language but a direct attack on an Ottoman imperial system that had once shared historical memory with the non-Turkish groups that had made up the Ottoman state.[66]

IDENTITY CRISIS

Was "Ottomanism" in actuality anything more than the name of our Government? Within the domains of the Ottoman State, in the Caucasus, Azerbaijan, Turkistan, Bukhara, Kashgar, in short, wherever we lived, we were genuine Turks.

By 1908, Turkish identity had reached crisis proportions. Ömer Seyfeddin, the author of "The Secret Temple," from which the above quotation comes, and a member of the Turkish Hearth Society (in 1914 he became the *Başyazar* [chief author/editor] of *Türk Yurdu*), expressed this crisis and this dilemma in the introduction to his 1918 book, *Ashab-i Kehfimiz* (Our Seven Sleepers).

After the Meşrutiyet [of 1908], I had spoken with most of our "Great Leaders." Their collective thoughts were approximately reflected in the following summation: "Ottomanism is a composite nationality. Ottomanism is neither Turkism nor being Moslem. Every individual living under the Ottoman administration, without regard to national origin and religion, is a member of the Ottoman nation!" However, this idea was nothing but an illusion, a fantasy, born of brains produced by the non-nationalist education system of the Tanzimat [reform] period.

It was not possible to constitute "a composite nationality" [*müşterek bir milliyet*] from the sum total of individuals who have separate religions, languages, moralities, histories, cultures and grounds for pride. Was "Ottomanism" in actuality anything more than the name of our government? It was not possible to call the Germans living in Austria "the Habsburg nation, the Austrian nation." Wherever he might be, a German is a German. Those of us who speak Turkish were a nation with a history of five thousand years, and with even older legends. Within the domains of the Ottoman state, in the Caucasus, Azerbaijan, Turkistan, Bukhara, Kashgar, in short, wherever we lived, we were genuine Turks.[67]

The Turkish Hearth Society represented the first organizational response to the identity crisis that had been exacerbated by the disintegration of the Ottoman Empire and the humiliating defeat during the Balkan Wars.[68] This response was a call, above all, for Turkism. It was in this environment, in this discourse, that Hamdullah Suphi made his pivotal speech on the Turkish house to the Turkish Hearth.

Thus Suphi's focus on the house as a Turkish house "where everything was Turkish" is the staking of a claim to a contested property and to a contested culture. He is staking a claim to the Ottoman past, wresting it from the groups that had once shared it. To give the adjective of "Turkish" to the wooden houses that covered a great deal of the Ottoman Empire's lands when that empire stretched from the Balkans to Jerusalem was to retroactively nationalize it. These houses had sheltered a variety of linguistic, ethnic, and religious groups, not all of them minority, and they had been produced by a variety of builders. Thus, Suphi's conscious anachronism was a highly political act, one that placed the house at the intersection of Turkism and nationalism and prepared the way for the Turkish Salon inside the Turkish Hearth Building, and for the Turkish room of Ay Hanım Efendi.

But Suphi's anachronistic act may not have been a contentious or belligerent one. By the end of World War I, Turkey had already been reduced to Anatolia and was referred to as Turkey both by Hamdullah Suphi and other post-"Young Turk" politicians. Furthermore, by the process of secession it was becoming, if not ethnically, at least religiously homogeneous. Certainly the groups who had once shared Ottomanness with the Muslim Turks, if indeed they ever had, had found other identities. Turkish nationalism had become a fact of history, and the Turkish Hearth Society and Turkish nationalism were not destroying Ottoman unity as much as recognizing that it no longer existed, and claiming what was left. The word Ottoman in fact had, at least in the remembered past, come to mean Muslim Turkish.[69]

Nonetheless, there remained a confusion abroad as well as at home about whether the Ottoman Turks who held on to the remnants of the empire really held on to anything at all. Hamdullah Suphi's speech, which seems to be about the Ottoman-Turkish house, addresses this issue head on, and we begin to understand how this Turkish house stood not merely for Turkish identity but for the Turkish homeland and the strength and tenacity of its civilization and culture. A somewhat long but telling quotation from the second half of Hamdullah Suphi's speech to the Turkish Hearth Society makes this poignantly clear:

> Yes, you know that Europe ships us whatever we need, from head to foot, from the army to the schools and even for the coffee shops. But we get these things directly from whom? We must think about this. Who serves as the middle men? The sellers remain in the hands of whom? We must think about this. I'm going to describe to you a conversation I had with a Frenchman. This man had been a correspondent for years for a newspaper published in Paris. I asked him the following question with profound emotion. "Could you please tell me something? This country [Turkey], which has been under such strong French influence that it could be said it was a part of France, on this Turkish soil on which millions have trod, in this old friendly country in which every millet, Muslim or Christian, has regarded it as a duty that its children be taught French in addition to its native language, your material and moral [manevi] advantages are a hundred times greater than those in Greece. So how is it that you sacrifice Turkey to Greece?" The correspondent had previously prepared his answer and asked me calmly and frankly, "Are you really patient? Speak to me frankly." "I know your answer. I am patient," I said. I will never forget what he told me: "First, where is this country that you call Turkey? We see before us one commercial nation, not one Greece and one Turkey, but two Greeces. One is the Greece that you know, the other is the one to which you give the name Turkey. In your ports and cities we see nothing that can be called Turkish life or Turkish commerce.... Pay particular attention to my final words. All the orders for goods to be shipped to your country are under the names [signatures] of a Kristodulos, or a Diyamandi, or a Yani, just like from Greece. When you see an Ahmed Efendi or a

Shakir Efendi as customers requesting products from our factories, then there will be a Turkey."[70]

It is in this context that Hamdullah Suphi made a claim on the Turkish house as "ours,"[71] and in this context that he saw the modernization and Westernization of the Turkish house as an invasion by the enemy. That his use of "the Turkish house" in rhetoric was more than just a proxy fight for independence can be seen in the host of publications about the Turkish house that he set in motion; these publications supported the theme that he had introduced in 1912 and carried his lamp through to the opening of the Turkish Salon in 1930. One of the most prolific of these writers was Ahmet Süheyl Ünver, who was a student of Hodja Ali Rıza's, a friend and admirer of Rıfat Osman, and a biographer of both. He was also a member of the Turkish Hearth Association.

AHMET SÜHEYL ÜNVER

These rooms are furnished in the true Turkish fashion and appeal to the national taste of those who enter them.

Ünver took up the Turkish house as a marker of Turkish identity in 1923, in an article called "The Oriental Room" ("Şark Odası"), published in the journal *Milli Mecmua* (National Journal).[72] In this article, Ünver focused on the interiors of old wooden houses, which he illustrated with his own paintings. He described four rooms, mainly their seating and window arrangements, but his emphasis was not on their configuration but on their beauty:

The sections [of windows] facing the room are in various styles with colored glass and are highly artistic. Those who look outside do so from plain colorless glass, but it is also beautiful.[73]

Although the title of his work is "The Oriental Room," he makes it clear that the rooms mark a specifically Turkish space: "These [rooms] are furnished in the true Turkish fashion (*asıl Türk tarzında*) and appeal to the national taste of those who entered them."[74] This is made even clearer when Ünver says that these rooms have changed over the ages, but "the ones that appeal to our taste are undoubtedly the ones [that remain] in the Turkish style."[75] He is quoted earlier in the discussion of Ay Hanım Efendi's "Turkish Room," where he also condemns the contemporary furnishing of "Oriental rooms" because they were not authentically Turkish but appealed to Western tastes. He further laments that the variety of styles that were once visible, along with the lifestyle that understood and underwrote them, "have unfortunately disappeared," and then he adds, "We have not been able to preserve today these wonderful pleasures/good taste [zevk] of our grandfathers who lived eighty years ago," referring to the moment the Ottomans opened themselves to the West with the Tanzimat Reforms.

By not specifying where these houses were, other than that one is from a village in Anatolia, Ünver makes the Turkish room and the lifestyle it represented belong to everyone's grandfathers, and thus to the entire Turkish population, situated in the traditional time of the past, regardless of city of origin or class. In a way similar to the Karagöz house-tasvir discussed in Chapter 1, the image of the room has begun to operate as a sign of the larger house, as well as of a large geographic area, the sign of an affective place (the center of social relations) and of (past) time. By describing a guest room (misafirhane) and the ceremonies that went on inside it, Ünver makes the entire house become a symbol of a way of life that was entirely Turkish, and thus he includes his entire audience. He also uses the pronoun "we" and adjective "our" to make certain that his appeal is emotionally felt and personally owned. In describing one of the illustrations, "a house-type drawn by my professor [üstad] the painter Ali Rıza Bey Efendi," he writes:

> It shows a room in an Anatolian village. We find one or two Levhas [calligraphic panels with Koranic verses] as striking; [these] beautiful written inscriptions, which express our own religious feelings, acquired a great place of respect in our old houses, but were not hung throughout in a disorderly fashion. . . . They were hung in a few, but the most important places, in the room.[76]

Although Ünver suggests that there are still a few people who remember the old houses and what went on in them, he refers to these people in order to frame the audience's sense of memory, and he is thus in the process of making collective memory. His ploy leads the readership to believe that they themselves participated in a shared or autobiographical memory when clearly they did not.

Ünver's interest in constructing a collective memory is not at all surprising because he wrote during the first years of the Turkish Republic; it might be surprising if his interests were otherwise. But the important question here is how and why he chose to insert a Turkish house into the national memory. Was it all begun by Hamdullah Suphi? Suphi's words fell on fertile ground, but certainly it was Ali Rıza Bey's textless images that brought Ahmed Süheyl Ünver into this dialogue.

Ahmed Süheyl Ünver (1898–1986) was a physician, an art historian, and an artist, as well as a writer. He entered the Mekteb-i Tibbiye (Medical School) in 1915, but at the same time he began to study at the Medresetü-l Hattatin (College of Calligraphy), from which he received his diploma in manuscript gilding and paper marbling in 1923. During this period he met Hodja Ali Rıza Bey and became his student.[77] Ünver studied watercolor and charcoal techniques with Rıza Bey, and this is reflected in his later style. The two men spent long hours walking the neighborhoods of Üsküdar and Istanbul drawing old houses, mosques, gravestones, streets, and fountains, and discussing the meaning of what they saw. But Ünver credits Rıza Bey with teaching him far more than painting, and describes their relationship as the key relationship of his life and the one that brought him to maturity:

> The painter Üsküdarlı Hodja Ali Rıza was one of my teachers. . . . [He said:] "Record everything that attracts you. Fixate our country's national architecture and houses. Don't over-value your comrades and don't annoy them. Take pity on the poor! . . . Run to their aid. Without being a Dervish have the humility of a Dervish. Work, but always be occupied with profitable work. Refine your spirit with beautiful words. Fill notebooks with beautiful paintings. . . . Love the small. Take pity on every type of creature. Be an exemplary patriot!"[78]

According to Ünver, then, Hodja Ali Rıza interwove his artwork with patriotism as they walked and painted during his formative years. They spoke about the famous men of history and their moral and religious behavior, so that the places that they drew were also infused with the values and ideas of past generations. In their loving father-son relationship, Hodja Ali Rıza would give Ünver his paintings and Ünver would write him poetry. Ünver called Rıza his spiritual guide (*"Ruhumun mürebbisi"*),[79] and when he said, "Whatever the Üstad did, I caught something from it" (*"Üstad ne yaparsa ondan birşeyler kaptım"*),[80] he meant both spiritually and materially.

According to Ünver, Rıza Bey "lived a life of perfection," and "he never died, but has entered our hearts with his works."[81] According to Ünver's biographer, Ahmed Güner Sayar, after Hodja Ali Rıza died in 1930, Ünver began to paint all Turkey through his hodja's eyes in order to be of service to

Turkishness.[82] Ünver wrote that he spent his lifetime trying to be just like his teacher and to hold on to his principles. "Whether or not I was successful, I cannot say for certain. But I have never strayed from the route."[83]

His paintings attest to his success, but so do his articles on the Turkish house. He wrote two more of them that I am aware of, one on the houses of Izmit,[84] in which he makes a plea for the Turkish Hearth Society to save one of them as a museum, as the houses are "valuable memories [hatıralar] that are one by one falling to ruin."[85] Although he does not suggest which house to preserve, he does highlight one of the largest and finest as an "original and unadulterated Turkish House" (orijinal ve saf Türk Evi). Another of his articles on the Turkish house also appeared in 1926: "Eski Türk Evinde Ocak" (The Hearth in the Old Turkish House).[86]

Ünver wrote all of his articles while he was a member of the Turkish Hearth Society; in fact, he had met Hamdullah Suphi and heard him lecture when he joined the society in 1915, along with his medical school classmates. By 1925, when he had published four articles on the Turkish house, he had been painting with Hodja Ali Rıza for nine years. He was, however, still studying medicine, for he never considered himself a painter.[87]

In 1925, Ali Rıza introduced Ünver to Rıfat Osman, perhaps because of their shared interests in medicine and art, and the two developed a life-long attachment. Rıfat Osman had published a textual history of Edirne in 1920, but soon afterward he shoved his documents and drawings of the Edirne Sarayı and neighborhoods into a trunk. It seems that he had become despondent when the rich library left by his father from the time of Abdül-hamid II had burned, then his own furnishings and books had been pillaged during the Balkan Wars (1912–1913) and again during the Greek occupation of Edirne in 1921.[88] The twenty-seven-year-old Ünver, however, was full of enthusiasm for Osman's work and began to help him organize his materials and return to painting. Ünver wrote an article about him describing his research on the Edirne palace, and in 1926 Osman's four-part article on the Turkish houses of Edirne was published in Milli Mecmua. Whether this last was in fact written by Osman himself or in conjunction with Ünver is unclear.[89] What is certain is that Ünver catapulted the work of Rıfat Osman into the public eye, where it remains a marker of Turkish identity to this day. They also developed a close relationship, and it was a terrible jolt to Ünver when Rıfat Osman, the second of his beloved teachers, died in 1933.

The ideas of Hamdullah Suphi are clearly at the intersection of the work of Süheyl Ünver, Rıfat Osman, and Hodja Ali Rıza Bey, and perhaps Celal Esad as well, for he provided an arena and a conceptualization that gave a national, patriotic, and textual voice to illustrate a historical work that had already begun. By the late 1920s, other writers had begun to take up his interest in the Turkish house.

Hamdullah Suphi wrote as a patriot, Süheyl Ünver wrote as an artist, Celal Esad Arseven wrote as an art historian. But beginning with Hamdullah Suphi, it was the house remembered as a player in Turkish history that began to take shape. This transformation is evident in a 1926 article called "The Houses of Ankara," by the Minister of Culture, Mübarek Galip, published in a journal for teachers called *Muallimler Birliği Mecmuası* (United Teachers Association Journal).

Galip's first sentence expresses his interest in the house in terms of a sort of proto-architectural history: "The first house began by turning Noah's ark upside-down" ("*İlk mesken Nuh'un gemisi'nin tersine cevrilmiş ile başlamıştır*").[90] Galip goes on to discuss the early influences of geography and climate on settlement patterns, tying all houses together visually (their rectangularity?) to Noah's ark. When he narrows his field to Ankara, he becomes, alas, less creative and more pragmatic, describing the Ottoman-period Ankara houses structurally: the use of sun-dried brick (*kerpiç*), the way the windows were inserted into the walls, and the decorative woodwork on the interiors. He differentiates between the decorative styles that predominated between the time of Mahmud I (1730–1754, "rococco") and Mahmud II (1808–1839, "the old embellishment"). Like Ünver, he laments that "as the days go by our beautiful houses are being destroyed" ("*Gün geçtikçe bu güzelim evler yıkılır*") and makes an appeal to the Ministry of Education to purchase a fully furnished house as an example of Anatolian works of art, and convert it into a museum for visiting and for research.

Several important themes are brought together here. First is Galip's call to make the house a museum so that people can see what their past looked like, as well make a place where the past is available for research. This call for museumization parallels Ünver's request voiced in his article on Izmit houses. As with the other writers who share an interest in Turkish houses, the sorrow at their destruction is not a call for preservation of either the houses, or the neighborhoods, or the old way of life. Certainly no one would or could suggest that these old houses should stand in the way of the progress represented by Ankara as the new capital of the republic. Instead, Turkish houses are presented not as Museum relics but as museum quality, not as relics to be dismantled and hidden in museums but as icons to be celebrated as museums. Galip does not consider how making a fully furnished house into a museum must remove it from the culture that gave it life; for him it celebrates the memory of that life and is an act of memory preservation. The final page of his six-page article has the poetry that decorated the interior walls of one old Ankara house, and it seems that he quotes this to show that he is fulfilling their call:

> Its atmosphere opens my heart,
> [how] could it not make me
> happy-hearted?[91]

The museum room and the idea of the museum house begin at this time to join text and illustrations at the heart of memory.

A second theme that is now clearly in focus is that the Turkish house is not merely a part of Istanbul but is Anatolian as well, and the Ankara house has become an important example of it. Ankara was at the center of the public eye as it became the new capital of the new republic in 1923 and the focus of an enormous building program both to house the influx of government employees and to construct a showpiece of the modern nation. To highlight the Turkish house in Ankara was to place it at the heart of Turkish history, and perhaps for this reason, Galip called this house the Ankara house rather than the Turkish house. But in a 1928 article titled *"Eski Türk Evi"* (The Old Turkish House), the Turkish house is described as spanning all of Anatolia. The author begins his work by saying, "while researching Turkish architecture in Anatolia, I found that the houses of many Anatolian towns were like those of Ankara."[92] How amazing that it surprised him.

But what is perhaps of the most significance is that these articles are all presented as "research" (*tedkik*). In this way, all the articles we have discussed are participating in the young republic's great emphasis on probing history for the deep and universal roots of Turkish culture; after all, could one ask for anything deeper or more universal than Noah? This "research" that blossomed in the new republic had recently been enlarged under the II Meşrutiyet by Fuad Köprülü and Ziya Gökalp, whose systematic study of Turkish cultural history stood on the shoulders of İbrahim Edhem Pasha, Osman Hamdi, and İsmail Galip, who studied Ottoman heritage.[93] Celal Esad Arseven was also a continuation of this tradition, which by the 1930s was entwined with the new republic's national history thesis.

The national history thesis posited that, with the right research, the roots of Turkish culture could be found in pre-Ottoman and even pre-Islamic times. The Turkish History Foundation (Türk Tarih Kurumu, or TTK) that was to be housed in the Turkish Hearth Building was explicitly founded to further this type of research. In 1928 the Turkish Hearth Society published Celad Esad's *Türk Sanatı* (Turkish Art), in which, for example, the Turkish house for the first time finds its roots in the tents of Central Asia.[94] Noah, of course, takes this one giant step farther (or backward). But what is visible here is the successful attempt to situate the Turkish house at the center of this discourse on what is to be remembered.[95]

Furthermore, when the Turkish house became the marker of the Turkish past and a subject of research, it began to become an archive in itself, a self-contained repository not merely of a lifestyle but of designs and structures that are specifically Turkish and therefore available for another important state project. It became available to be mined as the source for a new national architecture. Koyunoğlu saw this as a part of his project of museumizing a Turkish room in his Turkish Salon in the Turkish Hearth Building of 1925. In 1923, Süheyl Ünver was already a promoter of this idea. He didn't want to write heavily illustrated articles or to encourage others to publish illustrated books for the purpose of nostalgia ("The konaks which contain the harems and selamlıks are almost irrelevant to our modern way of life").[96] Rather, his was a call to action:

> My purpose is not just to publish a few illustrated articles in this study and to encourage specialists in architecture to preserve our heritage with large illustrated works, but to serve as a guide to others who want to build a functional and national house.[97]
>
> I would recommend to our respected architects that they visit Izmit in particular and study the architectural styles of its old houses.[98]

The idea of configuring a new national architecture to represent the Turkish identity that was being constructed at the same time was being discussed in many circles. In 1918, Ömer Seyfeddin's story "The First White Hair" ("*İlk Düşen Ak*") brought together everything that was at issue. A long passage from it is included here to give an example of how the idea of a national architecture was tied to issues of ideology and identity, and how these were being popularized and consumed, that is, how they were making their way into the collective imagination.

The main figure of the Seyfeddin's "*İlk Düşen Ak*" is a Turkish architectural engineer, trained in Paris, who returns home, only to experience a crisis of identity.

Yes, last year I was neither a nationalist nor an internationalist! I needed an ideal. However, an ideal could not be found and bought like ready-to-wear clothing. I liked literature very much. I thought of writing a novel, in fact I started writing it. . . . Then I thought of the scandal which would follow its printing. Famous—but for what?—engineer so-and-so has published a novel! This would have been akin to a famous Minister of Works writing a primer of religious education while he was still occupying his post! So as not to become a laughing stock, I gave up. I set as my ambition to read the publications surrounding the nationalist movement. Two months later, I summed up the thoughts I had gathered and came up with the following:

1. People who share the same language and religion belong to the same nation. The Turks are also a nation. However, since they have been living as an *umma* [Muslim religious community] they have neglected their own nationality. They have endeavored to resemble Persians and Arabs.
2. Upon becoming a nationality, it is necessary to modernize. Then they have attempted to imitate the "Franks" [the West].
3. However, Turks, just like other nations, have a distinct and separate personality in every branch of culture. They can progress when they discover this personality.

Then, I looked around. Authors were striving to write the spoken natural language; poets to produce the national literature, poetry, the national meters; jurists, to find the national jurisprudence; moralists the national morals; educators, the national upbringing. I started to seek the national art.[99]

Seyfeddin actually wrote when the First National Architectural Style was in full operation, a style that was then being taught in the architectural academy and that later led to the Turkish Hearth Building, designed by Arif Hikmet Koyunoğlu. This National Architectural Style had been applied to domestic architecture only rarely, for example by Vedat Tek, who designed what is today called the "*Vedat Tek Evi*" on Vali Konağı Caddesi in Istanbul's then very upscale area of Nişantaşı.

Vedat Tek's Turkish house had the plasticity or sense of movement associated with a conventional old wooden house, with protruding upper floors, but the facade was embellished by window shapes taken from a design rep-

The Vedat Tek house in Nişantaşı, Istanbul. Photograph by Carel Bertram, 1993.

Dinner at the Vedat Tek house. Courtesy of the Vedat Tek Family Archives,
P. Derviş and S. Özkan Collection.

ertoire of monumental religious architecture. That is, the purpose was not to celebrate the vernacular but to modify or even conceal it.

Although Seyfeddin, as part of the National Literature Movement, was primarily searching for a new literary style, his work also documents an early reaction against this architectural style that privileged an Ottoman monumental rather than a Turkish vernacular past. By the late 1920s this National Architectural Style was certainly out-of-date for the young republic. And although Koyunoğlu designed the Turkish Hearth Building in that style, it was the last of its type, and he, too, took up the banner of the Turkish house.

In 1928, as Koyunoğlu was in the process of building the national headquarters of the Turkish Hearth Society, he published an article in its journal, *Türk Yurdu*, titled "Turkish Architecture" ("*Türk Mimari*").[100] This is perhaps the final article written in Ottoman script that takes up the issue of the Turkish house. His second article on Turkish houses, "Ankara Houses" ("*Ankara Evleri*"), was published in *Türk Yurdu* in 1929, but it was written in the new, Modern Turkish alphabet,[101] signaling the seriousness and rapid implementation of the Kemalist reforms. After discussing how all art and architectural innovations have their roots in the past, he writes:

> Old Turkish houses, which are part of *our* old architecture *that has not been studied*—and which we consider today to be tumbled down buildings—were constructed in a *civilized manner* based on need, and incorporated certain hygienic requirements. . . . [Their] construction system, which was devised to separate the cold of the exterior from the inside of the building, should not be viewed as primitive. Flat roofs, which today prevail in all European construction, are built using a method called "*Hulç / Cement*," which is nothing but an imitation of the method of construction that has been applied for thousands of years in Erzurum. . . . Our old cities were composed of houses, which, for the most part, were built containing gardens. Making central gardens is accepted even today in city planning as the *most hygienic principle of urban architecture*. Indeed, societies have even been created to make propaganda on this point.

After describing the interiors, he continues:

> In short, the old Turkish house with its design and furnishings is a *monument of comfort*. The bedrooms, baths with marble basins, and

winter gardens [*limonluk*] show that hygienic requirements were fully considered in their construction.[102] (All emphases mine.)

Koyunoğlu has established that Turkish houses not only meet but anticipate modern conditions of light, ventilation, warmth, and hygiene, perhaps a necessary move in the face of the rhetoric associating Turkish houses with poor neighborhoods and dark, narrow, dirty streets. The words of the statesman and poet Ziya Pasha (1881) had stung hard and reverberated long: "I wandered in the land of the infidel and observed cities and stately mansions. I traveled in the land of Islam and saw nothing but wasteland and ruins."

Koyunoğlu, speaking as a respected architect, evoked an image of sophistication, for his Turkish house revealed intelligent design and material choices as well as a highly "civilized" Turkish aesthetic. Once this was made clear, the Turkish house was ready to be placed at the center of a "research program":[103]

Of this we are certain: it would be possible to establish successfully the design of a contemporary Turkish house inspired from these buildings. The result of a profound and serious study [of them] would undoubtedly be a success.... [We] expect from Turkish architects the modern Turkish house and its definitive form.[104] (Emphasis mine.)

Who was going to answer this call? The architect Sedad Hakkı Eldem was positioned by history to answer it. In 1924, Eldem returned from a childhood spent in Europe to continue the study of architecture that he had begun with the Bauhaus masters in Germany, and where he had also studied traditional architectural crafts and styles. He graduated from the Istanbul Fine Arts Academy (Sanayi-i Nefise Mektebi) in 1928. This was the academy that had been founded by his uncle, the Orientalist painter Osman Hamdi Bey. His great-grandfather was the historian İbrahim Pasha, his grandfather was the historian Galip Pasha, and his uncle was Mübarek Galip, the Minister of Culture who wrote the creative article on Ankara houses cited earlier. Eldem appears to have been groomed by history to answer the call of Koyunoğlu; he is remembered not for his place in this developing discourse on the Turkish house but as the man who brought the Turkish house out of obscurity. Between 1924 and 1928, he reacted against his teachers, who taught the First National Style, and went out onto the city streets to search its houses for their Turkishness.[105] Yet, although Eldem would become an important player in the 1930s, when he marked the Turkish house as a form to be used in a new architectural style, he marked it with as much amnesia as memory.

But between 1928 and 1931 Eldem was in Paris, studying with Le Corbusier. It was during these years that the Turkish Hearth Building in Ankara was conceived, finished, and opened with its Turkish Salon. The Turkish Hearth Association, which had been anonymously founded in 1911 by a group of physicians, opened with a grand ceremony: Hamdullah Suphi gave one of the opening speeches; İsmet Pasha spoke about the importance of this building to the future,[106] and Rıfat Osman was in the audience. (Hodja Ali Rıza died that year.)

These were the people who had drawn the pictures, written the text, and built the room that allowed shared and autobiographical memories to merge with ideology and to take on the weight of historical consciousness. Wittingly or unwittingly, this cohort had museumized and monumentalized the Turkish house, making it available for the collective memory of a people who had not experienced it themselves.

"Naim Efendi." Dr. İsmail Ali Bey in İstanbulun attire. Courtesy of Necdet Sakaoğlu.

THREE

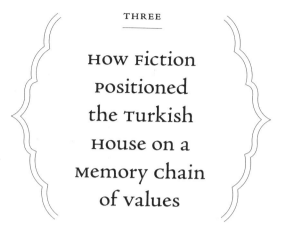

HOW Fiction
positioned
the Turkish
House on a
Memory chain
of values

WORKS ADDRESSED IN THIS CHAPTER

1873: *Zavallı Çocuk* (Poor Child), Namık Kemal
1875: *Felâtun ile Râkim Efendi* (Felâtun and Râkim Efendi), Ahmet Midhat
1876: *İntibah: Sergüzeşt-i Ali Bey* (Awakening: Ali Bey's Adventures), Namık Kemal
1891: *Turfanda Mı, Yoksa Turfa Mı?* (Is It Avant-garde, or Just Worthless?), Mehmed Murad
1918: *"Harem,"* Ömer Seyfeddin
1922: *Kiralık Konak* (*Mansion for Rent*), Yakup Kadri Karaosmanoğlu
1936: *The Clown and His Daughter.* Turkish version: *Sinekli Bakkal* (Grocery with Flies—the name of a mahalle), Halide Edib

USING LITERATURE TO UNCOVER THE MEANING OF THE TURKISH HOUSE

With the speeches of Hamdullah Suphi and the political efforts of the Turkish Hearth Society during the early part of the twentieth century, the old wooden house, the most important visual marker of Ottoman domestic space, began to be implanted in the public imagination as "the Turkish house." This erasure of the Ottomans through their Turkification was intensified with the success of the nationalist project, that is, with the establishment of the modern Republic of Turkey in 1923. In 1923, Ahmet Süheyl Ünver had titled his article in the journal *Milli Mecmua* (National Journal) "The Turkish House." In 1926, Mübarek Galip had written in the journal *Muallimler Birliği Mecmuası* (The United Teachers Association Journal) that old houses are an important part of "Turkish culture" and therefore must be preserved. In 1928, Arif Hikmet Koyunoğlu had written about "old Turkish houses" in the journal *Türk Yurdu* (Turkish Homeland). Celâl Esad Arseven, who began his career as a historian of Ottoman art, published his definitive and comprehensive *L'Art Turk* in 1939. This work described all Ottoman art and architectural monuments of present-day Turkey as *Turkish* art and architecture.

Between 1914 and the close of the 1930s, the old wooden Ottoman-period house took on the appellation "Turkish" in the Turkish imaginary and became a player in cultural identity. However, it was not the term *Turkish* that gave the house its depth of meaning. Rather, it was because the house was already coded with a rich and complex set of meanings that it became so important a companion in the move from Ottomanism to Turkishness. Furthermore, it is the content of this code that explains why the house has remained important in the Turkish imaginary to this day. Calling the house Turkish rather than old, wooden, or Ottoman confirms this importance because it brings its older meaning into the present.

The terms Turkish and Ottoman are, of course, highly charged in themselves and have been used polemically to mark political territory, as well as to designate huge universes of lived time and space.[1] But the charge of these terms is important to us because of the way in which they have intersected with the emotional charge of the house and with the highly complex, deeply felt, and even conflicting meanings that this house has called forth in memory and imagination. We have access to these older, deeper meanings through novels and short stories about them.

Literary sources such as novels and poetry offer levels of meaning to places that differ from those produced by political speeches, artistic production, or museumized rooms. The two categories also have their separate ways of conceptualizing space. Because literary works expose value systems that are not limited to national feelings of space but are concerned with a different problem of space, the invisible quotation marks around the term Turkish house can now be lifted. In this format I can uncover the meanings of the house that were not directly tied to particular historical or socio-ideological constructs, such as "Turkish identity" as it was inflected on the house by the Turkish Hearth Association, Ay Hanım Efendi, or Arif Hikmet Koyunoğlu.

Instead of this ideologically aligned "Turkish house," the words Turkish house (without quotation marks) can now be used to refer to the old wooden Ottoman-period houses and konaks in the land that is today called Turkey. These houses appear in the stories and novels of the 1920s and 1930s as places without political titles, for they are simply called "home."

1908 IN 1922: YAKUP KADRI KARAOSMANOĞLU'S *KİRALIK KONAK* (A MANSION FOR RENT)

In 1922, Yakup Kadri Karaosmanoğlu wrote *Kiralık Konak* (A Mansion for Rent). *Kiralık Konak* introduces us to the complexity of meaning and the heavily contested memory that surrounded the Turkish house as the new Turkish Republic came into being. I use it to show how the political rhetoric of the Turkish Hearth Society (*Türk Ocağı*), which led to a triumphant Kemalism, coincided with a quieter, multifaceted sense of loss and impending loss. A close reading of *Kiralık Konak* introduces the Turkish house as the carrier of some very specific values, such as that of "interiority" and, in a larger context, a deeply felt spirituality, and the Ottoman-Islamic rootedness of this spirituality.

Kiralık Konak is an appropriate centerpiece of this discussion because, by standing at the beginning of the new republic but looking back at the important years before, it is a chronological marker on a trajectory of memory that has roots in earlier literature and resonance in later ones. It helps us understand how the meaning of the Turkish house was affected by the genre of the novel, and also how the meanings assigned to the Turkish house were transmitted over time. *Kiralık Konak* does everything: the house, like a beloved uncle, is given deep emotional resonance, and as a symbol that evokes memories of the past, it exposes a turning point in this trajectory of memory.

Kiralık Konak does something else as well: it disrupts the memory that was being constructed by the authors writing within the ideology of the Turkish Hearth Society. Those writers conceived of the house in terms of an architecture that was created to enclose a place where "everything was in order," a place constructed to ensure light and spaciousness so that life would go on pleasantly, without discord. For Süheyl Ünver, the Turkish house had been carefully designed as "a monument of comfort, especially for women":

The Turkish woman lived pleasurably, not behind closed lattices but in konaks that provided pleasure, space and much joy. The colored glass [embedded in] plaster-of-Paris upper windows ensured that light would compensate for the darkness caused by the latticed ones below. For the Turkish woman the spacious and well-lighted world was full of pleasure.²

It was partly for this reason that the Turkish house was slated to be an archive of useful information about "Turkish" intellectual, aesthetic, and social history, as well as about construction methods. But *Kiralık Konak*, a konak that was for rent in 1917, is portrayed as standing at the end of this period of orderliness, and the novel bemoans its loss. As a novel, *Kiralık Konak* preserves—or constructs—the memory of this order by referring not to a comfortable Turkish wooden architecture but to a carefully delineated system of rules and hierarchies, a space of defined social behavior with the family's father at its apex. But the aging patriarch in *Kiralık Konak*, the Pasha Naim Efendi, no longer fulfills the role once expected of the head of an Ottoman household:

> In spite of everything, [Naim Efendi] was still the only authority who inspired fear and respect in the house. If only he would show a little force, it was still likely that everything would get back on course. But alas. . . .³

Thus, *Kiralık Konak* introduces an alternative image to the orderly image of the past, for over the years Naim Efendi's konak had come unglued. The remembered Turkish house does not always resonate with happy feelings; it is a house that has a history of internal conflict as well as a memory of wholeness, of a time when the social order and personal desires were aligned. The conflict that *Kiralık Konak* marks makes the chronology we are following complex and difficult to characterize simply or unilaterally, but it also gives the house richness and poignancy.

Kiralık Konak not only positions the Turkish house as the site of memory, it introduces the house as the site of a painful sense of rupture with the past, expressed in terms of a widening generational divide. Novels that predate *Kiralık Konak* make the evaluation of this rupture possible; in fact, novels that evoke the old wooden house give access to the emotional content of this rupture in the making. Furthermore, *Kiralık Konak* and the novels that preceded it suggest how the meaning assigned to the memory of the Turkish house entered into a much larger conversation that positioned this rupture as one between materialism and spirituality. In the context of this dichotomy, the image of the Turkish house took its place on the spiritual side of the divide, becoming, over time, a type of sacred text. Thus, *Kiralık Konak* introduces literary works as an important, even fundamental evidentiary base from which to uncover the meaning at the heart of collective memory.

Works of fiction can be analyzed in terms of the differences between what the author constructs and reality, exposing the agendas or perspectives of the author or his milieu. Contextualizing is thus crucial. But contextualization is not being used here to corroborate a model of constructed reality in which finding invented traditions results in positioning some real or objective narrative against the "falsity" of those traditions.[4] One reason that construction models are unproductive here is that they make finding any sort of continuity impossible. That is, literature can be a place of construction, but it is also a place that selectively reproduces the past. Therefore, a major value of contextualizing the novel is not to expose congruence with or difference from the real or unreal so much as to help us read from a contemporary reader's point of view. The contextualized novel shows how what is represented fits into as well as shapes the parameters of a believable sense of the past, of identity, of rupture and desire. This is not a question of constructions versus authenticity; rather, the novel is positioned as a player in a historical discourse, and thus in the activity of collective imagining and collective remembering. Furthermore, whether talking about fabrication, selectivity, or continuity, or whether finding "the Turkish house" or "the Ottoman house" operative in the construction of identities or in appropriating the past, one can know precious little about what is appropriated, constructed, rejected, selected, defined, or redefined without accepting the invitation of the novel to enter the house.

THE INTERIOR OF THE HOUSE AND THE QUALITY OF INTERIORITY

In Turkish society, entering the house[5] to discover its meaning has been problematic at many levels. The house has traditionally been *haram*, meaning a place "protected" by Islamic law (Shari'a) and Ottoman custom from the outside world. That is, at all levels of Ottoman society the concept of the house had embedded within it an important element of interiority and exteriority, of what was appropriately "inside" (*iç*, pronounced itch; the Turkish ç is "*ch*") and what was appropriately "outside" (*dış*, pronounced dish).[6] Within the house itself, behavior appropriate to the family was considered "*helâl*," or condoned by Islamic law (an Ottoman term for one's legitimate wife was "*helâllik*"). As described in Chapter 1, the house itself was divided accordingly, with a separate area reserved for men and their guests and another for the immediate family, or for women and their guests. In smaller houses there might merely be two rooms, or even a curtain for separation, but houses of any substance would have had an architectural division of some sort, and all had an operational separation that ensured certain rules of propriety could be easily followed.[7] The male and female areas could be side by side or in separate wings, or the male area might command the lower floor and the female the upper floors. Male family members and certain relatives were permitted by law or custom to enter the family part of the house, assuming there were no female guests there at the time. Thus, this inner, most protected, most haram area served as the general family living area when no outsiders, or those not permitted to be part of the entire family, were present. Although each culture and each period interprets Islamic law relatively, and therefore I do not use the Shari'a as my analytical framework, Lucy Garnett, who visited Turkey in 1890, indicates that this haram element of Islam was in full operation in the late Ottoman period:

> [T]he harem, far from being, as is so often supposed, a "detestable prison," is the most cheerful and commodious division of an Osmanli's house. The term, indeed, simply means a sacred enclosure, being applied in this sense to all the sanctuaries of Islam, and the haremlik is consequently the *sanctum sanctorum*, the place safe from all intrusion, in which not even the master may enter if a pair of galoshes at the door of the reception room announces that his wife has guests.[8]

The interiority of the house was visually separated from the exteriority and the foreignness of the outside, and it was the last area of the house to accept change. For example, although Western furnishings that were introduced to Turkey at the very beginning of the nineteenth century soon became signs of prestige and even fetishes, "as one moved into the more private domain, the inner sanctum of the Ottoman life, they ceased to exist."[9]

Perhaps the most protected interior space, however, was the emotional life of the people within the house. Discussing one's inner feelings or displaying emotional states in general was discouraged by a code of privacy that protected the inner person from the outside in the same way that the family was protected from the neighbors, the neighborhood, and beyond. Certain things were never discussed outside the house, and certain emotions were never expressed outside the self. The attribute of interiority, both for the house and for the people associated with it, forms an important matrix, if one difficult to pinpoint, that gives a specifically Turkish meaning to the way the Turkish house has been imagined and remembered.

Because Naim Efendi was a most interior [*içli*] and most polite man, no one would realize that he was being unhappy.[10]

The quality of having-an-interior (*içli*),[11] whether applied to a house or a person, is what is called here interiority, calling attention to this concept because of the deep associations it brings with it, connecting it to both the past and the house.[12] Interiority includes both a sense of sensitivity and reserve, and it appears in the background of my materials as a highly valorized attribute that attested to the dignity of the individual.[13] A proverb collected in the late nineteenth century—"The head is split inside the fez, the arm remains broken inside the sleeve"[14]—reinforces the point that disagreeable events and emotions are to remain covered from the outside. The concept of interiority, which runs as a leitmotif through these novels, is both an elusive and an important concept that is fundamental to understanding the way the Turkish house resonates in collective memory.

Interiority has spatial and emotional-psychological connotations, but it has a spiritual element as well. In Halide Edib's *Sinekli Bakkal*, the young heroine, Rabia, meets the educated and urbane Sufi dervish Vehbi Dede, who will become her music teacher and spiritual mentor. The first time Rabia sees him, she can't find his hands to kiss them:

> How was she going to find his hands so that she could kiss them? His hands must be some place inside the camel-hair colored cloak [*Harman*] that covered his whole length, all the way to the floor. Why didn't he reach out his hand to be kissed like other adults did? She slowly let herself look at her new teacher. The Dede, his tall form inside his long cape, bowed slightly forward, his head under the conical cap of the Mevlevi Order [*Mevlevi külahi*] tilted to the left, and in his behavior there was a note of expectancy. . . .
> As the child's eyes finally found the Dede's eyes, two thin arms emerged from his cloak and crossed in front of his chest and he greeted her with the Mevlevi bow of greeting, just as if she were a grown person.[15]

In *Sinekli Bakkal*, Vehbi Efendi stands for a sophisticated interiority that is both spiritual and cognitive and offered as an antidote to the spiritual poverty of the West and the ruthless materialism of the most extreme political reformers. It is this interiority, symbolized by the inscrutability yet kindness of his greeting, that predicts he will become the shelter of calm and tranquility in Rabia's life. At the same time, a sense of pain is associated with interiority, because a developed interiority was associated with the Sufi concept of the inner soul's painful striving to unite with God, giving this attribute another connotation of spirituality.[16]

Apart from any mystical association, the rules of Ottoman social behavior, which emphasized the well-being of the *mahalle* (the neighborhood) as well as the interior of the house, were organized so that activities and feelings would remain unspoken to protect the dignity of the house from curious neighbors or nonrelatives; certainly, the ability to keep one's emotions contained in trying circumstances was believed to keep the atmosphere calm and safe.[17] Walter Andrews has shown how excessive and indecorous displays of emotion, unless associated with the mystical-religious patterns of poetry, made a person the subject of general gossip, and how this could be a severe impediment to success within the rules of Ottoman society.[18] Interiority, then, had both spiritual weight and practical value.

Novels allow us to penetrate this double barrier of protection and interiority, of closed walls and closed emotions, and to investigate the emotional dimensions of domestic life, for the novel is the first mode to allow us entry into the house. Ottoman literary modes before the novel did not afford this opportunity. The Meddah theatrical tradition,[19] as well as the Karagöz puppet theater, used domestic settings as a backdrop, if at all, and never entered the house itself or analyzed the characters inside it. Karagöz plays, for example, used stock characters whose characteristics were known and expected. As for Ottoman poetry, when it had a setting it was a garden, but even this was always allegorical, and the psychological dimensions or development of characters was never an issue. Ottoman historical writing, such as myths, legends, and chronicles, was the only genre that approached a description of places and people. For example, Halide Edib, the author of *Sinekli Bakkal*, recalls reading Mustafa Naima (1665–1704), the most famous of Turkish historians:

> I got to reading Naima, the wonderful Turkish chronicler who reaches to the levels of Shakespearean psychological penetration in his very simple yet vivid description. . . . I had begun reading his almost incomprehensible and very formless old prose and till I could penetrate the hard crust of his language, and till his critical and intensely living presentation of facts emerged upon me, he succeeded in putting me to sleep. But the moment the difficulties of external form disappeared and I lost consciousness of the form as something apart, I had a wonderful vision

of individual souls, large crowds, and revolutions in life and action. He was opening my eyes to the psychology of the old Turks.[20]

Naima shows in one single revolutionary scene a singular power of representing the setting as well as the thoughts and the feelings of his time with an understanding which would sound true and real in any age.[21]

But not even Naima's unusual prose[22] entered the house, and so, before the novel, there was no possibility in Turkey of crossing the threshold of domestic space in a detailed, textual, or even symbolic way.

But novels, whether set in historical time or not, whether realist or not, are fiction. Clearly, if one is attempting to recreate the past by reading historical fiction, not only details of description but issues of authorial intention must be questioned.[23] But if one asks, what domestic settings were embedded in the imagination of the author (and by extension his particular milieu) as representative of the cultural conditions of the past? and how are these images given poetic intent or deployed as rhetorical devices? then there is no problem in separating the historical background from the fictional foreground, for one is looking for that exact conflation, the point where collective memory gathers and is made known. For example, the image of domestic space that emerges from *Kiralık Konak* is layered with the affective meaning that comes from the activities, intentions, and feelings that were associated in 1922 with the house of 1908.

Furthermore, a novel not only enlarges the setting but enlarges the perception of space in the reader, and thus operates to highlight and perpetuate a memory string of imagined images. Michael Boyd suggests that part of the reader's job "is to discover the nature of the role he or she has been asked to play,"[24] and he further suggests that different literary styles seek to train their readers in different ways of reading: "The self-consciousness of the artist about inherited literary modes and about habitual modes of perception will, it is hoped, be transferred to the reader."[25] The genre of the novel may force into speech and into thought things that had not been thought or spoken before, but these will always be interpreted within the context of the culture that writes and reads them.

Yakup Kadri was one of the most respected and frequently read authors of the early twentieth century in Turkey, and *Kiralık Konak* was one of his most read and most analyzed works.[26] The novels that you will get to know in this chapter are classics of their time, and what we find in reading them is that they not only invite us into the house but offer the chance to find images of the house that have been neither built nor depicted but were hidden in the context of discourse within the story and shared, often through poetic and symbolic language, between authors and readers. Thus, these novels allow us to investigate the depiction and the perpetuation of emotional space and the charge that it holds in memory.

THE HOUSE AS A MEMORY IMAGE

Kiralık Konak takes place in Istanbul from 1908 until 1917, or until the middle of World War I. It begins with the *II Meşrutiyet* (pronounced Meshrootiyet) or the Second Constitutional Period of 1908, when the Ottoman sultan lost, to a constitution, his absolute authority, and when the political and economic system that had provided sinecures, if not jobs, for the Ottoman nobility ended overnight. This change also meant that the Westernization and secularization of tastes and institutions that had begun in earnest in the last century lost their last impediment. Each character in *Kiralık Konak* represents a type of personality that was thought to be characteristic of this period of rupture. Naim Efendi, a retired pasha, a widower, and an Ottoman gentleman with an Ottoman upbringing who had once been a minister in the service of Sultan Abdülhamid II, represents the recent but suddenly obsolete past. He lives with his daughter, Sekine, his son-in-law, Servet Bey, his granddaughter, Seniha, his grandson, Cemil, a Polish governess, and a few servants. The son-in-law, Servet Bey, is the ultimate *"züppe,"* a forty-five-year-old dandy whose sole goal in life is to attain what he considers to be the height of Western (material) culture. Naim Efendi's grandson, Cemil, is a ne'er-do-well who at age twenty spends his nights away from home with his mistresses, or flirting and drinking in the Europeanized streets of Beyoğlu (pronounced Bey-o-loo; the Turkish "ğ" is silent). The granddaughter, Seniha, listens to stories of the West from her Polish governess, reads French novels, and aspires to a life of glamour and wealth. At the beginning of the novel, these three generations live together in a large konak in Cinangir (pronounced Jehangeer), on the edge of Beyoğlu.

In the late Ottoman period it was the custom for upper-class families to spend their winters in their urban konaks and their summers in their waterside yalıs along the Bosphorus. The Naim Efendi family had always made this yearly migration as well, alternating between their konak in Cihangir and their yalı in Kanlıca. When the novel opens, however, we learn that this year is different. "This summer, the Naim Efendi family had not moved to Kanlıca," is the opening sentence of the novel, and the rest of the story shows social life changing so quickly that the family structure of the Ottoman konak dissolves in front of us. The reader is shown why, in fact, the Naim Efendi family would never go to Kanlıca again.

Naim Efendi is portrayed as representing the last of the "true Ottoman" gentry, as having been educated in the refined "İstanbulin" period that had begun with Abdül Mecit (1839–1861). But his adulthood was spent in the "Ridingot,"[27] a period of moral and ethical as well as economic decay, led by the autocratic and paranoid Sultan Abdülhamid II. Thus, Naim Efendi, who was the same age as Abdülhamid, was a crossover personage, a representative of the high-level officials who, in this crossover, had been able to retain their refined manners but had lost their moral—and economic—savvy.

> Although he had seen many official and unofficial dirty affairs during his career [memur hayatında] [Naim Efendi] still had a deep respect for the government and the men of government. Naim Efendi was such a well-mannered person that one would never forget to add "Radiyallahû anh"[28] to the end of his name, and one would elongate the pronunciation of Pasha, and, above all, one would end his address with "hazretleri" just as one would for the saints and prophets. The greatest virtue of this type of person is their obedience and respect [itaat ve hürmet]. All their manners and ethical principles are founded on the meaning of just these two words. But apart from this, Naim Efendi had two more virtues, he was as affectionate as a mother and as fastidious as a widow. . . . A careless action, a rude word or a blot of oil on the vest would grieve him equally. But because he was a most interior (reserved) [içli] and a most polite man, no one would realize that he was being unhappy.[29]

Thus, Naim Efendi brought from the old, İstanbulin order his interiority, the demeanor of serenity that was rarely interrupted or ruffled by discussions of problems or by displays of emotion. "The Ottomans have never been so serene and clean and elegant as they were during the İstanbulin period,"[30] that is, during "the serious, elegant, and internalized [için için] traditional Ottomanness of the Abdül Mecit period."[31] Naim Efendi's wife had also epitomized the last of a generation that could make everything run smoothly. Before her death five years earlier, she had run the house in the old way, with an iron hand and a tight purse. It was this type of behavior that had made both Naim Efendi and his wife the last scent of a memory of an order that was portrayed as ending—or already ended. The role of the Ottoman patriarch (or the head of the family, when it happened to be a woman) was to keep the inside of the soul and the inside of the house running smoothly and serenely, in the same way that the sultan's responsibility was to keep the interior space of the empire in order: "A wife makes the house a home, the state makes the country prosperous," goes the proverb.[32] The sultan's patrimony was conceptualized both as the enclosure of a house and as an enclosed garden, analogies that made his authority parallel to that of the Divine. In the classic period, the pashas and viziers would run their households to replicate that of the authority above them,[33] and their power reflected that authority as well.

In *Sinekli Bakkal*, the young Rabia has reached an age at which she can legally choose whether she wishes to remain living in the house of her selfish grandfather, the neighborhood imam, or move to the house of her warmhearted father. The pasha of the neighborhood, Selim Pasha, is the arbiter and judge when it comes to where Rabia will live, and the imam agrees, saying, "I am ready to accept the pasha's decision as the sacred law."[34] In this way the large Ottoman households of the city were perceived as a microcosm of the palace to which they were linked through intricate patron-client ties (*intisab*) and by a kind of institutional reflection, and the poorer households were linked to the wealthier ones in the same way, depending on the konak pashas for authority and benevolence. "*Var evi kerem evi*": a house of wealth is a house of generosity.

According to the great "circle of justice" (*erkân-ı erbaa*),[35] the Ottomans understood that "the world is a garden, its walls are the state"—indicating that the government, which is tied to the Divine, provides an inner space that is safe, secure, and orderly. Andrews shows how Ottoman poetry seems to reflect a garden-like security and order in all its interior spaces. "The lands of the empire, the major administrative center, the palace, all partake of the garden analogy and the security of the home and the inner self." Each inner space has its own level of security. "Thus it is better to be home than out in public, better to be in the direct service of the Sultan than not, better a position in Istanbul than anywhere else, better to live in the Ottoman Empire than outside it,"[36] which is the ultimate punishment of exile. Thus the Ottoman symbolic universe,[37] or its matrix of cultural creations, shared understandings and shared values and beliefs, is conceptualized as a series of concentric (*iç-içe*) circles of interiority. These circles begin with God and His realm and move inward through His representatives, the sultan first, but also the great pashas in the large konaks of the mahalles and the family patriarch in the home, finally coming to rest in the soul. The house and the soul are

Sinekli Bakkal, *1984, cover. Reproduced courtesy of Atlas Kitabevi, Istanbul.*

at the inner, most protected, and arguably most sacred spot, infusing interiority with a transcendent significance[38] and making the house and the soul together a symbol of an orderly universe. Because this symbolic universe can be understood to be constructed of a hierarchy of actors, when each actor plays his role according to his assignment, such as the pasha making a decision in the neighborhood, with his reflected weight of political and divine law, the known world is both relegitimized and the universe feels as if it makes sense. There is a sense of wholeness.

However, in *Kiralık Konak*, Naim Efendi has abrogated his position of authority in the household[39] and is therefore responsible for the dissolution of the house and, by extension, the orderly universe it represents. Naim Efendi supports the material culture desired by his children and grandchildren out of weakness and short-sightedness, for he is without the guiding principles that once situated Ottoman authority within a higher system of values. His financial support of their fancy clothes, travels, and ultimately their move from the konak to an apartment is due to weakness, for he is in some cases offended but in all cases bewildered by the new lifestyle that has invaded his house and that, he knows, will ultimately bankrupt him. Here is the telling passage:

> Naim Efendi recently could not even understand the Turkish that was spoken or written, let alone the new instruments and new songs. Fifteen years ago he had picked up a book that his son-in-law had left. It had a red cover and the lettering was white. For a while he just turned it over in his hands; then he put on his glasses, and inspected the cover for a long time. He read the name of the writer, the title of the book, the date of imprinting; every symbol he could see, every word he could read, including the name of the author, it all looked peculiar. With great curiosity he opened the volume, but how could he read it? He tried to syllabify the words like a child in the first grade, but he couldn't even finish a sentence; or if he did finish, he couldn't understand what he had read. It was a novel from the "New Literature Movement."[40] But Naim Efendi had never read a novel in his life.[41]

The owner of this novel, Naim Efendi's son-in-law, Servet Bey, came from a respectable Ottoman family—his father was a judge (*kazaskar*)—but he had spent his youth in conflict with his upbringing, preparing for the day when he would escape to what he perceived to be its opposite, that is, Western European life:

[H]e would lie in his room on a *chaise-longue* staring at the ceiling, . . . on the one hand smoking his Dutch cigar, on the other hand singing some opera pieces in a quiet, rather scattered voice, killing time for hours; he had the right to do this in his own room. He always had a suitcase ready for a possible European journey and there was a hatbox next to it. When he was bored he would stand in front of the mirror and try on the hats one by one, and when he saw his head under the hat he would almost pass out from the ecstasy of looking at himself.[42]

When Servet Bey married Sekine, he moved into Naim Efendi's konak and proceeded to refurbish his father-in-law's home with European furniture. And not only that, but after the revolution (of 1908, when the Young Turks restored the constitution), he allowed no Turkish to be spoken in the konak at all. In line with the Westernizing and modernizing spirit of the Young Turks, only French was to be spoken. Thus, Servet Bey usurps his father-in-law's authority even though the author refers to him as an *"iç güveyi,"* a son-in-law who moves in with the wife's family instead of the other way around. This suggests that he is financially dependent on his in-laws—a position that was often seen as humiliating and humbling.[43]

But Servet Bey really wants not to Westernize the konak with new furniture and a new language but to abandon it altogether:

How can one live here? Look at the walls, look at the ceiling! What kind of a room is this? What kind of sofa! My god, please please save us as soon as possible! *Burada nasıl yaşanır? Allahım, sen kurtar, bir an evvel sen kurtar.*[44]

Eventually he is able, with Naim Efendi's money, to move with his wife and children to an apartment in Şişli, the most chic area of Istanbul.

Finally, one day, Servet Bey was relieved from his *"iç güveylik,"* which he himself had called *"canına tak"* [unbearable], and he moved to an apartment in Şişli, which was the deepest wish of his heart.[45]

Şişli (pronounced Shishli) was the more Muslim extension of Beyoğlu, which was the modern European section of Istanbul. Beyoğlu (comprising Pera and Galata) was almost an independent city, with a population in the second half of the nineteenth century that consisted mostly of non-Muslim Ottomans (Greeks, Armenians, and Jews) and Europeans, especially French

Istanbul. Surviving early twentieth-century apartment on Vali Konağı St., Nişantaşı.
Photograph by Carel Bertram, 1996.

and Austrian merchants; in 1920 the Russians swelled this population, bringing their balalaikas and ballet. The large trading houses and banks had their
headquarters there, and there were modern shops, theaters, and a variety of
European-style cafés and restaurants. Abdül Mecit (1839–1861) had encouraged the building of konaks to its north, in Nişantası, Teşvkiye, Pangaltı,
and as far as Şişli, but all these areas were soon overtaken by European-style
stone apartment buildings. Şişli was especially fashionable because it could
be reached by a tram pulled by horses; in 1913, as Servet Bey prepared to
move, the horses were replaced by an electric tram, and Şişli was becom-

ing the second area of Istanbul, after Beyoğlu, to have electricity and gas. Beyoğlu, and by extension Şişli, was the symbol of modernity, and not just for Istanbul but for the entire empire.[46]

When Servet Bey found the apartment of his dreams, he entered a state of childish rapture reminiscent of the way he had felt when looking at himself in the mirror as a youth. He changed from a taciturn and lazy husband to a man driven by desire. He was at the new apartment every day, arriving with the workers; he chose the furniture and the upholstery, and he put up the curtains himself, singing Western tunes as he worked.

It is to support this rapture that Naim Bey, who was raised to be polite and to take care of all the needs of his family, sacrifices his money. And it is for this reason, too, that the konak life led by the family father, with all the generations tied together physically and emotionally, splits apart. Sekine follows her husband reluctantly, as she realizes she is abandoning her father to an empty house.

> "What are you going to do here all by yourself?" she wailed, and as she
> said this, her eyes filled and she began to shake her head from side
> to side.
> "Me?" said the old man; "Daughter, don't you think about me . . .
> how many days of life are left to me? . . ."
> Sekine Hanım was sobbing. . . .
> "I'll come to see you every day." But still she felt no inner peace.
> "Dear father, I am going there but my thoughts are pulling me here. My
> heart is breaking."[47]

Naim Efendi is left alone in this konak, and for the first time he begins to weep.

> It was a very peculiar kind of sadness. He was like a man sobbing after
> his own death, mourning himself. . . . He kept saying to himself:
> "*Hey gibi Naim! Hey gidi Naim!* Just look at you, Naim, you old
> Naim. Poor Naim, how your luck has turned on you! What more are
> you waiting for? Why hold on? Isn't this enough? Isn't this enough?"[48]

As sad as Naim Efendi's personal loneliness might be, what is dying is the konak and its life-world. The meaning that the old wooden house, the Turkish house and the konak, holds is one of a unified social whole where the generations could act as a unit; it is a memory of a non-fragmentation, of wholeness. Sekine's move, unlike her husband's, is full of ambivalence, but the results are the same.

In the Ottoman-Turkish manner, social life was interior; it went on inside the house, and it was unthinkable—in fact, without Beyoğlu impossible—to lead a life on the boulevards or at restaurants or in European-style cafés, as Naim Efendi's grandchildren did. Outside Beyoğlu, men would meet in the evenings at the mahalle cafes or *kiraathanes*,[49] but the women and children would be at home and would receive endless visitors, or they would go visit other homes. Men of any standing at all would have a room in the house available for entertaining male guests, even if there were no *selâmlık*/harem division. Furthermore, the konaks of the wealthy were situated within the dense fabric of the mahalle, as neighborhoods were not at all segregated by class. A grand konak and smaller houses shared both a mahalle and a symbolic universe: the family of the konak was expected to open the home to people of the mahalle as well as help them solve their problems or find employment for their sons.[50]

Naim Efendi had been raised in this Ottoman-Turkish manner, in which the house or the konak was the center of family and social life.

> Naim Efendi spent all his childhood, all his youth in the most crowded konak of Istanbul, where he very much liked jovial company, talking with friends and the visits of guests. But ... now ... how was it possible to find the get-togethers, conversations, visits and guests of the old days?[51]

When his sister urges him to rent out the konak and live with her, we understand why Naim Efendi is loath to give up the one place that holds warm memories for him, even though his own family rejected the house and the interiorized life for which it stands.

The house proves difficult to rent, however, not merely because it is falling apart, dusty, and inhabited by mice, and not merely because Naim Efendi sabotages the effort by keeping the harem half of the house locked so that potential renters will feel unable to make a decision. It is difficult to rent because its meaning has been lost to a new generation of renters.

> These people were looking over the furnishings with scorn. It was as if the women, with their feet in shoes of the latest fashion, were loath to let them touch the floor. With each step they would stop and look around them and they would purse their lips, and each of them, as they

walked across the stone entry floor [taşlık] and up the stairs, said "honestly how dirty and unkempt this place is!" [Then the man] began to give a long lecture on the structure of the house to the woman next to him. "This is a type of architecture that has suffered degeneration. It is so decadent that it is impossible to find the origins of it. Our old ancestors lived in stone buildings." After the Tanzimat, a wooden house and a wooden konak style came into being.[52]

Naim Efendi in his bed hears them and begins to cough. (Certainly his distress comes from their criticisms and not because of their art historical inaccuracy, but the reader understands that by saying the old houses were stone and not wood, the renters show they have no idea of their own cultural heritage.) One of those hearing this cough says,

"Ah! Aman! What's that! Where does that voice come from?" The other one added: "As if someone is being strangled!" And the youngest jumped back and said, "Mother! Mother! don't go near that door. Someone must be dying there!"

Naim Bey heard all this . . . with difficulty he raised himself on his bed, holding the bedstead. Suddenly the door opened and many heads peered in. Naim Efendi with his white night cap and white gown was standing on the bed. The women screamed and immediately closed the door. Then he heard their voices from the corridor: "A dead man! a dead man! A corpse! Standing upright on his coffin.". . . "I saw it—it was moving, Vallahi! It was moving!"

Naim felt struck to the heart, and he fell back in his bed. Yes, it was just the way these unrefined women and inconsiderate women said, these women who were screaming at each other . . . and he said to himself, "You are contemptible! Just die already." And he coughed and gasped together.[53]

Yakup Kadri has made the konak the symbol of everything that is old. But at the same time that it is a memory of receding generational wholeness and of an empire's ordered and refined ways, it is also a memory of the empire's failure because of the government's inability to make intelligent decisions. For Yakup Kadri, the Turkish house is as much a symbol of the past as it was to Hamdullah Suphi, but with more complex and less fully positive associations.

This wooden konak, Naim Efendi, and the ways of the old empire are conflated, and all are weary. There is no one to take over this inheritance, neither strangers nor family. The konak is conflated with the past by its associations with Naim Efendi's interiority and through his memories, both of which give an emotional element to the memory of place. That is, his soul and his konak-life are inseparable. The meaning of the konak resonates with Naim Efendi's refined Ottoman lifestyle when "everything was in order," when people understood the meaning of manners and never showed their displeasure or emotions. It was a place understood to be ordered under a family patriarch, an *"aile reisi,"* and one believed that this order could hold the individual in the family and hold the family together physically as well as emotionally. Naim Efendi and his house stand for this aspect of the empire that is remembered as once intact but now being lost. This is the meaning of wholeness in *Kiralık Konak*: it is not a memory of perfect integration, but the house represents a place where conflicts had potential resolution within an ordered universe of meaning.

But now Naim Efendi has lost the ability to make good economic decisions; his konak and his empire are the final fragmentation of a possibility of wholeness. Naim Efendi sells off everything piece by piece, or has his representatives do so, until he is left with only a shell of an edifice. He sells his property in Çemberlitaş to pay for his granddaughter's French fashion tastes. Soon afterward, that property escalates in value because a tram line is laid in front of it. He refuses to sell his summer residence (yalı) because of his emotional attachment to it, choosing instead to sell his income-producing warehouse in Vefa. In the end, the yalı goes anyway, and then he must sell the furnishings in the konak. Eventually the konak is slated to be divided, by renters or purchasers, into autonomous apartments.

Naim Efendi represents an empire that had been in a state of economic, political, and cultural siege for more than a quarter of a century, that is, for his entire adult life. Let us assume that he was born in 1840. In 1878, after 100 years of no important territorial losses, the Ottomans lost control of Bosnia and Herzegovina, in their west, to Austria, and then Batum and Kars, in their east, to Russia. Naim Efendi, living in a novel set in 1908, does not know, but the author and reader do, that in less than fifteen years, the empire would be subjected to the humiliating Treaty of Sevres, signed on August 10, 1920, which attempted to institutionalize the division of the empire among foreign powers. Furthermore, just as Naim Efendi had allowed Servet Bey to invade the konak with Western furniture and language, so the empire had allowed foreign laws to invade it. The commercial treaties with England in 1838 and 1861, the Crimean War in 1853, the Treaty of Paris, and especially the Edict of 1853 all paved the way for the rise of European influence in the Ottoman state and indirectly facilitated the social and economic rise of a non-Muslim middle class with a European enclave in Beyoğlu. The "capitulations" that granted concessions to Western merchants in the interest of fostering trade predated the Ottoman regime, but they were reaffirmed during the Tanzimat and again under Abdülhamid II, so that non-Muslim foreign communities were able to govern themselves on Ottoman territory as if they were in their own nations—a serious infringement on Ottoman sovereignty.

Like Naim Efendi's decisions about his property, the empire's economic decisions were disastrous. One development abhorred by the Young Ottomans had been a newly instated Ottoman policy of borrowing money from abroad on terms that were ruinous to the empire and that led to complete financial collapse when there was an attempt to make payments.[54] In fact, this borrowing began in 1853 with Abdül Mecit's desire for a Western-style Rococo Palace, the *Dolma Bahçe*.

Whether Ottoman reverses were due to global economics or internal politics, the local understanding was that there was poor management at home. In Mehmet Murad's 1891 *Turfanda mı yoksa Turfa mı?* (Is It Avant-Garde, or Is It Just Worthless?), a novel that comments on the period of Abdülhamid II (1876–1909) and the need for bureaucratic reform, the protagonist criticizes the Grand Vizier for the incompetent management of the civil service:

> You say there is financial difficulty? One cannot [but] believe that there is financial difficulty seeing all the wastefulness around! Supposing there is financial difficulty; one doesn't see any attempt to solve it. Are you not the person having the responsibility and authority to take measures?[55]

When the Grand Vizier counters that the treasury has had to borrow from Europe merely to be able to make interest payments to maintain the status quo, Mansur retorts, "Are you not disturbed when you think of how the following generations will curse you because of the disaster your present policies will cause?"[56]

It is just as Naim Efendi says to his nephew:

> Every day I'm selling off something else from the house. First it was some of the extra things, I began with the fine china, and then the buffets, the tables, and the couches; now it's come to the beds and the

quilts. All the beautiful carpets in the *sofa* have gone, didn't you notice that when you came in, my boy?[57]

The konak, like the empire, had a heritage of wealth and beauty, but after a long period of deterioration its wealth was pawned, and even the blameless confused form with integrity. Naim Efendi is one of those seemingly blameless, although he condoned the behavior that the revolution of 1908 sought to redress. He discusses this in 1908 with his son-in-law:

The other day I visited Hasip Pasha in Erenköy. The poor man was in such a state that I felt sorry for him. It appears that the newspaper *Tanin* is talking about some embezzling and mis-appropriation that occurred when he was minister. However. . . .

His son-in-law demurs, causing the polite Naim Efendi, who cannot bear discord, to backtrack.

"Don't get angry," he said. "I didn't say that an accounting shouldn't be asked for, God forbid! Only think for a minute. I appeal to your conscience. How can an accounting be asked for from such an upright person as Hasip Pasha? . . . I assure you, he hasn't even five cents to his name. He gets by on his wife's money."[58]

The new generation denied the moral authority of these leaders and had no use for their universe, preferring the Western lifestyle that promised progress and reform. The houses that held this old life together were abandoned one by one. The first house that was rejected was the yalı, as it was too far from the Western entertainments of Beyoğlu. The new generation attempted to change the old house by making it Western rather than Eastern, by refurbishing it, by bringing in Western tutors and governesses, and finally by changing the language spoken in the house. But by finally moving out of the konak, Naim Efendi's children and grandchildren display more than their newly Westernized tastes: they show a complete rejection of the past the konak represents. When Naim Efendi and Servet Bey discuss the fate of Hakim Pasha after the 1908 revolution, Servet sums it up this way:

"All the old heads must be cut off, not just those of the dishonorable!" Naim Bey felt the savage allusion in this last sentence, but couldn't find the strength within himself to answer. He lowered his eyes and pondered deeply.[59]

Kiralık Konak ends with Naim Efendi's granddaughter, Seniha, in an episode in the Şişli apartment that shows the moral as well as material chasm between Naim Efendi and his grandchildren, and between what the past is remembered for and what the present forebodes. Seniha, although her grandfather's favorite, was a coquettish fin de siècle girl who had no guidance from her grandfather or her parents. Instead, she was influenced by her Polish governess and the characters in French novels. "Her only daily occupation from sunrise to sunset was bringing these young female types to life."[60] In fact, in *Kiralık Konak*, Seniha's escapades mark her as an immoral femme fatale, beginning with her love affair with her first suitor, Faik Bey.[61] The author even goes so far as to call her "whorish." By the end of the novel, Seniha has rejected Faik Bey as well as the love of her honorable and patriotic cousin, Hakkı Celis. Hakkı Celis stands as a counterpoint to Naim Efendi's rootless grandchildren, for Hakkı had been raised in the traditional and authoritarian environment of Naim Efendi's sister. But when he realizes his love for Seniha will bear no fruit, he becomes a nationalist, joins the army, and is killed in Çanakkale.[62]

A mere two weeks later, Seniha is at a gala party in her own home, flirting with German generals and businessmen who have newly emerged from the lower classes, having been made rich by the war.[63] One general hears the story of Hakkı Celis's noble death, and in an effort to impress Seniha says that he wishes to build a grand monument on the spot where Hakkı Celis fell. Hearing about her cousin's death makes Seniha uncomfortable. Her interest now is in showing off her clothes, with the intention of attracting the general's money, perhaps by taking him to her room after the meal. Unlike Naim Bey, who with his interiority is full of emotion but allows himself to show nothing, Seniha is full of words and postures but has no feeling. As the general leans over to see if he is making an impression, she sits still, all dolled up and looking beautiful. Thus at the end of the novel, the men and women of the new generation are posturing in their apartments, and Naim Efendi is dying of real emotions in a deteriorating house that no one wants to rent.

In *Kiralık Konak*, the house carries the burden of the past. It also becomes a protagonist, a player in a drama and a site of tension for both the readers and the characters in it. The konak is portrayed as the site where the personal and familial authority over the inside is receding: this "inside" includes the mental state of interiority that was remembered to characterize both the house and, by extension, the empire.

It is not that the meaning associated with the Turkish house derives from its association with privacy and enclosure (although this practice of privacy has made the interior of the house and its interior meaning difficult to access). Rather, the Turkish house is an integral part of a symbolic universe defined by enclosure and protection, and this universe has a spiritual dimension that legitimizes the activities that go on inside the house. What actually gives the house its meaning are the feelings of the people who live inside it and the way in which those feelings are crystallized by the stories and novels that depict behavior in this domestic universe.

The concept of interiority appears to be integral to understanding this crystallization. The word "iç" with its opposite, "dış," has a connotative base in Turkish that is consistently tied to meanings of interiority versus exteriority, but also to sincerity versus superficiality and home versus exile. "İç" is the inside, the inner substance, the heart and the mind. Although this is a realm that needs further textual corroboration, the examples seem to show that this sense of "having an inside" not only participates at a primary level in a matrix of Easterners and spirituality but also makes the house, which is the space of interiority, a fundamental marker of the East and the spirit, especially in contrast to the perceived exteriority, superficiality, and materialism of the West.

Understanding the development of the spiritual-material divide in literature and the role of the house as an arbiter in the tensions between them positions the Turkish house in a memory chain of values. The house had been imagined as a place of "spiritual and material tensions" before *Kiralık Konak*, as a part of a didactic literature that embedded this idea of tension into collective memory; in fact, "spiritual and material tensions" was one of the most familiar tropes of the nineteenth-century Ottoman Turkish novel.

THE TURKISH NOVEL: A SITE OF CONTENTION OVER CULTURAL VALUES, AND A PLACE FOR MORAL QUESTIONING

Thirty years before Ottoman authors began writing novels themselves, the novel as a literary form was introduced to the Ottoman world with the opening of its waters to the West.[64] The Turkish historian Niyazi Berkes suggests that the first real penetration of the West was marked by the appearance of steamships in the Mediterranean in 1828. He quotes the Scottish traveler, John G. Stephens:

Lately things have changed; the universal peace in Europe and the introduction of steam-boats into the Mediterranean have brought the Europeans and the Turks comparatively close together. It seems to me that the effect of the steam-boats here has already begun to be felt . . . I have no doubt that in two or three years you will be able to go from Paris to Constantinople in fifteen or twenty days.[65]

Certainly Western thought had penetrated the empire long before, for only eleven years after the appearance of these ships, the Tanzimat Reforms of Abdül Mecit (1839–1861) formally opened Ottoman lands to European, especially French, influences.[66] Abdül Mecit's bright hope for the Tanzimat was that an association with Westerners and the adoption of their political and economic practices would lead to a reversal of the military and economic decline of the Ottoman state.

These ships and the ensuing charter of the Tanzimat encouraged the importation of Western technologies and Western goods, but they also opened the way for the Western philosophies that would lead to a deep crisis in Ottoman thought. This crisis came about because the Tanzimat Reforms led to partial economic successes but to more obvious failures, and particularly to a radically increased dependence on European economies and a loss of Ottoman sovereignty.[67] The response was a rise in religious nationalism, represented by the Young Ottoman movement that began to emerge in the 1860s. The Young Ottomans suggested that at the heart of the philosophical issues brought about by the Tanzimat was the confrontation between the East and the West in terms of what was "essentially Ottoman" (and thus not to be changed) and what changes were necessary for progress. As much as the Young Ottomans wanted to emulate the West, and as much as they admired Western thought, they feared Western culture as a threat to that very identity that they wanted to create around a concept of Ottomanism. Thus, the nature and meaning of cultural experience began to be crystallized, causing a variety of polarizations and confusions.

The novel as a local form rather than as a translation into Turkish came into being in the middle of the intense discussion and confusion that the Tanzimat period fostered about what was necessary for progress, couched in terms of the West, and what was sacrifice, couched in terms of what elements of the East, that is, "Ottomanness," might be lost. Ahmet Evin discusses how novels, especially French novels, had been read by an Ottoman intelligentsia that had been educated in the new schools that were part of the Tanzimat program of reform; he shows how this group was a new class that knew foreign languages and had spent time in Europe, often in political exile. The authors who experimented with the novel were in addition politically active, and in the beginning many were members of the Young Ottomans.[68] Evin shows how these novelists, who were often journalists and scholars as well, saw their work as a didactic one and the novel as yet another arena in which they could educate the public about moral, social, and political issues. That is, although the form of the novel was Western and the style leaned toward the French realism that these authors were reading, the motivation was "not to capture life, but to say something about it."[69]

One of the primary issues of these authors was the role of women in Ottoman society, a topic that brought writers immediately into the house. Namık Kemal, the central intellect of the Young Ottomans, who combined a belief in the freedoms embodied in the French Revolution with an intense Ottoman patriotism, took up the issue of the inferior position of Ottoman women, especially Ottoman female slaves, and the denial of individual liberty that forced or arranged marriages represented.[70]

The clincher that these were intensely didactic novels is that their realism is often sacrificed to their message, a situation that can confuse the modern reader. For example, in 1873 Namık Kemal wrote the popular *Zavallı Çocuk* (Poor Child),[71] a play in which the young Şefika is in love with her cousin Ata but is forced to marry an old but wealthy pasha instead. The emotional setting is believable: Şefika, raised in the "interiority" tradition of Naim Efendi in *Kiralık Konak*, could never show her emotions. She would rather die, which in fact she does, leaving the reader with an image of a Turkish house ringing with her sorrowful words:

> I am worried and ashamed that my parents will find out my real feelings from my behavior and countenance. It is equally difficult to hide my true disposition from him [Ata]. If he understands my feelings toward him, then I shall die of embarrassment; if he does not, then of sadness.[72]

The year before, in 1872, Namık Kemal had discussed arranged marriages in an article titled "The Family" in the journal *İbret*:[73]

> You unfortunate mother, what is the reason for you to hasten marrying your very small daughter to the person you want, and not of her choice? . . . By forcing her to do so, you are only preparing her disastrous fate.[74]

With the reformist spirit of late nineteenth-century novelist-journalists, the image of the Turkish house became beset by the cries of mistreated slaves and young women married off by unfeeling parents to wealthy, aging men, and by the cries of prostitutes unfairly condemned, and by a disruptive polygamy; that is, the house was beset by issues of women's rights that reflected the Western philosophical stance of the Young Ottoman period. These complaints were a call for new legislation and new moral concepts, and thus served to mark the house as a place in need of statutory and spiritual reform. Namık Kemal summarized this image of the house as a place of conflict:

> The homes in a society are like the rooms in a house. Can one find comfort in a house constantly plagued by hatred and infighting? Could it prosper? Would happiness be possible?[75]

What is puzzling is that the research of the sociological historians Alan Duben and Cem Behar suggests that in Istanbul households at least, the age of marriage was late, not to mention that polygamy was rare. However, that arranged, forced child marriages might have been believed to be more common, or might have been believed to have been a problem in the less educated classes, which the reformers were trying to affect, might explain its insistent presence in contemporary literature. Or perhaps it was a straw man in the service of the didact's double mission: certainly, Namık Kemal attempted to embed two notions in the public consciousness, the first being the superiority of Western concepts of individual liberty and progress. Here the liberty of women could more easily be championed, as Duben and Behar suggest, against a situation of obvious degradation.[76] Or perhaps it was the world seen through Orientalist spectacles, as Edward Said would have defined Orientalism, that is, these Western-educated Easterners defining themselves through Western notions about polygamy, arranged marriages, and slavery of their own culture and time.

If the first notion refers to the championing of Western notions of individual freedom, particularly women's freedoms, the second notion that the Young Ottomans and didactic novelists of the late nineteenth century wished to address was that there were many Ottoman values that were superior to Western ones, and that these should be kept; in fact they must be fought for. For example, Namık Kemal and the Young Ottomans believed that Ottoman-Islamic religious or spiritual values were not an obstacle to progress, as the Western world seemed so fervently to believe, and that the political theories of the Qur'an and its interpreters provided the strongest guarantee of individual freedom.[77] As Berkes says, Namık Kemal "warned against the dangers arising from the widening gulf between the traditionalist conservatives and the imitative Westernists."[78] As one of the first Ottoman novelists writing in Turkish, Namık Kemal brought to the novel the search for what was of value in and essential to the preservation of Ottoman culture, and which elements of Westernization should be accepted as useful, which rejected as "over-Westernization" and therefore dangerous.

What is abundantly clear, however, is that with the very first Ottoman novels, the house became the site of contention over cultural values and the place for moral questioning.

1875: IN ORDER TO LIVE UTTERLY *ALAFRANGA*

The difference between what was perceived as the essentials of Western civilization and the essentials of Ottoman civilization, as well as the issues of the "blind" or "over-Westernization" of upper-class Ottomans, became the topics of novels as the Tanzimat period came to a close and the repressive era of Abdülhamid II opened. Abdülhamid II (1876–1909) suppressed the Young Ottoman and the later Young Turk movements and outlawed all mention of Tanzimat or reform, narrowing the discussions in literature to cultural rather than political issues.

Ahmet Midhat Efendi[79] was a Young Ottoman whose works cross over between these two periods, and in which perhaps the most important cultural paradigm emerges, that is, a polarity between the East and the West as a divide between a moral or spiritually superior East and a materially superior West. This concept was later "simplified" by emphasizing the positive, and characterizing the East as spiritual(-istic) and the West as material(-istic). This spiritual/material polarity is an important undercurrent of the late nineteenth-century novels and pervades the image of the house; it is a tension central to Ahmed Midhat's *Felâtun and Râkim Efendi* (the names of its two main characters) (*Felâtun ile Râkim Efendi*). Written in 1875, this novel is credited with introducing the character of the over-Westernized "*züppe*," or dandy, to the Ottoman Turkish imaginary,[80] a type we know from Naim Efendi's son-in-law, Servet Bey.

In *Felâtun ile Râkim Efendi*, it is Felâtun's father who begins the process of Westernization that will lead to the "züppefication" (*züppeleşmek*) of his son. He does this by leaving the traditional mahalle of Üsküdar in order to build a konak near the European area of Beyoğlu.

Felâtun Bey belonged to a Westernizing generation. His father, Mustafa Merâkı Efendi, was also a man with an *alafranga* disposition.... Although he himself was from Üsküdar and had a lovely konak with a garden and vineyards there; *in order to live utterly alafranga,* he had sold the lot regardless of price and had a new house built in a neighborhood of Tophane bordering on Beyoğlu. To give you an idea of his passion for *alafranga,* he had the house made of brick [instead of wood], so it would be unconditionally *alafranga.* Now in such a house in that kind of neighborhood, there was no question of an *alafranga* gentleman's filling up his house with the likes of black servants! Obviously Greek and Armenian servants were called for when *alafranga* friends came on their occasional visits.[81]

The two children of this "man with an *alafranga* disposition" are precursors of Naim Efendi's children and grandchildren. The daughter, Mihriban, is thoroughly spoiled. She was not taught the traditional homemaking crafts of embroidery or sewing because fine items were available outside, at the shops in Beyoğlu. Neither could she wash clothes, iron, or cook. The son, Felâtun (who prefers to be called by the Western equivalent, Plato), is given a spotty education by his foreign tutors, buys lavishly bound French books that he does not—and cannot—read, and spends his nights away from home in the cafés and streets of Beyoğlu and his days recovering from them. He dresses ostentatiously in his rendition of *alafranga* clothes, which are so tight that the pants split when he goes to a ball. When his father dies, he squanders his inheritance on his mistresses and gambling and finally is forced to leave the country altogether, taking a minor government post abroad.

His Western-style life is associated with material goods, particularly foreign ones, with purchasing clothes, and with spending money on entertainment. On a moral level his life is associated with "externality," the opposite of the enclosed life, which had "interiority" at its heart. It is a life meant to be lived in the public arena rather than in the protected privacy of the house and its circumscribed universe. The reader, who would have held the concept of interiority close to his heart, understood the severity of Felâtun's punishment for squandering his inheritance: exile, or *sürgün,* to the "exterior."[82]

In contrast to Felâtun's *alafranga* existence is the life of Râkim Efendi, who, although from a fatherless family, manages, through hard work and diligence, to become educated in Western and Eastern languages and literature and to become an outstanding economic success as a translator and tutor in the Westernized life of Beyoğlu. He has good relationships with Christian families, but he understands that they are "foreign/exterior" and therefore should remain separate from his interior life. He makes no attempt to assimilate into their culture, but selectively brings some of their culture home. Because of his morally superior, humble values, he continues to live in the small three-room house in a traditional neighborhood where he had lived with his widowed mother, when she was alive, and her trusty servant. After the death of his mother, he purchases a slave girl, Canan (pronounced Janan), to assist his old nurse. When he marries Canan,[83] he has her educated by his Beyoğlu friends. He brings home the Italian piano teacher, Madame Yozefino, who plays "*O dökülen kumral saç*" ("Those cascading brown locks o' thine"),[84] which is popular *alaturka* music. He also has Canan taught French; but he does not allow her to go out of the house unaccompanied.

Evin suggests that "Rakım's little, three-room house in a traditionalist quarter of Istanbul resembles the patrimonial household of the old Ottoman system,"[85] by which he means that it has a patriarch, a Circassian slave-girl, and a Nubian nurse, and that it maintains relations with "foreign" subjects such as Armenians and Europeans.[86] But it is also portrayed as the morally superior lifestyle, one that is not consumption oriented, that values warm human relations and time spent simply, inside the house.

Because Ahmet Midhat's purpose was a didactic one, he, like Namık Kemal, introduced a fundamental paradox. Felâtun and Râkim Efendi are portrayed as two contemporary types, but they are not real types, for the züppe was part of an "eccentric fringe,"[87] and in real life there were no cross-over types like Râkim Efendi at all.[88] Râkim Efendi, who guards his spiritual roots, is actually "a Westernized type in that he has the intellectual curiosity and the work ethic of the European bourgeois."[89] He works seventeen hours a day, inspiring Mardin to call him a "humorless, industrious prig."[90] In fact, both protagonists exist to inculcate the idea that success comes from taking the material and technical aspects of Westernization and bringing them into the Turkish house with its *Gemeinschaft* atmosphere and sensible clothes.[91]

The tensions that were in operation, therefore, were not merely between what was Eastern and what was Western but about how to isolate the useful material aspects of the West (such as pianos) while remaining true to the spiritual values that constituted the Ottoman-Turkish or Ottoman Islamic self.[92] This would mean, of course, that both material and spiritual would have to be defined, and these early novels introduce this dilemma of definition.[93]

What might have been considered aspects of the material world in a Western framework, or in the framework of a descriptive realism of the imported novel, was interpreted spiritually by the late Tanzimat authors. That is, although the mid- to late nineteenth-century authors, such as Ahmet Midhat and Namık Kemal, brought the space of the house into their novels and worked carefully to describe this space, this "real space" was given spiritual overtones because this was the interpretation that their culture put on "reality."

A clue to this different understanding of reality can be seen in one of the very first Turkish novels, *İntibah: Sergüzeşt-i Ali Bey* (Awakening: The Adventures of Ali Bey), written by Namık Kemal in 1876. Namık Kemal experimented with what it meant to describe a place, but he began with the trope of high Ottoman literature, which did not privilege how something "really looked" but how it affected the mental state of the observer:[94]

> Those who know Istanbul well know that not even Spring gives such inner pleasure or caresses the soul as does Çamlıca Pavilion.[95]

The goal of this type of description is not to see or to analyze, but to feel. Namık Kemal said that his object was not to investigate human behavior but to investigate the human soul; for him, realism was achieved if the story was kept within the bounds of credibility.[96] (And perhaps credibility here was related to the interior, the *iç*.) The above example clearly suggests that the Ottoman concept of reality had a strongly ingrained non-material content. As Andrews has shown in his work on Ottoman poetry, the emotional or spiritual content of one's relationship to people or places was seen as having an actual relationship to reality rather than a symbolic one.[97] One can only delight, then, in this paradox that allowed the spiritualism of places to become evident through a genre that was dedicated to laying bare the material world.

With this different understanding of the real, the emergence of the house as a spiritual edifice, even in realist novels, is not only less surprising, it is almost expected. Behavior was one of the vitally important aspects of the spiritual and an integral part of an Islamic worldview in which the acquisition of all knowledge was judged according to its moral purpose, which was to activate "right action" (*adab*) in the one who acquired it. In this way, the spiritual-material divide that was operating in these works was not the one familiar to Western thought, in which, simply put, things are opposed to ideas. Rather, it was the difference between a spirituality whose activities were related to some higher purpose rather than to a life whose activities were rooted in a secular Western scientific worldview composed of sensible experiences—often perceived as existing without any value restrictions at all.[98]

Thus, the late Tanzimat-period novels established the trope of the house first as an area of moral conflict, where decisions about the moral treatment of women and the family had to be dealt with. But because the quest to identify the spiritual dimension of Ottoman life was evolving from a comparison with what was unacceptable in, and what was desired from, Western behavior, the house became the site where this morally approved and spiritually appropriate behavior would occur. In this way, late Ottoman authors were casting realism in a strongly local—that is, strongly spiritual and emotional—way at the same time they were also grappling with issues of what was Eastern and what was Western. It was in this context that the East-West conflict became positioned as a spiritual-material one, with the old wooden house becoming situated on the side of the East and the spiritual.

However, although a change in favor of the Western and the material evoked a fear of the loss of what was Eastern and moral, it was also a fear that the moral underpinnings of the present would be lost for the future. That is, the higher moral values that are valorized in these early novels belong to a contemporary house, not to a house that is situated in a past, not to a memory of something that was lost to the present. The house as a memory of loss is introduced only in the twentieth century. *Kiralık Konak* was the first to bring this type of historical consciousness into focus, but *Kiralık Konak* was not the first literary moment when the present looked to the domestic past for moral or spiritual guidance. This happened four years before *Kiralık Konak*, in a short story called "Harem," by Ömer Seyfeddin.

1918: IT WAS THE NIGHT THAT WE REESTABLISHED THE HAREM[99]

Ömer Seyfeddin's 1918 "Harem" does not take place in a konak but in a modern Beyoğlu apartment in Şişli. But the memory of the old Turkish house, in terms of the behavior, morality, and spirituality that it represents, is a critical player in the story. "Harem" is about a young married couple, Nazan and Sermet, who have just separated after accusing each other of adultery. When they meet again at their apartment to retrieve their belongings, both profess outraged innocence, which they say they can prove because, as it turns out, each has kept a diary over the past three years of their marriage. As they read portions of their diaries aloud, the situation that led to their mutual accusations unfolds.

The problems all began at a party in their "salon" (living room, or parlor), at which time Sermet became jealous of Nazan's playful talk with a male friend of theirs. The description of this party, however, also shows not only the level of their *alafranga* life but how it is self-consciously contrasted to its *alaturka* counterpart, and what this means for those who must choose between them at a time when their relative meaning is still unclear.

On the night of the fateful party, Nazan wrote in her diary how she had devised a statistical method to compare European to Turkish behavior:

> Little by little our Turkish men have begun to kiss women's hands, too. But they are still afraid of it. They are not as daring as Europeans. They do it like so. . . . hardly touching! . . . But we are still improving on this. I looked at my statistics in the evening. Twelve Turks had come. For each one who kisses my hand, I fold down one page of my journal. If I feel it's a strong kiss, I make the fold a large one; if it is an embarrassed little kiss I make it small. My statistics came out well this time, I made five large folds and three small ones.[100]

Certainly the life of this innocently coquettish Nazan (whose account keeping parodies the materialist scientism associated with Western thought) is not one that longs for an enclosed life behind the screened windows of a Turkish house. That type of life is even beyond her imagination. At the party she speaks to a German guest, who, reminiscent of the foreigner in Seyfeddin's "The Secret Temple" (discussed in Chapter 2), wonders about "the *real* Turks."

> That poor woman kept asking me things about the Harem! She wanted to see window grills [*kafes*], screens [*perderler*], and a eunuch [*Harem Ağa*]. . . . "But these you can only see in dreams or novels dear Madam," I said. She didn't believe me. . . . She is searching in vain for a "pure Turk." I tried to enlighten her. I explained that the new generation has done away with segregation, that we only wear the *Çarşaf*[101] in the streets. In the salons the new women talk with men, and sometimes, even, only single men are invited, and I pointed them out to her.[102]

This observation leads the couple and the German guest to a discussion that shows us how what is Turkish is associated with the past and what is Western with the present, and how the values that each represents form a point of contention and confusion. Sermet, for example, professes not to like the old ways, not even to know them. Yet at the same time he longs for a lost sense of order, a firm structure to support values that he cannot quite define but which he knows must be part of his heritage and preferable to the artificiality of copying Western ways:

"I am not a retiring old father [*babayani*], I believe in order and progress [*intizam ve terakki*]. Everything should improve, and that means it will change; the present is not to resemble the past. But on one condition! That condition is order. Yes, everything will change. But gradually! . . . I couldn't live a life like my grandfather's. Not that I ever saw it, but he must have been sitting cross-legged, and eating with his hands, because even today at my family's in Fatih,[103] they all eat from the same tray. I couldn't wear baggy trousers [*şalvar*], I couldn't smoke a long-stemmed pipe [*çubuk*], I couldn't take snuff. But I hate being a monkey! I mean, imitating Westerners and Europeans! That's a very ugly thing, imitating Europeans, with their so-called 'etiquette.'"

"Oh, and do the Turks even have an etiquette?" asks Nazan.[104]

When her husband can't find an answer to this, she mimics old Ottoman manners, using the old Ottoman words:

> *Merhaba, Merhaba! Aleykümüsselam, hâkipayiniz, keyf-i âlınız, refika cariyeniz, mahdum bendemiz.*
>
> Good-day Good-day! A Peace be upon you! Your august presence! I wish you good health! My wife is your slave, my son your servant![105]

After which her husband confesses, "I am just trying to find what the essence of this *alafranga* life is, and what it means. [But] I can't find it!"[106] Sermet's Western life in a Western-style apartment has left him with a sense of strangeness, in a situation of anomie in the true Durkeimian sense of a social "normlessness" that occurs when older rules, habits, and beliefs no longer hold and alternatives have yet to arise. Certainly he has no historical or cultural basis for evaluating actions such as young men kissing young women's hands. Nazan has solved the problem by measuring Westernization according to its own scientific principles, that is, statistically. But Sermet is looking at it differently and is confused and uncomfortable, for the social rules that ordered traditional behavior were based on another system altogether. As Lucy Garnett reported in 1891:

> Hand kissing [is] the usual mode of respectful greeting; the wife kisses her mother-in-law's hand,—as also that of her husband—on the occasion of any family event, and also on special days, such as the opening of the Bairam Festival.[107]

In the Ottoman household, hand kissing was a show of respect and deference, it was behavior that was clearly understood to relate to the hierarchy of the family and society, and thus reaffirmed or stated one's place in the symbolic universe. We saw this, too, in *Sinekli Bakkal* when Rabia was confused when the Dervish Vehbi Dede did not offer her his hand to kiss. When he did not, she was then unable to take her social place by showing respect. But in Sermet's living room, hand kissing between men and women who are not related by older social norms disrupts the boundaries of hierarchy and asserts one's individuality and personal desires. Although *alafranga* hand kissing might seem to share a sense of respect with the Ottoman version, instead it is a flirtation that can conceal disrespect. Sermet notices that the foreigners who are kissing the hands of Turkish girls do not respect them, for when European men see a Turkish woman they say, "Ah, what a beauty you are! What a shame that you are Turkish. What a loss, what a loss."[108]

Nazan points out that her husband's discomfort with the West and his leaning toward a Turkish worldview mean that he wants to live in the past, which for her is both a distant conflation of *1001 Nights* and Pierre Loti, and a world where, perhaps, "everything was Turkish."

> [A]bove all, there are no foreigners. The streets are quiet and deserted, women are smoking nargiles, going about in yellow gilt slippers, chewing gum mastic. There are Harems with high walls, thick grills, black guards, and white eunuchs.[109]

It is in this atmosphere that we learn about that fateful night, when Nazan was playing a party game with a male friend as her partner. Her husband (who cannot understand how to evaluate this "intimate" type of behavior) became enraged and shouted at her to come talk to him alone, at which point all their guests, in embarrassment at this behavior, went home. Nazan was humiliated. Sermet thought they left because they understood, even approved of his anger.

After the party, Nazan realizes she must go along with Sermet's desire for her not to see men or she will lose him. They decide to see only their same-sex friends, and divide up the house accordingly, which is why Nazan calls this moment "the night that we reestablished the Harem."

Later, Nazan meets her male friend on the street and entices him to dress as a woman so he can see what is going on. But the man's wife discovers the plan, only she assumes that he is going to have a tryst with Nazan. She then dresses as a man, and enters "the *Selamlık*" to warn Sermet of what is about to happen. Sermet then goes into "the Harem," sees the man, and accuses his wife. His wife rushes after him to his rooms, sees the other woman there, and accuses him. As they read these diaries aloud, each realizes that the other was innocent, and they fall into each other's arms.

But this reconciliation does not dissolve the idea of the harem. Sermet holds to it, saying that the harem was an honorable part of the past.

When Nazan says; "I am happy . . . because it is a lesson to you . . . you understood that a Harem cannot separate men and women, it is such a place that hides the good as well as the bad. . . ." Sermet counters, "Don't talk that way, Nazan! Sacred is sacred and not to be judged."[110]

Sermet knows that the harem system will not work in his Beyoğlu apartment, but he also knows that it is allied to his longing for something that is missing. He thought he could find it in the harem, the system of known boundaries that shielded its members from the foreign and that gave familiarity, order, and security to the bonds of relationships. Sermet's use of the word *sacred* suggests that his memory of the harem carries the weight of a religious code, and he unconsciously suspects that this may stand for the larger code of meaning that he yearns for, the symbolic universe in which all meaning and action were integrated into an overarching universe of meaning. The harem encodes this memory of the past for Sermet, but he does not retain the belief system that supports it. The role-related rules of place, the rules of interiority and their boundary, the *haram* that organized the activities of large extended families, do not conform to Sermet's worldview, nor do they carry the weight of divine command. Although he thinks that what he has lost is to be found in the old Turkish house, it is actually to be found in the higher meaning that collective memory assigns this house. He has lost something spiritual and something sacred, and it cannot be analyzed. Sacred is sacred and not to be judged.

The nineteenth-century novel made the house the place where the values associated with a contemporary symbolic universe could be evaluated. It also made the house a place where Western artifacts such as the piano or Western habits such as the work ethic could be accommodated without penetrating one's interiority or sacrificing one's soul. As an antidote to the lifestyle of the züppe, the walls of the house could act as a separation from the exterior and thus from "foreign" values.

In the late nineteenth century, the moral or spiritual underpinnings of the past were conflated with those desired for the present and the future, making the house that contained them a symbol of continuity in much the same way as the house-tasvir of the nineteenth-century Karagöz play. This literary trope of value-laden continuity was the rhetorical position of the Turkish house that was available for Ömer Seyfeddin when he wrote "Harem" in 1918 and for Yakup Kadri when he wrote *Kiralık Konak* in 1922. But when Sermet invokes the past to give moral authority to the present, the effort of memory has begun.

Although this effort of memory is new in 1918 with "Harem," it is *Kiralık Konak* that marks the definitive turning point. This turning point is signaled by the clash between the generations, between Naim Bey and his children and grandchildren. The struggle between the generations existed in earlier novels as well,[111] but in *Kiralık Konak* it has become an irreconcilable clash that highlights a historic change at home.

This irreconcilable clash does not exist at the level of argument but at the level of the soul. Seniha's exteriority is the opposite of her grandfather's interiority, and this difference is not idiosyncratic or temperamental but refers to Seniha's full exposure to, and then full acceptance of, a Western lifestyle. This new lifestyle with its morally questionable exteriority is at the end of a process that led to both of her parents abandoning the family home, her father with lust for the new, her mother with poignant reluctance. The move from the house to the apartment that this generation makes was also a move from East to West.

This matrix of East/spiritual, West/material and older generation/new generation is epitomized by the anecdote we have all now committed to heart:

> [H]e couldn't understand what he had read. It was a novel from the *Edebiyat-ı Cedide Külliyatı*, the New Literature Movement. But Naim Efendi had never read a novel in his life.[112]

The *Edebiyat-ı Cedide Külliyatı* was made up of "Westernist" writers who privileged "the life of the European individual in which material comfort, scientific progress, and individual liberty reigned."[113] These authors wanted the entire package of Westernism, not just its material goods but the frame of mind that led to material progress. In fact, because their brand of Western materialism had an anti-Islamic element, they were attacked as atheists, even as "materialist atheists." Halide Edib characterized them as being "anti-religion," "anti-past" and as having "a childish craze for Westernization,"[114] a description that would have suited Servet Bey quite well. It was this subtext of the New Literature Movement, as much as its language, that was incomprehensible to Naim Bey.

The problem, then, was not that Naim Bey had never read a novel in his life. Naim Bey was no doubt a well-read man. He was born in the Ridingot period, when the well-to-do of good families knew Arabic and Persian as well as Ottoman. Perhaps the closest Naim Efendi came to reading realism was his encounter with his namesake, the seventeenth-century Ottoman historian Naima, who remained popular until his language style was finally unmanageable for twentieth-century readers, as Halide Edib noticed even before the script reform of 1928. Without a doubt, all the Naim Beys could recite by heart Hafiz, Ömer Khayyam, Nedim,[115] and other poets, and wrote their own poetry as well. The problem was that Naim Bey's literary background assured that his realism, or his brand of reality, was bound to a spiritual realism that considered emotions, behavior, and relationship as both the actual and the ultimate reality.

Naim Bey could not understand the novels of the New Literature Movement, and Servet Bey, who spent his youth looking in the mirror, could not understand the reality of Naim Bey, or the spiritual authority of his reality. There was no symmetry between their subjective realities and thus none in their identities—that is, in the ways they thought about their "real" selves.

Thus it is with Kiralık Konak that the generational divide is positioned as a divide between the material and spiritual aspects of values, which are again associated with two different domestic styles. When Servet Bey invades the interiority of Naim Bey's konak with Western furniture, the invasion is a double one: it is not only an invasion by the material culture of the West but an invasion by the West's belief in the materiality of culture. For Naim Bey, Westernism was undermining the true reality. But for Servet Bey, the old ways were sinking, and to circumscribe one's identity within the confines of an Ottoman Eastern system of ideas was to miss the boat.[116]

A cartoon from 1918 shows this divide in the middle-class urban family. A father with a fez reading the newspaper by candlelight in front of a Levha, or calligraphic religious motto, leans forward as the mother, wearing a headscarf and indoor slippers, says to her modern daughter in a skimpy dress and outdoor shoes, "Dear girl! What's going on? Did you just come from the hamam [public baths]?"[117] But the generational clash of Kiralık Konak alerts the reader, who is reading in 1928 or later, not only to the fact that the old

- *A kızım, bu ne hal? Hamamdan yeni çıktın galiba...*
- *Anneciğim, ev kadını, kocasının parasını iktisada gayret ederek sarfetmeli değil mi? Ben de bayramlık elbisem için kumaşa çok para gitmesin diye böyle kısa yaptırdım..*

Cartoon from 1918 of generational divide. "Dear girl! What's going on? Did you just come from the hamam?" Kılıç, 50 Yıllık Yaşantımız: 1923–1933, p. 114.

ways were no longer viable or legitimate but that the life of the konak that had stretched into history was over. *Kiralık Konak* also points to the historic moment when the house lost its legitimacy and became a marker of memory. This happened with that cataclysmic event in Ottoman history, the revolution of 1908, the date when the past suddenly arrived.

"These times were not like the old times. In the last two years, many traditions changed"[118] are the opening words of *Kiralık Konak*. On July 23, 1908, Abdülhamid was forced to replace his thirty years of absolutist rule with a representational government in the setting of a constitutional monarchy.[119] This meant that power changed hands overnight from the monarchy and a monarchy-controlled bureaucracy to a parliament, with its own bureaucracy. Most important, political and bureaucratic life became differentiated, so that the bureaucratic elite were no longer attached to the sultan by patronage and loyalty, a loyalty that had been strengthened, or complicated, by Abdülhamid's psychotic paranoia. In politics, therefore, there was a definite and sudden break with the past. The Ottoman state apparatus was totally dismantled and a clean sweep was made in the upper echelons of the civilian and military bureaucracy. The military and civilian pashas of the old regime, who had been accustomed to running the country without any accountability, and the scores of minor officials below them, who were either useless or corrupt and who owed their positions to nepotism, came up for review.[120]

The conversation between Naim Efendi and Servet Bey on reading of the disgrace of one of these pashas in the journal *Tanin* was a conversation that could have happened in many hundreds of households, and thus refers to the complexity of 1908 as a moment in shared memory. Two weeks after the revolution, *Tanin* began to publish lists of all the real estate that the corrupt pashas of the old regime had received as "royal gifts" (such as houses, apartments, office buildings, and farms).[121] The changes in all levels of government plus the massive celebrations by all classes of people throughout all of Turkey certainly situate 1908 as a date in the shared memory[122] that far exceeded the impact of major fires, such as the Aksaray Fire.

Thus, in 1908 the economic, political, and social system that had been the life support of the konak and the behavioral model for smaller houses was withdrawn. The likes of Naim Efendi (but not Naim Efendi himself, as he had resigned during a dispute two years earlier) lost their role at the palace, their sinecures, and their incomes; the patrimonial palace patronage system was suddenly terminated, and with it the role of the family father who controlled his household with his power, prestige, and purse. The three-generation Ottoman konak held together by this economic system, as well as the neighborhood structure that the konak supported, slipped off its foundations. In this situation the distance between the generations took on a new tension and a new meaning, for when the patriarch lost his ultimate rights over both the affections and the services of the new generation, he lost control of the future.

The year 1908 may appear to be discussed tangentially in *Kiralık Konak*, but it was such a strong aspect of shared memory that it colors the entire novel and makes the changes that are occurring understandable to the reader.[123] Changes that are considered the results of 1908 are on almost every page. As a retrospective ethnographic document, *Kiralık Konak* identifies what are remembered as outgoing and now outmoded role-related rules of place: Naim Efendi has lost his position as supreme head of the house because he cannot hold it together financially. More important, Naim Efendi has lost his role as moral arbiter, as the family patriarch who oversees cultural and moral continuity. In a conversation with her grandfather, Seniha says that although she understands that marriage is not a matter of love but of finance, she and her prospective groom will take care of the decisions and arrangements on their own: "For us marriage is not a matter of the heart. Nor is it a biological necessity. He [Faiz] and I both look upon it as a matter of accounting and of the mind; something to do with money."[124]

Perhaps Naim Bey would have agreed that marriage is a practical rather than a romantic issue, but Seniha's declaration indicates her complete severance from the traditional structure that had put marriage decisions if not completely then at least nominally within the family. Recall for a moment Şefika, who in Namık Kemal's *Zavalli Çocuk*, guarding her interiority, lamented in 1873: "I am worried and ashamed that my parents will find out my real feelings."[125] Seniha feels no such constraint when she says,

> Faik Bey isn't under his father's control if he wants to marry me, nor am I under yours if I decide to be with him. I am just about twenty! He is approaching thirty; we know each other much better than you know us. . . . If I wanted him now I would marry him; if he wanted me today he'd take me. But, I'm afraid, that's not what we want.[126]

With the loss of its underpinnings, the household can do nothing other than break up. Whether parts of the family move to apartments or not, Seniha, Hakkı Celis, and Servet Bey have become vectors shooting off in a variety of directions, while the stable and orderly konak life that Naim Efendi remembers for the reader turns to dust in front of our eyes, and we see its inhabitants becoming ghosts. Just as the future was a foreign country to Naim Efendi, the past was a foreign country to his grandchildren. The new generations could never again live a konak life.[127] It is this final rupture, this generational divide, that allowed the Turkish house to emerge in the collective memory as the gatekeeper to traditional time.

By the time of "Harem" and *Kiralık Konak*, and within the milieu of Ömer Seyfeddin and Yakup Kadri, the old wooden house and the old wooden konak had become a marker of the past. Yet paradoxically, by locking the spiritual lessons of the past into the space of the house, the Turkish house became available as an object of continuity and thus a major player in the field of identity. As the place where continuity was formally assured because it was where values were actually handed down from generation to generation, the Turkish house became the site where values could be stored in memory and thus became available as a socialization mechanism aimed at new generations who posited problems of compliance. The image of the Turkish house thus became the sign of the continuity that is essential if one is to identify with one's history.

Urban variety coded by dress in 1925. Logo banner of the magazine Türk Hayatı.

The new Turkish woman of the 1930s. Cover, Yedi Gün 12, no. 30.

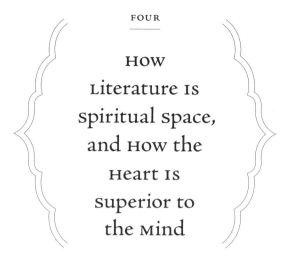

FOUR

HOW
Literature IS
spiritual space,
and HOW the
Heart IS
superior to
the Mind

Kiralık Konak was one of the last novels of the Ottoman Empire. It was written in 1922, at the end of the struggle for liberation, in the last year of the last Ottoman sultan, Mehmed VI.[1] In 1923 the Turkish Republic would be formally established, and before the end of the decade the new Turkey would institutionalize and canonize profound cultural changes as it worked to forge a modern nation. The author of *Kiralık Konak*, Yakup Kadri, was a nationalist, a supporter of Mustafa Kemal Atatürk, and a believer in the need for reform along Western lines. Yet neither he nor the rest of the Turkish population foresaw the extreme secularization measures or the break with the past that would be inaugurated by the Kemalist government in the mid-1920s.

In 1921, Yakup Kadri attended a religious service to commemorate those who had fallen in the war of independence in Anatolia. This memorial led him to a realization that the national struggle should not be for secular nationalism but for the deeper ideals of the people:

> Yesterday for the first time the common people, whom we had always despised as ignorant and idle, taught the intellectuals of this country some divine truths. One of these is that the heart is superior to the mind. Another is that apart from sincerity and devotion and simple faith, there is no way of salvation. The third is that there must be no separation between the nation and the religious community.[2]

By the 1930s, however, Kemalist secularization had institutionalized the material-spiritual polarization that had been used rhetorically to separate those who worked for Westernism from those who protected the status quo. With the ruptures caused by the new republic, this spiritual-material dichotomy took on both a new urgency and deeper poignancy, for the immediate spiritual world of the people had once more come up for reevaluation, and perhaps annihilation. For this reason, the novels of the 1930s that take place in a domestic setting are worth reviewing separately. These novels continue to use the trope of East versus West, but in ways that take us deeper into cultural identity and into the components of spirituality, as well as its boundaries.

Kiralık Konak established the Turkish house as a site of moral questioning, but also as a carrier of one's spiritual heritage from a past that had all but disappeared from the public realm. In fact, *Kiralık Konak* disrupted the memory that was simultaneously being constructed for it by Kemalist authors, who were conscripting the Turkish house for its "modernist" architectural components rather than for the affective, emotional qualities associated with a life that had been lived inside it, as we saw in Chapter 2. In *Kiralık Konak*, the Turkish house was allied with a concept of interiority that was a key element of the spirituality of this remembered affective past. What I would like to suggest now is that this memory of a valued interiority not only became more developed but eventually became part of a larger matrix. In the 1930s, within the context of the new republic's institutionalization of rupture, this memory, or this understanding, was used to disrupt a Kemalist, Orientalist-Western authority that was redefining Turkish identity from the outside. In the novel, an affectively understood house would be used strategically to reclaim authority by (re)presenting the Turkish self from its "authentic, Eastern" viewpoint—that is, from the inside. The house was the appropriate space to present this inside because it formed a matrix with interiority, spirituality, and historical consciousness. The Turkish house, and even its old Turkish exterior, were both represented and imagined as the deep Turkish interior.

In the 1930s, then, the Turkish house is enlarged as an image of tradition and the past, and of the values that are perceived as threatened by the present. As the site of the values of the past, it becomes an imaginative unit of social memory, or a memory image, that makes it an imagined site of socialization, as well as a place of refuge, safety, and continuity, and one of the markers of what constitutes the self. Thus, the Turkish house serves as a marker of a constitutive, holistic identity, which is a different kind of identity than individual identity or the social identity of nationalism; in fact, it often operates in opposition to both. This brings up the question of how identities overlap, their degree of constructedness, and the degree to which identities are a part of the conscious mind.

1931: PEYAMI SAFA'S *FATIH-HARBIYE*

The spirit is always great, the body destitute.

In 1931, Peyami Safa wrote *Fatih-Harbiye*, a novel in which the young heroine, Neriman, takes the Fatih-Harbiye tram line between her home in Fatih to European Beyoğlu, bringing into focus for herself and the reader exactly what would be at stake if she had made it a one-way trip.[3] The nineteenth-century Tanzimat novels made clear how Beyoğlu, on the northern side of

Istanbul. Postcard of the Fatih-Harbiye tram in Beyoğlu, on the Grand Rue de Pera, now İstiklal Caddesi.

the Golden Horn, was the accepted symbol for and the real place of a Westernized lifestyle. The neighborhood of Fatih, in the heart of the historic peninsula, was and remains to this day a symbol of the religious and social heritage of the Ottoman East.[4] In *Fatih-Harbiye*, Neriman's house in Fatih symbolizes the spiritual and emotional repository of non-Western life, and thus this novel continues the trope of siting the East-West dilemma inside the house, but it also shows how the house has become a much more developed spiritual authority of the past.

Neriman lives with her father Faiz Bey, their trusted servant Gülter, and their cat Sarman in an old-fashioned *çıkma-cumba*-style wooden house in Fatih. It has a *sofa* (an Ottoman-style living room) upstairs and a *taşlık* (an entry area paved with river stones) below, and when the front door closed, "the old wooden house shook and the window-panes rattled."[5] In this novel, everything about this house resonates with a warmth from the past.

> In this *mahalle*, in this house, with this gas lamp, this old man, and this worn out plaster, with this crooked cornice and these frayed satin curtains, surrounded by the aroma of this newly polished mouldy wood, Neriman saw that a person could be happy, and she remembered the cheery days that had been spent in this house.[6]

Neriman is thus a conservative girl but one who leads a modern life; she even has a sweetheart of several years, Şinasi (pronounced Shinasi), who studies *kemanje*[7] at the *Darü'l-Elhân*, the Music Conservatory. Şinasi is a young man from the same mahalle and is a talented musician whom Neriman's father loves as if he were his own son. In fact, the father and prospective son-in-law are very much alike. When Faiz Bey described Şinasi to others, he would say,

> He is silent and virtuous, with extraordinarily good manners and honorable by nature, and he has a compassionate heart. He has great emotional intensity, he plays the kemençe, and not only that, his name will be famous among the famous. When I listen to him I weep. I am enchanted by this boy.[8]

Furthermore,

> There were quite a few temperamental similarities between Faiz Bey and Şinasi: both could manage to stay quiet [*sessiz*] even when they felt enraged, and they were people who could keep their private things to

Istanbul. A house in Fatih, showing a "young Neriman" in the window.
Photograph by Carel Bertram, 1990.

themselves. When they sensed that others were curious, they kept their true selves enclosed inside [*kapanan ruhları içinde mahsur*]. And because of these [inner] feelings of pain and honor, they gave an [outer] appearance of dignity and suffering. Both of them very much loved the things of the East, Şinasi his *alaturka* music, Faiz Bey his Sufi literature.[9]

We recognize certain characteristics of Faiz Bey and Şinasi, for they are those highly valued attributes of what we have called interiority. It was this

"Faiz Bey with Neriman as a child" (Ali Saib Bey and his daughter, Berhiz), 1913. Courtesy of Elçin Gürkan.

Young women's oud lessons at the Darü'l-Elhân, *"The House of Melodies." From Paçacı, "Darü'l-Elhân," p. 557.*

interiority that characterized Naim Efendi, an Ottoman gentleman whose formative years were the middle years of the nineteenth century. *Kiralık Konak*'s Naim Efendi was in his late sixties in 1908; *Fatih-Harbiye*'s Faiz Bey is somewhere in his forties in 1926. Thus, although Faiz Bey's and Şinasi's world is the late 1920s, that is, the very first years of the new Turkish Republic, they are depicted as men who are grounded in Ottoman Oriental (*Şark*) culture.

Faiz Bey's daughter, Neriman, is the perfect soul mate for Şinasi, partly because of the affinity between Şinasi and Faiz Bey, partly because she "grew up in a pure Turkish environment,"[10] and partly because she is studying the oud, which is not only an Eastern, or local, instrument but is also the perfect partner to the kemençe. Because of their connection at the Darü'l-Elhân, we understand that Şinasi and Neriman play classical Turkish music together, a music that is tied to a non-Western tradition and that has affinities with religious feeling. Şinasi and Neriman are thus the perfect couple, alike in their interests and their upbringing. Because "they both looked like sister and brother and husband and wife,"[11] they should be destined to replicate the culture of the past in their shared future.

But the future that is imagined for this young couple is disrupted when Neriman becomes interested in the shops and life of Beyoğlu, which is not merely at the other end of a tram ride but a place that makes her look at her own life differently:

> Neriman got off at Beyoğlu. Just like most people who live in a genuinely Turkish neighborhood, she felt as if she had made a big trip. Fatih was off in the distance—it was far away. The distance wasn't even an hour by tram, but it appeared to Neriman as long as the way to Afghanistan, and she considered the difference between these two quarters as great as that between Kabul and New York.[12]

Not only is Neriman mesmerized by the Western life of Beyoğlu, but when she comes home to Fatih, she begins to look at it disparagingly:

> Darkness falls on these *mahalles* early. Neriman couldn't bear being at home at this hour of night. Even the little things she had never noticed before were now becoming important to her. She stretched out on the *minder* [cushion on the floor]. She was looking at the darkness that thickened in the small openings of those window-grills [*kafes*] that brought night early to the room. The small rectangular holes were losing their sharp contours and becoming circular. The white tulle cur-

tains darkened. This was the time when the sweet-sellers [helavcis] came by, [when] everything was silent, and one only sensed the voices of the helvacis. Like taffy [sakız], these voices stretched out and thinned as they met stickily in the distance, at the end of the street, and then were pulled away with the fading light, and were gone.

At this time, everything darkens and fades, and every living thing cowers. There are footsteps of one or two neighbors, late in coming back to the mahalle, their knotted bundles in their hands. Thinking that the night is a catastrophe, they knock rapidly on the house next-door; it opens and shuts violently. Thin smoke from the kitchens spreads through the entire street along with a light odor of coal [marsık] and oil. Then comes the call to prayer from the minarets of Fatih.[13]

Neriman's sense is one of oppressiveness: as it gets dark, people rush homeward and inward, we can almost hear their doors slam behind them as they close themselves off to the night. Later the reader is to find that this sense of oppressiveness is part of Neriman's imagination, a misreading under the influence of Beyoğlu, which had for so long been associated with lights, nightlife, vitality, and entertainment; where the night was anything but "a catastrophe." In her memoirs, which cover the years during which this story takes place, Halide Edib recalled a Beyoğlu that inspired what were called "hat and ball longings," that is, the desire to go out with a hat rather than a head scarf, and to attend dances.[14]

Neriman's introduction to Western ideas came from her mother's brother, who was educated in Europe and now lives in Şişli, that same upscale, highly Western neighborhood that had made Naim Efendi's son-in-law Servet Bey swoon in Kiralık Konak. But things only come to a head when Neriman meets Macit, a young man who is studying violin in the alafranga section of the conservatory.

Neriman begins to take secret trips to Beyoğlu with Macit, and to sit in the salon of Maxim's and to wear makeup and drink cocktails. Macit loses interest in the violin, and Neriman decides to stop her oud lessons because they are alaturka. She even considers entering the alafranga section of the conservatory. But when Macit invites her to a ball that will take place in a week, she is put in a terrible quandary. Her trips to Beyoğlu have put a strain on her relationship with Şinasi, not because she wishes to replace him with Macit (this is left unclear) but because she is attracted to the Western life that is against everything Şinasi stands for and everything that the two of them have in common. For this reason she has been lying about where she

A street in Istanbul ca. 1870–1910. Photograph by G. Berggren (1835–1920). Reproduced courtesy of the Library of Congress, Prints and Photographs Division, LC-DIG-ppmsca-03851.

Istanbul. Beyoğlu, the Grand Rue de Pera, 1912. Reproduced courtesy of the
Library of Congress, Prints and Photographs Division, ppmsca 05035.

spends her time, although both her father and Şinasi know the truth. Now, along with this cultural burden and her burdened conscience, there will be a financial burden as well. Her father gives her permission to go to the ball, because he wants her to be happy, but then walks the streets trying to sell family jewels to pay for a ballgown, returning at night with a worn and worried look.

But her father has a deeper worry, and that is that his beloved daughter has misinterpreted her heritage. Because of her attraction to the things of the West and because of her love for her father and Şinasi, Neriman is undergoing a deep crisis, "a secret interior, spiritual struggle" (*gizli bir deruni mücadele*), which she tries to sort out in her mind.

> In Neriman's eyes Şinasi was the family, the *mahalle*, the old and the Eastern, while Macit was the new, the West, and along with this he was mysterious and attractive adventures.[15]

Beyoğlu appears clean and orderly, with men and women walking together along its street of shops, or sitting together at restaurants with white tablecloths. In contrast, Fatih appears lethargic, disorderly, and unclean—it is the oppressiveness of that dark street of hers.

> *Allah razı olsun*, (with God's permission,) I myself hate it. The *mahalle* I live in, the house I live in, most of the people I talk to upset me. When I walk across the square in Fatih, groups of idle, feeble "*softa* types" [Muslim theological students] are sitting at the *Kahve* [Coffee Shop] . . . these idle men just sit in the coffee shops or in front of the mosque and watch the street.[16]

In a Beyoğlu perfume shop, as Neriman smells the light lovely aromas of essential oils, she is reminded of her childhood visits to Bayezit Square during Ramazan, where "under something like a tent, a man dressed like an Arab, among small, somewhat oily, dirty bottles, stood and sold scents."[17] It was with these images in her mind, and while being in a frenzy of guilt over the ball and over deceiving Şinasi, that Neriman tries to rationalize her attraction to the West. In defining the two cultures that are tugging at her soul, she has an epiphany:

> Neriman thought and suddenly understood why Easterners loved cats so much and Westerners loved dogs. In Christian houses there were lots of dogs, in Muslim houses lots of cats, —because Easterners resembled cats and Westerners resembled dogs! Cats eat, drink, lie down, sleep, give birth. Their life is spent on a cushion and passes in a dream; even if their eyes are open, it's as if they are dreaming, they are languid, lazy and day-dreaming creatures who can't stand work. Dogs are vigorous, swift, and bold. They do useful work—a lot of useful work. Even when they are sleeping they are wakeful. If they hear even the slightest sound, they jump up and bark.[18]

When Neriman's father comes home, she bursts at him with her new intelligence: "'Look!' she said. 'Gülter is sleeping and so is Sarman . . . [and] they're not the only ones who are sleeping, all of Fatih is asleep!'"[19]

Her wise and kind father understands her inner dilemma and gently offers another interpretation to the great East-West divide.

> There are some men who sit and think from morning to evening. They have a *hazine-i efkâr*, a treasury of ideas; I mean they are rich on the side of thought. Then there are some men who work on their feet from morning till night, for example, peasants . . . but the work that they do consists of laying four bricks on top of each other. At first people may appear lazy, but really, *velâkın!* they are hard working. Other people appear hard working, but really, *velâkın!* the work they do is weak. It's because one's work involves mental endeavors using the spirit, the other's work is physical and uses the body. *The spirit is always great, the body destitute.* The difference between what they do is because of this. (Emphasis mine.)[20]

Faiz Bey has succinctly summarized the East-West divide as one of the spiritual versus the material, placing what appears to be the hard work of material progress in an inferior position to the intellect.

From our point of view, this is an important summary, for, in its simplified polarization of East and West, it leaves out what was obvious to pro-Westerners, namely, that the West values the intellect, too. In fact, Faiz Bey shows how this stereotypical view of the East versus the West is communicated as a confusion and conflation of the intellect and the spirit, which are two separate things.[21]

But Neriman's spiritual struggle does not end with the discussion with her father. In another moment of internal despair, she asks the family retainer, Gülter, to tell her stories about her childhood, as those stories would always make her feel calm. These stories show how the arena of this life of the mind was often rooted in the house of the past.

> Your grandmother always had a book in her hand. Now, what history book was it. . . . You can be sure it was one of the great ones. . . . Wait, it's on the tip of my tongue: Hah! It was Naima's *History*. [Your grandmother] knew Arabic, and Persian too. . . . She would read to us and explain it. *That Konak was really a school.* (Emphasis mine.)[22]

This is the third time we have run into Naima. Naim Efendi read him in *Kiralık Konak*, as had Halide Edib, who remembered both his depth and how difficult he had become to read. That is, it would appear that Naima was remembered as a household standby of the past, and thus the inside of the house of the past was a world characterized by Naima's intellectual inquiry, as well as his concern with issues of moral behavior, honesty, and loyalty.[23] Faiz Bey and Gülter show Neriman what she seems to have forgotten with her changed perspective: that the inside of the house and the inside of the soul are a *hazine-i efkâr*, a treasury of ideas.

This view from inside the house has another purpose besides attributing a spiritual superiority to the East; the inside is presented with the intention of countering a Westernist gaze from outside it. This is something very different from conceiving of the house as a marker of an East-West spiritual divide, because the view from the inside marks the house as representing a different way of seeing, as well as a different way of being. It goes, in fact, to the heart of identity.

COUNTERING THE WESTERN GAZE

The Western gaze, or the Western stereotype of the East, which Edward Said called Orientalism,[24] considers Eastern social identity in terms of a binary with Western social identity. However, the purpose here is not to engage with the concept of Orientalism, which is a deep definer of the discourse about the East. An Orientalist model that uncovers stereotypes that Europeans developed about and projected onto the Middle East is a discourse about Europe. Here we focus on how these stereotypes were understood and confronted at home. Our interest is in Turkey. *Fatih-Harbiye* and other novels of the 1930s address this gap in the Orientalism model by presenting a local response, an Eastern acceptance or rejection of this Orientalist Western imaginary.

The Ottomans took on importance in the Western imagination as their armies advanced toward Vienna in the mid-sixteenth century. Europe depicted this Turkish threat as a threat to civilization itself, maintaining that the Turks had no civilization and no culture of their own due to their religion and to their inherently inferior nature. That is, the (Eastern) Turks, as the opposite of (Western) Christians, were lazy, dirty, and mentally and spiritually bankrupt.[25]

The military threat that the Ottomans imposed on the West in the sixteenth and seventeenth centuries was real, but the feeling of being threatened long outlived the threat, and the bigotry that it caused had a disastrous and longlasting effect on Western perceptions. When the balance of power shifted to the West, it could be argued that the bigotry begun of fear was maintained by the newly empowered as a way of keeping their power.[26] Furthermore, the negative image of the Ottomans was perpetuated in the nineteenth century by Ottoman sub-nationalist groups, that is, those within the empire who wished to separate from it both politically and psychologically. These separatist movements were supported in the West through an Orientalist rhetoric that continued a portrayal of the Turks as uncivilized. In 1875, William Gladstone, prime minister of Great Britain, published a pamphlet in which he protested Turkish atrocities against (formerly Ottoman) Bulgarian nationals:

> Let me endeavor very briefly to sketch in the rudest outline, what *the Turkish race* was and what it is. It is not a creation of Mahometism compounded with the peculiar character of a race. They are not the mild Mahometans of India, and not the chivalrous Saladins of Syria, nor the cultured Moors of Spain. They are upon the whole, from the black day when they first entered Europe, *the one great anti-human specimen of humanity.* Wherever they went a broad line of blood marked the track behind them; and *as far as their dominion reached, civilization disappeared from view.* (Emphases mine.)[27]

Many of these negative views were internalized by the Turks themselves, who identified with Western superiority in many areas. For these intellectuals, Turkish culture was seen to have basic flaws, as exemplified by a missing work ethic. At the same time that Gladstone was writing in Britain, Ahmet Lûtfi wrote,

> The material principle [of the West] comprises the rescue from idleness of the populace by the farmers, merchants and artisans and the re-strengthening of the principles that justify the production of wealth and discipline.[28]

Between the end of the Hamidian period (with the Young Turk Revolution of 1908) and the beginning of the new Turkish Republic, the issue of a morally and intellectually inferior East was addressed by every ideological persuasion—Westernists, Islamists, Ottomanists, and Turkists. A Westernist author of 1914 posited that this Turkish inferiority to Western culture existed at a deep level.

> It is nothing other than our own Asiatic Minds . . . our own degenerate traditions and institutions. . . . The power that is defeating us is none other than our own eyes which do not want to see, our brains, which do not know how to think.[29]

Or, as Neriman had put it, "they are languid, lazy and day-dreaming creatures who can't stand work."

Yakup Kadri, as we saw above, had looked at Turks from this Westernized stance until he was astonished by their strengths in the Turkish War of Independence: "for the first time the common people, whom we had always despised as ignorant and idle, taught the intellectuals of this country some divine truths."[30]

It is true that criticisms of outsiders sometimes merely mirrored the criticisms of insiders. Such was true of the critics of the dirty streets of Turkish cities. The turn-of-the century complaints by Istanbul citizens of urban mud and darkness were similar to travelers' reports, such as a *National Geographic* story on Ankara in 1924:

> The debris cluttered streets wind about between two-story houses. There is no sewage system, there are no sidewalks. In winter there is mud, fetlock deep, and in summer dust. At night, Angora, like all Turkish towns, is as dark as the inside of a camel.[31]

The image of dark, dirty, and oppressive Turkish streets, however, differs from the issue of urban uncleanness.[32] An example of this image of oppressiveness appears in the writings of Edmondo De Amicis, who came from Italy to Istanbul in 1874 and published his work *Constantinopoli* there. *Constantinopoli* was illustrated by Cesare Biseo, and these illustrations formed one of the only archives of neighborhood imagery until Hodja Ali Riza Bey. De Amicis's work was well read in Turkey, and serialized in the newspapers;[33] it was finally translated into Turkish in 1938.[34] In De Amicis's description of Istanbul:

> . . . the small wooden houses, are each one painted a different color; the first floor juts over the bottom one, the second floor juts over the first,

and the windows and cantilevered rooms [şahnişins] that are covered closely with wood screens, give the streets an air of concealment and despair. In some places these streets are so narrow that, over your head, the upper floors reach as far as to touch each other; and people, trapped all day in these houses, see the sky like a thin ribbon as they trample by. All the doors are closed. All the lower floor windows have iron grills. People believe themselves in a city made up of monasteries. If you hear a laugh, as soon as you raise your head to it, a pair of glistening eyes will disappear from behind the window grill. Sometimes, should you suddenly come upon a conversation going on between the windows of two houses, as soon as your footsteps are heard, the sound of it stops.[35]

By the 1930s the sense of darkness and oppressiveness had joined uncleanness as a deeply embedded trope invoked to support the replacement of the old wooden house with new ones. The architect İsmail Hakkı wrote in favor of modernism because

Above all else, the new architecture is a healthy architecture. . . . [T]his architecture does not allow one [to have] a life of dampness, microbes and dirt like the old ones.[36]

Fatih-Harbiye counters these Western-inspired views of Turkish life from the outside by addressing them from the inside, an inside that is represented by the inside of the house. For example, when Gülter tells Neriman her stories from the past, she talks about Neriman's grandmother, who made her konak a shrine of cleanliness.

"Ah," said Gülter, taking a deep breath and shaking her head. "Where can one find a woman like your grandmother today? How can I explain her virtues! So clean, so organized, what a refined woman she was! She would stand right next to the servants when they were cleaning and arranging things, she knew every single detail of house cleaning.

"Everything was in its place. . . . [T]he covers, the curtains, the shades [tenteler], everything was as white as snow, a person would want to kiss them! . . . if a person sat in those rooms for half an hour they would cheer up, and all their sorrows would disappear [içi açılır, gamı kasaveti gider]. . . . Ah, they knew how to be 'rahat,' to let go of their troubles."[37]

Neriman, who had been lulled almost to sleep by this story, wakes up on hearing the word "*rahat*," which is the pleasurable mental and physical state of being comfortable, calm, and relaxed, and says, "yes, always laziness!" Neriman speaks from a Western gaze that equates the lack of activity that rahat includes with laziness. To which Gülter replies, "But little lady! Nowadays does anyone work that hard? Where?"

By the 1930s, the long history of a Western view of the Turks had been crystallized in the discourses of the nations newly formed from the old Ottoman Empire. A Bosnian Serb summed up all these Turkish Muslim negativities that had kept them out of modern civilization:

> Over time, as a result of the assimilation of our Muslims with a Turkish way of life, Muslims added to their original Slavic mentality the worst characteristics of Oriental mentality: Oriental "*Yavashluk*" or lethargy, the habit of taking it easy [*rahatluk*], of not working hard, and the lack of ideas about practical and systematic work, [as well as] a spiritual indifference, fanatic self confidence and belief in special qualities, self boasting, and excessive sensuality. . . . The only way [to overcome this] is emancipation from Islam as a social religion. Islam must not be an obstacle to taking a part in the modern world.[38]

Gülter has addressed the dirty oppressive street by bringing the view inside the house; for when seen from the inside there is only cleanliness, as well as people who work hard and think large. Faiz Bey has also managed to disrupt the Western view of idleness by suggesting that it ignores what is inside the soul: "At first people may appear lazy, but really, [their] work involves mental endeavors using the spirit. The spirit is always great, the body destitute." That is, Faiz Bey and Gülter disrupt the Orientalist polarities that Neriman has begun to internalize, polarities of lazy versus active, useful versus useless, rational versus irrational, by bringing them into the house and into the spirit, which together are meant to represent the Turkish soul.

When the ideas and beliefs and values that make up one's life-world are contested or when a symbolic universe is threatened, the threatening external ideas must be interpreted to fit what is known and believed.[39] Faiz Bey and Gülter are doing this work of universe maintenance by translating what is seen from the exterior to what it really means, when seen from the interior. From a Turkish, and therefore "valid" perspective, what has appeared negative has been interpreted as positive.

Fatih-Harbiye's arguments are addressed to all the Nerimans who have been influenced by uncles educated in Europe, or by trips to Beyoğlu, but also to a republican insistence that "the Oriental mind" was inferior to the Western mind because it defined itself in terms of morality and spirituality rather than in terms of a secularity that led to progress.[40] Faiz Bey also addresses the wider, more complex contemporary world of Turks, the intellectuals and the rising middle classes who have begun to be educated with Kemalist ideals. That is, the fascination with the West and the internalization of its perspective had threatened the symbolic universe at the intimate psychological level, as well as at a more concrete political one.

The importance of "perspective" is critical here. For although a discussion of an internalized Orientalist gaze has uncovered a conscious, or at least implicit, strategy to counter it, our discussion has also uncovered something less conscious and therefore deeper. Because Faiz Bey and Gülter counter the foreign and the Western gaze with a perspective from the inside, we have been introduced to a constitutive way of seeing that is a part of interiority (which is a way of being). And this whole interior is framed by the old wooden house.

The Western gaze that Neriman has internalized is one of the aspects of the rupture with the past that the house represents at a time of insistent change. But the larger issue is not what has been misinterpreted but what is at stake, what is in danger of being lost or abandoned as the rupture continues to widen. In *Fatih-Harbiye* and the works that follow it,[41] the Turkish house is the location where these issues are taken up, and therefore the house becomes the place where rupture might be healed with a promise of continuity.

CONTINUITY AND RUPTURE

There were still curtains on the windows, yet was anyone inside? And if there was, who?

In Neriman's period of internal struggle, the old Turkish house was the sign of continuity; it continued to exist in its run-down condition but with a memory image of an interior made strong by a strong father with a strong spiritual heritage. It was an icon of the past that sanctioned traditional behavior, with its promise of wholeness and happiness, because it was the place where the universe made sense. In fact, in *Fatih-Harbiye* there is the depiction of a particular house that actually represents this opportunity for continuity: it is an old and worn-out "tahini-colored" wooden house with a

Istanbul. Fatih Mahallesi. "House of the Ghost of the Konak." Note the Şahniş
protruding into the street. Photograph by Walter Denny, 1990.

şahniş that protrudes into the narrow street. Neriman and Şinasi would pass
it every day as they walked home from school:

> Every part was run down, the windows had lost their rectangularity,
> the eaves had lost some of their planks, the zinc cladding had fallen
> in. . . . [T]his Konak was in such ruin that even a three year old child
> could push it down. . . . [But] there were still curtains on the windows,
> yet was any one inside? And if there was, who?[42]

Over the years, Neriman and Şinasi would imagine that there was an old man inside who was watching them, and each time they walked by they would add to their story about him, until he felt entirely real.

> [H]e had a long white beard, the cap [takke] that he put on his bald head was plain and simple, he sat to the right of the şahniş, by the right-hand window and fiddled with his prayer-beads, his lips always mumbling a prayer. He would think, but he wasn't thinking about people or work; he had large ideas about the world, about humanity, about God and death. When he heard a footstep on the street, his trembling head would look out the window behind the grills, and when he would see Neriman and Şinasi walking by, he would shut his eyes and pray that they were happy.[43]

Who is this old man who looks so much like Naim Efendi in *Kiralık Konak* but is the ghost of the konak and the voice of tradition? When Şinasi and Neriman walked by during the tense period of her inner struggle, when she was struggling with her "hat and ball longings," Neriman was

> caught up with a strange feeling, as if she had heard a footstep in the house; then she thought the door opened and she thought she saw the image of the old man on the threshold. He still had his prayer-beads in his hands, [but] this time his face was as white as his beard and his night cap; and he asked with eyes that tried to conceal a deep, sad astonishment: What has happened, children? What has happened to you?[44]

The ghost of the konak wants Şinasi and Neriman to be together as before, when there were no disruptions in—or threats to—the continuation of traditional life. In spite of the ghost's interiority ("he asked with eyes that tried to conceal"), Neriman feels his emotions deeply, if diffusely. In fact, this vision is so disturbing to Neriman that she faints in Şinasi's arms.

The diffuseness of her feelings and what the konak stands for—and what is at stake—is made clear as the story progresses. Neriman does not give up her plans to go to the ball or her enchantment with Beyoğlu until she hears a story that truly unnerves her. While at her Europeanized cousins' apartment in Şişli, she meets the grieving mother of a young Russian girl who had left her childhood sweetheart for a wealthy Greek. When the girl realized that her new lover was a sham, she tried to return to her sweetheart, but he would not take her back, and she committed suicide. Here, the reader is to understand that the enticements of the "foreign" are shallow, that accepting them is a rejection of one's own heritage, and that the results can be fatal. Neriman, who is not as clear as the reader but who is nonetheless shaken to her roots, enters a reverie in which she imagines herself begging Şinasi for forgiveness. But in Neriman's reverie, Şinasi always takes her back.

Just as the Russian girl had left her heritage for a "foreigner,"[45] Neriman begins to interpret leaving Fatih for Beyoğlu as a contemptible, almost traitorous, and now potentially dangerous act. She might lose Şinasi, who represents the communal past that ties her to her own individual future happiness. Sobbing to herself that she is not "contemptible" (alçak), she boards the tram from Beyoğlu to Harbiye, to return home.

Neriman arrives in Fatih with a childish eagerness to tell her father and Şinasi of her new epiphany and her spiritual return, but since they are at a gathering of friends from the conservatory, she tells her news to the trusty Gülter, and then goes to join them. She arrives in the middle of a discussion, which quickly becomes a tribunal. Because she has abandoned her oud lessons and has been attracted by Turks who have become Westernized, the men turn their discussion to her, and thus accuse her of abandoning her culture.

> When Neriman chooses a new instrument, it means she is choosing a new culture. The oud and the violin symbolize two different cultures![46]

The men at the gathering compare Neriman's rejection of the oud to the impending closing by the Atatürk government of the alaturka section of the Darü'l-Elhân, and thus she becomes part of the threat to the Ottoman-Eastern musical tradition, and by extension a threat to all of Ottoman-Eastern culture. That is, Neriman's actions do far more damage than threatening her personal happiness, they undermine an entire way of life. Clearly, when Neriman's music teachers attack Neriman for being influenced by the West, it is a veiled attack on Atatürk and the entire Republic, in fact so lightly veiled that one wonders how it got through the censors of the time. Their anger at Neriman for abandoning the oud was also their anger at the nation for abandoning the Ottoman religious and cultural heritage that alaturka, or "Türk klasik musiki," represented.

The musicians and music teachers from the alaturka section of the Darü'l-Elhân are, in fact, participating in a much larger, contemporary discussion of the meaning of culture and civilization, a discussion that the reader would know well: that is, the distinction, if any, between "civilization" and "culture."

"Civilization" and "modernity" were associated with Westernization and the universality of technology, whereas culture and "tradition" were associated with the East and its own spirituality. But these men have decided that culture and civilization are of a piece, and therefore if any aspect of Western culture is accepted, its entirety is accepted. Therefore, the discussion of terminating the *alaturka* section of the conservatory, or the choice made by an individual for Western music, symbolizes the choice of one culture and the rejection of another.[47]

It is for this reason that Neriman's actions are so dangerous, and she feels it acutely. This attack clarifies Neriman's view of herself as being contemptible, for the repercussions are larger than she could have imagined. Şinasi himself had interrupted the discussion to make this point. Yes, he said, however one looks at the duality, some of "our girls are becoming *züppes*," meaning that they had left the culture of the East, or Ottoman culture, for that of the West.

> "And it's not just that they are becoming *züppes*! They are letting us down [*sukut ettiriyor*]!"
>
> Neriman was startled, and began to pull at a lock of her hair. *Sukut!* [Let down!] Şinasi was talking about *sukut*! This word, for a girl like Neriman had always had a romantic intensity. *Sukut!* The word rammed at her head like hard wood. . . . *Sukut!* But she, unlike the Russian girl, had *not* fled with the Greek lover, she was *not* contemptible! She had just given up the idea of going to the ball![48]

Finally Neriman is able to tell of her spiritual return, which makes everyone happy; and in the last few pages of the novel, Şinasi, Neriman, and Faiz Bey go back to their own houses among the other sleeping houses of Fatih and fall into a sleep of relief. Because Neriman's decisions have been made correctly, in favor of Eastern traditions, in favor of the right music and the right spouse, and because the men have done their job of telling her what is right, everyone falls asleep easily, and with a good conscience.

Faiz Bey had reinterpreted the sleep of the cat, changing the association of sleep from one of laziness to one of spiritual depth. The sleep of the cat had allowed the reader to focus on the Orientalist stigmatization of the East, and Neriman herself had made the connection to the East and to Fatih in particular when she cried, "All of Fatih is asleep!" The interpretation of the sleep of the cat as the sleep of the spiritually attuned gives meaning to the fact that all the residents of Fatih are now asleep *in their houses*. The final scene that is framed by the sleeping houses of Fatih and the falling into sleep of the protagonists suggests that the rupture with the past with its spiritual offering has been healed, at least for tonight. The old house offers a place to imagine continuity with the wholeness and safety that traditional life was perceived to have made possible, although it is in fact a dream that is becoming harder and harder to recall.

The depth and dimensions of the spirituality that the Turkish house called forth in memory in the first decade of the new republic were profound. The past that was represented by Kiralık Konak's Naim Efendi in his konak in Cihangir was a moribund past. But by the 1930s, in the face of the innovations in society, the (post-)Ottoman patriarch has pulled his act together and revitalized tradition.

Naim Efendi had represented the Ottoman nobility remembered in part for their refinement; he was the "İstanbulin," with his careful interiority, his sense of orderliness, and his strong sense of family responsibility. Naim Efendi's house was portrayed as a potential antidote and a potential barrier to the spiritual superficiality of the West, if only he had but used his authority wisely or at all.

Faiz Bey's house in Fatih-Harbiye, where he has discussions with Şinasi about Sufi literature and where he reads the classics of Eastern religious literature, the Mesnevis of Rumi, the poetry of Sa'di, Ömer Khayyam, and al Ghazzâli,[49] and where he is a connoisseur of alaturka music, has a richer, more developed, and more stable offering. Faiz Bey's house, like Neriman's grandmother's clean konak, where everyone read or listened to Naima, is a "treasury of ideas," a hazine-i efkâr. That is, his old wooden house is the repository of the spiritual strength of the East, with all its connotations of correct moral behavior. The spirituality and spiritual heritage that emerge in these works are becoming clearer. In part they are the treasury of insight and ideas of Islam in its broadest sense, yet in a sense specifically understood and continuously invoked. This remembered spirituality does not refer to an individual's private religious beliefs or convictions but to the higher moral authority of the Islamic system, a symbolic universe of interrelationships and morally defined behavior, supported by a rich intellectual tradition. Discussing this symbolic universe is another way of discussing culture, for it is not a symbolic universe defined by the five pillars of Islam[50] but a universe that connects everything, even one's internal interiority, to a larger system, and where a carefully articulated order is mediated by the intermediaries of the great Islamic thinkers and artists. It also includes the system of authority, the series of concentric circles of authority that began with God and His realm and moved inward, toward the home and the soul. In Halide Edib's 1935 *Sinekli Bakkal*, Rabia's music teacher, the Italian pianist Peregrini, who stands for a "rational" West that has a great deal to learn from the "spiritual" East, says, "Islam to me is not a religion, it is a way of living, a mere label and a code of human relationships."[51]

The emotional charge of the memory that surrounds the house is a spiritual one in just this way. The meaning for the present that memory gives to this old house is one of wholeness, in that this meaning operates within the sanctions of religion writ large, and for the happiness of its members. It is a place that has an answer for the pain of rupture.

CONTINUITY AND RUPTURE

We are facing a spiritual chaos, unrest has developed in men's souls.

The sleep of Fatih heals—in the imagination—a rupture with the past that was long in the making. The changes of 1908 permanently restructured the household and the mahalle, but by the time *Fatih-Harbiye* was published, in 1931, this rupture had increased in dimension and scope. By 1930 the Turkish population had seen a complete secularization of the institutional spaces that had once been a part of the Ottoman Islamic polity. Without a doubt, the intensity of these changes came as a shock to the entire population.[52]

Between 1923 and 1926 a cabinet system was instituted, and the caliphate, which had linked the state to religion, was abolished.[53] There was a thorough Westernization of education: the religious schools and dervish lodges, the *medresses* and *tekkes*, were closed. The religious foundations (*Evkaf*), with their mosque-centered and mosque-administered social services, were handed over to the state, and visits to the graves of the sultans and saints were prohibited. The secular Swiss Civil Code was adopted in 1926, the same year that the Darü'l-Elhân was closed. Among other things, the Swiss Code gave women new rights, abolishing polygamy and repudiation. In 1925 the law on general apparel encouraged women to wear Western clothing in public. Although the mahalles remained the basic units in the urban fabric of the city, after 1927 layman were appointed as local headmen (*muhtars*), taking over many of the prerogatives that had previously belonged to religious leaders. In 1928 the Arabic alphabet, which had been associated with Islam, was exchanged for the one used by the Christian world. The state was thus "freed" from its Ottoman and religious past, and religion was made into one of the state's most strictly supervised departments.[54]

This process of secularization included what has been called the "desacralisation of politics" and the "deconsecration of values."

> *The desacralisation of politics* [means] the abolition of sacral legitimating of political power and authority, which is the prerequisite of political change and hence also social change, allowing for the emergence of the historical process.
>
> *The deconsecration of values* [means] rendering transient and relative all cultural creations and every value system [including] religion and worldviews having ultimate and final significance, so that in this way history, [and] the future, is open to change.[55]

The desacralisation of politics was especially swift and harsh, and hit at the heart of a system of authority that had given meaning to life by tying together the political, the personal, and the spiritual. The deconsecration of values went hand in hand with a system that integrated the political and the social, thus dismantling an older symbolic universe piece by piece.

In 1928 the philosopher Mehmet Emin (Erişirgil; 1891–1965) wrote of the Turkish people,

> We are facing a spiritual chaos. As a result of the destruction of the institutions of religion which came down from the past, and which were found incompatible with national life as well as [with] modern civilization, unrest has developed in men's souls.[56]

But the public reaction to secularization was carefully controlled, for the state monitored all cultural activity. Even Namık Kemal's nationalistic play, *Vatan Yuhut Silistre* (The Motherland or Silistra), was banned because of its rallying cry, "Long Live the Ottomans" and "Long Live the Sultan,"[57] even though it referred to the battle over Bulgarian Silistra and the play had been written half a century before. And even Yakup Kadri, who was known as a rather staunch Kemalist, was censored in 1929. His play *Sağanak* (Downpour) portrayed a family split between an anti-Kemalist father and elder son and a Kemalist younger son and his sister-in-law. The elder son had conspired against Atatürk with a secret organization and was sentenced to death, throwing the family into turmoil. It is said that the play was banned because the sides were not portrayed in sufficiently black-and-white terms.[58]

The Ottoman state had been identified with the personal rule of the sultan, who was also the caliph of Islam, but the Kemalist republic portrayed this ruling system as outmoded and incapable of competing with the European nation-state system. Furthermore, the Islamic basis that gave legitimacy to the Ottoman state was seen as the primary obstacle to material progress, and thoughts that countered this view were considered seditious.

Secularization was a political motto that not only marginalized the lifeworlds that had been based on Islamic identity but issued sanctions against their expression. But the appearance of the spiritual element in the literature of the 1930s suggests that the old house and konak had become the space in those margins that the old life-worlds could still inhabit, and the only place left to play out the microcosm of what had once been a unifying and legitimizing system of belief and behavior. More important, the house had become the only place to struggle for its future.

In *Fatih-Harbiye*, Faiz Bey and Şinasi understand this, and therefore their struggle is a conscious one:

> Şinasi pulled Neriman strongly toward the past and its customs [*maziye ve an'aneye çekti*]. He was almost a young Faiz Bey. He had been working for years to mitigate the yearnings for the new in Neriman's soul. But this had not been easy on Şinasi.[59]

After Neriman had come back to reclaim her heritage, after she had given up the ball and taken up the oud, Şinasi and Faiz Bey negotiated the crooked streets of Fatih like victors on a triumphal way. Although their sleep in Fatih can be seen as a metaphor for being spiritually attuned, at the end of that day, Şinasi's sleep is also that of a warrior who has won a battle. When Şinasi got into bed and thought things over, "he found it all satisfactory. More than the honor of his victory, he was feeling the peace of it."[60]

Faiz Bey, too, understood that a battle had been won. As he goes off to sleep, he opens his book of poetry, of *"gazels,"* and like a child who believes that the random opening to a page will reveal one's fortune, he opens his book and reads a refrain from al Ghazzâli: *"'Harp bitti'* it says. The war is over."[61]

In *Fatih-Harbiye*, the struggle is spiritual, but if it is specifically Islamic, this is covertly expressed. There are clear references to religion when Neriman is repelled by the *"softa* types" who appear lazy and useless, or when the oppressiveness of her own street in Fatih is punctuated by the muezzin's call to prayer. Both are later reinterpreted favorably. The books that Faiz Bey reads and the music that Şinasi plays refer to Islam as well. But because the religious aspects of the Ottoman past were highly politicized, it is unclear if the continuity (which the house represents) was specifically religious. Is it that religion was renamed "house" in order to be remembered? There are no clear references to Islam, yet the mode of sacredness appears to have its own terms of reference: it is emotionally rather than theologically informed, and bound to the sacred bonds of the family and the Ottoman system of wholeness that we have uncovered in all the novels under discussion. It is this system of wholeness that the head of the family, the *aile reisi*, struggled to maintain in his old wooden house, which was the bulwark that could protect older values from being rendered "transient and relative."[62]

THE FOUNDATIONS OF WHOLENESS

Faiz Bey as *aile reisi* and Şinasi as his prince-elect struggle to keep the wholeness of the system intact, but neither one is the hero of the story. Neither is Neriman. In these stories, such as *Kiralık Konak* and *Fatih-Harbiye*, the protagonist is not an individual seeking a narrative history within the family or the community but a community or family protecting itself from just such an event, that is, from the individual becoming the protagonist. This struggle is shared by family and individual alike, with the family struggling to enclose, and perhaps ironically the individual struggling to remain inside.

When Şinasi and Faiz Bey feel that their struggle is over, Neriman sighs a reciprocal sigh of relief, and her sleep brings her the peace of a clean conscience and acquiescence. Earlier, she had taken the oud on her lap, and the music had given her "an exact solution to [her] feelings of renunciation [*feragat*]. [The music] moved like a soft brush, down from the top of her soul, and swept away . . . the impossible things of her desires."[63]

The author considers Neriman's interior struggle as part of a family struggle. Her epiphany allows the family to function as a whole, with all the hierarchies intact, and all its threats ("the impossible things of her desires") removed.

The family as protagonist appeals to a validating history in order to maintain itself in the face of threats to its sense of cohesiveness. The appeal is to the past as it was depicted in Neriman's grandmother's house ("That konak was really a school") rather than to the personality of the grandmother; it is an appeal to the "treasury of ideas and insights" that were read in the house, and thus to the system of Islamic scholarship that provided its moral foundations.

If the family is seen as the representation of a worldview in which the spiritual happiness of the individual is only possible, in fact only conceivable, within a context of the harmony of the system, one begins to understand how it is the family—and the house that enclosed it when it was intact—represents continuity with the past, and thus a bridge that heals the rupture brought on by the present.[64] The system that the house frames has a hierarchy with a prominent father at its apex, but it is a hierarchy that is remembered as wholeness rather than tyranny.

Evin has pointed out that in novels such as Halit Ziya's 1898 *Aşk-ı Memnun* (Forbidden Love),[65] the household is characterized as a community, "the harmony of which depends on personal bonds of loyalty," that is, "a community loyalty patterned according to the Ottoman patrimonial system."[66]

Evin's use of "patrimonial system" is not discussed fully, but he clearly uses it to mean something other than the system addressed here. The words patrimonial and patriarchy carry such strong authoritarian weight that one might be loathe to use them at all; they detract from the unique life-worlds that these novels position in memory, a life-world of order and tranquility, most often represented by the father but not imposed by him. In the early twentieth century, it is a memory that seems to have forgotten or been relegated to a more distant past, a system that arranged marriages between "too-young daughters" and "too-old pashas," a system that left Şefika to sob over Ata, as we read in Chapter 3.

In the 1930s, Faiz Bey is a loving father who wants his daughter to be happy; he is not a tyrant. Neither is he a reactionary. He has encouraged Neriman to further her education in the conservatory, which means that she has an active life outside the house; after all, it was less than a decade earlier that girls had entered universities, and only then to sit behind a curtain.[67] In fact, the opening of a conservatory of music, along with a National Theater that used Turkish actors, was an innovation that came in the wake of the Second Constitutional Period of 1908.

Faiz Bey is not even upset that his daughter visits Beyoğlu; rather, he is anguished that he does not have the money to buy her a dress for the ball. However, within Faiz Bey's universe, tranquility or happiness comes from conduct appropriate to a system that values behavior and relationships that are bound up with daily life (*hayatla iç içe*).[68] Faiz Bey perceives himself as acting for Neriman's happiness, not his own, but with the understanding that happiness is not idiosyncratic but systemic, and thus her happiness is everyone's happiness; it is a family happiness.

The point is not that no single person can be happy outside of the system that the house represents but that *Fatih-Harbiye* is a biography of this shared struggle rather than the biography of an individual's struggle; therefore it must take place inside the house, where wholeness resides. Happiness is an interior phenomenon that comes with everyone's peace of mind. The happiness at the end of the story is possible because the struggle has been won by everyone, and therefore the system is intact. Faiz Bey's clone, Şinasi, will marry Faiz Bey's daughter, and this endogamous marriage (iç evlenmesi) will ensure that the system remains intact.

But the system was not intact, and the successful resolution of *Fatih-Harbiye* stands at the crossroads of nostalgia and moral lesson, with the imagined Turkish house at its center. Not only was the Turkish house no longer being built (Faiz Bey's house could hardly be maintained, although its moldy wood was polished daily), but the *alaturka* section of the conservatory had been officially closed by the time *Fatih-Harbiye* was written, and the music that had been taught at the Darü'l-Elhân would soon be officially discouraged on the public airwaves. It is also unlikely that the books that Faiz Bey reads, that give substance to the spirituality of the house, could be understood by Şinasi's generation, even if they wanted to understand them, and certainly not by their children. Faiz Bey's generation was at the tail end of the culture that he wanted to replicate. One of Faiz Bey's "contemporaries," Hüseyin Cahit Yalçın (1874–1957),[69] wrote in his *Literary Reminiscences* that he "did his utmost to read his father's favorite book, *The Seals of Wisdom* of Ibn al-Arabi.[70] But alas, in vain! This book conveyed simply nothing to him."[71] This is the exact counterpart to Naim Efendi's problem: Naim Efendi could not understand the novels of his son-in-law; the sons and sons-in-law could not read the literature that shaped their fathers.

The biography of the family in the house in *Fatih-Harbiye* is an effort of memory, and it has encoded within it a deep sympathy. And yet, because it is the place where there is a struggle for continuity, it also is a place that represents an opportunity to return. The house, then, has two strong, seemingly opposite meanings. It represents a system and a life-world that are over, yet it also represents a recuperable heritage that can be chosen instead of the lifestyle of modernity.

Both of these points are evident in one of Peyami Safa's later novels, *Cumbadan Rumbaya* (*From Cumba*—that Ottoman-style protruding window—to *Rumba*), published in 1936. This novel, by continuing the association of the old house with "the father,"[72] makes clear again how the house filled a microcosmic space within a symbolic universe that had once radiated from God and the sultan inward toward the neighborhood and the house, resting at last with the family father, the aile reisi. But the house in *Cumbadan Rumbaya* also stands for a system that is not merely a part of memory but is intact enough to beckon the protagonist and the reader to return and to remain.

THE PLACE WHERE HER FATHER GREW UP, AND
SHE HERSELF WAS BORN

In the novel *Cumbadan Rumbaya*, the neighborhood of old wooden houses of *"Karagümrük"* and the spiritual values they represent are encoded in the word *cumba*, the protruding bay of the wooden house. *Rumba* stands for the nightlife of Beyoğlu by calling to mind the balls and ballroom dancing that it had brought to Turkey and that became a sign of modernism.

Cemile (pronounced Jameeleh), the heroine of *Cumbadan Rumbaya*, is a cross between Neriman and the poor Russian girl of *Fatih-Harbiye*, for she is attracted to the wealth of the West and becomes one of a group of women who have ostensibly attached themselves to Westernized Turkish men in the hope of marrying into that life. According to this trope of the shallow *female* over-Westernized *züppe*, if marriage does not materialize, the woman becomes a mistress, selling her soul for material pleasures or security. Whether or not these types were real or apocryphal, there was a ditty that described them, and *Cumbadan-Rumbaya* begins with it:

Ol bir salon gelini	Be a salon bride
Koy kalbime elini	Put a hand on my heart
Kıvır ince belini	Wiggle your narrow waist
Kalblere vur bir zımba	Put a staple on their hearts
Rumba da rumba, rumba!	Rumba and rumba, rumba![73]

Cumbadan Rumbaya is a more complex novel than *Fatih-Harbiye*. Unlike Neriman, the heroine, Cemile, is almost completely seduced by the *alafranga* lifestyle (although a few of her Beyoğlu friends turn out to have good hearts with "traditional" Karagümrük values). But like Neriman, Cemile carries a strong sense of love and respect for her family and her neighbors in Karagümrük, where the doors of her house had always been open to them. In 1961, Önol referred to the life in *Cumbadan Rumbaya* as "those close-knit [*iç-içe*—interior to interior] times"[74]—that is, the times when people's souls felt connected.

Also like Neriman, Cemile has a love interest who pulls her back to her roots, and, as in *Fatih-Harbiye*, a turning point in *Cumbadan Rumbaya* involves the old wooden house. Before moving to Beyoğlu (Taksim), Cemile so desired the Beyoğlu life that she had hatched a plot to have her old house burn so that she could move to an apartment. Although she later changed her mind, at the beginning of the novel the old wooden house represented the life that Cemile thought she wanted to erase. Instead, she is able to move to an apartment financed by her admirer, where she begins to lead a Beyoğlu life.

But while at a party given by a wealthy Egyptian princess in Beyoğlu, Cemile gets a phone call from her mother to tell her that their Karagümrük house and neighborhood are on fire, a very believable scenario in the aging areas of Istanbul. News of the fire puts into perspective for Cemile and for us what this loss, a loss that she once craved, would mean.

> A great compassionate sob stuck in her throat. Karagümrük is burning! The house where she herself was born and *her father grew up!* The poor *mahalle* was burning! Who knew now how the poor and old were sobbing. . . . Hafize, my dear little Hafize, "Auntie" Hafize . . . [and] Hamdune, poor Hamdune! Oh Dear God! *Aman Yarabbi!* (Emphasis mine.)[75]

Our "good-hearted" ("*iyi kalpli*") Cemile's first thoughts are for her neighbors, whom she knows live financially marginal lives, are ill, and are not insured. But as the reality of the fire sinks in, we see how she identified her own house with her father as well.

> Shutting her eyes, she took a deep breath. Karagümrük was burning. The place where Cemile was born, the room suspended above the garden, the green-ceilinged room where her father had died . . . the *sofas* that rang with their singing, all were burning. Suddenly, and who knows why, the edge of the dining-room door met her eyes. . . . Her father had marked her height each year on such a ledge from the time when Cemile was three until she was twelve. . . . Even when Cemile had reached the age of fourteen or fifteen she would stand in front of these marks to see how much she had grown, and tried to figure out the difference. On the days when her father was dying Cemile, without letting anyone see, would kiss these marks. . . . Now she was thinking that this wooden piece was also burning in the fire . . . "hih" . . . she said, drawing in her breath.[76]

It is in this context that Cemile calls herself "treacherous" for having abandoned her "*samimi*" (intimate) neighborhood, and for having considered burning her house in order to leave it for what she finds is a superficial *alafranga* life, where men cheat on women and where, she is shocked to learn, no one believes in God.

Aman Yarabbi! Oh Dear God! Me, me, crazy woman, me, treacherous woman, shameful woman, how can I get it into my head that my own house and street are burning without being ashamed?[77]

In spite of the fact that Cemile's house has burned down and Neriman's conservatory is closed, it would appear that each has been asked to make a life-defining choice between two social systems. In this way, the reader is led to choose something that the past, with its code word of "house," represents, and therefore that *must still be felt to exist.*

In *Fatih-Harbiye*, Neriman is accused of being a züppe because she is mesmerized by the "hat and ball" life of Beyoğlu and because she gives up her *alaturka* music. Neriman chooses to go home, calling herself *"alçak,"* "contemptible," because she almost didn't. Cemile wants to be driven by a chauffeur and to drink champagne at parties where women wear high-fashion clothing; she is accused by the people of Karagümrük[78] of no longer being "our Cemile." When she realizes the inherent value of these neighbors in contrast to her inner desire to destroy that life-world, she calls herself "treacherous" (*"ben, hain karı!"*).[79]

By calling themselves contemptible and treacherous, and by choosing to return home, Neriman and Cemile have made a new type of choice, one that was not imagined before this period. This element of choice is fundamental to the message of Safa's two novels and gives the Turkish house a new layer of meaning. By choosing to go home, Neriman and Cemile show us how the Turkish house has become an icon of continuity, a bridge between the past and the present. I will return to this idea of choosing continuity yet again.

OUR HOUSE, OUR FAMILY, AND OURSELVES WERE ALL ONE BEING. WE UNITED WITH THE PAST IN THEM, WE STRETCHED OUR ROOTS INTO THE PAST WITH THEM.

The Turkish house, as a marker for the still vital or still recuperable life-world of the Ottoman Islamic system, was not shared by everyone. One could argue that its viability or even vitality was a dream that was desired only by the less Western-minded. And certainly there were some who felt that the emotional content of the Turkish house was hardly recuperable at all, and that the house was becoming not only a memory but an effort of memory.

Yakup Kadri had already shown that the rupture with the past was taking place inside the konak. The Westernist author and journalist Hüseyin Cahit Yalçın, mentioned earlier, suggested that without the actual physical space of the house, its emotional value was not recuperable, and therefore it was marking the memory of a divide between the past and now, and a memory of loss. His 1935 article *"Ev Sevgisi"* (Affection for the House) reminds us that, along with efforts of recuperation and continuity, the effort of memory had begun.

> So in this sofa our grandfather had died. In this room our mother had coins sprinkled on her head when she became a bride. Our house, our family, and ourselves were all one being [*vücut*]. . . . [Its] wood, its boards, its nails . . . none were made of lifeless stuff. Each was from a part of us. They lived along with us, and they brought us a message from our past, from our grandfathers and grandmothers. We united with the past in them, we put out our roots into the past with them.[80]

When Yalçın wrote about the old wooden house in *"Ev Sevgisi,"* he conceptualized it in much the same way as Safa, as the paternal home both in the sense that it had ancestral, familial ties and as a spiritual base. And like Cemile in *Cumbadan Rumbaya,* Yalçın saw the old house as the place where both a personal and a family narrative were plotted.[81] For Yalçın, it is this attachment to one's roots that defined what was meant by affection for the house, by *ev sevgisi.*

> A source of pleasure and devotion that is in danger of being lost in the new way of life is: affection for the house [*ev sevgisi*]. Both large and small families had their parental [patriarchal] home [*baba yurdu*]. We opened our eyes to the world in a house that looked out onto a narrow street with broken pavements, whose exterior view was blackened by rain and gales. No matter whether the house was large or small, it had a garden. Every part of the garden was cultivated by our own hands. When our mothers and fathers showed us some old apricot trees, they explained that they had been planted by our grandfather with grafts that had come from somewhere they didn't know, and that they had played under these trees when they were children.[82]

The house connects its occupants to the remembered past (grandfathers and grandmothers) and to immemorial time ("planted by our grandfather with grafts that had come from somewhere they didn't know"). The house fuses autobiography with what went before; it is a collective memory of affection. The feeling of love that was bound up with the house was a love for the family and the past, and this affective memory was the source of one's tranquility. Yalçın saw this tie to the past as threatened by modern living and its spaces.

> Today . . . we are separated from the hearth of our fathers [baba ocağı]. Our old houses burned, or were torn down. We were unable to live in them, and when a buyer appeared we sold them to the destruction crew. And they destroyed with a crash and a snap, right in front of our eyes, the old buildings that formed our family history and that had collected in them all the bitter and sweet days that we lived. . . . In our great homeland we are left as if we were homeless and with no nest.[83]

Yalçın addresses the loss of the old wooden house itself, but even more so, he laments that without the house, the connection that memory made to the past was threatened:

> And the worst of it is, we are even indifferent to the bitterness of this. Because we find ourselves left far—not just materially, but spiritually— from the family hearth and from the love for the house . . . the meaning of the word "house" has been lost.[84]

For Yalçın, the physical loss of the house meant the loss of continuity, not a plea for it. For him the choices imposed by the rupture with the past were definitive. Like Neriman's music teachers, who suspected that all choices were all-or-nothing choices, Yalçın might have said that "when one chooses an apartment, it means one is choosing a new culture!" Thus, although there was disagreement on where the house sat on a continuum of memory, Yalçın and Safa (and Yakup Kadri as well) were in complete agreement that the Turkish house was the site of the spiritual values of the Turkish heritage. Yet Peyami Safa and Hüseyin Cahit Yalçın are good examples of very different political voices and forces having a shared imaginary; it is this that underlies a discussion of the Turkish house as a marker of a broad-based identity.

A case could be made that Peyami Safa was both an Islamist[85] and an Ottomanist who used his valorization of a non-Western lifestyle to conceal the degree to which he was disturbed by the rapid and unidimensional secular and Western focus of Atatürk's republic. In *Fatih-Harbiye*, Safa positions the East (Şark) against the West (Garb), choosing Arabic-Ottoman words to do it.[86] In fact, he almost never uses the word Turk or Turkey, instead choosing the word East (Şark). The classical literature that his Faiz Bey reads is

Persian or Arabic, and to counter Neriman's condemnation of Easterners as lazy, he writes:

> [Faiz Bey]—Look, the clock behind you on the stand has been invented by an Easterner [*bir şarklı icat etmiştir*] in the time of Harun al-Rashid,[87] and the book in my hand is written by an Easterner [*bir şarklı yazmıştır*].
> [Neriman]—Oh well, that black covered book . . . who reads it besides you?
> [Faiz Bey]—Many people read it—besides you.
> [Neriman]—Oh, they're all lazy people and daydreamers.
> [Faiz Bey]—No, the Europeans read it too. There are many translations of this book in the West and anyone there can read it. The man on the street reads it, the upper classes read it. *Velâkin!* You're the only one who doesn't read it! This type of work doesn't exist in your school anymore. If you ask an English girl about Sa'di, she'll know. [But] you, even though you are an Easterner [*sen, Şarklı olduğunu halde*] you don't know. Whose fault is that? Yours—or Sa'di's?[88]

"The East" for Safa is the *ümma*,[89] the community of Islam, which was arguably a deeper identity to him than the Turkish nation that only diminished it. Although he was remembered at his death for being a nationalist, the writings at the time of his death only lightly veil his anti-Atatürk, anti-secularist feelings. In the quote above, he is clearly against the new educational system that privileged scientistic and rational Western teaching. In a 1945 issue of the conservative journal *Büyük Doğu* (The Great Orient), the editors published the answers to a questionnaire titled "INTROSPECTION among seventy-five famous Turks with respect to every aspect of their careers and work."[90] One of the questions asked was, "Should the teaching of morals and the sacred be a part of the school curriculum?" Peyami Safa answered, "Yes!"[91] Safa was remembered for his strong religious and politically conservative feelings,[92] and after his death, in 1961, he was toasted as a religious "martyr" for his political activities.[93]

Peyami Safa (1899–1961) and Hüseyin Cahit (1874–1957) were cohorts,[94] and although both were nationalists, their vision of the nation differed, as Hüseyin Yalçın was a secularist and a staunch supporter of the republican ideology.[95] When the Second Constitutional Period (II Meşrutiyet) was proclaimed in 1908, it was Yalçın and his friends who had begun the journal

Tanin, the journal that had listed the offending bureaucrats, including Naim Efendi's friends.[96] Later he became the sole owner of *Tanin*[97] and the leading voice of *Yedigün*, the most popular journal of its time.

Yalçın was born during the years between the birth of Naim Efendi's son-in-law Servet Bey (b. ca 1862), who read novels from the *Edebiyat-i Cedide*, and the birth of Faiz Bey (b. ca 1880), who spent his evenings reading classical literature. Remember that Yalçın had tried to read his own father's classical books, but they meant nothing to him. It was only French literature that held any resonance with the world he both knew and desired.

> What were the forces that had delivered my mind from the swamps of scholasticism, the forces that opened new horizons before my eyes, the forces that freed my soul from bondage? I find today that it was the French language and culture above all things which was responsible for my awakening.[98]

This statement stands as a refutation of Peyami Safa's epigrammatic use of the East as a trope to reposition culture and even daily life within the framework of the Ottoman Islamic world, with a rhetoric tied to the Arab past and its authors, such as al-Ghazzali. Yalçın had attacked this Arabism at the turn of the century as a means to keep the empire from entering the future.

> This talk of Oriental culture, Islamic civilization, [and] the sciences of the Arabs, was repeated constantly in every writing, and on all occasions in order to anaesthetize the nation, in order to prevent it from joining the stream of life of the West passing us nearby.[99]

Yalçın himself was attacked for translating Caetani's ten-volume *History of Islam (İslam Tarihi)*, as it was believed to be intensely anti-Islamic and even sacrilegious.[100] Thus, unlike Peyami Safa, Yalçın was neither an Islamist nor a proponent of the East. When Peyami Safa answered "Yes!" to the question, "Should the teaching of morals and the sacred be a part of the school curriculum?" Hüseyin Cahit Yalçın answered, "No!"[101]

Yet Hüseyin Cahit and Peyami Safa were talking about the same house, the same old wooden house that we are now calling the Turkish house. Both gave it a similar affective meaning and a similar centrality. Through these houses, a cultural sense of self could retain the memory if not the specifics of the Ottoman life-world. Yakup Kadri shared this imaginary as well. Like Yalçın, Yakup Kadri was a strong supporter of Atatürk, although he lost favor with the regime in the early 1930s because of his Marxist journal *Kadro*.[102] Thus all three authors had different political leanings but shared an image of the old wooden house as the spiritual foundation of their own heritage, showing how this image cut across ideological or political associations.

In fact, to the extent that Naim Bey's konak in Cihangir and Faiz Bey's wooden house in Fatih shared like spiritual values with Yalçın's "large and small houses," the affective meaning of "konak" and "house" are conflated in the imagination. This is an important point, for although the konak, the yalı, the köşk, and smaller wooden multistoried houses can be discussed in terms of their differences, that is, the size of their ground plan, or the size of the incomes that sustained them, their differences seem to disappear—or merge—in the affectivity or emotional charge that they brought to the imagination. It appears that the image of the old wooden house contained then, as it does now, a similar memory, whether the old house was large or small, rich or poor, inhabited by secular nationalists or by religious revivalists, as long as it was Turkish (that is, ours). If indeed there once were socially or culturally significant class differences, they lost that difference in the memory of the house, and thus memory crossed economic and class lines.[103]

That the affective meanings of the image of the Turkish house crossed ideological and economic lines emphasizes the uniform base that these meanings were coming to have at a time of intense change and rupture. Because of these intense changes in social life, there was, seemingly, a choice to be made between the life-world that was imagined to exist in the house of the past, and the life-world that was imagined to exist in the rapidly unfolding present and in the apartments that symbolized it. Neriman and Cemile were asked to make this type of choice, one that was not imagined before this period. In older novels, the overly Westernized dandy, the züppe, had represented a choice *not* to be made. The züppe as defined in *Araba Sevdası* or *Kiralık Konak* was a cautionary figure marginalized by satire rather than a figure to emulate. The cost factor of the *züppe* life also limited it to an elite few. Thus, even in *Kiralık Konak*, life-world choices were not being presented so much as differences were being defined.

But by the 1930s the differences had narrowed. The life-world changes that had taken place demographically, institutionally, and architecturally had invaded the daily life of the entire literate urban population. Urban life now involved spending time in the space of modernity that Beyoğlu stood for. If one didn't enter Beyoğlu via a tram ride, the way that Neriman had, or rent an apartment, as had Naim Efendi's daughter Sekine and his son-in-law, Servet Bey, and also Cemile, then one entered via the republican imaginary presented in every magazine and newspaper. *"Harem"* had already exposed the wider base of the Westernized elite and removed it from a züppe rhetoric, and the lifestyles of Naim Bey's children and grandchildren had become common lifestyles, even though their habits confused their elders or caused them real pain.

Because of this penetration of modernity there could, in fact, be no real choice offered of returning to the old way of life. Neither could one return to the old house. Because the houses were no longer being built, because Naim Efendi's konak was to be rented, because the houses in Fatih had no electricity, because the houses in Karagümrük had burned down and could only be replaced by apartments, and because even the "House of Melodies" had lost its Turkish voice, all lifestyle choices either did now or were clearly destined soon to involve abandoning the old house itself. Thus, when Safa suggests choosing a "cumba" instead of a "rumba," or when he praises the old, moldy wooden house where Neriman knew "she could be happy," he seemingly suggests choosing something physically unobtainable.

But the choice was felt to be a real one because the Turkish house was considered a structure of feeling more than a structure of wood. It is for this reason that it was affectively attainable and available as an image of continuity. In the early republican period the image of the Turkish house was a mixture of memory, existence, and desire, and held the possibility of mediating between the past and the present. Perhaps the house may be called a dialectical image in the sense that Walter Benjamin envisioned: "an image of the past that carried the desires of the past generations into the present."[104] As a dialectical image the Turkish house held a place of vital importance, for it was imagined to be capable of healing a strongly felt but unclearly articulated rupture. Because the old house was a physical representation of the ineffable quality of the symbolic universe, of an all-encompassing Ottoman-period life-world that had no terminology but was alive with emotion, it was a physical representation of identity: of one's history and desire, happiness and being at their most basic level.

The Turkish house became the place that resonated with a sense of a self within one's culture at a moment of change, and it seems clear what the fundamental aspects of this identification included, and how these felt. The Turkish house situated identity within a symbolic universe that was rooted in the past and experienced through the family. The emphasis on the family father gave authority to this domestic image of culture, and gave some of the details in the narrative that tied identity to the symbolic universe of the past. The image of the house, with a father connected to larger values, made it a place where one might imagine replication of values, providing a place for continuity. Thus, the Turkish house, as a literary representation, was a place where socialization of the new generation could take place, albeit by a mental association with the story, or symbolically.

The cross-generational demands of cultural continuity had been ruptured in Naim Efendi's konak. But Faiz Bey's house, as the place that stored the values of the past, allowed a potentially rebellious new generation of readers to have, along with Neriman, a sort of face-to-face interaction with a remembered culture. This made the house a place where change could be evaluated and negotiated.

Because the idea or image of the Turkish house was the place where what was perceived as "Western" or "modern" culture was copied and integrated as well as where it was rejected, it marked a present that was aligned with choices for change. Bhabha calls this integration "cultural translation," the process that leads to cultural merging, or "hybridity."[105] Turkish cultural identity was not defined simply, and it was not defined by a simple past. Instead, it included this activity of cultural translation; perhaps identity must always include the ambivalent and discriminating self. The imaged and imagined Turkish house represented the viewing point from which a culturally defined self looked at change and at the "other," and therefore represented the self in transtion, as it was deciding just how to adapt. Faiz Bey, who represents the cultural past, is comfortable with Neriman's public life with Şinasi, and Cemile's modern lifestyle is not at issue, only her values. In the early republican period, then, these authors used the Turkish house to portray cultural identity as a dialectic with the new rather than in opposition to the new. The Turkish house operated as an image that made an authoritative version of the past available to the present, providing cultural identity and cultural continuity: a place for an ongoing construction or definition or placement of the self. Benjamin's dialectical image tied the past to the present. This dialectic makes the house the place where the two could be in an active dialogue for acceptable changes. In this way the Turkish house was a symbolic space that provided an alternative to the dominant public republican discourse that repudiated the past; instead, the image of the house allowed one to imagine the self within a present that could be felt as a part of the real past, and allowed one to combine the social, spiritual, domestic, and private meanings of both.

There is, in fact, a visual (rather than descriptive) representation of the Turkish house as an image of an identity that is rooted in the past but looking out toward and negotiating the new. I offer this as an image of the house as "past present." It is a drawing of the house that positions one's constitutive self in engagement with the exterior world, and thus acts as both a memory image and an image of collective identity.

THE VIEW FROM THE BACK STREETS

In the late 1930s, the 20,000 readers of the popular magazine *Yedigün* were offered a series of articles by Halide Edib titled "*Arka Sokaktan Görüş*" (View from the Back Street). The banner drawing at the top of each article was one of a classic mahalle street of old houses, a street that could have illustrated Edib's *Sinekli Bakkal*, which had recently run as a monthly serial and had then been published in book form.[106]

Sinekli Bakkal begins:

> This neighborhood of narrow back streets had taken the name "*Sinekli Bakkal*."
>> *Bu dar arka sokak bulunduğu semtin adını almıştır: Sinekli Bakkal.*[107]

Thus the banner illustration relates the articles to *Sinekli Bakkal* and to Halide Edib as its author, but it also recalls her roots in the Turkish mahalle, as we know from her memoirs,[108] and identifies her with the symbolic universe shared by Rabia, Naim Efendi, Şinasi, Neriman, and Cemile in the complicated new world of the new republic. Halide Edib, one of Turkey's

"Arka Sokaktan Görüş" (*View from the Back Street*), Halide Edib's banner logo.
Yedigün 8 (Şubat): 9, 1938.

most public figures, stood at the center of the complexity of this contemporary life, for she represented a fierce modernism and a fierce nationalism, as well as a strong sympathy for Islam.[109] The banner drawings of Turkish houses, by association with Halide Edib, who was rooted in the past but engaged with the modern, stood for this rootedness and this engagement as a specifically Turkish cultural condition.

What is extremely telling, however, is that the articles these houses illustrate have nothing to do with quaint houses or even local news. The "View from the Back Street" series is not about Istanbul, it is not about Turkey, and it is not about Turks. Halide Edib is writing solely about events and ideas outside Turkey—about the Paris Opera, revivals or reinterpretations of Greek theater, the American judicial system, Indian film stars, and London pubs.

These houses were felt to be a natural representation of the Turkish self, looking out at the world. It is not that the author or reader lived in those streets or even wanted to live in those streets. Surely most of them did not, as every one of those roofs leaked. In fact, the rising middle-class readership no longer lived in the neighborhoods that were still characterized by those houses, and those neighborhoods no longer supported the mahalle culture described in *Fatih-Harbiye*.[110] Yet the novels discussed here show how the deepest identity of the readers still inhabited those streets in memory, and therefore marked their identity.

What makes these depicted houses particularly interesting and particularly appropriate for these articles, then, is that they represent the Turkish reader's Turkish cultural identity as it is coming to terms with the present, for as images in *Yedigün*, with its insistence on the modern, they are striking images of the traditional in a sea of modernity. That is, these old houses would have a shock of familiarity among the less familiar, among ads for refrigerators and articles about women giving intimate dinner parties.[111]

Halide Edib consciously addressed this difference by naturalizing her Western subjects as "back street people" like "our own back street people" (*bizim arka sokak halkı*), broadening them occasionally to include even Turkish intellectuals (*arka sokak münevverleri*).[112] Thus, these houses represent Turkish culture in the act of cultural translation, a process that the republican discourse and the forces of history in general were making an important part of consciousness. This image of the Turkish house marks an identity that is rooted in the past but not fixed in it, an identity that is in the process of taking its place in the Kemalist imaginary of *Yedigün*.

In their works, neither Peyami Safa, nor Hüseyin Cahit Yalçın, nor Halide Edib, nor Yakup Kadri before them name this house "Turkish." The houses of Naim Efendi and Faiz Bey are called Turkish here not just because the houses are described as konaks or with protruding cumbas but because the novelists are depicting the life-worlds of the urban population of that place called Turkey. These novels speak of Turkish identity. Safa, in fact, with his insistent use of "East" or "Oriental" (*Garb* and *Şark*) rather than "Turkish," positions the cultural sense of self in an Ottoman life-world, or at least in a life-world that has no Turkish national affiliation, with all of Turkish nationalism's secular connotations. The Turkish house is tied to Turkish cultural identity here, although the literary works themselves show that the meaning of this identity is clearly complex, spreads in time and space, and can elude naming. However, it appears that the houses that stand behind Halide Edib's views of the exterior world are in fact the houses in the back streets of collective memory and thus corroborate the old house as a marker of this identity. An article by Hüseyin Cahit says it explicitly:

> If, when I enter the kitchen with its wide fireplace on a ground paved in Malta stones, I can't say that this is where my aunt was given sweets for her first day of school, then I can't feel in my spirit the mysterious and charming ties of family life. The *baba ocağı* [paternal hearth] plays a very large part in creating our spirituality [and] our identity [*hüviyet*]. . . . We want . . . our family, our life, [and] our spirit that our father's house creates. . . . The impersonal life of these apartments that confront us is a dark chasm [*ucurum*] that swallows up these holy things.[113]

The sense of rootedness is in an Ottoman period past, but the Turkish house does not convey an Ottoman identity. Rather, it is an identity full of simultaneity, an identity of negotiating with the past in a very Turkish present. It is for this reason that the Turkish house is a place of constitutive cultural identity; it is the place where identity could be formed and could continue to be reformed again within a space of origins.

It was *Kiralık Konak* that took the older trope of the house as a place of moral identity and rooted this moral identity in the symbolic universe of the past. Thus it was *Kiralık Konak* that gave the house the sense of pastness that origins and formation need. This is the whole thrust of collective memory. In *Fatih-Harbiye*, the remembered space of the past was also defined as the old wooden house, but one that allowed a place for the past to continue the formative functions that collective memory assigned it. Unlike Naim Efendi's house, Faiz Bey's house was not shut off from the present by intimations of demise but was a place for the most basic self to remain alive and evolve while other definitions of self were being transformed or erased. It is for this reason that the Turkish house became such a vital and long-lived sign of identity. It became the sanctuary for memory when no other place was available. It was thus positioned as the bridge in a time of rupture, a source of identity at a time of identity crisis. It was a place to negotiate this rupture, to figure out how to use and evaluate the past in and for the present.

Although it may seem anachronistic to call this old wooden house "the Turkish house" and to align it with Turkish cultural identity, by bringing the past into the present, this alignment becomes clear and valid. Literary works both uncover cultural identity and contribute to the meaning of what increasingly was being called "the Turkish house." The movement that began in 1912 (when Hamdullah Suphi described the old house as a place "where everything was Turkish") was taken up with enthusiasm in the 1930s, the time when cultural identity, the term *Turkish*, and the old wooden house became permanently merged in the Turkish imaginary.

Anatolia. Juxtaposition of the new and the old gives a quaint atmosphere to the Turkish house. La Turque Kemaliste, *no. 18, April 1937.*

FIVE

The
New Turkish
Landscape
and the
Desire to
Remember

I even began to have doubts that I had ever lived in that wooden house.

The konak life of Naim Efendi came to a close in 1908. In 1910, perhaps somewhat prematurely, Ahmet Midhat wrote in his novel *Jön Türk* (*Young Turk*) that "today the expression *konak yavrusu* (a konak-chick, or mini-konak) has become an expression that is out of use and forgotten. 'Konak' is gone, let alone mini-konak."[1] In 1927, the twenty-four-year-old journalist and historian Refik Ahmet Sevengil described konak interiors as if his readers had no image of them, including how the seating was organized around the wall and what covered it.[2] I say that this was somewhat premature, as authors like Yakup Kadri and Peyami Safa have shown that konaks, yalıs, and wooden houses were not only alive in the contemporary collective memory but had a strong resonance as a true spiritual home. They were both a space of retreat from the fearful aspects of modern culture and a mental stage on which to play out these feelings, a place to come to terms with modernity and identity.

However, it is true that before the middle of the twentieth century, the palatial konaks of the viziers and the mahalle pashas, such as Rabia's mentor Selim Pasha in *Sinekli Bakkal*, had all but disappeared as residences from Istanbul and the provincial capitals. Those that remained had been transformed into schools or government institutes, such as the Darü'l-Elhan, where Neriman and Şinasi studied music in the 1920s. The smaller konaks, the *konak yavrusu*, or the slightly larger types lived in by extended families such as Naim Efendi's had been subdivided into smaller units or torn down. Faiz Bey's wooden house in Fatih survived somewhat longer; perhaps it is still there today. But with the rapid modernization and population changes of the new republic, it soon became an anachronism and an anomaly, and only the newly urban shared domiciles under its roof.

I would like to position the memory that was held in these novels and stories within the architectural landscape that had begun to develop during this period of change, especially the architectural landscape that was being advertised as symbolic of the young republic. Two types of republican-era architecture are relevant here. The first is the modernist house style called "*kübik*"; the second is the style of public architecture called the Second National Style, which incorporated formal elements of Ottoman-period domestic architecture. Although the first, the kübik, actually served to bring into focus what was disappearing—that is, Turkishness—still, both the kübik and the Second National Style were counterimages that worked to contest or erase the primacy of meaning and normative values that the narrative (textual) image of the Ottoman-period house had come to represent.

THE PROBLEM WITH THE NEW HOUSE: EARLY MODERNISM IN TURKISH DOMESTIC ARCHITECTURE

Modernism in Turkish architecture was a conscious strategy of the Kemalist revolution. The new Turkish Republic refined and reforged the principles of nationalism and populism that had flowered during the period of the II Meşrutiyet, the period when Hodja Ali Rıza Bey and Rıfat Osman were painting urban landscapes of wooden houses, when Hamdullah Suphi was positioning them as a symbol of Turkish nationalism, and when Ziya Gökalp was giving this nationalism its theoretical support. By 1931, Atatürk had codified "Revolutionism" as one of the ideological themes of the Turkish Republic, along with "Etatism, Republicanism, Nationalism, Populism, and Secularism." Revolutionism was actually a lightly veiled code word for modernization along Western lines. In fact, the words revolution and modernization were often synonymous, and articles that discussed the modernization of art and architecture had titles such as "Revolution in Art and Architecture."[3]

Modernization had already been given visual expression in the West in the architectural movement called modernism, and Turkey was quick to adopt this style. Architectural modernism had been developed and refined in Europe and America by Mies van der Rohe, Frank Lloyd Wright, Walter Gropius, and Le Corbusier. Le Corbusier was an especially vocal theorist of modernism as the ultimate expression of the rational, the universal, and the secular. In terms of domestic architecture, he conceived of the ideal house as "a machine for living," with designs based on engineering achievements in bridge building and steamship construction and on modern institutional materials such as concrete and sheet glass. His popularity in the West was brought home to Turkey by the Turkish architects who had studied with him, such as Sedad Hakkı Eldem, or by other Western-educated architects who were invited to Turkey to design and to teach; their work and ideas were featured in popular publications as well as in professional journals.[4]

The spirit of the modernist movement in architecture that had taken over the West, and that movement's emphasis on universalism rather than regionalism, was suitable for a new republic that was eager to identify with European civilization. Modernism was chosen by Atatürk and quickly put in service to make a public visual statement that "modernization" was in force; that is, that the young republic had made the transition from an Islamic-Eastern-Ottoman cultural base to a Western one. Ankara, as the new capital, was to be built as a symbol of these new ideals, and its success was regarded as synonymous with the success of the regime.

Modernism in architecture replaced Turkey's First National Style (ca 1917–1927), a style that had made the official transition from a nationalism based on Ottomanism to the Turkish nationalism of the new Turkish Republic. The First National Style was historicizing, with decorative programs meant to recall Ottoman religious architecture, but with a structure that was rooted in the West, in terms of both forms and materials. It was a style used almost exclusively for monumental buildings, especially for the first public buildings in the new capital in Ankara. But Atatürk was not happy with this style: it took too long to build,[5] it demanded expertise in Ottoman crafts that no longer existed, and it required materials that were too expensive. Most important, the First National Style privileged a past that Atatürk wanted to discredit and erase as a site of solidarity and loyalty.

The last official building that was built in this style was Arif Koyunoğlu's Turkish Hearth Society Building in Ankara, begun in 1927, shown and discussed in Chapter 2. But even as it was being built, a radical move toward modernism in architecture, with its faster and cheaper construction methods, had already begun. Sometimes referred to as the functional-rational style,[6] it was championed by the state and the press and led by Theodor Post, Bruno Taut, Paul Bonatz, Clemens Holzmeister, and especially Ernst Egli,

Ankara, School for Girls, 1930. Ernst Egli, architect. From La Turque Kemaliste.

who took charge of the architectural curricula in the Turkish Academy of Fine Arts.

These foreign architects were given most of the major government commissions,[7] leaving private and residential architecture to the local Turkish architects whom they had trained. Although most of the population would come to live in engineer-designed concrete block apartments, there was an important entry into house design by Turkish architects, and their houses were publicly discussed and desired. They, too, were modernists, and although they were neither restricted nor supported by public sector funds, their house designs accepted the purist movement of Le Corbusier, whose modernism fit Atatürk's needs perfectly.

A PRESSURE COOKER AND A PICTURE WINDOW:

THE TURKISH *KÜBIK*

There is here no longer any question of custom, nor of tradition, nor of construction, nor of adaptation to utilitarian needs. Contour and profile are a pure creation of the mind; they call for the plastic art.[8]

The cubic house (*Kübik Ev*) was the modernist, Bauhaus version of domestic architecture preferred in Turkey. These houses were reinforced concrete

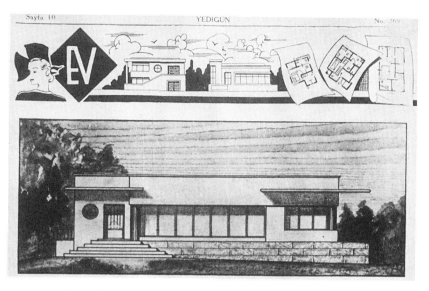

Banner for series on modern homes: A kübik house. Yedigün 269:10, 1938.

structures with unadorned surfaces; they had a flat roof, wide glass windows, rounded building corners and entrances, cantilevered terraces, and simple cubic volumes covered with cement. These were the first new houses of the republic built in Ankara, but they graced Istanbul and the smaller towns as well. As an internationally recognized symbol of the new and the modern, the scientific and the rational, and as a highly visible ideal in contemporary Turkish magazines, these houses were carriers of the desire to be modern, with all its attendant norms and values.

The Turkish architects who were designing these local modernist houses organized their own Association of Turkish Architects (*Türk Yüksek Mimarlar Derneği*) in 1927 in Ankara. Inspired by the French architectural journal *Aujourdhui*, which privileged the work of Le Corbusier, in 1931 they began their own journal, *Mimar/Arkitekt*, which became one of the longest-living magazines in the world.[9] Its founders were Zeki Sayar, Abidin Mortaş, and Abdullah Ziya Kozanoğlu. These young architects gathered at night to talk about modernist styles, about the cubic house and about Bauhaus, and saw themselves as revolutionary leaders of modernization.[10] It was they who adopted the Kübik house as one of the first symbols of modernism in Turkey[11] and as a form meant to change the meaning of domestic space, for the republican discourse on modernism had a strong domestic component, with the house as the center of a small nuclear family.[12]

The meaning of the new house was explained in popular journals that discussed at length how to furnish a "modern interior" in order to lead the life of the republican ideal, with motherhood as a national duty and the home as the space of national renewal.[13] The wife, living without servants or a mother-in-law, was to be responsible for the home, and the new kitchen designed for her was referred to in magazine ads, such as in the "Home" and "Furniture" sections of *Yedigün*, as the *kadın salonu* (the woman's room or woman's domain). The modern house was applauded because it needed little upkeep, allowing the mother to spend several hours a day outside, for example at the park with her children.[14] Women were also encouraged to work outside the home, and therefore the idealized environment was a house with the necessary labor-saving devices of modern life, such as electric dishwashers and pressure cookers. The idealized republican-era house introduced a life that was that of "the European [where] the house is a special and private place reflecting [one's] *individuality*."[15] The modern woman was portrayed as faced with modern dilemmas, whether to work outside the home or to find personal satisfaction inside, and in the nuclear family. In 1932 a (Ms.) Muzaffer wrote in the woman's journal *Muhit* that she had worked outside the home for many years but found it *personally* unsatisfying and full of the anxieties produced by a desire for money:

> I had spent the years before I added a child to my family life at work entirely outside our house. I had a rather good paying job at the Ziraat Bank. I had earned the respect and confidence of the establishment. I was so identified with my work that I found it laughable that an educated and intelligent girl could live enthusiastically by taking care of a house, and as a wife and mother.[16]

But when she quit her job and moved to a small house, she found a fulfilling life in self-improvement activities, in reading the classics so that she could talk intelligently to her husband, in giving little dinner parties, and in raising a garden and raising her children. Women, although encouraged to have professional lives outside the house, were also idealized as the center of its operation, or at least conceived of as equal partners with their husbands. There was also some fear that women would embrace this freedom with such gusto that they would never return to take care of the home. In any event, the emphasis had shifted to the house as the center of individuals, making individual decisions about their own happiness. This emphasizes, too, the changed role of the father, who was no longer depicted as the sole spiritual authority of the house and the source of its stability. Actually, there was no image of spiritual authority attached to the modern house at all. In fact, the feelings that the house calls forth in *Kiralık Konak* and *Fatih-Harbiye*, of a deep interior identity but with moral and traditional attachment to the larger family and mahalle, were being reworked as a republican exteriority, with an insistence on the nuclear family and kitchen appliances. In the 1930s and early 1940s the deep feelings of the old house were politicized as both anti-modern and anti-republican, making interiority, family, and spirituality hard to talk about openly. But clearly a lifestyle based on an isolated nuclear family instead of the larger one set in a mahalle, a lifestyle that privileged individuality instead of the group and that focused on the outside rather than the inside, was a revolutionary change.

The house had been an important site of modernization in the late Ottoman era as well. In the late nineteenth century the Ottoman "tray culture" was replaced by eating at tables, and a piano had become the centerpiece of social gatherings,[17] both of which signaled Western tastes and a desire to change one's cultural identity. Naim Efendi's son-in-law Servet Bey's refurnishing of his father-in-law's konak with Western furniture is but one example of the painfulness of this process. As early as Ahmet Midhat's book of etiquette in 1894,[18] books and articles had given readers a model for living a contemporary life in a contemporary home; these primers of the Occidental lifestyle continued til the mid-1950s.

But whereas in the late Ottoman period, the symbols of social change had privileged the interior, the new revolution involved the exterior of the house as well. These houses built in the kübik style were pierced by large plate glass windows that opened out to the public street. Thus, the examples of this new international style that covered the pages of *Mimar/Arkitekt*, as well as the weekly issues of *Yedigün* and other popular magazines of the early 1930s especially, were the exact opposite of the inward-looking Ottoman house that was set above the street and that enclosed a large family within its garden walls. It was these depictions of small houses ("*Küçük Evler*") that hoped to redefine the tastes of the middle classes in every urban center. Even in the remote Anatolian town of Safranbolu they said that every bride hoped for

> a Motherless husband
> a smokeless chimney
> a pressure cooker
> and a picture window[19]

Although kübik houses were indeed built, they were more of a modern-ist ideal than a reality, and even in Ankara there were very few, certainly far fewer than one would expect from their appearance in magazines and from the ideological service they were called on to perform. Modernism was an elitist move, and the few kübik houses that were built were commissioned and owned by a small group.[20] In actuality, most of Istanbul and Ankara's small houses were not kübik, just concrete.

However, the desire to be modern surely extended to a very wide class that consisted of the many military and civilian officials who were the most important members of the "newly modernized" population of Ankara. This population could not be accommodated in architect-commissioned houses but were housed in projects of tiny homes and small apartments.

But the ideal kübik house that was continually in the public gaze, if out of the public reach, could be appropriated, at least as it applied to interior design, even by apartment dwellers: they need only purchase the inexpensive modern furniture, called "cubic furniture" (*kübik eşya*), and they could be linked to the entire project or ideology of modernization just by sitting down. In the 1930s, to live in the kübik house, or in its cheaper concrete replacement with cubic-style furnishings, would be to live at the end of history, in the era of cleanli-ness and health, that is, in the era of hot water and electricity: "On entering

Government villas, Yenişehir, Ankara. La Turque Kemaliste, no. 20, August 1937.

the house from the street, no pressure is felt in the lungs/liver. . . . The walls are plain, with a cheerful tone [and they] inspire people to cleanliness."[21]

Following Le Corbusier, the metaphor of cleanliness to represent the new was joined by one of light as one of the most important images of modern living. In a 1927 issue of *Hakimiyet-i Milliye* (Sovereign Nation), the new style of house was contrasted with the old: "The founders of new Ankara want simple and comfortable houses. . . . This attitude represents great progress from the past . . . the grills adored by Loti no longer decorate the windows of the new city. Modern hygiene demanding ample light and air . . . has vanquished one of the oldest traditions."[22]

In the 1930s, a journalist in the weekly magazine *Yedigün* wrote, "Whereas the moonlight reigned in the old houses, the rule of the sun is beginning in the glass-enclosed buildings of today."[23]

This rhetoric of light and cleanliness versus dark and unclean is a part of an Orientalist model of East versus West. But it was also part of modernism's international rhetoric. In Turkey, as the kübik, concrete, and plate glass were internalized as defining a preferred architectural space, there was an alienation from the traditional. That is, the kübik house called to mind another, unnamed house, the "large wooden houses with spacious 'sofas' no longer appropriate for our machine age with its changes in mentality and lifestyle."[24]

What the government required and modernism expected, in Istanbul, Ankara, and elsewhere, was that the new republic's population would come out of the dark ages, obliquely aligned with the old wooden Ottoman-period house, and into the light of modernism, clearly identified as the concrete kübik, or at least with concrete. Thus, the modernist rhetoric arguably kept the old house alive in memory as that which should be left behind during the march toward the present.

Yet at the same time, old houses were kept alive in the imagination because of a parallel dissatisfaction with architectural modernism. The affective or feeling aspect of modern architecture had been criticized by authors such as Yalçın in his *"Ev Sevgisi"* article in 1935, but the architecture itself was also addressed in literature. In his 1934 *Ankara*, Yakup Kadri ridiculed the newly modern "Republican Bourgeoisie" of military and civilian officials who had abandoned the old-style house in favor of the kübik:

> They too used to live in a house with a tower and overhanging eaves. Later, like all the other families, they were affected by a consuming urge for the Modern. Hakkı Bey outdid everyone else in the matter

of a house and displayed the first example of the cubist to everybody. Hakkı Bey's house became the first of the buildings with glazed corners, lacquered doors and ceilings hollowed out for concealed electrical installations.[25]

When Yakup Kadri described the interiors of the new houses, it was abundantly clear that the kübik was not universally accepted: "Couches like dentists' chairs, seats like operation tables, sofas resembling the interiors of automobiles, and finally, scattered all over these, some weird, grotesque knick-knacks."[26]

Thus it might be said that the kübik was not only not universally accepted as a national house, it brought the old house to mind. This was the old house, of course, that the earlier republicans had begun to portray as a symbol of the Turkishness of the new nation. But these nationalists had truly conceived of "the Turkish house" as an image in the imagination, for it was not to be rebuilt or restored. Rather, it was conceived of as an inspirational image. In 1923, the Turkish house that Suphi had tied to Turkish heritage through "our grandfathers" had been offered by Ünver "as a guide to others who want to build a functional and national house."[27] In 1927, Arif Hikmet Koyunoğlu had designed a Turkish Salon in the Turkish Hearth Building, hoping that "Turkish" domestic forms would become the basis of a new national architecture.[28] Although the kübik was offered as an architectural style that would represent the republic as quintessentially modern, it was met by a parallel discourse that remembered the Turkish house as not only local but "modern at its core." If it were to experience a revival, the 1930s would have been its time.[29]

DISMANTLING THE TURKISH HOUSE: SEDAD HAKKI ELDEM, THE SECOND NATIONAL STYLE, AND THE NEW TURKISH HOUSE

By the early 1930s it was becoming clear that a distinctively local national style was necessary, at least for public buildings. In 1934 the new Commission of Buildings under the Ministry of Public Works decreed that "a Turkish National Style" should be developed, although what this style was to look like was not specified. The architectural profession was certain, however, that this new architecture should be designed by Turks and that it should have a "Turkish" form. In part this was a way to protest their secondary position vis-à-vis the European architects to whom the government routinely awarded its commissions.[30] In part, however, there was a sense that a national architecture would not be "authentic" if it wasn't rooted in the Turkish collective memory and experience. When the Austrian Clemens Holzmeister arrived in Ankara in 1927 to begin a long career of designing state buildings, Arif Hikmet Koyunoğlu wrote a newspaper article "welcoming" him:

> Welcome Holzmeister. It is an appropriate [time to] open a new architectural era in this country. . . . Yet it is necessary to think of a Turkish modern architecture that this nation will like. Ankara is a new capital, [but] only Turkish architects can determine the identity of this city. Architect Holzmeister is a talented person with a respectable position. But he is not the person to understand our country's revolution, and build its edifices.[31]

There was a sense, then, that a national architecture should be rooted in the experience and knowledge of the people of Turkey as well as be relevant to Turkish history, for only in this way could it tie the present to the past and the past to a place.

In 1927 Sedad Hakkı Eldem had been a student of architecture at the Turkish Fine Arts Academy, spending his free time drawing the old houses and palaces of Istanbul.[32] In 1928 he had left Turkey to study the modernism of Le Corbusier in Paris and to continue his research on old Turkish houses. In 1930 he returned to Turkey to join the faculty of the Academy of Fine Arts. Thus, by 1934, when the Commission of Buildings called for a Turkish national style, Eldem was ready, poised at the crossroads of Turkish history.[33] Eldem was the one architect in a position to crystallize the general feeling expressed in essays and editorials: that there was a need for an architecture that was both modern and national, and that it should be designed by a Turk.

Thus, in 1934 Eldem began his now famous seminar on national architecture at the Fine Arts Academy in Istanbul, which he organized around the Turkish house as the definitive element of a national style.[34] It is at this moment, then, and with this seminar that the old wooden Ottoman-period house could be made fully and permanently *Turkish*.[35]

Eldem set up a curriculum in which his students went into as many towns in Anatolia as they could to intricately document their remaining vernacular architecture—that is, "Turkish houses"—with drawings, photographs, and measurements.[36] These students were convinced that they were accessing something that was essentially Turkish when in fact they were appropriating for themselves forms that had been designed, built, and lived in by

Jews, Christian Greeks, and Christian Armenians, as well as Muslims of various ethnicities, and all of them during the Ottoman period.[37] Perhaps it is Eldem's voice that is heard in the dissertation of one of his students, who wrote on the houses of Ankara:

> We can read the Turkish character inside these houses [and] we have no difficulty in feeling the Turkish taste in their architecture and their decoration. All of the buildings of this type have a single spirit [ruh], the Turkish spirit.[38]

Eldem analyzed and synthesized this information in order to understand the Turkish house according to a set of typologies, such as room placement, window types, and roof eaves,[39] which he considered to be their common and thus essential characteristics. It was these typologies that were to be made available as a resource for a national style.

Eldem's seminar also marked the moment when Turkish architects began to be trained in increasing numbers, all of whom, by participating in Eldem's collecting and typologizing, were groomed to value the aesthetics of the Turk-ish house as an icon of Turkishness. In 1937 an architectural department was opened in the Istanbul Engineering School (which became Istanbul Techni-cal University in 1946). This department followed the lead of Eldem, so that both departments directed dissertation work toward the documentation of Turkish vernacular forms. By the late 1940s, more than three hundred prac-ticing Turkish architects in Turkey had been trained in these departments.[40]

The Turkish house was now positioned for a revival and thus might have been restored visually to the place that it deserved emotionally. If this had happened, the architecture of the 1930s and early 40s would have had an important place on the trajectory of memory about the Turkish house, with all the changes and reinterpretations in meaning that the idea of memory implies. But this did not happen, for the Second National Style was not a discourse about the Turkish house, or even about houses. It was a discourse about public architecture, nationalism, and modernism.

In 1940, Eldem published his first definitive statement on this national idiom, "Toward Local Architecture" ("*Yerli Mimariye Doğru*"), in which he suggested how the inspiration for modern public buildings would come from Anatolian residential construction methods, materials, and styles.[41] The structural forms that Eldem identified as salient to the vernacular and the domestic were to be used as the basis for the entire national style, which com-prised primarily public buildings; but private and domestic buildings were

Istanbul, Taşlık. The Oriental Café, Şark Kahvesi, 1947. Sedad Hakki Eldem, architect. Photograph from Arkitekt, *1950, 207–210.*

included as well.[42] The most common exterior design element of the Second National Style, and one used by both foreign and local architects, was the protruding bay or *cumba*. In his own practice, Eldem used this Turkish residential form on buildings such as the Faculties of Sciences and Letters (*Fen ve Edebiyat Fakülteleri*) of the University of Istanbul in 1944, built with Emin Onat.

These buildings carry the projecting cumbas and eaves and the uniform windows of the Turkish house, as well as references to domestic interior ceilings. One of Eldem's most beautiful buildings, now gone, was the Oriental Café (*Şark Kahvesi*), which emphasized the cumba or the windowed room that projects from the upper story, with its row of uniform windows. One of his most famous buildings does this, too. This is the Social Security Complex in Istanbul (1963–1970).

Although completed after the close of the Second National Style, the Social Security Complex continues its program of using local forms with new materials.[43] The Social Security Complex recalls the spatial use of a *mahalle*. Although its series of cumbas are concrete, it is sensitive to the mahalle in scale and sense of movement and enclosure.[44]

The use of residential forms in public buildings was not out of line with Ottoman practices: mahalle medresses were often externally similar to mahalle houses; what looked like a konak on the outside was often a school

Istanbul. Social Security Complex, Yildiz Mahallesi, 1976–1978. Sedad Hakki Eldem, architect. Photograph by Carel Bertram, 1990.

on the inside; the mahalle pasha's konak often operated as a court of justice; and the external walls of urban warehouses (*hans*) might be articulated with cumbas and protrusions that were similar to domestic ones. Therefore, although it is tempting to suggest that the Second National Style blurred the visual lines between domestic and public forms, this blurring had historical precedent.

But what is important in terms of a trajectory of the image of the Turkish house is that the Second National Style of Architecture was never an attempt to revive or even recall what the Turkish house meant, that is, the interior lifestyle that these older forms enclosed. Because of their use on public buildings, the message of these domestic forms was purely an external message of national identity and national unity. Typologizing the house served this purpose directly, as it ignored references to differences, whether they were regional or ethnic, related to class or to use, and thus eliminated any discussion of cultural purposes served. House forms such as projecting eaves, cumbas, and rows of windows that were purified of the particularities of the population became acceptable signifiers of the collective past of a single "nationality."

Look for a moment at Eldem's Oriental Café in Taşlık, Istanbul. Indisputably elegant and tragically destroyed during the construction of Istanbul's Swiss Hotel, the Oriental Café looked like a giant cumba or *şahnişin* with exaggerated eaves; it had an upper story with no lower one. Still, with its veneer of wood and beautifully proportioned windows, it recalled more than anything else a view of the house from the street. But this modern cumba was not a house, it was a café. And unlike the mahalle café, which was always at ground level and frequented by neighborhood men, Eldem's café served as a restaurant for the Westernized elite, making it closer in function and conception to the Viennese café than to the traditional Turkish *kahve*.[45] Thus, to the extent that the Second National Style was an attempt to synthesize modernism and regionalism in order to provide a sense of historical continuity, it was doomed to failure. When the house was fragmented into its typological essences and then when these fragments were repositioned in places that were foreign to their origins or use and unrelated to their original scale and proportion, these new buildings lost the ability to become players in memory. Rather, they became reminders that the Second National Style was a mark of discontinuity, if not of a memory disorder. The dismembered house-that-was-not-a-house could not recall to memory the lived or valued past, and may well have provided a sense of loss rather than a sense of place. Further confusing the meaning of these forms, in Eldem's case at least, was his use of Turkish house forms on buildings that were not signifiers of Turkishness in anyway at all, such as the Dutch (1973–1977) and Indian (1976–1980) embassies in Ankara, with their projecting eaves and modular windows.

But Eldem, and the other architects who worked in the Second National Style, built houses too. However, even these houses existed outside the margins of the imagined Turkish house and worked consistently, even consciously, against memory.

THE MOST IMPORTANT MESSAGE IS THAT THE OLD TURKISH HOUSE IS CLOSE TO THE MODERN HOUSE OF TODAY TO A SURPRISING EXTENT.

In 1936, Sedad Hakkı Eldem built a home for Atatürk's close friend, Ahmet Ağaoğlu, in Maçka, below Nişantaşı, the neighborhood adjacent to Şişli in Istanbul.[46] It was a house within the modernist, "kübik" vision but one in which he carefully incorporated formal elements of the Turkish house. The exterior of the Ağaoğlu house had two projecting rooms that were suggestive of the Ottoman cumba. These cumbas had defined the profile of the house-tasvir in the Karagöz puppet theater and had signaled a particular way of life in From Cumba to Rumba. However, the Ağaoğlu cumbas do not project over the street to catch the breezes and expand the view but are positioned over front and side gardens, and are thus not a part of the streetscape. On the front of the house, the cumba is a rounded protrusion of the inner oval sofa, which acts as a şahnişin, but its overhang provides no shade for passersby, although it does project over the entry door. But the massing of the window glass of these cumbas makes this house quintessentially kübik, even though these windows are protected from the sun by emphatic Ottoman-style eaves. Bozdoğan calls the stylistic references to the Turkish house a "tradition-conscious gesture."[47] On the inside, the oval, Baroque-style sofa is not given its traditional central position in the house, in which it once opened to private rooms. Rather, the Ağaoğlu sofa has become a Western sitting room that is separated from a Western-style bedroom and dining room. It is not a choice reminiscent of most Turkish houses, and it is not made of wood.[48]

Another residence of Eldem's, the Ayaşlı Yalı, on the Bosphorus, built in 1938, was more identifiably "Turkish" and praised for its local character. It was built for Münevver Ayaşlı (1909–1999), a novelist who knew the life of the old yalis and wrote about them.[49] As part of a modernized Bosphorus Yalı, its facade was characterized by a row of uniform windows, which became a signature of Eldem's and reappears throughout the following decades as a

Istanbul. Nişantaşı/Maçka Mahallesi, exterior of the Ahmet Ağaoğlu house, 1936–1937.
Sedad Hakki Eldem, architect. Arkitekt, *1938, 213–217.*

Istanbul. Nişantaşı/Maçka Mahallesi, interior of the Ahmet Ağaoğlu House, 1936–1937.
Sedad Hakki Eldem, architect. Arkitekt, *1938, 213–217.*

type in itself. That is, the Second National Style house represented neither a continuing evolution nor a reconstruction or revival but a conscious and conscientious vector of modernism. But it was a Turkish modernism. One rationale of Eldem and his students for using Turkish house forms for residential architecture (as opposed to their semiotic purposes on public buildings) was that the Turkish house was thought to be already quintessentially or prototypically modern, and the typologies of the Turkish house were used to prove this.

In 1942, Eldem gave a lecture titled "The Turkish House" at the Ankara Halkevi[50] in which he denigrated the kübik style that was filling the urban landscape: "But what kind of Kübik [do we see]? Imported kübik. One resembles a German house, one Italian, the other French. But a real Turkish house? This you will not find."[51] He then explains that the way to develop a nationally sensitive Turkish architecture is to base it on the old house: "[M]any nations are able to find a modern architecture by grafting on to their old architecture. And we too, have no other way to go but this."[52]

When he describes and evaluates the old Turkish house, however, he uses modernist criteria:

> The system of built-in furniture demanded in the modern house exists in ours from the old days. [In the old Turkish house,] besides cupboards, there are niches [hücre], shelves, lamp niches, clock niches, every thing is thought of as part of the house and is built in to its walls. Heavy portable furniture is not to be found. Isn't this fundamental to what is required in all modern houses? Furthermore, the bedroom can be used as a sitting room during the day. In Europe doesn't everyone have divans that can turn into beds? Aren't American beds that can be hidden in a closet a modernized version of our old bed? Furthermore, aren't Europeans now making the same wide seating [sedirs] that we used to sit on? Aren't the fireplaces that we had in our rooms being replicated in today's fireplaces? And above all, isn't the local tile that is used in the houses of Rumeli[53] just like the tile that they are making in Germany? . . . The most important message is that the old Turkish house is close to the modern house of today to a surprising extent.[54]

For Eldem, the Turkish house satisfied the most crucial element of modernism: universality. Le Corbusier had made universality basic to the modernist project when he said, "I propose one single building for all nations and all climates . . . a universal logic devoid of historical and regional references."[55] In 1928, Koyunoğlu had established that "Turkish houses" not only met but anticipated modern conditions of light, ventilation, warmth, and hygiene. So it was natural that by the 1930s, the Turkish house was promoted as a universal house, perhaps the "original" universal house. And, as we have seen, Koyunoğlu had even put out a call: "We expect from Turkish architects the modern Turkish house and its definitive form."[56] Therefore, all that was necessary to find a "modern," yet local, Turkish domestic architecture was to put traditional eaves onto concrete houses that were built according to modernist principles.

Eldem was not alone in the thought that a new Turkish house could be made from the elements of the old one, given a modernist cast, and be cast in concrete. Even non-Turks, such as André Gabriel (the French archeologist and architectural historian of Anatolia), claimed that Istanbul houses were actually modern and would yield better results than cubist architecture if only wood were replaced by concrete.[57]

The Turkish house that was prototypically modern thus served an important ideological purpose; it made "Turkish culture" seem to be both a universal culture and a modern culture. But as a modernist project, the fragmented, typologized, and then reconstructed Turkish house could not serve a mnemonic function.[58] Because Eldem's Turkish house is not an "evolved" Turkish house or even a "simulated" Turkish house, and therefore not a believable Turkish house, one that recalls visually the matrix of meanings embedded in memory, that is, the interiority of the inhabitants or their relationship to the street and the mahalle, it could at best become a memory site with its memory removed. For its purpose was to evoke and support a modern lifestyle, that is, individual actors or the nuclear family divorced from the mahalle.

Nonetheless, Eldem's work was clearly pivotal for the image of the Turkish house in the public imagination, for it was his project that cemented the old wooden house as the visual centerpiece of Turkish collective memory. Although the appellation "Turkish house" had been in use as a nationalist concept since the very beginning of the republic, because of Eldem's work, the work of his students, and his own visibility as a teacher and lecturer, it became permanently linked to the old wooden house from this moment on. Eldem's students' fieldwork, on which he based his modules and typologies, was consistently based on the timber-framed Ottoman-period house. Eldem's own drawings include some stone and mud-brick houses as well as wooden ones, and he was interested in the wide spectrum of Anatolian vernacular, not all of which is wooden. Nonetheless, his own work supported the timber-framed house as the quintessential Turkish house.

Thus it was Eldem who catapulted the old wooden house into the position of the Turkish house par excellence, and it remains the sign of the Turkish urban heritage to this day. Furthermore, it was Eldem who embedded in the imagination the idea that the Turkish house was intrinsically modern, although as we have seen, this idea had been taken up before. The speech that Eldem gave at the Ankara People's House (*Ankara Halkevi*), from which I quoted extensively above, emphasized this modernity to "a large and interested audience."[59] This speech was then published in the Halkevi's central journal, *Ulku*, and in the *Turkish Touring Association Bulletin* as well.[60]

Although I have discounted Eldem's houses (or others built in the Second National Style) as contributing to the longevity or meaning of memory, his articles and speeches made a direct contribution to a contemporary popular awareness of the Turkish house as an imaged and imagined place.[61] However, Eldem's greatest contribution to the Turkish imaginary was through his students, and thus to the future of scholarship about the Turkish house. This is a lasting tribute to him, and it cannot be overstated. The format of research that Eldem's students followed, that is, drawing, photographing, and describing, set the precedent for studies of the Turkish vernacular that continue to this day. Although it is only recently that scholars have included cultural questions in their work, those who followed Eldem's careful descriptive procedures continue to produce rich sources of information for preservationists and historians alike.

When popular works on the Turkish House began to appear in the 1970s, they carried Eldem's voice. These popular works both privileged the old wooden house and showed how it had been made forever modern. This was especially evident when they applied notions from architectural modernism such as Le Corbusier's concept of "human scale" to the Turkish house. For example, there is a shelf that runs the circumference of the room between the ceiling and the top of the sash windows. This shelf defines the useful sector of the room and therefore is used for display items but not for items of daily use. Above this shelf are the nonopening, decorative windows, below it are windows that can be manipulated for light and air. Küçükerman, who wrote the earliest popular books on the Turkish house, suggested that this "man-shelf relationship" (*raf-kişi ilişkisi*) represented the human scale and humane quality of the Turkish room (see page 29).[62]

Very few houses were actually built in the Second National Style. And, except for Eldem's yalıs, the houses that were built were soon torn down and forgotten, verifying their inability to find a place in the Turkish imagination. Furthermore, even the most nationalist of its designers were consistently eclectic, suggesting the wide range of client demand. Eldem himself was fully so. In 1934, the same year that he established his seminar for a national architecture, he designed the Electric Company building in Fındıklı, Istanbul, using the purist modernism of Le Corbusier.[63] In 1936, as he was designing the Ağaoğlu house, he was also building a Japanese modern house on the island of Büyükada off the coast of Istanbul. With the new economic structure and international leanings of Turkey that developed after World War II, the Second National Style project was all but abandoned, and in 1950 Eldem, as the local consultant for the Istanbul Hilton, ushered in Turkey's complete immersion in the International style.

Eldem, even as the exemplar of the Second National Style, had no interest in repeating or even preserving the past; he only wanted to go back to it to get somewhere else. That somewhere else was modernity. His historicizing architecture, whether public or domestic, and although brilliant and memorable individually, was therefore a method to un-think the past. His own buildings, and buildings of those who designed similarly, did nothing to preserve the image of the Turkish house as a memory image; rather, they served to give the built Turkish house a definitive closure. In fact, as we have seen, architecture by itself can never preserve meaning, for meaning does not reside in it but in the realm of thought. The novels I have discussed underscore how meaning exists in accumulated ideas about behavior and belief, and how it is then preserved in the imaginary of collective memory, to be awakened and "felt real" by contemporary emotions. Thus, although the Second National Style was seemingly a struggle to perpetuate old memories by giving them modern meanings, it could do no such thing, as it untied this emotive connection between memory and old buildings. It might even be said that the Second National Style, although in part a response to the kübik, which had no tie to local memory, produced an amnesia—an amnesia that made people forget that what they really wanted to do was to remember.

And a longing for memory did emerge. It emerged at the end of the 1930s, along with the formal rejection of the kübik; it took shape in the 1940s, and continued into the 1950s, after which Turkish society and its urban fabric changed again. Thus, the meanings that became embedded in the Turkish house, along with the effort concerted to remember and preserve it, continued to resonate even after most of these houses had disappeared.

Istanbul. A disappearing Ottoman konak. Photograph by Carel Bertram, 1996.

Amasya. The first intrusion of concrete and apartment buildings, in the 1950s. Amfora, Ocak 1993, 4.

THE DESIRE TO REMEMBER

Why was there a desire to remember? Obviously, memory is a key to cultural identity and emotion-laden values, and the house is one of its important sites. But why, beginning in the late 1930s, was there a sudden interest in memory? Why was memory felt to be in jeopardy? There were two immediate reasons, and a third as well.

First, the old houses that we have identified as sites of memory were disappearing. The konaks, wooden houses, and quiet streets of the Ottoman neighborhoods were being sold and rebuilt, the gardens of the summerhouses were being subdivided into apartments. As a corollary to this, the population of the new neighborhoods had changed with the sudden influx of immigrants from former Ottoman provinces or the Anatolian countryside.[64]

Second, the people who could remember the Ottoman period, the cohort who had lived in a pre-1908 life-world, the world that had taken on the shape of the past, were gone or aging; and now their children would have only second-hand memories to relay. In this way, the past was seen to be "slipping away."[65] Even Neriman, born about 1908, depended on stories about her grandmother in order to access the "real life" of the konaks.

The loss of houses and the impending loss of people to talk about them generated a rush to collect and preserve a past that was related to one's grand-

Amasya. A mid-nineteenth-century Armenian house in Amasya, now the İlk Pension. Photograph by Carel Bertram, 1992.

mothers and grandfathers, that is, to preserve the memories the old houses held. One of the first to collect the memories related to houses and neighborhoods was a student of Hodja Ali Rıza Bey's, Sermet Muhtar Alus (1887–1952). A journalist and a novelist, he gathered anecdotes about Istanbul life at the time of his own childhood, that is, at the turn of the twentieth century, as well as from "as far back as anyone could remember," that is, Istanbul in 1848, in the "İstanbulin period."[66] In 1936, at the age of forty-nine, he began a series of articles in the journal *Tan* (Dawn) called "What Do the Old Konaks Have to Tell Us?" (*Eski Konaklar bize neler anlatıyor?*),[67] which told about the owners of konaks, yalıs, and köşks and the "life" they had lived. For example, he wrote about the yalıs that had been built over the water on pilings and that still could be seen "up to 30 or 40 years ago."

> They were in an *alaturka* architectural style, their upper floors had çıkmas, their eaves were overflowing, and they were impractically large with twenty to thirty rooms. Below them were portals for the caiques [*kayıkhane*] that were entered from a little door—really just an opening with shutters. . . . First of all, these *kayıkhanes* were there to shelter the rowboats, secondly, they were there to store water for washing the *taşlıks* . . . and third, this [covered area] was a "sea bathing area," a term known to mean "the women's bath." So if you heard loud shouts, shattering laughter, and the shrieks of children, know that the Harem section was uncovered and out bathing.
>
> Now, I'm going to tell something I heard not from Latife, but from her older sister-in law, who's now gone: One morning at İstinye, at her Grandfather's yalı, when she was 13 or 14 years old, she opened the door of the *kayıkhane* to go into the water. Suddenly, what did she see on the step? A mermaid! Above the waist she was a person, below the waist a fish, and what was she doing? Combing her golden blond hair!
>
> "I saw her with my own eyes, as clear as the day," she swore. Some of us believed her, but some of us just laughed and let it go as naiveté.[68]

Alus exemplifies a type of writing that collects not just solid information on structures but also anecdotes that express something less solid and more intimate and emotionally evocative than, say, the family lineage of the inhabitants. Another writer, Abdülhak Şinasi Hisar (1888–1963), was a master of this genre of double collection, as can be appreciated from his description of the yalı that belonged to Zeynep Hanımefendi:

The large yalı that Zeynep Hanımefendi and her husband Yusuf Kâmil Pasha had built in Bebek was made from plans drawn by Garnier, the architect of the Paris Opera House. It was painted the color of redbud blossoms . . . and with its great pinkness it became famous as the most beautiful and grandiose of yalıs. A friend of the Pasha's who came to see it said, "For God's sake, don't court the evil eye! You must hang a *nazarlık* [apotropaic blue bead] on it right away!" But the owner of adjacent yalı, Ali Pasha, answered for him: "Our *yalı* will suffice as a blue bead, as it is just next door."[69]

Abdülhak Şinasi Hisar and Sermet Muhtar Alus were not the first to write about the near past of "old Istanbul," nor did this type of writing begin in the 1930s.[70] In 1921 and 1922, just before the declaration of the republic, the popular writer Ali Rıza Bey (1845–1926)[71] (as opposed to the painter Hodja Ali Rıza Bey) wrote a series of articles about old Istanbul called "Life in Istanbul in the 13th Century AH" (the eighteenth century CE) (*Onüçüncü Asr-ı Hicride İstanbul*).[72] And in 1910, Abdülaziz (1850–1918), a contemporary of both the writer Ali Rıza and of the painter Hodja Ali Rıza Bey, wrote of the life of the previous century (although his work was not published until 1995).[73] Both Abdülaziz and Ali Rıza wrote to document change and preserve memory;[74] Ahmet Rasim (1864?–1932), quoted extensively by Reşad Ekrem Koçu, belongs to this genre as well. But there is an important difference between these two generations, that is, between these pre- or early twentieth-century "documentary" writers of memory and those whom I am about to discuss: although earlier writers participated in a new interest in memory collection, including disappearing values and customs, their interest was not in disappearing houses, and to the extent that personal lives were discussed, it is not the house that frames them. By the mid-1940s, however, the Turkish house had become a centerpiece of memory collection.

This can be seen in the conscious attempt at memory collection that was made in the mid-forties by Reşad Ekrem Koçu (1905–1975), who organized in fascicle form the first *Encyclopedia of Istanbul* (*İstanbul Ansiklopedisi*). Koçu had studied Ottoman history with Ahmed Refik Altınay[75] and later wrote hundreds of articles about Istanbul in almost every contemporary magazine.[76] His encyclopedia project was a labor of personal devotion and personal memory collection as he wrote most of the articles himself, based on information he collected during his own walks in the city. Although Koçu's fascicles never went beyond the letter "G,"[77] and thus never reached

"Konak" or "Yalı," his encyclopedia takes much of its character from the old wooden houses of Istanbul. Not only does it include articles with titles like "Wood Construction" (*Ahşap Yapı*), "Wooden Houses" (*Ev, Ahşab Evler*), and "Cumba," it also includes specific neighborhoods and streets. These articles were richly illustrated with houses, frequently based on those drawn by Hodja Ali Rıza Bey or Cesare Biseo,[78] or even with Koçu's own drawings, under pseudonyms such as "A. Bülend Koçu."

In fact, Koçu was so devoted to wooden houses that he included an excerpt from Ahmed Rasim's 1864 story "The Beautiful Helene" ("*Güzel Eleni*"), which is about prostitutes at the end of the Abdülhamid era.[79] Koçu devoted several pages to it because it gave such a vibrant account of the past. The lively scenes that he chose are actually descriptions of the intimate interiors of an old wooden house in Saraçhanebaşı, and he included an illustration of it from the story.

Although Koçu could have included more intellectual history and less social geography, as does the 1993 *İstanbul Ansiklopedisi*, one could certainly argue that to catalogue Istanbul up to the very recent past was to catalogue wooden buildings.[80] But what is more interesting is that these articles, although in the formal venue of an encyclopedia, express a sadness and a loss that attest to Koçu and his colleagues' desire, in their hours and hours of walking the streets, to collect remnants of "the disappearing past."

> Wooden buildings [once] surrounded the city . . . Today . . . every day a wooden house or a *köşk* is being destroyed and a concrete apartment built instead. And as each of these wooden buildings' gardens are destroyed, day by day, Istanbul loses its greenness. To this tragic sight we must add the . . . *gecekondu* [squatters' houses] that have been erected by immigrants from the Anatolian villages who have come in like a flood.[81]

There is no discussion of the architectural structure or plan of these houses, only what has now become (but may not have been then) the standard description of facades and interiors, reiterating their intrinsic value and beauty. However, information on structure was being collected at this time by Eldem's students, who had been dispatched to Anatolia to collect information on whatever was left of its wooden houses and wood-based urban fabric. Koçu had understood that this information was needed to fill a void in his own depiction of the disappearing house: "In our national libraries there is no book called *Istanbul's Old Wooden Houses*. Authorities in the

Architecture Department of our Fine Arts Academy, such as Professor Sedad Eldem, are zealously making very valuable studies in this area, but these studies have not been published as a comprehensive work."[82] Koçu was aware, too, of the movement to use wooden houses as a basis for a national architecture: "Today it is impossible to find wooden buildings in order to make the national style known."[83]

Koçu's good friend Sermet Muhtar Alus had collected memories of life inside Istanbul's konaks, Eldem's students were collecting measured drawings of wooden houses in Anatolia, and Koçu collected information about their location in Istanbul and marked each as a sadly disappearing image of national heritage.[84] Thus, from the late 1930s into the early 1950s, there was a frenzy of collection of memories, information, ideas, and feelings with a common centerpiece of the Turkish house.

But there was also a revival of the move to collect the old houses themselves. In 1945, in a lengthy article in the *Turkish Automobile and Touring Association Bulletin* called "Old Turkish Houses" ("*Eski Türk Evleri*"), the nationalist Cafer Seno asked the city to "collect" a few of the remaining houses as museum houses in order to protect the disappearance of the national heritage:

> Yet, while in the process of this change, wouldn't it be possible to hide away and protect for tomorrow, in a corner of the city, [the] nobleness and purity . . . of the old Turkish *mahalle*. . . . Especially the old Istanbul houses that the old Turk valued on the inside more than the outside, [and where,] inside these houses, good taste and emotion created a very lovely and meaningful lifestyle? . . . It would be useful to have a building with the spirit of that time in it.[85]

The "process of change" that the author refers to is not merely modernization in general but the changes to the urban fabric that were being implemented under the direction of Henri Prost, who had been given the task of planning Istanbul in 1936. The Turkish Touring and Automobile Association was the first voice of opposition to his plan, which they made clear by inviting Prost to hear Hamdullah Suphi, Abdülhak Şinasi Hisar, Emin Erkül (the former mayor), and Ali Fuat Cebesoy (Minister of Public Works) speak against any sacrifice of Istanbul's urban "picturesqueness."[86] This meeting marked the beginning of an organized voice for preservation that led to the establishment of National House Museums, a project that was first verbalized by Ahmed Süheyl Ünver and Mübarek Galip, Sedad Hakkı Eldem's uncle.

The call for a house museum was part of a call to collect memory. Although it can also be discussed as a project of nationalism, it was certainly conceived as a mechanism and a technique to conserve memory itself at a time when memory was seeming elusive. The passion for collecting has been identified as a characteristic of the beginnings of modernity. Terdiman conceived of the advent of modernity in relation to what he called "a memory crisis," which occurred when rapid changes put people's connection with the past "under pressure." He suggested that "modernity" itself can be characterized by the sudden appearance of numerous texts that attempt to capture memory, and it is these that indicate both an "epochal rupture" and the perception by those who were living within this rupture "that the world had decisively changed."[87]

But what made this arguably typical condition of modernism unusual for Turkey was the third reason that memory had become an issue: during the time of epochal rupture, the republican world had not only created a milieu where "anything that had to do with Ottomanism must be replaced with its opposite," it had also imposed an official amnesia. The institutionalized forgetting of the Ottoman past included erasure of the Ottoman script, Turkification of the Ottoman language, and changes in clothing; but more important there was an official control over the appearance of Ottoman references in Turkish cultural products, such as theater, including the texts of Karagöz plays, literature, and historiography. Even Yakup Kadri was censored. Thus, through the 1920s and even into the early 1940s, written histories, which are important sites of memory, consciously ignored the recent past in favor of a preoccupation with pre-Ottoman and thus "deeper" roots.[88] As the recent past became unspoken and unthought, it began to feel ineffable, and the hold on it tenuous. Thus, in Turkey, as people woke up to the fact that the urban landscape was not just changing but had already changed irrevocably, and with no other visual or verbal memory sites available, they began to ask, "Was it all a dream?"

I EVEN BEGAN TO HAVE DOUBTS THAT I HAD EVER LIVED
IN THAT WOODEN HOUSE. I FELT AS IF I HAD BEEN SUDDENLY
PRODDED AWAKE AFTER SEEING IT IN A DREAM.

In this period the compelling images of dreams, the unconscious, the ineffable, and the liminal join the collection of hard data as a way to approach memory. In 1939, at age sixty-four, the art historian Celal Esad Arseven "awoke" with a feeling of longing to see the house of his childhood (*Çocukluğumda oturduğumuz evi görmek hasreti uyandı*). But when he returned to his old

"The Voice of the Yogurt Seller," by Celal Esat Arseven. Yedigün, 1939, p. 15.

neighborhood,[89] he found everything so changed that it "shocked his memory." The gardens were dried up and empty, and most of the houses were now made of concrete. The wooden ones that remained, and his was one, were barely standing. Sadly, he walked away from his house and into the square to search for the little shop where the old hunchback had once sold odds and ends. As he walked, he heard the voice of the yogurt seller, and this sound was so unchanged that it carried him back to the past. He then found the shop he was looking for and stood peacefully in front of its glass windows, which were filled with toys, reed pipes, whistles, blue beads, wooden matches, and Karagöz puppets.

However, this vision in the shop window turned out to be caused by a dream state:

Suddenly, [the toys in the window] disappeared; they had hidden behind the Mt. Kaf[90] that I had heard about in fairy tales. [And then] it seemed to me that my mother was calling me! She was asking anyone in the street: Did you see a child? With a knit cardigan [şam hırka]?

With a cap [*takke*], and with slippers [*terlik*] on his feet? He was playing just here. . . . . I don't know what happened! If you see him, tell me.
Tell him that his mother wants him.[91]

The loss of the visual past put Arseven into a state of memory disruption,
a state that made time feel as if he were in a dream, although it is perhaps
unclear whether it was the past that felt like a dream or whether it was the
interim, the entire republican period. Only the voice of the yogurt seller and
Arseven's own heart made the connection with the past.

In the mahalle there was neither the sound of the *hallaç*[92] nor of fright-
ful dogs. Neither the squeaking of a baby's hammock nor the splash of
the fountain. Every kitchen garden a ruin, every tree a "*kübik*" house.
I looked, but everything seemed changed. The *mahalle* was changed. I
don't know why my heart still hadn't changed. Like the voice of the
yogurt seller.[93]

Arseven, foreshadowing the old man in the Istanbul cartoon, was hardly
the only person to have a confused sense of time. When Cafer Seno asked the
Istanbul municipality to preserve some old houses as museums, he argued
that they had already become "a hazy dream in the memory of the elderly"
and an impossible image for the young.

Especially the old Istanbul houses that the old Turk valued on the
inside more than the outside. Inside these houses they created a very
lovely and meaningful lifestyle, with good taste and with emotion. Ah,
now that old Istanbul mahalle is but a dream. The old Turkish houses!
Peaceful in spirit and with an inner life of comfort . . . and with the
tranquility and solitude of the receding, beautiful past.[94]

In a story called "*Ahşap Ev*" (The Wooden House), published in the popular magazine *Selected Stories* (*Seçilmiş Hikâyeler*),[95] the Turkish house stands
for the world of childhood, but also for this shared experience of loss: not
merely of childhood and its memories of one's own and one's family's past but
of the house itself. This sense of loss is intensified by a fear that the house
may never have existed at all.

Our house had been built right up against the large walls left from the
Byzantines, and our family had been raised there for five generations.[96]

Its wide *sofas* and *taşlıks*, its wide rooms with lowered windows and with rows of cupboards, this was the wooden house that described all the riches of my childhood world, and my memories were stacked in every corner. Until my father died, it could never cross my mind that we could live in a different house.[97]

When the family is forced to move to an apartment, the young boy and his mother find that they cannot forget the old house, for "something is always missing" that belonged to it, and although the boy refers to what is missing as physical, his sense of longing, and the reader's understanding of the deeper meaning of the old house, make it clear that he is referring to a spiritual void.

We moved from the wooden house to a rented flat on the outskirts of the city. . . . Often, my mother and I watched the lights that came through the window from the tram, and the people walking under the trees, and we thought that the wooden house was forgotten. [But] then we would search for things that had been in one of its big cupboards, and we'd hunt around for a few minutes, but we never found them.[98]

The boy begins to have a more and more tenuous relationship with the past. As he reaches adulthood, the (now) young man is exposed more frequently to the modern world, making his memory lose nothing of its intensity or poignancy but most of its clarity. It is at this time that he begins to wonder if that old house hadn't all been a dream:

I even began to have doubts that I had ever lived in that wooden house. I felt as if I had been suddenly prodded awake after seeing it in a half-happy, half-fearful dream. It seemed like a film.[99]

In the end, he finds he cannot even bear to go back to look for that "old home that was sleeping inside me," that "wooden house that had lived in me for years as a sacred trust."[100] His fear is too great that he will find everything gone or changed and that his past is missing, perhaps only dreamt, perhaps only alive in dreams.

BURSA SLEEPS IN THIS DREAM EACH NIGHT

The past as a dream state was not merely a random feeling that we have accessed anecdotally through stories and memoirs. It was a true state of what can truly be called a collective unconscious: the past as a dream state was unconscious in that dreams always signify something submerged, and it was collective because of the wide base of its expression.[101] In fact, this collective feeling that the past was held in a dream state was given a conscious voice in the work of Ahmet Hamdi Tanpınar.

Ahmet Hamdi Tanpınar was a writer, poet, historian, and literary critic who began to work with images of the subconscious to signal not only that the past should not be ignored but also that it was recuperable, as it lived on in a dream state. For Tanpınar, the dream was an image of hope, for an accessible past meant the possibility of resolving what he saw as the most pressing problem of the modern, urban, educated Turk: the inner duality (ikilik) felt as people straddled a chasm of space, between the East and the West, and a chasm of time, between the past and the present—that is, the chasm between the republican world, as it was being mediated in political rhetoric and social discourse, and the Ottoman life-world that was inaudible, below the surface.[102]

Although this duality had been addressed in novels over the previous half-century, as with Ahmet Midhat, Yakup Kadri, Halide Edib, and especially with Peyami Safa's Neriman (who suffered "a secret, interior, spiritual struggle"), Tanpınar made this a major concern of his literary production. He brought it to public attention and gave its condition a conceptual framework and even a name: duality (ikilik), represented on the one hand by the fully Kemalist "new man" (Yeni Adam)[103] and on the other by the person who had not yet "awoken" to this condition, the sleepwalkers of his novel Sahnenin Dişindakiler (Those Outside the Scene [or Off-Stage]), who saw "life through a heavily gilded mirror of the past." Individuals had some of each inside them, but many refused to remember or acknowledge their inner sleepwalkers. Thus Tanpınar wanted a third space, grounded in the reality of the past, in order to make possible an authentic self. He was for historical consciousness, with its political, social, moral, and aesthetic depth, and against amnesia.

> It's as if we've lost the essence of our wealth and history; we're left in a values crisis. We accept everything without taking in the larger meaning of any of those things, and everything we accept, we then hide away under lock and key in some corner of our minds.[104]

His famous poem, "Time in Bursa" ("Bursada Zaman"),[105] written in the early 1940s, suggests, comfortingly, that Bursa's Ottoman past, represented by its tombs, mosques, fountains, and old gardens, is still alive, and although it is living in a dream state, this past gives vitality to the present. Thus the poem speaks to those who had (accidentally or conveniently) forgotten the past, as well as to those who lamented its loss.[106]

> In Bursa, the courtyard of an old mosque
> Water gurgling in a small fountain
> A wall remaining from Orhan's time
> A plane tree just as old . . .
> A serene day . . . all around . . .
> A melancholy left behind from a dream
> Smiling at me . . .
>
> As if at each moment the day, the hour, the season
> Lives the past of the city.
> The dream, still on these stones, smiles,
> Even the noiseless glance of the pigeon
> Rings out with an endless illusion.
>
> Bursa sleeps in this dream each night
> Every dawn it awakes with it and smiles.

The image of the Ottoman past as a dream, and those who were still dreaming it as sleepwalkers, was both pervasive and apt. When religion, social norms, and the political organization of the past became unapproved as topics of open discussion, when the once full and open Sufi orders went underground, when the books that had been the standbys of the past were hidden in shelves and cupboards, their language obscure and their writing inscrutable, when the houses one had lived in could only be seen in artistic renditions or faded photographs, and when even the names of one's grandparents and grandmothers were hidden in history, it was as if the life-world of the past had withdrawn into the darkness and silence of sleep.

Although somewhat different from the trope of dreaming, the trope of sleep is a familiar one. It had been used by the early European nationalists who saw themselves as awakening from a deep sleep that had lasted from the time of their originary and epic past. This was an especially useful trope for groups for whom a nationalist consciousness was new, because by depicting themselves as late risers, it meant that their sleep had been especially long, certainly epochal, and had thus concealed the deep antiquity of their origins. As these newly awakened groups began to "recover" their pasts, especially their "original" languages and customs, they felt that they were "re-discovering something 'deep down' and 'always known.'"[107] The Turkist movements of the II Meşrutiyet had used this trope and had given the name "awakening" (hal-i bidar) to their project of educating the population about this newly recuperated, formerly shared Turkish past.

Because Turkish culture had generated an awakening, Ottoman Culture had been "put to sleep"—in order not to interfere with it. But Ottoman sleep differed substantially from that experienced by the sleep of a Turkish (nationalist) culture. Turkish culture had seemingly been in a deep sleep since the time of the Central Asian shamans, or at least since the mythic Dede Korkut.[108] But Ottoman culture had just dozed off, with its memories and consciousness barely beneath the surface, still spoken in the code of novels, liminal in the mind, and thus in-the-ready. It slept with one eye open. This threshold state posed a threat to the Kemalist modernism of the 1920s and early 1930s, but it was a promise of redemption to Tanpınar in the 1940s, especially now that the Ottoman period was sadly but more safely in the past.[109]

What the trope of sleep offered to both Turkists and Tanpınar was its attractive interiority. Sleep is a deeply interior state, with a meaning seemingly unknowable to outsiders, and characterized by an inaudability; it is therefore both open to interpretation, yet, arguably, authentic. It was used as an acceptable metaphor for the "true" spiritual strength of the East (recall Neriman's sleeping cat). Thus the sense that the sleeping past held something authentic to the Turkish soul also attested to a feeling that something authenticating to the soul was missing in the present. Tanpınar recognized that "this something that was missing" was a sense of connection, without which there would never be a wholeness; that is, duality would continue and integration would be impossible.

> Our most important question is this: *Where and how* are we going to connect with our past? . . . So long as we recognize this, we shall take hold of our lives and our creative work.[110]

One longed to connect not with the events of recent history, but the life-world that had been erased in the rush to become a secular, *"yeni adam"*: "We search for part of ourselves in these old things, which we think we lost in our battles within our souls."[111]

Thus it was not merely a question of Ottoman time, it was a question of the transcendent values that had once been secure in Ottoman space. All that was left of that space was the house, which people were frantically trying to remember. Thus, *how* the connection would be made would be through memory, by waking up from the amnesia of sleep, and acknowledging the existence of the recent past. The *where* of this connection with the past, as is shown in stories from this period, was in the memories enclosed in the Turkish house. The Turkish house had become the site where the past took place.

In 1951, in a story called "Bygone Days" (*"Geçmiş Günler"*), published in the *Selected Stories Magazine* (*Seçilmiş Hikâğyeler Dergisi*), the old wooden house both existed in a liminal space and was also the place where the new generation could make a connection with the past through an effort of memory. In this story, which takes place in the present (of 1951), a father takes his young adult daughter back to his old family house in an unnamed provincial town, where he has not been since before she was born.

When they arrive at the house, having taken the keys from the local grocer, they find that the *taşlık* (stone entry floor) and the whole interior of the house are shining clean, for the house is being cared for by "Ayşe Abla." But Ayşe Abla is not there. Her whereabouts are unclear, and the reader wonders why she was not expecting them. As the daughter enters the old wooden house, she is startled by its beauty, but at the same moment startled when she sees her reflection in the glass of the dark interior. The interior is dark because a light bulb has blown, so the father finds a new one from the cupboard.

Thus we have a strange meeting with the past. The people one expects to see are somehow hidden, and no one is expected. But, like ghosts, their presence is felt. The daughter sees her own image, as if she were coming to greet herself from inside the house, a ghost of an ancestor who looks like her, her roots; or perhaps this is who she might have been if times had not changed. At the same time, there is a sense that nothing has changed in the interim, for the father easily finds a light bulb, just where it should be. The house exists in the liminal, in a dream state that is ready to awaken and offer back the past.

The mood is reminiscent of the dream state of the past evoked by Yahya Kemal in his poem "Evening Music" (*"Akşam Mûsikisi"*) written a few years earlier, which takes place in gardens of the historic mansions of Kandilli:

> At Kandilli, in the old gardens, when
> Evening drops down her curtains one by one,
> Sadness is tinged with happy memories.
>> No one is coming,
>> No one is expected . . .[112]

Both the father and the daughter have come to ask something from the past. He is looking for happy memories related to the people who are, alas, no longer there. The daughter is looking for some connection to the past, and for memory itself.

When they walk upstairs, the father says,

"Look, this is *my* room."
"This is *your* room?" "Yes."
  Then she wished she could have a room like that, and also that she were a contemporary of her father, so she could talk about the old life. If I were my father's friend, he would tell me many things [she thought].[113]

But this does not happen, and her father tells her nothing about the past, although he came there wanting to show it to her; in fact, they decide to cut their trip short and return to Istanbul. For the father, the house represented his history in the warmth of the people who are missing. For the daughter, what is missing is the chance for a connection to the past, through memory. This father and this daughter do not find what they are searching for, but this does not negate the fact that there was a cultural expectation that the house was the place to look. They are like the young man in "The Wooden House" ("Ahşap Ev") who believed that "what was missing" in his current life could be found in the cupboards of his old house. Thus, although their house is empty of people, it is full of potential voices from "bygone days." It holds memory in a type of emotion-laden dream state, suspended in liminal time (almost a liminal space), as Tanpınar had described time in Bursa.

Yahya Kemal evokes this conflation of time, the liminal, sleep, dreams, and the memories of the past that are still alive, in the conclusion of his "Night Music."

> Now wandering phantoms cause recurrent shivers,
> And darkness, coming in at every door,
> Is by her footsteps clearly manifest.
> . . .
> Then, as the world retreats from seeing eyes,
> On this night of a thousand and one nights
> A dream, as though within a dream, begins.[114]

Yahya Kemal was Tanpınar's mentor, and Tanpınar dedicated *Beş Şehir* to him. But neither was nostalgic. What Tanpınar wanted, perhaps following

Yahya Kemal, was not a nostalgic return to the past but a "return to *ourselves*" ("*Kendimize dönmek*"), to the self that had been lost when Ottoman culture went to sleep, and when time and memory had been interrupted by looking for one's authenticity in the West or in Central Asia[115]—that is, anywhere but home.

In fact, Tanpınar did not want to return to who he authentically had been, but to find who he had authentically become. It was for this reason that authentic memory was needed.

> Why is the past pulling us to itself like a bottomless well? I know very well that what I am looking for are not the people of the past; I am not nostalgic about their time either. How much satisfaction is there . . . to stroll in Istanbul, in the year I was born, at a Ramadan Fair, wearing a fez on my head . . . amid the mixture of smells of rose attar, cinnamon oil and all kinds of spices? . . . I have to figure out how much I would gain and how much of the authentic parts of myself I would have to throw away. [We can appreciate the past with the accumulation of experience] and with ourselves that have become more clear cut between two different worlds of values, that made us internally richer.[116]

Thus the wholeness that was attributed to the past was really a feeling that was available to the present. The feeling of wholeness would come when the rupture was mended, and a complete individual could appear.

Tanpınar understood the importance of memory as it was later conceptualized by Terdiman, who discussed it as the essential characteristic of periods that follow times of intense rupture:

> Memory stabilizes subjects and constitutes the present. It is the name we give to the faculty that sustains continuity in collective and in individual experience. Our evidence for it may be as indirect as Freud's evidence for the unconscious, but it is an essential postulate in our attempt to explain how the world remains minimally coherent, how existence doesn't simply fly apart.[117]

Tanpınar marks a moment when Turkish historians were waking up to Ottoman history, and also another moment, when Turkey's Ottoman urban fabric was undergoing its last destructive burst. Although the 1930s had been characterized by a nationalist historiography, even Atatürk at the end of his life rejected the thesis that all Turkish history could be traced to Central

Asia. During the 1940s there was a liberalization in historiography as well as an increased interest in the recent past.

But at the same time that the recent past was opened up to scholarship, its remaining urban housing stock was finally destroyed. This was due to the enormous housing shortage following World War II, but also to the increasing importance of the United States as a role model, with its skyscrapers and high-rise apartments. When the Republican People's Party, which had been in power since the foundation of the republic, lost the elections in 1950, the country was taken over by the political populism of Adnan Menderes, who set into motion a process of easy and cheap construction (*Yap-sat*) that allowed the destruction of the remaining traditional fabric of most urban areas. "Menderes' image of the city had two ingredients: Modern apartments and cars."[118]

The old houses and konaks that had not been destroyed or relegated to slums found themselves surrounded by concrete buildings that made their old private life impossible and their gardens ugly. Buildings such as Reji Nazırı Şükrü Bey's konak,[119] which had stood for a century between Aya Sofia and Sultan Ahmet, were sold or abandoned in the early 1950s.[120] The year 1950, then, marks a turning point in Turkish history, a finale for the visual domestic past, a finale for those who could remember it, and an opening up to looking back.

IF WE DON'T SEE THE LINKS THAT I SEE IN THESE PICTURES,
WE WILL BE CUT OFF FROM EVERYTHING. THIS WAS THE FINAL
PHASE, WE WON'T BE HAVING BETTER THINGS THAN THIS.

I was born in the large red-colored yalı *of my grandfather, Kazasker Siruzığzade Hacı Tahir Efendi, in the year 1866 on the 6th day of March in Salacak Mahalle in Üsküdar, on a spot overlooking the sea. Today there is only a rather large empty plot where it once was.[121]*

This passage was written by Cemil Topuzlu, who had been the first mayor of Istanbul, just as the Menderes urban "renewals" were picking up speed. Topuzlu's dream was an Istanbul of wide, straight (and mudless) streets, and his five-year plans foresaw much of the way that the historic peninsula looks today, with the Golden Horn lined by a wide avenue and the wide avenue lined with three-story commercial buildings. Topuzlu believed that modernization along Western lines could only benefit the city that he loved. Yet whether he expected his own neighborhood across the water in Üsküdar to

A house in Üsküdar. Hodja Ali Rıza Bey. From Erhan, Hoca Ali Rıza, p. 69.

be rebuilt with concrete apartments is quite uncertain. Topuzlu was born two years after Hodja Ali Rıza Bey, who was also born in Üsküdar, in the Ahmediye Mahalle, and among the konaks and houses that were the subjects of his drawings, and where he took long walks with his student, Ahmet Süheyl Ünver.

Topuzlu was part of the final cohort who might have seen the two books that Ünver wrote on Hodja Ali Rıza Bey in 1949,[122] and who still could have recognized in them scenes from his own lived past, for he was born in 1866 and died in 1958. If his cohort was the last of those who might have lived some of their childhood in the "traditional" way, that is, before the II Meşrutiyet, which began in 1908, then Topuzlu's peers included Mustafa Kemal Atatürk, Halide Edib, Hamdüllah Suphi, Yakup Kadri, Abdülhak Şinasi Hisar, Peyami Safa, and Faiz Bey, who was Neriman's father.[123]

In the early 1950s, when Abdülhak Şinasi Hisar went to see Hodja Ali Rıza's paintings at Galatasaray Lisesi, in Beyoğlu, he wrote about the feelings that seeing these old houses generated in him and the types of memories and emotions they evoked. Perhaps Topuzlu would not have shared these feelings, yet Hisar provides us with an important moment of memory. That is, he is not summarizing the life of the past according to one who lived it but giving memories in the form of the summary feelings that these images of old houses evoked. What these images evoked in him would be inscribed onto the house for the next generation, a generation who would view these images within the context of this inherited collective memory. Abdülhak Şinasi Hisar may not have realized that he was a conduit of memory on a trajectory of collective memory, but he knew that he was standing at an important moment when he said, "If we don't see the links that I see in these pictures, we will be cut off from everything. . . . This was the final phase; we won't be having better things than this."[124]

This is also a moment when art and literature come together, for Hisar described Rıza Bey's poetic paintings with his own poetic prose.

DID YOU FORGET, DO YOU REMEMBER, IS IT IN YOUR MEMORY, THEY SAY?

When Abdülhak Şinasi Hisar first looked at Hodja Ali Rıza's paintings of houses and neighborhoods, his memory was suddenly awakened, as if from a forty-year sleep. The imagery he used, however, is not of his own sleep but of sleeping houses, and of a time that is either sleeping or waiting in the realm of the inaudible.

> In Haydarpaşa, there is an old pink house near a white wall overlooking İbrahim Ağa's field, on a day like all other days, in an afternoon, living the same [old] day of its life, it is sinking into memory and dreams. . . . And isn't this a miracle that this painter evokes in me things that were thought to be mute, all these walls, these closed windows, and these buildings seen from outside . . . call out from me a creative voice. . . . What one sees with the eyes is remembered by the heart.[125]

What is evoked for Hisar are feelings of love, affection, loss, and sadness. Love is evoked because these images touch his deep interior (için içinde), as if the houses in them were members of his own family. In this way he presents them as not only close to his heart but as his most immediate heritage. Of course, these paintings are not of his own family's houses, but they are so like them that they recall how he lived and where he used to walk, and they certainly housed someone's own aunts and uncles, or somebody's mother, or someone he once knew. In this way he includes every reader in his act of remembering.

Houses that look like the old women of olden times . . . and the colors of the *yalıs* of olden times are like their cloaks. . . . I love these pictures so much [because they] give me the feeling that they are the containers of time. What lives here, is what we lived in the past. [They] all remind me of some life we have previously lived, and how [it felt to leave them] on those sad Sunday evenings when I would return to school with my heart full of feelings of anticipation of how I should hug them again come the first vacation day.[126]

Hisar's feelings of love, family, heritage, and palpability, depicted with a wide brush of sadness and loss rather than with the detailed brush of description, summarize the feelings of family and belonging that the house had come to evoke in the novels of the 1930s, and it is these feelings that will remain attached to the houses as their images reappear in the ensuing years. These are feelings that will flash up when one is looking at images of houses and will seem to be evoked by no other place: feelings that the past exists in a space of wholeness, with a promise that memory can supply "the something that is missing," if you remember not to forget.

All of these houses are woven through with feelings and are looking at me with tearful eyes, asking "did you forget, do you remember, is it in your memory," they say?[127]

Although Hodja Ali Rıza painted neighborhoods as well as river-front houses, the wholeness that Hisar is remembering here is that of the yalı life of the upper classes. He understood that this was a separate world, so separate that its members couldn't quite understand the movement toward nationalism. This is clear from another article in this same collection, in which Hisar tells us some of the essence of what he remembers and what is missing:

The Bosphorus was like a lake with each *yalı* bound to the other by the spiritual connection of the water, which was like a huge secret maker of solidarity and unity. Everyone regarded each other with benevolence—besides which, out of the corner of one's eye, they were supervising each other's morality. With its old unity, with the zeal of the night watchmen [*bekçi baba*], with the somewhat-educated mosque-caretakers, with the supervisors of religious time [*muvakithane memurları*], and with the moral simplicity and well-being of religion, all of the Bosphorus neighborhoods were eventless through

the centuries, and without disputes, without violence, without mur-
ders, without arson, and without thievery. Today, even if we wanted to,
we would be unable to organize more of a miracle of civilization than
the one that has gone by.[128]

Abdülhak Şinasi Hisar was one of the last to interpret memory from a
position of autobiography. (That is, he was not reporting his experiences for
the future but remembering an experienced past.) After this moment, which
he portrayed and symbolized so well, the images of the old wooden houses
that appear in text and art become like the poem about Aksaray that was discussed in Chapter 2. The poet who wrote "Our Love was the most devastating fire of Aksaray" lived through love but not through the fire. Similarly, the
creators of textual or visual images of houses that appear from the middle
of the century and beyond experienced a void without ever having lost their
own houses. By the 1950s, love and loss, fires and houses had entered the collective memory. The houses, like the fires, had taken on meaning from the
shared memories and real feelings of the people who at one time had felt as if
they were communally experienced.

Thus the Aksaray fire provides a viable analogy because, although it was
a single event that happened to many people, the similar way in which it was
experienced made people feel as if they were experiencing the same thing at
the same time, and the fire entered memory in that way. In fact, one could
argue that it entered memory in the space reserved for experiencing any fire
in a neighborhood of wooden houses. In the same way, the loss of wooden
houses as expressed by those who were collecting memories was a shared
feeling of loss, as if they were all reexperiencing a loss suffered in a single
fire rather than by the fire of history. Thus, like the fire of Aksaray, events
that were autobiographical in nature were also communally experienced and
became part of a shared memory.[129]

This phenomenon is made clear by the memories chosen to be collected
by authors such as Sermet Muhtar Alus, who collected stories about the
"harems" of women and children bathing beneath their summerhouses, or
of Latife's sister-in-law, who saw a mermaid there. These stories are bits of
reality, anecdotes that take the past both out of the realm of scholarship and
out of the dream state, and put them into the personal, the intimate, and the
interior. These stories would be "remembered" by those who experienced
them as well as by the children, nieces and nephews who heard them long
after the house was gone; or if they did not remember that story exactly, it
reminded them of a similar one. The events collected by Alus, each of them

idiosyncratic yet endlessly replicable in emotional memory, helped to tie memory into a collective whole, and tie it to the house.

The realm of emotions is a part of every discussion on the Turkish House, and it could be argued that every level of memory resonates because of it. Emotional attachments are always genuine, and therefore always personal and autobiographical. What is "felt real" has its own place in the brain, and represents a specific way of knowing. If this is true, if "the felt real" is an important part of what was felt to be "missing" from the past, then it is not missing at all but known, felt, and remembered all at once. Unlike the fire of Aksaray, the Turkish house evoked a feeling that was a shared feeling of love and continuity as well as loss. The houses were lost to the fires, perhaps, but the spiritual closeness could still be felt. The emotions evoked by the collected stories about the house, a sense of sweetness, naiveté, or just plain human foibles, were understood because they were felt, but perhaps only in the realm of the private: inside the house, inside the soul and apart from the difficult march toward progress, the hard work necessary to change to a life organized around scientific principles, rationality, and the political demands of the new secular society. The memory of the house was something that felt real and attainable, but not within the minimalist spaces and hard-edged furnishings of the kübik and the modern. Perhaps these old houses spoke to emotions of rapture as well as to memories of rupture, and to a reality that was not driven by science, rationality, and exteriority and all that was necessary to be a part of the modern world. The stories told by Alus and Hisar, and the feelings evoked by the old wooden house, far more than the lack of thievery, continue today to remind the present of what it is that feels most real to the self.

Vaclav Havel characterized this memory dichotomy as part of the postmodern situation.

> Today, for instance, we may know immeasurably more about the universe than our ancestors did, and yet, it increasingly seems they knew something more essential about it than we do, something that escapes us. . . . By day, we work with statistics; in the evening, we consult astrologers and frighten ourselves with thrillers about vampires. The abyss between the rational and the spiritual, the external and the internal, the objective and the subjective, the technical and the moral, the universal and the unique, constantly grows deeper.[130]

Sometime in the 1950s, with the last of Abdülhak Şinasi Hisar's cohort, and with the final evisceration of cities by the Menderes mentality, the memory image of the Turkish house takes deep root. In fact, one could say that, like the fire of Aksaray, the image of the Turkish house continues to glow red in the Turkish imagination.

1950S AND BEYOND: THE SECOND HALF OF THE CENTURY

But Yüksel!! You can't go on living without the spirit of the konak!

Reflected in the glow of the image of the Turkish house are all of the iconic meanings and messages that entered the imagination and settled in it. These images became more and more important in the succeeding decades among those who seemingly could not remember without the "collections" that collective memory provides.

Walter Benjamin has shown how images of the past that flash up in the present are those that bring the desires of the past into the present. The images that he addresses are images that are created by past generations, which he considers to contain desires that are still "true" and relevant for the present, and thus speak to the something that is "true" about both.[131] "Every image of the past that is not recognized by the present as one of its own concerns threatens to disappear irretrievably."[132] Following Benjamin, one can find these messages of continuity that flash up in the present in the imagined Turkish house, which provides a space of legitimacy for the concerns and characteristics of former life-worlds that remain valid in the present.

A project, however suggestive here, of looking at images of the Turkish house for the desires that collective memory brings from the past is a different project than looking at how images of the past are used to construct memory or to rewrite the past. It also differs from projects that uncover the appropriation of the past. Thus, following Benjamin, but highlighting emotion as much as desire, one can emphasize continuity rather than construction.[133]

In the early part of the second half of the twentieth century, one of the issues of the past that still felt real was the rupture between the generations. Furthermore, just as in *"Harem"* and *Kiralık Konak*, the house was the site in which to look for the spiritual rootedness of the pre-1908 past. This is clear in both Yusuf Ziya Ortaç's 1953 novel, *The Three Storied House* (*Üç Katlı Ev*), and Necip Fazıl Kısakürek's 1964 three-act play, *The Wooden Konak* (*Ahşap Konak*).

The Three Storied House takes place in a large residence in Saraçhanebaşı, near Fatih, in 1945; *The Wooden Konak* takes place in the early 1960s on the Beyoğlu side of the Golden Horn, in Nişantası. Both concern houses with three generations: a grandfather who represents religion and rootedness, a middle generation that is "lost," either to Western decadence or to economic conditions, and that is therefore lost as a link in a chain of values, and the grandchildren, who are threatened by this break in continuity.

In *The Three Storied House*, the three grandchildren weather the storms of change, in a great part because of the love and spiritual strength of the grandfather-pasha and his wife. In *The Wooden Konak*, however, continuity is more clearly threatened, and the role of the house as its keeper is more specific. Recai Pasha, who lives on the top floor of the wooden konak with his wife, Hacer, is a religious man whose widowed daughter on the middle floor has spent all of her money on card gambling and on morphine, and, let it not be forgotten, on ugly and uncomfortable modern furniture. But the grandson, Yüksel, understands what his grandfather and the konak stand for. As an architecture student he has made a model of the konak as a class project, but presents it as far more than a material object: "Yes . . . they assigned it saying it should be conceived as a physical layout, but I'm treating it as a spiritual one."[134]

As Recai Pasha begins to understand the depth of corruption of his children, he decides to set his konak on fire rather than leave it as an inheritance. But he leaves it symbolically to Yüksel, who, by the way, has also taken a new interest in religion. As the flames start, he tells Yüksel to grab the model of the konak and to run into the garden so that he can throw him the *levha*, the calligraphic religious motto that protected the konak. Naturally, Yüksel is frantic and begs him not to enter the house, but Recai Pasha runs into the flames, saying:

"But Yüksel!! You can't go on living without the spirit of the konak!"
And as the *levha* is caught by Yüksel, we hear Recai's dying words:
"Yüksel! Save this as a trust . . . save this in trust. . . ."[135]

Thus the Turkish house in the 1950s and 1960s, long after it has disappeared as a viable dwelling on the ground, remains a place to play out the difficulties of coming to terms with the new, just as it was for Neriman in *Fatih-Harbiye*, for it has become a symbol of the transcendent values that would make the process acceptable. The *levha* adds clear religious significance, just as did Faiz Bey's Sufi literature, but it is also the legacy of the house felt by the young man in *The Wooden House*, who felt that the house "that had lived in me for years was a sacred trust."[136]

Yusuf Ziya Ortaç's and Necip Fazil Kısakürek's houses are images taken from collective memory, although both are arguably constructed by crossover authors, as Ortaç was born in 1895 and Kısakürek in 1905. Yet the threat of rupture with the past that began with Yakup Kadri clearly resonates for the contemporary reader at mid-century, making these houses sites of collective emotion as well. In fact, rupture still feels real into the 1970s, even if its dimensions, and what is felt to have ruptured, begin to change.

In 1973, Yusuf Atılgan wrote *Anayurt Oteli* (Motherland Hotel),[137] which also takes place in a konak, but this time in an unspecified provincial location. And instead of three generations headed by a grandfather who has values to transmit from the past, this konak has been turned into a hotel and is run by Zebercet, the last member of a once thriving Ottoman family. Zebercet is a lost soul. He does not marry, he wastes his reproductive potential on a non-wife, and in the end he commits suicide. The konak itself cannot save him because it has lost its identity as a konak, and it no longer functions as such in his life or in his memory; it is a hotel. Furthermore, the connectivity that it once housed is gone. Flashbacks represent the konak as once being very densely inhabited and thus a container of interrelational complexity, but the social relations that made up the life of the konak when it was "alive" are now conspicuously absent.[138] It is now a place of exteriority rather than interiority, a place open to strangers and empty of family. Thus, *Motherland Hotel* does not allow a recuperation or a continuation of the wholeness of the past, not because there is no memory of real people and real events, but because without a real connection to that life, Zebercet suggests an almost existential emptiness of one who is emotionally unable to identify with a history that should be able to give meaning to his own life and to his environment, and thus that should be able to bind him to a Turkish collectivity.

In *Motherland Hotel*, the rupture between the past and the present, with all the implications for the future, is still played out in the house, but the sense of being in a period of transition is not felt. Naim Efendi's konak had something that was crumbling and decaying, as well as something valuable to be preserved. *The Wooden Konak* had forgotten what was exhausted from the past but remembers the lessons it might still live by. In *Motherland Hotel*, the reader is meant to "recall" what appears to be gone—connectivity and the value of it. Zebercet is lost, but the reader who experiences this tragic sense of loss "recognizes this concern as one of its own." With the assistance of *Motherland Hotel*, the reader's emotional memory is aroused and he cannot forget to remember, even in 1970.

There has been a shift in emphasis, then, from the time of Ahmet Hamdi Tanpınar's stress on connecting to the past to give a sense of wholeness, to *Motherland Hotel*'s emptiness, and inability to give meaning either to the past or to the present. Yet Tanpınar was correct when he characterized the interest of the present in the things of the past as a search to find what is missing.

> Alas, one quickly gets tired of gilt ceilings, silver objects and past memories. No, we definitely don't love these things for their own sake. What attracts us to them is the feeling of void they create in us. We search for part of ourselves in these old things, which we think we lost in our battles within our souls.[139]

Zebercet's interiority has been replaced with an inner void, and whether this represents him alone or the emotional offering of the republic, *Motherland Hotel* points to the continued value of interiority, the *"içlilik"* that we remember from Naim Efendi, Faik Bey, and Şinasi.[140] The konak in *Motherland Hotel* is a memory image with a warning message: anomie will ensue if the connection and the connectivity that the reader is expected to know are broken and if memory is forgotten.

> YOU ARE FULL OF DOUBTS. COME IN, OLD MAN, LET ME
> RELIEVE YOU OF YOUR DOUBTS. COME INSIDE AND HAVE
> A CUP OF OUR COFFEE.

Issues of rupture and connectivity continue to be relevant into the present, and the house remains the place to look for relief. In the 1990 cartoon of the old man's childhood house, he remembers what the past had offered, but thought that this offering was lost to the present. As he passes what appear to be the ruins of his heritage, his childhood home, he is surprised to find it still inhabited by "the beauty of the past," who opens the door.

> Old man (stuttering):
> "I, I didn't think anyone was living here."
> Gorgeous but refined Young Thing in Ottoman Costume (The beauty of the past)
> "You are full of doubts. Come in, old man, let me relieve you of your doubts. Come inside and have a cup of our coffee."[141]

The old man's fear was that "the Turkish house," the place designated to hold the most intimate and important part of the past, held something irretrievable. Perhaps, like the boy in *"Ahşap Ev"* (*The Wooden House*), he feared that the past has been a dream. If it were empty, a frightening rootlessness

The gorgeous woman at the door. (from left to right) *"I, I didn't think anyone was living here." "You are full of doubts. Come in, old man, let me relieve you of your doubts. Come inside and have a cup of our coffee." From Gülgeç, "Hikâye-i İstanbul," İstanbul Dergisi 17 (1996), p. 118.*

would take its place. But the cartoon offers relief by refreshing memory, and thus suggesting that the past still lives (accessible—if we knock on the door of the Turkish house), and thus that the memory of what was valued is still a value. The cartoon does not make this specific: the reader is expected to "know" what collective memory has assigned to the house, but certainly it includes the warmth of hospitality as well as good Turkish coffee.

But in the 1990s, as the old man was sipping his coffee, he could also have entered the old Turkish house by picking up a coffee-table book, such as *The Konak Book (Konak Kitabı). The Konak Book* is a study of "the evolution of the traditional Turkish house [that] reached its peak in the konak."[142] It is an excellent introduction to the wooden residential form that spread from Istanbul to the provinces, falling within the genre of books about the Turkish house that began with Sedad Eldem and his students. It is not a book about Turkish culture, for the reader enters the past only through photographs; he or she must bring his or her own (collective) memory of the life-world that these photographs conceal.[143] This coffee-table book can serve as an alternate way to enter the house of the past, because it stands for yet another genre of images in the trajectory of collective memory, and that is the reconstructions and restorations of "real" Turkish houses that began to emerge in the 1970s.

In the 1980s "nostalgic communities" of "Turkish houses" begin to appear as memory images on the Turkish landscape, including Kemer County, Sedadkent, the *Hıdıv Köşkleri*, (Khedive [Viceroy] Kiosks), and the Beykoz Konaks, which sponsored the writing of *The Konak Book* to entice or grace the coffee tables of those interested in buying their houses. *The Konak Book* made certain that potential buyers of nostalgia would make the appropriate connection with the past.

Gated communities attempt to convince the purchaser that their Turkish houses replicate (or at least call to mind) a traditional neighborhood, and

Kemer county houses, Istanbul. Photograph by Carel Bertram, 1999.

many of their advertisements refer to a sense of lost community.[144] Sedad-kent's advertisements go so far as to add an image that is reminiscent of the old *Bekçi* or night watchman who ensured that all the residents of his neighbor-hood were home and inside by nightfall and spent the night in safety. Recall Hisar's words above: "with the zeal of the night watchmen [*bekçi baba*] . . . all of the Bosphorus neighborhoods were . . . without violence, without mur-ders, without arson, and without thievery."[145]

The Turkish houses that are being purchased in this new form carry a common desire for a relief from Zebercet's isolation, as well as an upper-class preoccupation with protection from burglaries. Perhaps, too, they offer relief from fears shared with the cartoon character who feels that he has lost his past and is stuck in a memoryless modernity; perhaps they seem to say, "Let me relieve you of your doubts. Come inside and have a cup of our coffee." If so, these gated nostalgic communities operate as living reminders of still active desires (as well as operating to "provoke desire"[146] and thereby make a sale). As spaces that legitimize real feelings, nostalgic reproductions show the desire to connect both with "the something that is missing" in modern life (even if only in the imagination) and the "place of origins" for values strongly held.

As images in the Turkish imaginary, nostalgic communities (along with the Turkish house as a museum house or a hotel), deserve a discussion all their own.[147] Certainly it is worth investigating further whether a yearning for the rich interiority of the symbolic universe of the past can be satisfied by a view of its exteriors (for the interiors of nostalgic housing are decidedly modern) or whether the scenography of the museum or the hotel, or of Turk-ish houses restored as a street of "the authentic past," could possibly seduce or satisfy memory. Perhaps these communities should be discussed as *con-tributing* to feelings of rupture, as they make the distance of the past from the present palpably absolute.

Not every image of the Turkish house in the late twentieth century or early twenty-first century can be traced in a linear fashion to the feelings and strategies of the formative years of the republic; at the very least, any con-necting chain of events and associations is complex. For example, the emo-tions associated with the Turkish house at a time when identity building was a vital activity of a secularizing state may differ from those forty years later, when the old house became the centerpiece of a conservation and restoration movement that began among the leftists and leftists-turned-liberals in the 1970s.[148] Yet I believe that the association of this house with a shared memory of wholeness continues, and that it began at the beginning of the last century and continues to this day. When we look at the cartoon of the old man entering a dilapidated "Turkish house" and imagining the world of the past, we can understand some of the warmth and safety that the cartoonist felt in his own family life, and how he connects his spiritual universe to the past, perhaps even to his grandfather. This might also explain why a middle school child from Istanbul chose the Turkish house to represent her ideal future. Understanding the emotional resonance of the Turkish house might also help us understand some of the attractions it offers as a coffee-table book or a gated community.

Nonetheless, images of the past must always be investigated with a sensitivity to changing ideologies and to contemporary populations. In the early republican period, images were used conspicuously in an attempt to forge a common past. The Turkish house today remains an icon of the past, but the limits, contents, and ownership of the past are again in flux and subject to manipulation. For example, today, and since 1998, a row of Turkish house facades is used as a centerpiece of Istanbul's celebration of Ramadan. Are these symbols of a shared life-world with links to the spiritual past felt by Peyami Safa and his successors? Or are these images an attempt to associate Istanbul with an Ottoman revival in which the late Ottoman period has become suddenly religious? The desire of the municipality may be penetrated, but the way that these houses resonate with continually new Istanbul populations from Anatolian villages remains to be investigated. Their autobiographical and shared memories rarely contained a Turkish house, but their collective memories, it appears, certainly will.

But what will this image mean? The real Turkish style houses that newly "Istanbulized" Anatolians see today are either the restored or repaired wooden houses of the fabulously wealthy or decaying structures that are the unclean abodes of the very, very poor. Do these real structures enter the imagination, or does the image of the house have a life of its own, built, for example, on images in Turkish children's books? Those images are part of the legacy of its positive associations with a felt spiritual wholeness, which, I would argue, remain a part of a contemporary symbolic universe.

The meaning carried by the imagined Turkish house cannot be summarized in a single sentence or in a single work. The poet Edip Cansever (b. 1928) lamented the loss of konak life for just this reason: once the real life within these houses was gone, its legacy to the future would be summarized, and its depth of meaning simplified.

The breeze brings these back . . .
The breeze brings back its memory
    —a red konak
and its whimpering,
    a sick konak,
And the owl that is perched on the roof,
    the fun that was had on the wooden balconies
And all of its conversations,
    now collected into a single sentence,
And its silence
    —that has become as large as a monument,
A konak
    —and how splendid it was to be a konak,
The breeze brings these back.[149]

Certainly the image of the Turkish house that survives in the Turkish imagination today reveals important truths, and one of these is that other truths have been concealed. When considering the development of the affective resonance of the Turkish house, one might ask, "Whose house?" Yet the Turkish house that is "remembered" in the Turkish collective memory has a hegemonic voice that has been carefully preserved. It is not the voice of nationalism or national unity, although it has operated in its service; rather, it is the voice of an upper-class elite, originally an Istanbul elite, a voice that began when their lifestyle was threatened, first by modern innovations and demographic changes and finally by the movement of power away from the Istanbul families to the bureaucrats of Ankara. The image of the Turkish house carries the voices of this educated Istanbul elite who wrote about the house, drew its portraits, and later worked for its preservation as a national monument to what had once been their way of life, when Istanbul was "the real Istanbul" and before Istanbul "became a village." To the extent that they are the authors who preserved memory, they are responsible for their house becoming a national one. It is because of them that when the Turkish population finally awoke to look at the past, they found themselves all in the same house.

Perhaps it is impossible to have a collective memory that does not have a hidden hegemony to unify it. How could it be otherwise, when defining a Turkish collective memory assumes that Turks exist as a collective? For this reason alone, collective memory is in the service of national unity in a population of Turks who may privately consider themselves to be Kurds, Laz, or

Georgians, Sunni, Shi'a, Alevi, or Bektashi, not to mention those who consider themselves Armenians, Greeks, or Jews, with each group carrying its own separate memories and versions of history and its causes.

The reifications of the Turkish house as a museum or a hotel, and especially as a gated nostalgic community, can be seen as the care taken to preserve the hegemony of the Istanbul elite.[150] But images of the Turkish house are far too ubiquitous in the Turkish imaginary to classify them as images of the elite alone or to give them a single voice. Although the Turkish house may carry idealized images of a harmonious, pre-Western pre-republican social order, that image has, at least, been democratized. Perhaps the conflation of *konak* and *house* is a part of that democratization. In today's Turkey there is an underlying belief that everyone has roots in a Turkish house.[151] This is in spite of the great population movements and immigration into the cities by people whose grandparents never saw one. Yet the children of these migrants take pride in the old houses that their parents could only afford as slums, and have become active preservers of their heritage.[152] Perhaps it is in part because these same children, whether Kurd, Laz, Georgian, or "Turk," or from Istanbul, Anatolia, or Rumeli, are exposed to children's books that continue the memory of a common house.[153]

But there is another voice, or another hegemony, that is carried by the Turkish house as we saw it represented in the Istanbul Municipality's re-creation of a "traditional" Ramazan, with its street of Turkish house facades. Adults and children from every background participate in this celebration with the understanding, perhaps a "new understanding," that they are participating in something from their own past. Perhaps the Turkish house is the shape of their encounter with what they think the present cannot offer, but, as a player in emotional memory, maybe it is the shape of something that they know quite well, and that therefore feels both real and lost, collective and personal, past and present, all at the same time. For it is the force of emotions that makes this amalgam of time and spaces possible and believable.

Certainly the image of the Turkish house as it is imagined in the Turkish collective memory is an amalgam; it is an amalgam of the finest characteristics and deeply felt transcendent desires that its culture has to offer, and it is a way to validate them and keep them current. And if it "creates" the past, the image of the Turkish house continues to create a past of carefully constructed ideals. For this reason alone, the memory of the Turkish house does important cultural work.

Memory, as William James said, is "the association of a present image with others known to belong to the past."[154] But the Turkish house is also an image that creates the future, an image of expectation, which according to James "is the association of a present image with others known to belong to the future."[155] This, as James saw, is the other side of memory, and the Turkish house owes much of its longevity to its position at the crossroads of memory and expectation. The winning painting of the middle school student of her ideal tomorrow, a landscape covered with Turkish houses, attests to this, for it takes a present image of the past and imagines it in the future. This is another part of the cultural work done by the imagined Turkish house. The fact that this drawing could be conceived, the fact that it was understood by her teachers, and the fact that it was accorded first place in the school competition all attest to the activity of a collective memory that continues to give monumental significance to a house made out of wood.

Istanbul Neighborhood. Photograph by Fred M. Donner, 1983.

The cast of characters

Both the Young Turk revolution and the National Movement were very much the work of a single generation, the people born between 1875 and 1885.[1]

1665–1704	Mustafa Naimi
1785–1839	Mahmut II, Sultan 1808–1839
1790?–1848	Esad Efendi
1823–1861	Abdul Mecit I, Sultan 1839–1861
1820	Felâtun Bey's father, the "man with an *alafranga* disposition"
1830–1876	Abdul Aziz, Sultan 1861–1876
1840–1888	Namık Kemal
1840–1904	Murat V, Sultan 1876
1840	Naim Efendi in *Kiralık Konak*
1842–1918	Abdülhamit II, Sultan 1876–1909
1842–1910	Osman Hamdi Bey
1843–1909	Cesare Biseo
1844–1912	Ahmet Mithat Efendi
1844–1918	Mehmed V (Mehmet Reşad), Sultan 1909–1918
1845–1926	Ali Riza, the author
1847–1913	Recaizade Mahmut Ekrem
1850–1918	Abdülaziz Bey
1850–1923	Pierre Loti
1855	Felâtun Bey of *Felâtun and Râkim Efendi*
1861–1926	Mehmed VI (Mehmed Vahideddin), Sultan 1918–1922
1862	Servet Bey, Naim Efendi's son-in-law in *Kiralık Konak*
1862–1893	Nabizade Nazim
1864–1930	Hodja Ali Rıza Bey, the artist
1864?–1932	Ahmet Rasim

1864–1943	Hüseyin Rahmi Gürpınar
1866–1958	Cemil Topuzlu Pasha, first mayor of Istanbul
1866	Tevfik/Tewfik, Rabia's father in *Sinekli Bakkal*
1867	Sekine, Naim Efendi's daughter in *Kiralık Konak*
1867–1945	Halit (Halid) Ziya Uşaklıgıl
1868–1944	Abdül Mecit II, Caliph 1922–1924
1873–1942	Vedat Bey (Tek)
1874–1933	Rıfat Osman
1874–1957	Hüseyin Cahit Yalçın
1875–1971	Celâl Esad Arseven
1875–1924	Ziya Gökalp
1880	Recai Pasha, grandfather of Yüksel, in "The Three-Story House"
1880	Faiz Bey in *Fatih Harbiye*, making him twenty-six when Neriman was born and forty-six at the time of the novel, in 1926
1880–	Ay Hanım Efendi (if she is fifty when she gives her tea parties)
1880–1983	Clemens Holzmeister arrives in Turkey in 1927
1881–1938	Mustafa Kemal Atatürk
1881–1937	Ahmet Refik
1882–1964	Halide Edib Adıvar
1883–1961	Osman Nuri Ergin
1883–1952	Memduh Şevket Esendal
1884–1920	Ömer Seyfeddin
1884–1958	Yahya Kemal Beyatlı
1885–1966	Hamdullah Suphi Tanrıöver
1887–1965	Le Corbusier
1887–1952	Sermet Muhtar Alus
1888	Rabia in *Sinekli Bakkal*, making her twenty in 1908
1888–1963	Abdülhak Şinasi Hisar
1888–1982	Arif Hikmet Koyunoğlu
1889–1974	Yakup Kadri Karaosmanoğlu
1890–1966	Mehmet Fuat Köprülü
1891–1965	Mehmet Emin (Erişirgil)
1892–	Seniha, Naim Efendi's granddaughter in *Kiralık Konak*
1893–1974	Ernst Egli, arrives in Turkey in 1927
1893–	Sermet Bey in *Harem*, age twenty-five in 1918
1895–1967	Yüsuf Ziya Ortaç
1896–1953	Sedat Simavi

1898–1986	Ahmed Süheyl Ünver
1898–	Nazan in *Harem*
1899–1961	Peyami Safa
1901–1962	Ahmet Hamdi Tanpınar
1901–1987	Malik Aksel
1905–1993	Samiha Ayverdi
1905–1975	Reşad Ekrem Koçu
1905?–1973	Sadberk Hanım
1905–1983	Necip Fazıl Kısakürek
1905–1966	Aptullah Ziya Kozanoğlu
1908–	Neriman in *Fatih-Harbiye*, making her eighteen in 1926
1908–1970	Irfan Orga
1908–1988	Sedat Hakkı Eldem
1909–1999	Münevver Ayaşlı
1915	Cemile in *Cumbadan Rumbaya*, making her twenty in 1935
1915	Yüksel in "The Three-Story House," making him twenty in 1935
1919–1999	Salah Birsel
1921–1989	Yusuf Atılgan
1921?	Yaşlı Adam, the cartoon character in "Hikâye-ı İstanbul," making him seventy-five in 1996
1923	Oktay Akbal
1928–1986	Edip Cansever
1930–	Güngör Dilmen, author of "Our Love was the most devastating fire of Aksaray"
1939–	Önder Küçükerman
1944–	Ahmet Turhan Altıner, architect, journalist, historian
1947–	İsmail Gülqeç, cartoonist

Notes

INTRODUCTION

1. Terdiman, *Present Past*.

2. In *Simulacra and Simulation*, Jean Baudrillard argues that our postmodern culture is a world of signs that have fundamentally broken with any reference to reality.

3. A portion of this work appears in preliminary form in Bertram, "The Ottoman House in the Turkish Imagination."

4. Thompson, "Reception Theory and the Interpretation of Historical Meaning," 251 (emphasis mine). See also Holub, *Reception Theory*.

5. See almost any analysis of the work of Mahmoud Darwish, but also Parmenter, *Giving Voice to Stones*.

6. See Khan, "Memory Work: The Reciprocal Framing of Self and Place in Émigré Autobiographies," and Bastea's "Storied Cities: Literary Memories of Thessaloniki and Istanbul." Also see how Bastea includes the literary imagination as a player in *The Creation of Modern Athens*, where the city is shown to be "a remarkable balancing act between a radiant myth and a miserable reality," as Georgiadis puts it in his review of this book in *The Journal of the Society of Architectural Historians*.

7. Evin, *Origins and Development of the Turkish Novel*; Sönmez, "Turkish Women"; Parla, *Babalar ve Oğullar*.

8. Lachmann, *Memory and Literature*, 15. But see also Vervliet, *Methods for the Study of Literature as Cultural Memory*.

9. Duben, "Nineteenth and Twentieth Century Ottoman Turkish Family and Household Structure"; Duben and Behar, *Istanbul Households*.

10. Kandioti, "Gendering the Modern."

11. Göçek, *Social Constructions of Nationalism in the Middle East*.

12. His major works are listed in the Bibliography. He is also discussed in Chapter 5. See also Bozdoğan et al., *Sedad Eldem*.

13. See the still useful Küçükerman, *Anadolu'daki Geleneksel Türk Evinde Mekân*

Organizasiyonu Açısından Odalar. More recently, see Kuban, *The Turkish Hayat House.*

14. *Modernism and Nation Building* was published in 2001, two years after my manuscript was presented as a doctoral dissertation entitled "The Turkish House: An Effort of Memory" (1999, Department of Art History, UCLA). Although I have incorporated as much of the current literature as is feasible in revising the dissertation for publication, most of my references to Bozdoğan are to her earlier work.

15. A term introduced by Pierre Nora to describe places of collective memory that hold ideas about the nation, which may include actual places, such as buildings or monuments, but also, and more tellingly, political traditions, rituals, national celebrations, and textbooks. In my work I have used Nora, *Realms of Memory.*

16. Benjamin, "Theses on the Philosophy of History," 168.

17. James, *The Principles of Psychology,* 425.

18. Ibid.

CHAPTER 1

1. Lefebvre, *The Production of Space,* 39.

2. Üstünkök, "Ten Years with Seventeen-Ten."

3. For a discussion of the Türkiye Tarihi Evleri Koruma Derneği from its inception through 1993, see Balcı, *Türk Evi ve Biz.*

4. The word *taht* comes from the Arabic *tahta,* meaning "below, under"; *tahtani* thus means "the lower floor" of a two-story building.

5. *Fevkani* derives from Arabic *fawqa,* "above, over"; Ar. *fawqānī* is used to refer to the upper levels of the house, in opposition to the *tahtani.* See A. T. Altıner, *Konak Kitabı.* For a discussion of an Anatolian konak, see M. Winfield, "The Yakupoğlu Konak."

6. *Hayat* means life; thus, the *hayat* could be considered analogous to a living room.

7. The word *oda* is seen to derive from the word *otağ,* or tent.

8. The Arabic word *haram,* "harem" in Turkish, refers to a space restricted to those who follow certain rules, where anything profane is prohibited. It is thus a sanctuary. An example is the *Haram as-Sharif,* or Noble Sanctuary, which is the platform that supports the Dome of the Rock and the Al-Aqsa Mosque in Jerusalem. The ultimate harâm is the Ka'ba, the holy sanctuary at Mecca. In the house, the harem is a sanctuary restricted to women and those men who meet requirements of relationship or age.

9. For a discussion of how the structure of a house, such as door and window sizes, has been approached for social information, see Pavlides, "Architectural Change in a Vernacular Environment."

10. Hutchins et al., "Sign and Symbol," 730. Augustine, in the fourth century, was discussing the spiritual truth of the Eucharist.

11. For the conception of space as a symbolic structure of relations created by society and modeled after social relations, see Durkheim, *The Rules of Sociological Method*, and the "social semiotics" of Pavlides, "Architectural Change in a Vernacular Environment."

12. James, "Conception," n. 17, in *The Principles of Psychology*.

13. And, *Karagöz: Turkish Shadow Theatre*.

14. See Siyavuşgil, *Karagöz: Its History*. Ahmet Hamdı Tanpınar wrote that the Karagöz plays were so much a part of Ramazan that there were actually twenty-eight separate plays, one for each night. Tanpınar, *Beş Şehir*, 71. Hacivat and Karagöz were so embedded in late Ottoman culture that they were used as the stars of numerous political cartoons of this period to convey widely understood personality traits. See, for example, Çeviker, *Nişan G. Berberyan*.

15. There is also a garden pavilion or köşk that is not a residence, although it may be used that way in some cases. For an example, see Göktaş, "Karagöz Shadow Shows," 37. The garden pavilion is also a popular motif in Ottoman-period embroidered textiles, made for both domestic and court use. Examples of these embroidered kiosks, as well as kiosks that resemble Shirin's house, or the *Şirin'in Köşkü*, can be seen in almost every published collection of Ottoman embroideries. See, for example, Barışta, "*Özel Müzelerimiz ve Koleksionlarımız*," 21–23.

16. The story of Ferhad and Shirin, a type of Romeo and Juliet, is a Persian one. In its Turkish Karagöz form it retains its Persian characters, except that the Turkish version is sweeter because Karagöz enters the story and manages to unite the two lovers, who remain apart in the Persian original.

17. There are two forms of house-tasvir. The main one is Karagöz's house. This always shows the cumba in profile. Hacivat's house also has a cumba, but since it is usually shown straight on, it is not as clearly read as a protrusion. Contemporary viewers would have understood it, however. See the drawing of Karagöz and Hacivat onstage in Chapter 2. I am grateful to Hayâlî (shadow theater puppeteer) Emin Şenyer for his detailed information about the use of the tasvir, or puppets and images. See also Şenyer, "Traditional Turkish Puppet Shadow Play."

18. Hutchins et al., "Sign and Symbol," 732. Emphasis mine.

19. Refer to Bozdoğan et al., *Sedad Eldem*. See also U. Alsaç, *Kültür ve Tabiat*.

20. Eldem, *Türk Evi*.

21. Tanyeli, "*Anadolu'da Bizans*" ("Housing and Settlement Patterns"), 466. Faroqhi's research in Anatolia suggests that the second story (above the ground floor) of the Ottoman-period house was introduced in the seventeenth century as an import from Istanbul. Thus, the Ottoman house type as we know it today represents an eastward expansion of the Istanbul or Bursa form. Faroqhi, *Men of Modest Substance*, 214.

22. Eldem, *Türk Evi*, 284–285.

23. Ibid., vol. I, A:41.

24. Oleg Grabar suggests that the renderings of the house form in the thirteenth-century *Maqamat* of al-Hariri relate to the scenes and props of contemporary shadow theater. Grabar, "Pictures or Commentaries," 84–104.

25. James, "Conception," n. 17. "What we began by calling the 'image' or 'copy' of the fact in the mind, is really not there at all in that simple shape, as a separate 'idea.' Or, at least, if it be there as a separate idea, no memory will go with it. What memory goes with is, on the contrary, a very complex representation, that of the fact to be recalled plus its associates, the whole forming one 'object' known in one integral pulse of consciousness and demanding probably a vastly more intricate brain-process than that on which any simple sensorial image depends." James, "Memory."

26. Siyavuşgil, *Karagöz*.

27. The Ottoman mahalle was not a loose geographic entity but a well-defined area with its own government offices and an organized social structure. For some discussion of the mahalle and its late Ottoman types, see Kandioti, "Gendering the Modern."

28. For a discussion of republican intervention into Karagöz productions, including monitoring by the Ministry of Internal Affairs and the rewriting of plays and characters to serve state ideology, see Öztürk, *Karagöz Co-Opted*.

29. Choay, *L'Allégorie du Patrimoine*.

30. Renda, "Wall Paintings in Turkish Houses," 711–735.

31. For a discussion of these paintings, see Renda. Rüçhan Arık has found similar paintings of architectural scenes of Istanbul on late nineteenth-century metal trays and boxes for home use; he attributes their style and subject matter to the influence of Western artists working in Turkey, including those in the postcard trade. Arık, "Landscapes in Trays."

32. An undated metal tray with a scene of Istanbul, Galata, Galata Bridge, and the Marmara has a suspicious similarity to the Amasya Şadırvan Canopy. See Arık, "Landscapes in Trays," 10.

33. See, for example, the urban illustrations in the 1810 "*Musavver Iran Sefaretnamesi*" of Yasincizade Seyyid Abdülvahhab Efendi. Unat, *Osmanlı Sefirleri*, figs. 32–36.

34. Tanyeli, "*Anadolu'da Bizans*" ("Housing and Settlement Patterns"), espec. 454.

35. Ibid.

36. James, *The Principles of Psychology*, 425.

37. According to Robert Maynard Hutchins's paraphrasing of William James: "The object *remembered* or imagined need not be physically present to the senses like the object *perceived*. The object imagined need not be located in the past like the object remembered, nor, for that matter, need it have any definite location in time and space. . . . It need have no actual existence. It may be a mere possibility. . . . As

the object of memory is an event that no longer exists, so the object of imagination may be something which has never existed and never will." Hutchins et al., "Memory and Imagination," 134.

38. How Istanbul "really" looked is not at issue here. Certainly there were, at the time of the student's drawing, neighborhoods of the type of houses that this young artist represents, for example in Cankurtaran, the area on the Marmara side of the Sultan Ahmet Mosque, abutting today's Akbıyık. But these houses were in a state of decay. Furthermore, her drawing depicts the areas across the Golden Horn from Cankurtaran, in Ortaköy, where neighborhoods like these had not existed for several generations.

39. Boyer, *The City of Collective Memory*, 67.

40. Tanpınar, *Beş Şehir*, 59.

41. Terdiman, *Present Past*, 3.

42. Ibid.

43. Lowenthal, *Geographies of the Mind*.

44. Bakhtin, *The Dialogic Imagination*, 13.

45. Another poetic reading of rupture is Larry McMurtry's *Walter Benjamin at the Dairy Queen: Reflections on Sixty and Beyond*: "Because of when and where I grew up, on the Great Plains just as the herding tradition was beginning to lose its vitality, I have been interested all my life in vanishing breeds."

46. Eldem wrote that "the major architectural traditions finally died during the lifetime of Mongeri." Eldem, *Türk Evi*, 208. Giulio Mongeri was an Italian architect who, from 1909 until 1930, taught at the Academy of Fine Arts (*Sanayi-i Nefise Mekteb-i Âlisi*) in Istanbul, under the directorship of Osman Hamdi Bey.

47. For a personal memory of fires and changes of fortune in Istanbul in the early twentieth century, see Orga, *Portrait of a Turkish Family*. For maps of Istanbul's fires up to the middle of the nineteenth century, see Atasoy, *İznik*, 18–19.

48. Çelik, *The Remaking of Istanbul*, 52.

49. See Hüsameddin, *Amasya Tarihi*, 92, 111, 113, 128, 185, 203, 234; and Demiray, *Resimli Amasya*, 52.

50. Pekean, *Te inchpes Hruandanin aghjike Berdakaghak hars tarin*, 303.

51. In his biography, Irfan Orga recalls the fire in his neighborhood of Sultanahmet in the early years of this century. Orga, *Portrait of a Turkish Family*.

52. Tanpınar, *Beş Şehir*, 63.

53. Curtis, *The Turk and His Lost Provinces*, 116.

54. According to Çelik, "Kârgir construction was defined as having stone supporting walls on the lower levels and brick walls on the upper stories." In addition, there were two types of kârgir: *tam kârgir* (completely kârgir), in which the beams and roof structure were of iron or copper, and *nim kârgir* (partially kârgir), in which the beams and roof structure could be of wood. Çelik, *The Remaking of Istanbul*, 52.

55. For example, two fires in 1887 and 1908 in Arnavutköy, an urban village up the

Bosphorus from Istanbul, destroyed 373 houses, which were then rebuilt in timber, although with a changed street pattern and a revivalist style of architecture. Nayır, "Arnavutköy."

56. See Denel, *Batılılaşma Sürecinde İstanbulda* (Changes in the Conception and Exterior of Residence in Istanbul), for a list of all the proclamations and codes regarding the height of buildings, as well as the materials used in their construction, until the end of the nineteenth century. His list of regulations regarding the height of residences and the width of streets spans the years 1725–1883. It also has many of the relevant texts of these codes.

57. Tekeli, "Nineteenth Century Transformation of Istanbul Metropolitan Area," 38.

58. Ibid. For an example of such a map, and the visual difference these maps made to the urban fabric of Izmir, see the 1905 "Plans for the Central Business Area of Izmir" and the suggested post-fire urban plans in Atay, *Tarih İçinde İzmir*, 143 ff. For Istanbul, see Çelik, *The Remaking of Istanbul*, 49–81.

59. Çelik, *The Remaking of Istanbul*, 52.

60. Ibid., 55.

61. Ibid., 58.

62. In 1903 the Armenian *Illustrated Geographical Dictionary* (*Badgerazart Pnashkharhig Pararan*) criticized the old part of Amasya as having very narrow and crooked streets by comparing them to the only neighborhood there, Savadiye, where the streets were at least a little wider. Badgerazart, *Badgerazart Pnashkharhig Pararan*, 128.

63. Ortaylı, *İstanbul'dan Sayfalar*, 36.

64. Çelik, *The Remaking of Istanbul*, 50.

65. Ibid., 52.

66. Aksel, *İstanbul'un Ortası*, 13.

67. Çeviker, *Nişan G. Berberyan*, 150.

68. Ibid., 227.

69. Aksel, *İstanbul'un Ortası*, 13.

70. Kalem, *Kalem Journal*, 1–2.

71. Çelik, *The Remaking of Istanbul*, 63.

CHAPTER 2

1. This was the title of Güngör Dilmen's poem in *The Turkish Pen*. It was also the title of an earlier play, which was the winner of the 1989 İş Bankası Grand Award for Literature.

2. Güngör Dilmen, really a playwright rather than the poet I characterize him as, was born in 1930. The fire in the Aksaray neighborhood of Istanbul was extensive

and devastating, and by the end of it far more than two thousand buildings, mostly dwellings, were lost. Sakaoğlu, "Yangınlar: Osmanlı Dönemi," 427–438.

3. Lara, "The Stories We're All In Together."

4. Koçu, "Aksaray Yangınları," 539–542.

5. "Alus, Sermet Muhtar," 232–233.

6. This cityscape has since become the backdrop for the annual Ramazan celebration in Sultanahmet.

7. Tanyeli, "Osmanlı Barınma Kültüründe Batılılaşma-Modernleşme" ("Westernization-Modernization in the Ottoman Wohnkultur"), 284–297.

8. What a wonderful phrase! Is there a counterpart, I wonder, such as Eastern-Occidented?

9. Alafranga literally means "in the manner of the French." Because the French were the first to colonize and affect the Middle East, "Frenk" or "Frang" was the first word for these foreigners and their customs; the term was then extended to all Westerners.

10. The historic peninsula is the area enclosed by the old walls of Constantinople.

11. Nazim, Zehra.

12. Evin, Origins and Development of the Turkish Novel, 189.

13. Seyfeddin, "The Secret Temple," 270–273. The charm of this story lies in the credulousness of the European guest, who interprets everything he does not understand, such as laundry piles, as Oriental exotica. We know it was written before 1920 because Ömer Seyfeddin died in 1920.

14. Pierre Loti is the pseudonym under which the French novelist Julien Viaud wrote novels of romantic encounters in Istanbul.

15. Orga, Portrait of a Turkish family. Western sources take this Westernization of interiors back to the mid-nineteenth century: In 1845 the traveler Charles White wrote, "In proportion as intercourse with Europeans extends, fashions and customs vary, so that an important change is rapidly taking place in the furniture of houses. Thus, in those of wealthy persons, chairs, sofas, tables, consoles, mirrors, wardrobes, chandeliers and a variety of Western essentials may be seen, Indeed, the Sultan's private day-apartments, at Tcherghan and Beshiktash are furnished more in the European than the Oriental style. Fireplaces or stoves alone are wanting to give them the appearance of the most commodious French or German Salons. The middling classes are also making some progress. . . ." (Emphasis mine.) White, Three Years in Constantinople, 174–175, as quoted in Sönmez, "Turkish Women in Turkish Literature of the Nineteenth Century," 3.

16. Another example of a memory image is the use of the wooden house facades that lined the hippodrome in the Ramazan celebration in 1998, depicted and discussed in this chapter.

17. Taylor, "On the Shores of the Bosphorus," 50–52; Barışta, "Özel Müzelerimiz ve Koleksionlarımız," 17–26.

18. Büyükdere was the first area to break with the homogeneity of Ottoman housing and establish a European physiognomy. Tanyeli, *"Anadolu'da Bizans,"* 467.

19. Taylor, "On the Shores of the Bosphorus," 50–52.

20. The upper row of windows made of stained glass set in plaster lost their popularity in Istanbul in the mid-eighteenth century, when plate glass became available even to the middle classes. It remained in use in the provincial capitals until the mid-nineteenth century. Tanyeli, *"Anadolu'da Bizans,"* 460–463.

21. Baydar, *Hamdullah Suphi Tanrıöver,* 5.

22. Halide Edib (sometimes spelled Edip) was educated at the American Girls College in Istanbul and was considered the crowning success of the missionaries who ran the school. The memoirs of the president of the college, *Under Five Sultans,* "opens with an unveiled picture of Halide Edib on the inside cover, and the inscription reads, 'Halide Edib. Bachelor of Arts, Constantinople Woman's College, Author, Educator, Statesman.' The photograph is a symbolic depiction of both the work of the American women and the beginning of a new life in the modern Republic of Turkey." Başcı, "Shadows in the Missionary Garden of Roses," 112, quoting Patrick, *Under Five Sultans.* Edib was the only female member of the Turk Ocağı until 1918, when she helped rewrite its constitution to make women eligible for membership. Edib, *Memoirs,* 325. She was known for the intensity of her feminism and not only was active in the war of independence but also became a permanently public figure after her speech at the famous Sultanahmet meeting of 1919 following the occupation of Izmir. She served on the Western front, first as a nurse and later as an interpreter, press advisor, and secretary to Mustafa Kemal.

23. Edib, *Memoirs,* 323. The validity of Halide Edib's memory of a unified Ottoman consciousness is outside my topic, as pertinent and provocative as it may be. The Tanzimat Reforms, however, had sought to address the inequalities between Muslims and non-Muslims and to guarantee equal legal rights to all peoples living within the Ottoman domain; it promised to regularize tax assessment and collection and to improve the conscription methods and training of the military. Also promised was greater participation in local government by minorities.

24. Turkism arose, along with Islamism, Pan-Islamism, and Pan-Turanism, as an alternative form of identity to Ottomanism. The idea of a Turkish as distinct from an Ottoman or an Islamic loyalty began with the Young Turks in Paris, who separated from the Young Ottomans. See Lewis, *The Emergence of Modern Turkey,* 155, 343–353.

25. This awakening mirrored the Greek awakening that preceded it. For example, even before the revolutionary movement began in earnest in Greece, Greek ballads such as those of Vlachavas (d. 1809), the priest-*klepht* leader who rose against the Ottomans, rang with these words: "'Will you turn Turk, Diakos mine, change / your faith / Make obeisance in the mosque and leave / the Church?'/ But Diakos answered him, and spoke angrily; / 'Go, you and your faith, you infidels, / to

destruction! / *I was born a Greek, and a Greek I will die!*'" Volkan and Itzkowitz, "Greeks and Turks."

26. Lewis, *The Emergence of Modern Turkey*, 350.

27. Abdülaziz Bey (1850–1918) wrote in his memoirs about the "awakening," its relationship to educating the public, and the Türk Ocağı of 1912. Abdülaziz, *Osmanlı Adet*, 5.

28. Baydar, *Hamdullah Suphi Tanrıöver*, 56.

29. Ibid., 55–57. Halide Edib was not one of the founding members of the Ocak; it had been founded in secret by students of the medical school in 1911. But she was soon to be an active member. In 1918 she and Hamdullah Suphi, Mehmet Emin, Ağaoğlu Ahmet, Ziya Gökalp, Köprülü-zade Fuad, and Hüseyin-zade Ali Bey were the Science and Culture (*Hars ve İlim*) organizing committee members. Enginün, *Halide Edip*, 49.

30. The building was opened as the *Türkocağı* (Turkish Hearth) Building on May 23, 1930, but very shortly afterward, on June 10, 1930, following the closure of all Türkocağı centers, for reasons still unclear, it was handed over to the Republican People's Party. In 1932 it became the center of the *Halkevi* (People's House) organization and continued to be used by them until after the elections of the 1950s, when all Halkevis were closed down. It is now the Museum of Painting and Sculpture. Başkan, *Ankara Devlet Resim ve Heykel Müzesi*, 82–84.

31. It seems almost sacrilegious to relegate Mustafa Kemal Atatürk's history and importance to a footnote. He was the charismatic leader of the Turkish Nationalist movement who led the military campaigns that would lead to a successful war of Turkish independence. He became the Turkish Republic's first president, and it was his vision and clout that made the first years of the republic an almost military move toward secularism, Westernization, and modernity. His name and his vision are behind this move as it is addressed and readdressed in this book.

32. Yavuz, "Finding a National Idiom," 54.

33. Koyunoğlu wrote that Atatürk took a special interest in every aspect of its design, and would appear at the work site to see how it was progressing. Altıner, "*Arif Hikmet Koyunoğlu*," 45–46.

34. Bozdoğan, *Modernism and Nation Building*, 36. The First National Style begins a series of styles and movements that attempt to capture the moving target of Turkish identity. We will address many of these movements here. For a visual catalogue of buildings in these styles, see http://www.archmuseum.org/galeri_resimler .asp?fotoid=24&id=6&exid=4. The categories on this Web site are Foreign Architects of the Young Republic; The New Approach Towards the Contemporary Movements; A New Perspective on National Architecture: 2nd National Architecture Movement; The 1950s and Modernism; the 1960s; and the 1970s to the Present.

35. Koyunoğlu, "*Ankara Evleri*," 46–47.

36. Koyunoğlu, "*Türk Mimari*," 197–199. Koyunoğlu remembers Atatürk's dis-

cussion with him, as the building was in process, for a need to have a modern Turkish architecture that was different from other modern national architectures. Altıner, *"Arif Hikmet Koyunoğlu,"* 46. Atatürk's interest in a national architecture stems from Ziya Gökalp's ideology of Turkism, which privileged the construction of a "Turkish culture" with deep historical roots that could serve as the building blocks of modern culture.

37. Yavuz and Özkan characterized Koyunoğlu's buildings, such as the Ministry of Foreign Affairs and the Museum of Ethnography, as "monumental with extravagant front elevations, usually hiding modest structures behind them." Yavuz, "Finding a National Idiom," 62.

38. Razi, *"Ay Hanımefendi,"* 19.

39. Hisar, *İstanbul ve Pierre Loti.*

40. Ünver, *"Şark Odası,"* 626–627.

41. Razi, *"Ay Hanımefendi,"* 19.

42. Alonso, "The Politics of Space, Time, and Substance," 387.

43. Ottoman citizens did not have formal last names until the time of the republic. A name in parentheses, here, Hamdullah Suphi (Tanrıöver), is the surname taken by 1934, when they were required by law.

44. Altıner, *"Arif Hikmet Koyunoğlu,"* 44.

45. The text is written in Ottoman script, as this predates Atatürk's script reforms. I am indebted to Gary Leiser for his sensitive translations of these Ottoman passages. Suphi, *"Eski Türk Evleri,"* 1216–1221.

46. The Tanzimat Reforms were a type of perestroika. They were a series of "reorganizations" begun in 1839 under Abdül Mecid I (1839–1861), with the goal of using Europe as a model for what were seen as necessary changes in the Ottoman Empire. They followed Sultan II Mahmut's (1808–1839) restructuring of the bureaucracy, most notably in the creation of Western-type ministries of foreign affairs, the interior, and finance.

47. Suphi, *"Eski Türk Evleri,"* 5:1216–1221.

48. Suphi, *"Eski Türk Evleri,"* 6:2063–2069.

49. Refer also to the changes in the urban street pattern discussed above, and see Tekeli, "The Social Context of the Development," 9–33.

50. Tanyeli, *"Osmanlı Barınma Kültüründe Batılılaşma-Modernleşme,"* 284–297.

51. Kostof, *America By Design,* 7.

52. Arseven, *"Türkiye'de Tanzimat Devrinden Sonra Resim,"* 143.

53. Ibid., 128–160. Arseven, *"Türk Sanatı Tarihi, menşeinden bugüne kadar."*

54. There were other artists who included houses in their landscapes, especially Hüseyin Zekai Pasha (1860–1919), of whom Arseven said, "He was the first impressionist painter of Turkey . . . [and he was] like a museum of the Bosphorus Yalı." Ibid., 151. Together with Hodja Ali Rıza Bey and a few friends studying at the Kuleli Askeri İdaresi, he appealed to the school director and pioneered the founding of an

art studio. Ahmet Ziya Akbulut (1860–1919) and Halil Pasha (1857–1939) also had houses in their artistic repertoire. See Berk, *Türk ve Yabancı Resimde İstanbul*, and Tansuğ, *Çağdaş Türk Sanatı*, 60–62. Hodja Ali Rıza, however, made the neighborhood and its houses his prime subject, and was loved for it.

55. Yetik, *Ressamlarımız*.

56. Yaman, *"Osmanlı Ressamlar Cemiyeti,"* 176–177. Sayı, *"Ali Rıza'nın Hayatı ve Eserleri,"* 100. Vecih, *"Ankara Resim Sergisi Münasebetiyle,"* 9–15.

57. Yetik, *Ressamlarımız*, 110.

58. Ünver, *Dr. Rıfat Osman'a göre Edirne Evleri ve Konakları*, ii.

59. Osman, *Edirne Rehnuması*. Interestingly, although his paintings are of residences, both palatial and mundane, his textual work on Edirne catalogues monumental architecture only. (This remains an important source of information on Edirne's mosques, churches, synagogues, bridges, markets, fountains, and streets.)

60. He was also an active photographer, but his photographs of Edirne's houses remain unpublished to date.

61. Begun in 1889 as secret societies of progressive university students and military cadets, the Young Turks were a group of intellectuals who worked for the establishment of constitutional monarchy. Their politically dominant era was from 1912 to 1918.

62. Işın, *"Celâl Esad Arseven Üzerine,"* 3.

63. Arseven, *Constantinople: De Byzance*, 247.

64. Ibid., 243.

65. In the same year that Suphi gave his speech to the Turkish Hearth meeting, Arseven's *Constantinople* was published in Turkish.

66. In 1908, with the proclamation of the constitution (the II Meşrutiyet) Enver Pasha had opened Turkish arms to all nationalities. But this show of brotherly love was temporary, and may even have been an attempt to win German support, which soon became unnecessary, and his open arms turned to armaments.

67. Seyfeddin, *Ashab-ı Kehfimiz*, 9. English translation courtesy of H. Paksoy.

68. The Balkan defeat was received by the Turkists in particular as a spur to national regeneration. Akçura wrote in the 1914 Turk Ocağı journal *Türk Yurdu*, "We have been defeated. The Bulgar, the Serb, the Greek—our *subjects* of five centuries, whom we have despised, have defeated us. This reality, which we could not conjure up even in our imaginations, will open our eyes, will serve as a terrific slap in our faces to turn our heads in sane directions." (Emphasis mine.) Berkes, *The Development of Secularism in Turkey*, 358.

69. For example, women's journals published between 1886 and 1923 indicated that their pages were "open to Ottoman women"; however, Demirdirek has shown that "Ottoman" seems to have meant the Muslim-Turkish community, as such usage of the term was the common practice at the time. Jewish, Armenian, or Greek women

were not contributors, and the language of the publications addresses Muslim Ottoman women. Demirdirek, "In Pursuit of the Ottoman Women's Movement," 67.

70. Suphi, "*Eski Türk Evleri*," from another sensitive Ottoman translation provided by Gary Leiser.

71. In Halide Edib's semi-autobiographical story of the Turkish struggle for independence, *Shirt of Flame* (*Ateşten Gömlek*), she talks about how the Beyoğlu side of Istanbul was full of Christians who sneered at the Muslims until a Muslim demonstration took place that made them afraid to come outside. "We walked across the bridge. Armed and all-powerful Pera had gone through a panic expressed by 'the Turks are coming' and no one was on the streets. For a moment we had the dreamy and unreal feeling of possessing our own country." Edib then explains, in a note to her readers: "Pera—usually filled with native Christians. In times of alarm they shut themselves in their houses." Edib, *Shirt of Flame*, 39.

72. Again, I am deeply indebted to Gary Leiser for his timely, insightful, and even witty translations of articles in Ottoman Turkish.

73. Ünver, "*Şark Odası*," 627. Thanks to Gary Leiser for the translation from the Ottoman.

74. Ibid., 626.

75. Ibid., 627.

76. Ibid., 627.

77. Sayar, *A. Süheyl Ünver*, 191.

78. Ibid., 202. This is from one of the many dossiers of Ünver's mostly undated memoirs and drawings held in the private collection of his daughter, Gülbün Mesara. Other dossiers are at the Süleymaniye Library.

79. Ibid., 237.

80. Ibid., 475.

81. Ünver, "*Ressam Ali Rıza Beye Göre*," 7.

82. Sayar, "*A. Süheyl Ünver*," 476.

83. Ünver, "*Ressam Ali Rıza Beye Göre*," 7.

84. Ünver traveled to Izmit in 1923 and made over eighty drawings during a week-long visit. He describes houses that were built between 1160 AH and 1195 AH that are now "suffering from neglect." Ibid., 143.

85. Ünver, "*İzmit Hatıraları*," 1165.

86. Ünver, "*Eski Türk Evinde Ocak*," 1098–1011.

87. Ünver finished his medical studies in Paris in 1927–1929. In 1930 he entered academic life at the Istanbul Medical School (*Tıp Fakültesi*).

88. Sayar, "*A. Süheyl Ünver*," 156.

89. According to Sayar, in 1926 Rıfat Osman invited Süheyl to Edirne to give him an intimate tour of the city. Ibid., 157. And in 1928, Süheyl was working on Osman's Palace materials, organizing it into a book. Ibid., 182.

90. Galip, "*Ankara Evleri,*" 354. I admit that Gary Leiser and I laughed with astonishment when he first translated this from the Ottoman, but over time, it's beginning to make sense.

91. Ibid., 359.

92. Nürettin, "*Eski Türk Evleri.*"

93. İbrahim Edhem Pasha wrote *Usul-ü Mimarığ-i Osman*, or *L'architecture Ottomane*, which was published on the occasion of the Ottoman Empire's participation in the Vienna International Exposition in 1873. Osman Hamdi was the founder of the Imperial Museum of Antiquities (*Asar-ı Atika Müzesi*) and the Fine Arts Institute (*Sanayi-i Nefise Mektebi Alisi*).

94. It was this book that was later expanded into the 1939 *L'Art Turc*.

95. Nürettin's article is in *Fikirler*, the journal of the Izmir Halkevi, but Galip's audience is the teaching community; thus he offers the Ankara house to teachers as a resource for teaching history while at the same time making an open plea, as Minister of Culture, to the Minister of Education.

96. Ünver, "*Edirne Evleri,*" 669.

97. Ibid., 670.

98. Ibid., 668.

99. Seyfeddin, "*İlk Düşen Ak,*" 67–68. Translation reproduced by permission of Hasan Paksoy.

100. Koyunoğlu, "*Türk Mimari,*" 197–199.

101. Koyunoğlu, "*Ankara Evleri,*" 46–47.

102. Koyunoğlu, "*Türk Mimari,*" 42.

103. Koyunoğlu's 1929 article, "Ankara Houses," reiterates that domestic architecture is at least as valuable a marker of Turkishness as monumental architecture:

Just as the large and official buildings of Turkish architecture show a strong individuality, old Turkish houses show some beautiful types. In architectural research, small buildings designed for residence are very significant, just like large monuments that contain a great character.... It is very important to investigate our old houses because an old house is like the fulcrum [*içtima*] of an era, it is a document of national thought and of its older people; it is a measure of the aesthetic feeling of the people who lived inside it (Koyunoğlu, "*Türk Mimari,*" 45).

104. Ibid.

105. Bozdoğan, "Sedad Hakkı Eldem of Turkey," 44.

106. *Türk-Yurdu* (1930), "*Türk Ocakları Merkez Binası,*" 79–81, plus many unpaginated photographs.

CHAPTER 3

1. For example, the term Ottoman has been used retroactively to define a time of inclusivity, an idealized period when multiculturalism was institutionalized. Amy Mills is currently working on this retroactive image as it has persisted in Istanbul's Kuzguncuk neighborhood. See Mills, "Boundaries of the Nation." Çolak, "Ottomanism vs. Kemalism," investigates contemporary Tukish Islamists' reinvoking a memory of Ottomanism as a critique of Kemalism in the 1990s. It may be noted, however, that a policy of greater emphasis on Turkification marked the career of Mahmut II (1808–1839), but this slowly gave way to a more inclusive vision of society, heralded by the Tanzimat, which admitted non-Muslims to coveted "Ottoman status" by opening careers in the military and bureaucracy to them. It was the Tanzimat that sought to guarantee all peoples living within the Ottoman domains their lives, property, and honor; promised to regularize tax assessment and collection; and to improve the conscription methods and training of the military. It was "the Young Turks," along with liberal Ottoman exiles in Paris, whose inflammatory journal *La Jeune Turquie* envisaged a union under which all races and creeds would live and progress together. Thank you to Tracy Lord for emphasizing that the terms "Ottoman" and "Turkish" have long histories that predate the Republic of Turkey, and meanings that are as overlapping as they are contrastive.

2. Ünver, "*Türk Evi*," 667.

3. Karaosmanoğlu, *Kiralık Konak*, 29.

4. For more on this idea, see Friedman, "The Past in the Future: History and the Politics of Identity."

5. I am indebted to the insightful Tracy Lord for the concept of the novel as a method of entering the house.

6. Ottoman society has many parallels with other Islamic societies, but diverges in important ways as well. For this reason I avoid putting Ottoman society in any larger framework. For the connection between sanctity and the house in Islam in general, see Schimmel, *Deciphering the Signs of God*, and Campo, *The Other Sides of Paradise*.

7. Tanyeli contests the notion of a functioning privacy. His research of *waqfiye* (endowment) records suggests that only the smallest minority were able to meet the costs of separation ("modesty—just as is true everywhere at all times—appears to be viable for a small minority who are able to meet its high monetary cost"). Tanyeli, "*Anadolu'da Bizans* (Housing and Settlement Patterns)." One might consider, then, that the idea of the harem and the selamlık were constructed memories, an upperclass or elitist dream of the past. However, mid-nineteenth-century newspaper ads of houses for rent or for sale in Istanbul describe house after house with selamlıks and harems of varying sizes. "*Koçu Ev*," 5402–5403.

8. Garnett, *Turkish Life in Town and Country*, 51.

9. Tanyeli, "*Osmanlı Barınma Kültüründe Batılılaşma-Modernleşme* (Westernization-Modernization in the Ottoman Wohnkulture)," 288.

10. Karaosmanoğlu, *Kiralık Konak*, 29.

11. Here, *iç* (interior) is combined with *li* (with). "*İç*" carries a variety of significant meanings in Turkish, including the heart, the mind, the soul, and their inner recesses, and the inside story, or the heart of the matter. It can also connote a sense of secrecy.

12. I am indebted to Tracy Lord for turning my focus toward "*iç*" and its implications of interiority. She has explored the concept of interiority in post-1980s Turkish culture. In this work, Lord suggests that the novel, itself "a medium of interiority," operates in parallel to the house as interior space. "In contrast to existing genres of literature of the late Ottoman period, the Western novel tends to focus on psychology both analytically and as a narrative, as well as on domestic space. And when it talks about activity of any kind, cultural or psychological, the novel brings a setting with it." Lord, personal communication, September 1998.

13. Göçek suggests that images of the Ottoman as "refined and introverted" were constructions that originated in the new print culture of the last quarter of the nineteenth century. She attaches them to a matrix that includes the characteristics of "very knowledgeable in Western music and literature, conversant in a Western language, positivist, attributing value to human beings, and subscribing to a Western style of life." Göçek, *Rise of the Bourgeoisie, Demise of the Empire*, 119. If this is so, what we are seeing is how this construction was only partially accepted by the early twentieth century. Naim Efendi, after all, had never read a novel in his life. Faiz Bey, however, whom we meet later on, fits this bill.

14. *Baş yarılır fes içinde, kol kırılır yen içinde (kalır)*. Yurtbaşı, *A Dictionary of Turkish Proverbs*, 291.

15. Edib, *Sinekli Bakkal*, 39.

16. Dane Kusić maintains that Sufism is a part and parcel of Turkish culture, history, politics, everyday life, and identity. Sufism is not just a religion; in Turkey it is a shared way of being, or even better: a shared existence that is known to, and lived/experienced by many Turks; thus, it was not something that could be easily discarded (as Atatürk may have tried), and not something that Turks may want to forget. He cites, for example, the resonance of Sufism in Turkish popular music of the late twentieth and early twenty-first century. "Arabesk music, as well as other modern musical genres, are memorial mirrors in which Sufi existence reflects and bounces off." For example, "popular music, even 'pop' Turkish music today, is often characterized by a type of internal pain and suffering that can be understood as a modern rendition of the older trope, i.e., the soul's search for union with the Divine. Listeners may feel comfortable with this, but not know why." Personal communication, September 1998.

17. Mardin, "Cultural Change and the Intellectual," 213.

18. Andrews, *Poetry's Voice, Society's Song*, 116.

19. The *Meddah* is an Ottoman-period one-act, one-man dramatic play in which the narrator also performs the various characters.

20. Edib, *Memoirs*, 232.

21. Ibid., 262.

22. The great scholar, politician, and historian of the Ottomans, M. Fuad Köprülü (1890–1966), singled out Naima as the Ottoman historian "who possessed descriptive powers of the first order" and who "gives vivid historical analyses of historical characters." Köprülü, "*Naima*," 952.

23. Ivo Andrić, for example, has been severely criticized for substituting romantic mythology for history, and I wrestled with this problem in my first readings of him. See Bertram, "Kafana, Konak."

24. Boyd, *The Reflexive Novel*, 174.

25. Ibid., 29.

26. See, for example, Mutluay, *100 Soruda Çağdaş Türk Edebiyatı* "*1908–1972*," and idem, *Elli Yılın Türk Edebiyatı*. *Kiralık Konak* was also one of the required readings in the high school curriculum of the 1950s. See, for example, Nisari, *Metinli Türk Edebiyatı*.

27. The *İstanbulin* and the *Redingot* refer to two types of male Ottoman attire that denoted different periods and different outlooks, although both had a connotation of "Europeanized." The İstanbulin was a long dark military frock that came into fashion with the Tanzimat period of Abdül Mecit II. It was called *İstanbulin* because Istanbul tailors invented it. Take a look at the image of "Naim Efendi" at the beginning of this chapter, although in fact this is the physician, Dr. İsmail Ali Bey. The İstanbulin was not limited to the elite, for all strata of government, from janitors to the pashas, could wear it, and it was particularly favored by soldiers and secular university students. Its Westernness was in opposition to the heavily padded and turbaned clothing of the religious intelligentsia. The *Redingot* (from "riding coat") was a cutaway or tuxedo jacket worn by the men who were attached to the bureaucracy of Abdülhamid II, so it had a connotation of elitism, but also of obsequiousness and hypocrisy. "The *Redingot* men said *bonjur*" (the Turkish spelling of "bonjour"), and this lasted until the revolution of 1908. Sakaoğlu, "İstanbulin," 253.

28. A formulaic expression used after naming any of the companions of the prophet, meaning "May God be well pleased with him."

29. Karaosmanoğlu, *Kiralık Konak*, 29.

30. Ibid., 20.

31. Ibid., 22.

32. *Evi ev eden avrat, yurdu şen eden devlet.* Yurtbaşı, *A Dictionary of Turkish Proverbs*, 249.

33. Tanyeli, "*Anadolu'da Bizans* (Housing and Settlement Patterns)," 463.

34. Edib, *Sinekli Bakkal*, 85.

35. Mardin, *The Genesis of Young Ottoman Thought*, 95–100.

36. Andrews, *Poetry's Voice, Society's Song*, 155.

37. According to Peter Berger and Thomas Luckmann, symbolic universes are "universes of meaning" or theoretical traditions that integrate meaning and institutional order in a symbolic totality, and thus create a whole world. In a symbolic universe, "institutional roles become modes of participation in a universe that transcends and includes the institutional order. Experiences belonging to different spheres of reality are integrated by incorporation in the same, overarching universe of meaning." Berger and Luckmann, *The Social Construction of Reality*. Geertz discusses culture as a type of symbolic universe when he argues that culture is "public" because meanings are necessarily the collective property of a group. When we say we do not understand the actions of people from a culture other than our own, we are acknowledging our lack of familiarity with the imaginative universe within which their acts are signs." Geertz, *The Interpretation of Cultures*, 12–13.

38. I believe that Walter Andrews's work on Ottoman poetry is the most creative work done to date on this ineffable yet delineated concept of interior and exterior space that includes the mundane and the divine, positioning them in this matrix of connectivity. Andrews, *Poetry's Voice, Society's Song*, 152–154. See also Duben and Behar, *Istanbul Households*, 78.

39. Ottoman households were under the jurisdiction of their oldest male, and generations frequently lived together in his house until he died, after which they might establish separate households. The line of authority and respect devolved from him, and this was made clear by terms of address that indicated a person's authority according to age and sex. Duben and Behar, *Istanbul Households*, 225–226. Duben and Behar call this system a "gerontology." Lucy Garnett explained the system when it was working at the end of the nineteenth century:

> The relations between the various members of a Turkish household, and the way in which the younger show respect towards their elders, appear somewhat curious to Europeans. If a man's mother resides permanently under his roof, which is not unusual, his wife's position in the house is but secondary, and she is required to defer to her mother-in-law's wishes in all things. . . . The wife may not seat herself at table before her husband's mother, nor be the first to help herself to dishes, nor may she smoke a cigarette in the presence of the "First Lady" unless the latter invites her to do so. It no doubt often happens that a good deal of friction exists between two ladies occupying these relative positions; but these prescribed rules must be all the same observed. . . . In all matters of Osmanli family, and also generally of social etiquette, precedence depends on age. If, for example, a married Turk has a sister residing in his harem with his wife, the elder of the two would enjoy precedence of the other; and similarly, if he has three children, the eldest and the youngest boys and

the second a girl, she must defer to her elder brother, while the younger boy, spoilt and indulged though he may be, must give way to her in anything that affects their common interests. Nor do the youthful members of a family presume to sit cross-legged before their elders. (Garnett, *Turkish Life*, 52–53)

Kandioti says that "The Ottoman patriarch represented central features of the old order: hierarchy, fixity, and absolute authority." Kandioti, "Gendering the Modern." For another discussion of the patrimonial household system in the Ottoman Empire, see Findley, *Bureaucratic Reform*, 30–39.

40. I discuss the New Literature Movement, the *Edebiyat-ı Cedide Külliyatı*, below.

41. Karaosmanoğlu, *Kiralık Konak*, 22–23.

42. Karaosmanoğlu, *Kiralık Konak*, 25.

43. In Istanbul, young men often moved into the households of the father-in-law, following the system of the Imperial Palace, where the "*damat*" or son-in-law played an important role. However, Karaosmanoğlu refers to Servet Bey according to the Anatolian counterpart of the damat, that is, the "*iç güveyi*," who was considered anything but desirable. See Duben and Behar, *Istanbul Households*, 78–79.

44. Karaosmanoğlu, *Kiralık Konak*, 156.

45. Ibid.

46. Karpat, *Ottoman Population*, 97; "'Şişli,'" 184.

47. *Babacığım, gözüm arkamda gidiyorum. Yüreğim parçalanıyor.* "Dear father, I am going there but my thoughts are pulling me here. My heart is breaking." Karaosmanoğlu, *Kiralık Konak*, 156.

48. Ibid., 158.

49. These reading rooms were established when newspapers became popular. Newspapers were also read aloud here. "The first Turkish Newspaper, *Takvim-i Vekai* (Calendar of Events), a sort of bulletin, was published by the government in 1831. . . . The newspaper had a rather unusual feature, which attracted readers and gave the press a high status: the Sultan often wrote the leading article. Indeed the sight of a newspaper carrying the ideas of the Sultan was an intellectual revolution in itself." Karpat, *Ottoman Population*, 97.

50. This is portrayed in depth in the novel *Sinekli Bakkal* and discussed in Duben and Behar, *Istanbul Households*, 29–32.

51. Karaosmanoğlu, *Kiralık Konak*, 22.

52. Ibid., 178.

53. Ibid., 179.

54. Lewis, *The Emergence of Modern Turkey*, 172.

55. Evin, *Origins and Development of the Turkish Novel*, 123.

56. Ibid.

57. Ibid., 208.

58. Karaosmanoğlu, *Kiralık Konak*, 29–30.

59. Ibid., 109.

60. Ibid., 28.

61. The "feminism" of Karaosmanoğlu never included extramarital sex, which was the ultimate degradation, destroying the bonds of the family. See also Karaosmanoğlu, *Sodom ve Gomore*.

62. The 1915 Battle of Çanakkale (Gallipoli), or the Dardanelles, the strait that leads from the Mediterranean via the Aegean to Istanbul, was a disaster for the Allies in WWI because they had underestimated the power of the Turks, who had joined the Germans at the end of 1914. Although casualties were high on both sides—about 252,000, or 52%, for the Allies and 300,000, or 60%, for the Ottomans—the heroic leadership of Mustafa Kemal raised the morale of the Turks as they began to conceptualize and then fight for their new status. Mustafa Kemal was soon catapulted into the leadership of the Turkish national liberation struggle that began in 1919. By the time the republic was declared in 1923, and when he became its first president, he had taken on the name Atatürk, father of the Turks.

63. As a result of the inflation caused by World War I, those on fixed incomes, such as military and bureaucratic salaried classes, teachers, and pensioners, were faced with hardships and sudden poverty. The exorbitant prices these classes had to pay filled the pockets of tradesmen and speculators, who were later disparagingly referred to as "the 1332 [1916] merchants," or the "war rich." Duben and Behar, *Istanbul Households*, 46.

64. Turkish literature has been divided into schools or periods according to a variety of criteria, the most popular one being that of style. I use the terms "Tanzimat literature" or "Tanzimat authors" quite loosely; by extending this term from 1838 to 1908 it would include all literature in Turkish that reacted against a classical literature based on Arabic and Persian forms and language. Many literary historians would refine this into a Tanzimat period that extended from 1860 to 1880 (Şinasi, Ziya Pasha, Namık Kemal, and Ahmet Mithat Efendi), the *Servet-i Fünun* authors of 1880–1896 (including Tevfik Fikret and Halit Ziya Uşaklıgıl plus Hüseyin Rahmi Gürpinar, who was not a member but supported this group), and the *Fecr-i Ati* group, which included Yakup Kadri Karaosmanoğlu at the start of his career. These movements combined with independent authors to create a modern Turkish literature. What has been called a national literature came into being between 1911 and 1923 and included Ziya Gökalp, Ömer Seyfeddin, Yusuf Ziya Ortaç, Yakup Kadri Karaosmanoğlu, Halide Edib Adivar, Necip Fazil Kısakürek, Peyami Safa, and Ahmet Hamdi Tanpınar, many of whom are discussed in Chapter 5. Atiş approaches the fifty-year period preceding the republic as encompassing four political vectors: Pan-Ottomanism (Namık Kemal), Westernism (Tevfik Fikret), Pan-Islamism (Mehmet Akif), and Pan-Turkism (Ziya Gökalp, Ömer Seyfeddin). She discusses a nationalist literature that spans 1900–1940 and the effect of

pre-republican literature on the creation of a distinctively Turkish literature. Atiş, *Structural Analysis of Five Short Stories.*

65. Stephens, *Incidents of Travel*, 176–177, quoted in Berkes, *The Development of Secularism in Turkey*, 138. In fact, steamship travel shortened the travel time from Istanbul to Marseilles from six weeks to six days. Karpat, *Ottoman Population*, 97.

66. The Tanzimat Reforms, which weave through this discussion, were a "Charter of Reforms" proclaimed on November 3, 1839, by Abdül Mecid, who had been on the throne for a mere five months. The ideas embodied in the reforms were not Ottoman but ideas of freedom and equality that began with the French Revolution and were crystallized in constitutional government. The Tanzimat period, which included the attempt to implement these reforms, with a perhaps primary goal of catching up with the perceived superiority of the West, lasted from 1839 until 1876. The Tanzimat claimed such principles as "the security of life, honor, and the property of the subject, [and] fair and public trial of persons of all religions in the application of these laws." Lewis, *The Emergence of Modern Turkey*, 105. It was a period when Europe began to exert influence in a variety of fields, primarily economic. Restrictive economic practices were abolished and a policy of free trade with Europe was begun, even though many of these changes compromised Ottoman sovereignty. One effect was an increase in the urban population, especially in Istanbul, which attracted a cosmopolitan population of European colonial subjects. Furthermore, it was the non-Muslims who were in a position to benefit from the European economic penetration. Berkes, *The Development of Secularism*, 139–141. Ozankaya characterizes the Tanzimat like this:

> The purpose of the Tanzimat reforms was not to create a democratic nation-state based on scientific progress; far from it. The purpose . . . was to strike a balance between [the Sultan's] interests and those of the colonialist industrial powers. . . . While assuming the responsibility for guaranteeing the freedom of conscience, life, property and residential immunity of [non-Muslim] merchants associated with the great Powers. . . . [T]o the Turkish Moslem population [however] its purpose was proclaimed to be "greater adherence to the Şeriat." And an entire period based on a double standard was thereby initiated. (Ozankaya, "Reflections of Şemseddin Sami," 130)

67. For a discussion of the increase in foreign trade and its repercussions, see Berkes, *The Development of Secularism*, Chap. 5.

68. According to Berkes, "Perhaps the greatest change/effect on the Muslim upper classes was from a political and intellectual point of view, and that was the rise of an intelligentsia trained in the new urban secular schools—primarily the *Mühendishane* (Engineering Academy) and the School of Medicine—as opposed to the religious schools or Medresses. The Medresses continued to operate, however,

leading to a bifurcation into 'religious' and 'secular' educational life." Ibid., 177. For the implications of the new educational system on the formation of a new Ottoman class structure and the operation of print culture in this formation, see Göçek, *Rise of the Bourgeoisie*.

69. Evin, *Origins and Development of the Turkish Novel*, 40. Evin suggests that it was partly because of this didacticism that the Turkish novel was unsuccessful as a "Realist novel," as one cannot both write with the intention to convince and write with the intention of objective portrayal. For a discussion of the development of the novel in Turkey, see ibid., 41–78; Finn, *The Early Turkish Novel*; and Tanpınar, "*Türk Edebiyatında Cereyanlar*." For a discussion of these authors as an example of the strategic use of print culture as discussed in Anderson's *Imagined Communities*, see Kongar, "Turkey's Cultural Transformation," espec. 48. For a list of issues discussed in these novels, see Esen, *Türk Romanında Aile Kuruma*.

70. Houses of prostitution were also a subject of articles and novels; see Ahmet Midhat's *Henüz On Yedi Yaşında* (Just Seventeen), 1881, which may refer to the author's second wife. Besides the discussion of houses of prostitution, it paints a Turkish house of controlled women. "If I were going to stay locked up in a house with a woman who was just mine, I'd get married. I don't need a wife; I need a prostitute. I can do whatever I want with her and have my fun. When I get tired of her, I find another." Ahmet Midhat, *Henüz On Yedi Yaşında*, 105, quoted in Finn, *The Early Turkish Novel*, 14–15.

71. *Zavallı Çocuk* was written in 1873 and performed in 1874 at the Gedik Pasha Theater, with separate performances for women on the nights of Ramazan. It was reprinted in general works in 1908, and many were printed without permission after that, but the original, first published in 1873, was reprinted for the seventh time in 1890. Silay, *An Anthology of Turkish Literature*, 617.

72. Sönmez, "Turkish Women," 9.

73. *İbret* was the journal published by Namık Kemal and Ebüzziya Tevfik with the goal of spreading the ideas of the Young Ottomans. Ahmed Midhat joined this project in 1872.

74. Quoted in Sönmez, "Turkish Women," 19.

75. Quoted in Duben and Behar, *Istanbul Households*, 195. For another opinion of women in the household, see Sönmez, "Turkish Women."

76. Ibid., 139–140. This issue was brought to my attention by Kandioti, "Gendering the Modern."

77. For a discussion of Namık Kemal as a Young Ottoman, see Mardin, *The Genesis of Young Ottoman Thought*, 283–336. For a continuation of the discussion of Islam as an obstacle to change, see al-Attas, "The Islamic Worldview."

78. Berkes, *The Development of Secularism in Turkey*, 215.

79. Often referred to as Midhat Efendi, but not to be confused with Midhat Pasha, who was a state administrator active in promoting a constitutional regime,

first under Murad V and then under Abdülhamid. Ahmet Midhat did, however, take his name from Midhat Pasha, who had been his early patron and enticed him toward constitutionalism.

80. Evin, *Origins and Development of the Turkish Novel*, 82. For a discussion of the *züppe* and "over-Westernization," see Mardin, "Super Westernization in Urban Life." Midhat's work could also be seen as a comparison between the morality of the old wooden houses of the mahalle and the "deteriorated" (Westernized) moral state of the great Ottoman konaks. But since Ahmet Midhat wrote many journal articles about the "deterioration" of Istanbul konaks, by which he meant their restoration in European style, with their Turkish furnishings replaced by European ones, the dichotomy is not between the simple mahalle house and the konak but between the Western materialism and the Eastern morality that these were used to represent. Orhan Oktay has parsed many of Ahmed Midhat's articles and novels for their themes and related them to his other writings. See Okay, *Batı Medeniyet Karşısında*, espec. "*Eski ve Yeni Ev Düzeni*," 92–101.

81. Midhat, *Felâtun ile Râkim Efendi*, 3–4, quoted in Finn, *The Early Turkish Novel*, 15–16. Ahmet Midhat was known more for his topic than his prose, as this quotation exemplifies.

82. "The house of exile is the house of affliction" (*sürgün evi vurgun evi*) says the *Redhouse Dictionary*. The traditional Ottoman punishment was banishment from the protected circle, banishment to the outside, and many proverbs from the Ottoman period attest to the pain of being sent to the "*yaban*," the world of strangers, beyond the family and the social circle.

83. Perhaps the only contemporary novel that does not depict slaves as mistreated.

84. The line continues, although it is not in the novel: "*O dökülen kumral saç, canımı yaktı ey peri.*" A poetic translation of this, done by Ahmet Turhan Altıner, is "Those brown locks o' thine cascade pain in my soul, O fairy!" It was written by the Armenian composer Nikoğos Ağa (1836–1885), a student of Dede Efendi (1778–1846), one of the greatest composers of Turkish classical music. Great Armenian composers and theorists of Turkish music, such as Hamparsum Limonciyan (1768-1839), also a student of Dede Efendi's, were considered fully Ottoman. The architect Ahmet Turhan Altıner is seen giving a tour at Dede Efendi's house in Chapter 1.

85. Evin, *Origins and Development of the Turkish Novel*, 84.

86. Evin discusses the house and community patterned according to the Ottoman patrimonial system when he discusses *Aşk-i Memnun* (Forbidden Love), the 1898 novel by Halit Ziya Uşaklıgil. In this example, the household defies stratification, and its harmony depends on personal bonds of loyalty. Ibid., 18.

87. But the züppe certainly existed. Mardin saw the literary protest against the züppe as arising from the redistribution of wealth associated with their lives. Their economic lives were contrary to what I discuss as the accepted life of the pre-1908

mahalle, that is, instead of money belonging to an office, for example, the sultan or a pasha who would redistribute it according to the rules of patronage, the new rich would take it out of circulation and keep it for themselves. This was abhorrent both to the masses and to those who could not profit from the new status of private property, that is, the first modern intellectuals who were the authors of these novels. Mardin, "Cultural Change and the Intellectual," 419–423.

88. Mardin, "Super Westernization," 406.

89. Evin points out that in order for Rakim to be a successful entrepreneur, that is, to "strive and succeed," there would need to be an entrepreneurial class. Since there was none, Rakim can be said to represent a group that is imagined rather than real—an ideological construct. Evin, *Origins and development of the Turkish Novel*, 87–92.

90. Mardin, "Super Westernization," 406.

91. I have used Ahmet Midhat to show how Tanzimat literature might be characterized by its use of the trope of the house, apartments, and interiors as part of the east/west spiritual/material *alaturka/alafranga* discourse. But see also Şemseddin Sami's 1872 *Taaşuk-i Talât ve Fitnat* (The Love of Talat and Fitnat). Although written to demonstrate the evils of forced marriages, his descriptions of the physical environment, especially interiors, make the protagonists appear in a milieu compatible with their social classes. Recâizade Ekrem's 1886 *Araba Sevdası* (In Love with Carriages) takes place in 1869–1870, a period when the konaks of the bureaucratic elite were still located in the old part of the city, surrounded by their *mahalles*. The hero, Bihruz Bey, like Ahmet Mithat's Felatun Bey, is a züppe who squanders a fortune on clothes and insists on speaking French whether or not anyone understands him. In 1898, Halit Ziya Uşaklıgil wrote *Aşk-i Memnun* (Forbidden Love), in which the spacious and elegant Adnan Bey mansion, with its crystal chandeliers, stands for the deeply rooted problems of a traditionalist culture versus Westernizing groups.

92. This is the tension and the strategy that were theorized by Ziya Gokalp as *"hars"* (culture) and *"medeniyet"* (civilization). *Medeniyet* is either Western or universal and refers to the scientific and the rational. Its import and its assimilation into Turkish culture can be beneficial. *Hars*, on the other hand, must be preserved at all costs, as it is local and what gives a nation its unique identity.

93. Mardin is one of a group of scholars who have long recognized the supreme importance of the spiritual and moral dimensions of Turkish cultural life. For example, he has suggested that the züppe character that originated with Felâtun Efendi (and continued with Servet Bey in *Kiralık Konak*) was a signal of its "traditional" opposite, an Ottoman value of nonconspicuous consumption. (Perhaps this is worth investigating as an attribute of interiority.) Mardin traces a revulsion of conspicuous consumption to the economic practices and ideologies of the guilds, as well as to its dangers in palace life. In his work he uses Bihruz Bey from Recâizade Mahmut Ekrem's *Araba Sevdası* to stand for the entire züppe class. Mardin, "Super Western-

ization." In this novel, Bihruz Bey is infatuated with material aspects of Western civilization and sacrifices his father's fortune for a horse-drawn carriage.

94. For a discussion of the influences of the Ottoman literary tradition on the Turkish novel, see Evin, *Origins and Development of the Turkish Novel*, 65–74. What we are seeing here is that investigating the spiritual dimension of the Turkish house opens an alternative discourse on the Ottoman and then the Turkish novel, different from approaches that trace its origins in realism or naturalism, its political thrust, or its didactic intent. Evin, for example, shows how authors such as Ahmet Midhat were influenced by French positivist thought and by realistic authors such as Zola, who depicted the domestic environment in order to examine people in their own true settings. Evin, *Origins and Development of the Turkish Novel*, 103.

95. Kemal, *Initbah: Sergüzeşt-I*, 16.

96. Evin, *Origins and Development of the Turkish Novel*, 74.

97. Andrews, *Poetry's Voice, Society's Song*, 114–115.

98. According to al-Attas, "Islam does not concede to the dichotomy of the sacred and the profane; the worldview of Islam encompasses both *al-dunya* (this world) and *al-akhirah* (the world to come)." al-Attas, "The Islamic Worldview," 215. See al-Attas for a discussion of the worldview of Islam prepared for a late twentieth-century Turkish Muslim audience. See Schimmel, *Deciphering the Signs of God*, 228–229, for another discussion of the *dunya/al-akhira* dichotomy.

99. *Haremi yeniden tesis ettiğimiz gece*. I am indebted to Leslie Peirce for calling this work to my attention.

100. Seyfeddin, "Harem," 133.

101. The *çarşaf* was a long coatlike overgarment worn by women, usually with a veil over the lower part of the face. After the law on general apparel in 1925, it was no longer required street attire.

102. Seyfeddin, "Harem," 132.

103. Fatih is a conservative neighborhood in the old city of Istanbul. See the frontispiece map and the discussion of *Fatih-Harbiye* in Chapter 4.

104. Seyfeddin, "Harem," 134.

105. Ibid. Ahmet Turhan Altıner read this and other Ottoman passages aloud with the intonation of an Ottoman İstanbulin so that the full message would not escape me.

106. Ibid., 137.

107. Garnett, *Turkish Life*, 52.

108. Seyfeddin, "Harem," 138.

109. Seyfeddin, "Harem," 140.

110. Ibid., 164.

111. See, for example, Sezai's 1899 *Sergüzeşt: Bir Esir Kızın Romanı* (Adventure: The Story of a Slave Girl) and Hüseyin Rahmi's 1889 *Şik*.

112. Karaosmanoğlu, *Kiralık Konak*, 22–23.

113. Berkes, *The Development of Secularism in Turkey*, 295.

114. Edib, *Conflict of East and West in Turkey*, 199.

115. "Hafiz" (Shemseddin Muhammad of Shiraz, b. ca. 1320) was the most acclaimed lyric poet in Persian history. His poetry reveals an intimate familiarity with five centuries of Persian literature, knowledge of Islamic sciences, and competence in Arabic (Hafiz 1997). "Nedim" was a seventeenth-century Ottoman Court poet who challenged conventions by integrating local linguistic and cultural elements into a tradition, which until then had remained essentially "foreign." Silaym, *Nedim and the Poetics of the Ottoman Court.* "Ömer Khayyam" (ca. 1048–1131) was a Persian poet, astronomer, mathematician, and author of *The Rubiyat*.

116. The East-West divide is clearly an important part of the discourse of modernity as it was being felt in late Ottoman and early republican Turkey. However, that it was a part of the contemporary discourse does not make it a true dichotomy. İlhan Tekeli suggests that from a later vantage point, that is, today, we see that this divide was a misperception of the project of modernity, which was a universalizing project. This is why, Tekeli says, it is not the same thing to see oneself transforming from an "Easterner" to a "Westerner" as from a "pre-modern" to a "modern" person. In the former there is a loss of identity, whereas the latter is realized through internalization of a universal process, without an identity loss. Akıncı, "İlhan Tekeli's 'Modernization Project.'"

117. The text of the cartoon continues with the daughter's response: "But Mom! Shouldn't a housewife work to conserve her husband's money? Because I didn't want to spend too much on my holiday dress, I had them cut it short." Kılıç, *50 Yıllık*, 114.

118. *Zamanlar artık eski zamanlar değil, iki sene içinde pek çok adetler değişti.*

119. The Revolution of 1908 is popularly referred to as the beginning of the Second Constitutional Period (II Meşrutiyet), with the First Constitutional Period being the short-lived one at the beginning of Abdülhamid's rule in 1878. Aykut Kansu suggests that a thirty-year interval, with a concomitant thirty-year underground resistance, qualifies the Second Constitutional Period as something far greater than the mere reinstatement of a once lost document. He argues persuasively that 1908 was the revolutionary turning point in Turkish history, marking the true end of the Ottoman Empire and the beginning of modern Turkey. He argues that Kemalist historians and Kemalist-driven ideology have dismissed this obvious truth in order to portray 1923 as the almost mystical moment when Turkey began a nondisruptive but successful movement from tradition to modernity under the reforms of Atatürk. But these theories deny any place to the internal struggle and resistance to the political and economic system that was occurring, and to the changes that followed its overthrow. Kansu, *The Revolution of 1908 in Turkey.* In any event, the revolution was a bloodless one. Abdülhamid gave in to the revolutionary movement led by the Committee for Union and Progress (İttihat ve Terakki Cemiyeti) that had taken on

guerrilla proportions in Macedonia and Thrace, and avoided immediate deposition by "restoring" the constitution of 1878.

120. Kansu, *The Revolution of 1908 in Turkey*. Also Findley, *Bureaucratic Reform*, 294–295.

121. Kansu, *The Revolution of 1908 in Turkey*, 139.

122. For a description of these celebrations and the reaction of the population in general, see ibid. and Edib, *Memoirs of Halide Edip*.

123. The revolution of 1908 was followed in rapid succession by a series of major events that marked 1908 as a major turning point: changes in sovereignty in Istanbul served as a signal to Austria to annex Bosnia and Herzegovina, for Bulgaria to proclaim independence, and for Greece to annex Crete. This was followed by the Italo-Turkish War of 1911–1912, the First and Second Balkan Wars of 1912–1913, the First World War, which included the occupation of Istanbul and other cities, and then the Turkish War of Independence (1918–1922). Duben and Cem's in-depth retrospective interviews indicate that it is 1908 exactly that entered the collective memory as the time that ended the era of "konak life." Duben and Behar, *Istanbul Households*, 200. Cemil Topuzlu, who was the first mayor of Istanbul (1912–1921 and 1919–1926), wrote in his memoirs that his life fell into three periods: "1. 1866–1908: From my childhood up to the proclamation of the Meşrutiyet, 2. 1908–1920: From the proclamation of the Meşrutiyet to the time that I left Istanbul, and 3. 1920 to today [1950]." Topuzlu, *80 Yillik Hatiralarim*, 5. It is interesting that the proclamation of the new Republic of Turkey is not one of these turning points. Halide Edib wrote of the celebrations that followed the proclamation of the II Meşrutiyet:

> "The memory is so intense that to this day I cannot think of it unmoved. I think of it as the final embrace between the simple peoples of Turkey before they should be led to exterminate each other for the political advantage of foreign powers and their own leaders."
>
> But as Halide Edib was listening to the crowds, her grandmother was crying:
>
> "It means the end of everything," she said. (Edib, *Memoirs of Halide Edip*, 272)

Halide Edib also uses 1908 as the end of her novel *Sinekli Bakkal*, in which it signifies the end of Ottomanism as a system, for good or for bad, and the hope of a synthesis with the West. Recall also that Siyavuşgil suggested that the entire Karagöz play screen or stage represents the typical and thus generic mahalle of Ottoman Istanbul as it existed "until 1908." See also Orga, *Portrait of a Turkish Family*, for a memory of the years between 1908 and the Balkan Wars as the disintegrating years of the extended household. Just before the war, Orga's father, Hüsnü, tells his mother that a war is coming and his business is bad, and that "perhaps it is time to sell the house." Although this is what happens, Orga's grandmother's reaction reminds us of Naim Efendi's: "'Nonsense,' came my grandmother's voice crisply. 'Why should a war in Europe make any difference in our lives? All my children were born in this house, Hüsnü, and two of yours. I came to it when I was only thirteen and I would rather die than leave it now'"(Orga, 46).

124. Quoted in Duben and Behar, *Istanbul Households*, 101.

125. In Gürpınar's 1916 *Kadın Erkekleşince* (Women Turning into Men), set in the middle-class Istanbul of 1916, a girl too shy to show her love for a young man is presented as "a girl of the last century." Duben and Behar, *Istanbul Households*, 100.

126. Ibid.

127. For a list of novels that take up the disintegration of konak life, see Esen, *Türk Romanında Aile Kuruma*, 247–248. This list spans the years 1925–1975.

CHAPTER 4

1. In 1922, Mehmed VI was replaced by Abdül Mecit II (1922–1924), who was merely a caliph and thus had no temporal authority.

2. Ergin, *Muallim Cevdet'in Hayatı*. See also Lewis, *Making of Modern Turkey*, 401.

3. Harbiye is the area just beyond Beyoğlu, about where Nişantası and Teşvkiye come together. It takes its name from the Military Academy (*Mekteb-i Harbiye/School of War*), where Hodja Ali Riza Bey was a student and later a teacher. It was the end of the line for the trip from Fatih to this Westernized section, and therefore represents "Beyoğlu." See the frontispiece map for the tram route.

4. Halide Edib wrote in her memoirs that "Fatih, as the center of great theological colleges (medresses), was always opposed to Westernization. Great mutinies in Turkish history were led by the eminent hodjas and the theological students at Fatih, and these mutinies put forth the religious pretext, their usual war-cry being, 'We want Sheriat,' meaning the holy law." Edib, *Memoirs*, 276.

5. Safa, *Fatih Harbiye*, 23.

6. Ibid., 45.

7. The *kemençe* (*kemanje*) is a three-stringed Middle Eastern lute with a long neck that is played with a bow. Because of the long neck, it is held vertically, resting on the player's knee.

8. Safa, *Fatih Harbiye*, 55.

9. Ibid., 55–56.

10. Ibid., 57.

11. Ibid., 56.

12. Ibid., 30.

13. Ibid., 40.

14. Ibid., 229. The idea of a fancy ball and ball dress was one of the tropes of

modernity, known by many although experienced by few. See Kandioti, "Gendering the Modern."

15. Safa, *Fatih Harbiye*, 58.

16. Ibid., 26.

17. Ibid., 31.

18. Ibid., 46.

19. Ibid., 47.

20. Ibid., 295–296.

21. The life of the mind can have a spiritual value put on it, and there is a life of the material world on which spiritual value can be placed. The thing and the valuing of the thing are separate. Thus we are left with a false dichotomy. However, see the following footnote for an Ottoman example of this way of thinking. Thanks to Ann Bertram for this insight.

22. Safa, *Fatih Harbiye*, 77.

23. An example from Naima's *History* shows his consistent conflation of historical writing with moral advice: "Earlier, at sunrise, Dede Kurd had come to the Pasha and said, 'My Sultan, if it is your intention to kill Assaf, that is out of the question at this time, for you have given him a written safe-conduct as well as the towel.'" (A lavishly embroidered textile indicated that the bearer had the favor of the Ottoman Sultan, in this case that a promise had been made and must be honored.) Thomas, *A Study of Naima*, 7.

24. Orientalism is a way of coming to terms with the Orient that is based on the Orient's definition based on a European, Western experience. This concept is the brainchild of Edward Said, who wrote, "Anyone who teaches, writes about, or researches the Orient—and this applies whether the person is an anthropologist, sociologist, historian, or philologist—either in its specific or its general aspects, is an Orientalist, and what he or she says or does is Orientalism." Said, *Orientalism*, 1. Later he wrote, "Orientalism can be discussed and analyzed as the corporate institution for dealing with the Orient—dealing with it by making statements about it, authorizing views of it, describing it, by teaching it, settling it, ruling over it: in short, Orientalism is a Western style for dominating, restructuring, and having authority over the Orient." Ibid., 3. It is very close, then, to what Kiril Petkov calls "textual attitude," or the specific way to conceive of foreign people. Petkov, *Infidels, Turks, and Women*.

25. Schick discusses the Orientalist tropes of the women of Turkey in which "the idleness and indolence of Harem women is a recurring theme in Orientalist discourse." Schick, "The Women of Turkey as Sexual Personae," 95.

26. In 1786, the Englishwoman Lady Elizabeth Craven was angered by the laziness of the people of Istanbul: "I have even seen people who sit on the seashore watching the kites in the sky or children getting into boats and taking trips for a whole day, from morning to evening." Craven, *A Journey Through the Crimea*.

27. Gladstone, *The Bulgarian Horrors*, 11–13.

28. Ahmet Lûtfi was the imperial historiographer to Abdül Aziz, Murat V, and Abdülhamid II, and author of an eight-volume *History*. He wrote this in 1875. Quoted in Göçek, *Rise of the Bourgeoisie*, 118.

29. Berkes, *The Development of Secularism*, 346.

30. Lewis, *The Emergence of Modern Turkey*, 401.

31. Major Robert Imbrie, *National Geographic*, 1924, quoted in Leiser, "A Brief History of Ankara," 40. Travelers' reports of Istanbul often referred to its unclean streets. Baron de Tott, who lavishly praised the beautiful panorama he saw in 1755, went on to complain about the dirtiness of its streets. The memoirs of a doctor named F. Maynard, published in 1855 by Alexandre Dumas (1803–1870), reported "narrow, rutted, muddy, dark, filthy streets that never saw sunlight or fresh air." The filth of the city is reiterated by Mark Twain in his *Innocents Abroad*.

32. See Mitchell, *Colonising Egypt*, for the effect of a European view of the East as unclean in Egypt during the closing decades of the nineteenth century.

33. Nirven, "*Cumba.*"

34. Koçu, *Constantinopoli*.

35. Koçu, "*Ev, Ahşab Evler,*" 5403.

36. Hakkı, "*Yeni Mimari Değişikleri.*" We discuss the Turkish acceptance of the rhetoric of architectural modernism in more depth later.

37. Safa, *Fatih-Harbiye*, 76–77.

38. Prokić, "*Muslimani u Bosni,*" 35.

39. According to Peter Berger, there are two modes of universe maintenance: therapy and nihilation. "Therapy re-socializes the deviant individual into the objective reality of the symbolic universe of the society. Nihilation liquidates conceptually everything outside the Symbolic Universe, by denying the reality of those external objects. The ultimate goal here is to incorporate. The negation of one's own universe is subtly changed to an affirmation of it." Berger, *The Social Construction of Reality*, 112.

40. The (formerly Pan-)Turkist Ahmed Ağaoğlu wrote in 1928:

If the West is superior in the material then it is due to its totality—its virtues and its vices. The Eastern system is permeated by religion at all levels and this brought decline, while secularization of the West brought superiority. If we want to survive we have to secularize our view of religion, morality, social relations, and law. This is possible only by accepting openly and unconditionally the mind as well as the behavior of the civilization which we are bound to imitate. (Ağaoğlu quoted in Berkes, *The Development of Secularism*, 465)

See Chapter 5 illustrations to see the house that Eldem built for Ahmed Ağaoğlu.

41. See especially Ortaç, *Üç Katlı Ev*, and Kısakürek, *Ahşap Konak*, and the discussion at the end of Chapter 5.

42. Safa, *Fatih-Harbiye*, 66–67.

43. Ibid., 67.

44. Ibid., 68.

45. The words "foreign" and "foreigner" may be used interchangeably with "strangers" to refer to all those who are "exterior" to the context—non-nationals, non-neighbors, non-family members, and non-co-religionists. In writing his memoirs in 1977, the painter and writer Malik Aksel (1901–1987) still used the word "foreigners" (*yabancılar*) for minorities, meaning Greeks and Jews.

> At the time of World War I it was mandatory to put a sign with one's name on shops.... It was the command of Enver Pasha ... a boycott against the *yabancı*. One day in Kumkapı, Nişancı Düriye Hanım went to the Bakkal [local shop] and said, "My son, tell me, are you a *Gâvur* (unbeliever) or a Muslim? You know we can't buy anything from *Gâvurs* because the punishment is large." [To which the shop owner replies:] "My name is Mehmet, my father's name is Ahmet, I can put my hand on the Qur'an." "God bless you," she said, "they frightened me, that is why I'm asking you." (Aksel, *İstanbul'un Ortası*, 271)

46. Safa, *Fatih-Harbiye*, 118.

47. The music teachers understood the political nature that a decision to close the conservatory meant: "Let's not forget that the people who are making these decisions, when they are at home or meeting together, don't listen to any other kind of music than *alaturka* music." Ibid., 121. Atatürk was known to have listened to Turkish music at home, but said that "[although] we will like *alla Turca* music until we die ... real music is Western music." Nalbantoğlu, "Architects, Style, and Power," 44.

48. Ibid., 119.

49. Celâleddin Rumi (d. 1273) was a mystical poet and the eponymous founder of the Mevlevi or "whirling" dervish order. A *mesnevi* is a poetic form that Rumi brought to perfection. Sheik Sa'di of Shiraz(1213?–1292?) was a Persian poet known especially for *The Orchard* (1257), a verse collection illustrating Islamic virtues, and *The Rose Garden* (1258), a collection of stories, anecdotes, poems and maxims. Ömer Khayyam was a Persian poet, mathematician, and astronomer famous for his *rubiyats*, a rhyming poetic form. Abu-Hamid al-Ghazzâli (d. 1111) remains even today among the best-known of mystics and scholars who gave a deeper ethical dimension to the fundamentals of Islamic belief.

50. The five pillars of Islam are the five actions required of the true believer: the attestation of faith (that is, declaring "There is no God but God, and Mohammad is the Prophet of God"), prayer five times a day, ritual fasting, pilgrimage to Mecca if affordable, and the giving of charity.

51. Edib, *The Clown and His Daughter (Sinekli Bakkal)*, 273.

52. In the case of the population in general, the struggle for independence was exactly that: a struggle for independence from foreign occupation, whether that foreign force be governments or the non-Moslem elements of the Ottoman population. Postcards that commemorated the end of the Greek occupation of Izmir, Bursa, Kütahya, and Edirne make this clear. For example, thousands of postcards were printed and sold with a *"Mehmetçik"* (Turkish soldier) kissing the hand of Osman Gazi, the eponymous founder of the Ottoman Empire, depicted in front of his sarcophagus in a setting that equates him with a Muslim saint (Özal, *Cephelerden Kurtuluş Savaşı'na*, 543). We know that sultans and saints were conflated in the religious imagination, at least of this period, from the fact that visits to the graves of the sultans and saints were prohibited in the republican period, as mentioned below. These images attest to a popular belief that the struggle for independence was at least in part a struggle to insure the future in the name of the past, that is, in the name of an Ottoman heritage that embraced its Turkish-Muslim heritage.

53. In the Ottoman Empire, the sultan was also the caliph, or the leader of the entire world community of Muslims (to the extent they believed he was the legitimate leader of their body politic). In November 1922, as the empire came to a close, the office of sultan was abolished by the National Assembly, the proto-republican government, with their capital in Ankara. The sultan had left Istanbul a month before, to take refuge in Malta, under the protection of the British. He was no longer the sultan, but the position of a moral leader of a unified Muslim polity as caliph was left intact. This position passed to the sultan's cousin. The National Assembly proclaimed Turkey a republic in October 1923. In 1924, it created a constitution that deemed it the sole place of national sovereignty, thus abolishing the caliphate. And with this formal ending of the sultanate, the parliament sent all members of the Ottoman (royal) family into exile, ending the 625-year rule of the Ottoman family dynasty.

54. For a discussion of the institutional changes that were part of a revolutionary move to construct a new national consciousness, as well as the strong sanctions against dissenting opinion, see Zürcher, *Turkey, A Modern History*, 173–214.

55. al-Attas, "The Islamic Worldview," 231–232. According to al-Attas, the third component of secularization is "the disenchantment of nature," a term and concept borrowed from the German sociologist Max Weber and meaning the "freeing of nature from its religious overtones ... so that man can act upon it as he pleases." Ibid.

56. Berkes, *The Development of Secularism*, 492.

57. And, "Atatürk and the Arts," 225. The play was first performed in 1873. Because of its nationalism, it was banned then and Namık Kemal was exiled to Cyprus. After the Second Constitutional Period (*II Meşrutiyet*), it was performed again, only to be banned again in the first years of the Turkish Republic.

58. Ibid., 226.

59. Safa, *Fatih-Harbiye*, 58.

60. Ibid., 129.

61. "The war is over. Those who have died lie on the battleground. All their cries, their cries of hatred and malice are silenced. The silence that follows the hurricane of mankind, how well it shows how empty these things are!"

62. Perhaps this is why, in a 1930 issue of the magazine *Kalem* (Pen), a satirical glossary called "*Yeni Kamus*" (The New Dictionary) defines "*Çile*" (the period of isolation and spiritual trial demanded of new dervishes, or others attempting to cleanse their souls) as "*Aile Reisliği*" (heading a family). Kalem, "*Yeni Kamus*," 5.

63. Safa, *Fatih-Harbiye*, 127.

64. A great number of works from this period have the family as the protagonist instead of the individual, such as Reşat Nuri Güntekin's *Yaprak Dökümü*. Nutku suggests that until the 1950s, domestic conflicts were treated from "the traditional viewpoint of harmony." For this subject in novels and the early Turkish theater, see Nutku, "A Panorama of Turkish Theater," 251–252, and Esen, *Türk Romanında Aile Kuruma*, 247. See also "*Sağanak*" (Downpour), by Yakup Kadri Karaosmanoğlu, discussed above.

65. *Aşk-i Memnun* was serialized in *Servet-i Funun*, nos. 413–479, January 1314/1898 to May 1316/1900.

66. Evin, *Origins and development of the Turkish Novel*, 219. The external-internal dichotomies I am presenting are not gendered, in that they do not signify a "feminine" interior/domestic versus a "masculine" external world. Although gender issues are beyond the scope of this discussion, I note that the protagonists in both Safa's *Fatih-Harbiye* and *Cumbadan Rumbaya* are young women. This may remind the reader that Atatürk persuaded most authors to have female heroes; it may also suggest that the house was not felt locally to have problematic gender issues, or it might suggest the importance of gender in the presentation of issues of compliance and control. For the suggestion that in this era, fathers and daughters had a special role, the father, losing his patriarchal distance, "giving birth" to the new daughters of the modern republic through warmth, support, and intelligence, see Kandioti, "Gendering the Modern."

67. The Kemalist vision of women working outside the home was opposed by religious conservatives, but also by many republican intellectuals; Peyami Safa was one of these, as was Hüseyin Cahit Yalçın. But working outside the home was not the same as being educated outside the home, which was a strongly shared ideal of the intellectual elite from before the turn of the century.

68. Özcan, "*Açılış Konuşması*."

69. I suggest that Faiz Bey was born in 1880, which would make him twenty-six when Neriman was born and forty-six at the time of the *Fatih-Harbiye*, in 1926.

70. Ibn al-'Arabi was a twelfth- to thirteenth-century Muslim mystic. His "*Fusus*

al-Hikam," which has been translated as *The Seals of Wisdom,* is one of the most well-known and profound of all Sufi works. Yalçın's comment on him refers both to language and to content.

71. Berkes, *The Development of Secularism,* 291.

72. To discuss the father as a major code for the macrocosm may or may not overstate the case of the real situation, but its important insertion in memory is certainly clear. Even when late Ottoman and Turkish novelists began to use the genre of the novel to "open the doors of the house," the unwritten rules of *haram* may still have remained in place. The interaction between a genre that forced entree into a private domain in a setting that was architecturally closed according to very specific cultural codes needs exploration. Thus, whether the novels were written by men or by women, interpersonal relations and the role of mothers may have been carefully protected, and thus seem to be ignored or represented sketchily for reasons of convention. Nonetheless. a strong tradition of representing the house as the father's house exists. (Thanks to Tracy Lord for instigating this discussion.) For examples of the father as the dominant figure in the house, see Naim Bey and his konak in *Kiralık Konak,* Arif Paşa and his konak in Sedat Simavi's 1940 *Hürriyet Apartman,* Hacı İsmail Paşa's house in Yusuf Ziya Ortaç's 1953 *Üç Katlı Ev,* and Recai Paşa's konak in Necip Fazıl Kısakürek's 1964 *Ahşap Konak.* In 1928, Salih Zeki (Halide Edib's teacher and first husband) yearned for his homeland in the 1928 poem *"Babamın Evi"* ("My Father's House") ("I search in my dreams for the birds on its roof"), as does the protagonist in Orhan Kemal's 1949 *"Baba Evi."*

73. Safa, *Cumbadan Rumbaya,* 4. This is a ditty that would have been sung on the streets by the lower classes both to mock and show envy. Being a "salon bride" means you can get anything you want, you can bond people to you with a staple just by wiggling your waist.

74. Önöl, *"Cumbadan Rumbaya,"* 3623.

75. Safa, *Cumbadan Rumbaya,* 346.

76. Ibid., 348.

77. Ibid., 346.

78. Ahmet Altıner, former editor of *Arkitekt,* has coined the word *"mahallezens"* for the "citizens" of a single mahalle, that is, the mahalle neighbors.

79. Safa, *Cumbadan Rumbaya,* 346.

80. Yalçın, "Ev Sevgisi," 5.

81. Postmodernist theory suggests that the loss of a life narrative leaves nothing but fragmentation. Anderson suggests that identity, because it cannot be remembered, must be narrated. Anderson, *Imagined Communities,* 196. For a discussion of narrative emplotment in a Turkish context, see Şerif Mardin's presentation of Necip Fasil Kısakürek's life trajectory in Mardin, "Cultural Change."

82. Yalçın, "Ev Sevgisi," 5.

83. Ibid.

84. Ibid.

85. For a discussion of the Islamist, Westernist, Turkist, and Ottomanist stances, see Berkes, *The Development of Secularism*, 360–428.

86. *Şark* was being replaced by *Doğu*, and *Garb* by *Batı*.

87. Harun al-Rashid (786–809) was the caliph—ruler of the Abbasid Muslim empire centered in Baghdad. He is remembered for a flourishing of the arts and sciences, and idealized in *A Thousand and One Nights*.

88. Safa, *Fatih-Harbiye*, 49–50.

89. In Turkish, "*ümmet*" means a community of the same religion. "The" *ümma* refers to the "*ümmet-i Muhammed*" or the community of Muhammed, that is, all Muslims.

90. This difficult title, "İş ve Eserde Her Telakkiden 75 Türk Meşuru Arasında Nefs Muhasebesi," was translated for me by Gary Leiser.

91. *Büyük Doğu*, November–December 1945, unpaginated.

92. Peyami Safa wrote both under the names Safa and Server Bedai. He contributed to almost every contemporary journal, including the very conservative pro-Ottoman journal, *Son Havadis* (Recent Events), as well as *Yedigün* (Seven Days) and *Büyük Doğu* (The Great Orient). He produced his own *Kültür Haftası* (Cultural Weekly) in 1936 and *Türk Düşüncüsü* (Turkish Thought) between 1950 and 1960.

93. Kurdakul, *Şairler Yazarlar Sözlüğü*, 14. Peyami Safa was not, however, a reactionary. Note, for example, his article on women wearing bathing suits; he suggests that this is not shameful but eminently healthy. Safa, "*Utanmaya Dair.*"

94. Along with Yakup Kadri (1889–1974). Yakup Kadri, the author of *Kiralık Konak*, was also a nationalist, but of a different stripe. He was a strong supporter of Atatürk, although he lost favor with the regime in the early 1930s for his Marxist journal *Kadro*, which proposed the development of a literature based on a lifestyle of social responsibility in opposition to individualism. Ertop, "Trends and Characteristics of Contemporary Turkish Literature," 152. Yet Yakup Kadri shares with Cahit and Safa a memory of the old wooden house as the spiritual foundation of the Ottoman past.

95. One could also argue, but I do not, as it is not borne out by the characters, that Safa's novels were polemics against women entering the public sphere. See, however, his article, "*Türk Modern Kızı.*" Bozdoğan translates this passage, saying, "Though he emphasized the need to 'open wide the windows of the house and the mind of the Turkish girl to the outside, to nature and to society,' Safa nonetheless added: 'Some fools talk as if the Turkish revolution intends to move the Turkish girl's center of operation from home to the street. They talk as if hatred of family, hatred of marriage, and hatred of children are the primary features of modern sensibility. From time immemorial, every woman's center of operation has been her home: so will it be for the modern Turkish girl and woman. Through sun, air, books, and radio, this center, this home, will be flooded with all the amenities, interests, and excitement

of both nature and the society outside.'" Bozdoğan, *Modernism and Nation Building*, 197–198.

96. Although Hüseyin Cahit may have been a member or supporter of the "loyal opposition party" and the Progressive Republican Party as well. The PRP folded when the government closed all newspapers and journals that were not official organs. Zürcher, *Turkey: A Modern History*, 179–181. *Tanin* was one of these, and Cahit was sent into exile between 1925 and 1927. Koloğlu, "Hüseyin Cahit Yalçın," 205.

97. Ibid., 414.

98. Yalçın, *Edebî Hatıralar*, 26, quoted in Berkes, *The Development of Secularism in Turkey*, 291.

99. Ibid., 298.

100. Berkes, *The Development of Secularism*, 370.

101. Büyük-Doğu, November–December 1945, unpaginated.

102. Ertop, "Trends and Characteristics of Contemporary Turkish Literature," 152.

103. Of course, there were social and class differences, but the concept of class was, perhaps, not as divisive as in Western society. As mentioned in Chapter 1, mahalles were integrated in terms of economics and occupations, and social mores and norms were more shared than different. Tanyeli, who finds that most stereotypes of Ottoman neighborhoods are not corroborated by *waqfiye* (endowment) data, agrees with this. "Housing of a particular standard exhibited no concentration in a particular urban area. On the contrary, every district could be noted to display roughly the same scale of standards." Tanyeli, "*Anadolu'da Bizans* (Housing and Settlement Patterns)," 441. One might also consider how the house was in the service of a Kemalist discursive affirmation of the non-class character of Turkish society, which was basic to the construction of a "totalizing national identity" (Keyman, *Kemalism, Modernity and Tradition*, 9), or one could argue that this non-class-consciousness was in fact deeply rooted. There were, as we have seen, architectural or structural similarities between the konak and the ev (house). Arseven refers to this in his *L'Art Turc*: "The difference between a konak and a house is not too large" (97).

104. Quoted in Scarparo, "An Analysis of the Video *One Way Street* and of Walter Benjamin's Dialectical Thinking."

105. Ibid., 226–227.

106. The serial "Sinekli Bakkal" was published in *Haber Akşam Postası*, nos. 1352–1485, from 11 İlkteşrin 1935 to 24 Şubat 1936. It was published as a book in 1936 by Ahmet Halit Kitapevi, Istanbul. Enginün, *Halide Edip Adıvar'ın Eserlerinde Doğu ve Batı Meselesi*, 541–542.

107. Edib, *Sinekli Bakkal*, 1.

108. Halide Edib's memoirs were first published in English in 1926. I am not certain that excerpts were available in Turkish before it was published as a serial with

the title *Mor Salkımlı Ev* (The Wisteria-Covered House) in *Yeni İstanbul* between 1951 and 1955. Ertop, "Trends and Characteristics," 149.

109. *Sinekli Bakkal*, which the logo illustration of *Turkish Houses* recalls, expressed Halide Edib's attachment to the mysticism of Islam. She was criticized for this sympathetic portrayal when *Sinekli Bakkal* was reviewed in *Yeni Adam*, and called "a new Pierre Loti." Ibid., 150. In 1923, in her memoirs, she wrote: "I believe that a child who recites a sura from the Koran in her own language every night will inevitably be convinced that Islam expresses a spirit which encompasses all humanity" (quoted in Zürcher, *Political Opposition*, 92). In 1924 she and her husband said of Atatürk's secularization, "things have gone too far." When a plot against Atatürk's life was discovered in 1926, her husband felt it wise to leave the country, and the two of them moved to England (ibid., 92). She continued, however, to write and speak in favor of the new republic. Edib, *Conflict of East and West in Turkey*.

110. Halide Edib was living in the United States when she wrote these articles. In the same years, Arseven described a return to his childhood neighborhood to find that the wooden houses that remained were falling down, most replaced by modernist houses. Arseven, "*Yoğurtcunun Sesi*." See Chapter 5.

111. *Yedigün*, which belonged to Hüseyin Cahit Yalçın, was a prime example of the Kemalist imaginary. The covers generally had a "modern Turkish woman" (see Chapter 4, page 146), and its articles were about modern living, including a series on women's fashions and one on the modern house, with ads for modern appliances that suggested an already Westernized readership. Its pages were filled with photographs of what contemporary life was meant to be: one of young men and women together at school, in the workforce, and in competitive sports; or articles about the intellectual life of famous people, including Hamdullah Suphi (Münir, "*Büyük Elçimiz*") and Yakup Kadri (Münir, "*Yakup Kadri*"). Although there were occasional historical pieces, these were primarily of the Ottoman "classical" period, not the recent past, with only a rare article of personal nostalgia.

112. Edib, "*Arka Sokaktan Görüş: Yuvarlanan Kırklar*."

113. Yalçın, "*Ev ve Apartman*," 5.

CHAPTER 5

1. Tanyeli, "*Osmanlı Barınma Kültüründe Batılılaşma-Modernleşme* / Westernization-Modernization in the Ottoman Wohnkultur," 284.

2. Sevengil, *İstanbul Nasıl Eğleniyordu?* 154.

3. See, for example, Vedad, "*San'at'ta İnkilap*" (The Revolution in Art); Bedrettin, "*Minarlıkta İnkılap*" (The Revolution in Architecture); and idem, "*Türk İnkılap*" (The Turkish Revolution). Bozdoğan has made this observation as well. Bozdoğan, "*Modern Yaşamak: Erken Cumhuriyet Kültüründe Kübik Ev*" (To Live Modern: The Cubic House in the Culture of the early Republic), 327.

4. His ideas on the house as a machine were translated by Adnan Cemgil in 1928 in *İnsan*, a journal of art, culture, and philosophy.

5. When Arif Koyunoğlu was building the Türk Ocağı building, he found that the foundations that had been laid did not meet his standards. Atatürk arrived as they were being destroyed with dynamite and said, "For God's sake, Hikmet, we are trying to build Ankara and you are blowing it up!" Başkan, *Ankara Devlet Resim ve Heykel Müzesi*, 82.

6. Sometimes called modern functionalism. For a discussion of this movement see Batur, "To Be Modern."

7. Between 1927 and 1936, only one major public building in Ankara was designed by a Turkish architect. This was an exhibition building for the National Economy and Savings Society, built in 1933. This society had responded to the Depression by sponsoring a campaign to use domestic products rather than foreign ones, and the exhibition hall was to display these products. Tekeli argues that it was no coincidence that a "domestic" architect was chosen in this ideological climate. Tekeli, "The Social Context," 17.

8. Le Corbusier, *Vers une architecture*, 11–12.

9. The original name of the journal was *Mimar*, which means architect in Arabic as well as in Ottoman and even in modern Turkish. However, Atatürk wanted no names that had Arabic or Ottoman connotations. In 1933 a Finnish journal was introduced called *Arkitekti*. Since the Turkish Language Association considered Finnish and Turkish to be closely related, that name was deemed acceptable, and *Mimar* was changed to *Arkitekt*. Information courtesy of Ahmet Turhan Altıner, one of its former editors.

10. This information is from Ahmet Turhan Altıner, former editor of *Arkitekt*.

11. See for example, Mortaş, "Evlerimiz."

12. By 1923, the traditional extended family had largely been replaced by the nuclear family, a trend that began early in the twentieth century, if not before.

13. Bozdoğan has made this point in "Modern Yaşamak" (To Live Modern), 317. She also reminds the reader that the role of women as standing at the heart of national change began much earlier. See Bertram, "Restructuring the House, Restructuring the Self," for a discussion of the late Ottoman period when progressivists argued that the emancipation of women was a prerequisite for civilization (i.e., entree into Western civilization) and that women as wives and mothers should be educated because they were responsible for future generations.

14. Ziya, "Ev Döşemesi ve Bugünkü Ev Kültürü," 46.

15. Bozdoğan, "Modern Yaşamak," 317. Also see this for a selection of the model homes that were published in popular magazines, with their instructions on how to arrange the furniture in a modern house.

16. Muzaffer, "Memuriyet Sizin Olsun," 46.

17. I am indebted to Tanyeli, "Osmanlı Barınma Kültüründe Batılılaşma-

Modernleşme / Westernization-Modernization in the Ottoman Wohnkultur," and especially to Bozdoğan, *"Modern Yaşamak,"* for their comprehensive discussions of the role of the house in the late Ottoman and Kemalist periods. See also Tekeli, "The Social Context," and Batur, "To Be Modern."

18. Mithat, *Avrupa Adab-ı Muaşereti yahud Alafranga.*

19. Tayla, *"Türk Evi."*

20. Nalbantoğlu discusses how Turkey's modernity did not rise from the roots but was an official policy implemented by a bureaucratic and professional elite. Nalbantoğlu, "Between Civilization and Culture," 20. For a discussion of the problems of housing the newly urban, the refugee population after the war of independence, and the refugees that arrived after the population exchanges with Greece, see Sey, "To House the New Citizens."

21. Ziya, *"Ev Döşemesi ve Bugünkü Ev Kültürü,"* 47.

22. Batur, "To Be Modern," 77.

23. Çadırcı, "The Neighborhood," 322.

24. Ziya, *"Binanın İçinde Mimar,"* 60.

25. Quoted in Batur, "To Be Modern," 77.

26. Çadırcı, "The Neighborhood," 325–326.

27. Ünver, *"Türk Evi,"* 670.

28. Koyunoğlu, *"Türk Mimari."* Arif Hikmet, however, did not take his own advice. Instead, he designed a model village house that carried no mark of regionalism, either in form or in sensitivity to traditional family practices of privacy from the street. See Nalbantoğlu, "Between Civilization and Culture," 72.

29. Since the first publication of this work in its dissertation form (1999), Bozdoğan has investigated the demise of the love affair with the kübik because of its not-Turkish, that is, not-local vision. For this and Safa and Yalçın's (expected) as well as others' participation in this renunciation, see Bozdoğan, *Modernism and Nation Building,* chap. 6.

30. Nalbantoğlu, "Architects, Style, and Power."

31. Ibid., 44.

32. See Bozdoğan, *Sedad Eldem, Architect in Turkey,* for an analytic biography of Eldem.

33. The exact reason behind a call for a new Republican National style is complex. Tekeli suggests that official interest in a national style grew from Turkey's post-Depression alliances with fascist Germany and fascist Italy, which were constructing buildings in their own nationalist styles. Tekeli, "The Social Context," 20. Alsaç suggests that it was a response to the pressures of World War II, including a need for nationalist feeling while surrounded by hostilities, or a response to the unavailability of imports during the war. He also suggests that it could come to fruition only after the death of Atatürk (1938), who had insisted on consistent Westernization rather than regionalism. Alsaç, "The Second Period of Turkish National Architecture,"

92–95. Aslanoğlu has suggested that the call for a new national style reflects Turkish architects wanting to take control of the profession from foreign ones. Aslanoğlu, "Evaluation of Architectural Developments," 24. Tekeli adds that the concern of the Turkish architects was not ideological but economic (and for that reason welcomed foreign architects as professors so long as they did not compete for commissions). Tekeli, "The Social Context," 18. Nalbantoğlu makes a convincing argument that the Nationalist discourse itself was appropriated by Turkish architects as a strategy to take power over an architectural profession that was in the hands of foreigners. Nalbantoğlu, "Architects, Style, and Power." Alsaç, "The Second Period," 98, also gives a psychological explanation, suggesting that revivalism is a natural and necessary step before moving forward, that the search for the past, for what is lost, reveals the irrationality of such a search, clearing minds so they can concentrate on the present or the future.

34. Vernacular architecture as a sign of the newly national is a common occurrence (perhaps related to the revival of interest in craftsmanship, exemplified in the Bauhaus movement). Although I have traced the emergence of interest in the Turkish house, it is beyond my scope to discuss how this choice compared with similar choices in other settings, although I refer the reader to the work of Dušans Jurković and Josip Plečnik in Slovenia; see Moravanszky, *Competing Visions*, and Niedhardt and Grabrian in Bosnia. See Alić, *The Appropriation of the Ottoman Heritage*, and Spasojević, *Arhitektura Stambenish*.

35. Bozdoğan has reminded me that Behçet Ünsal attributes the initial idea for the establishment of the National Architecture Seminar at the Academy not to Eldem but to Ernst Egli (Behçet Ünsal, 1973). It would be interesting to consider whether the Second National Style would have made use of domestic forms if it had not been for Eldem. But see the preceding footnote.

36. Five dissertations on Anatolian houses were published by Eldem's students as monographs in the 1950s: Komürcüoğlu, *Ankara Evleri*; Eser, *Kütahya Evleri*; Berk, *Konya Evleri*; Erginbaş, *Diyarbakir Evleri*; and Çakiroğlu, *Kayseri Evleri*.

37. "The pre Modern Ottoman world was a stranger to ethnic-ideological fragmentation in relation to housing structures. It is certain that local variations were great. But the origin of the differences, just as in all vernacular traditions, lay not in conscious preferences or a desire to create a group identity; they were accumulations that had been unconscious in the social imagination for centuries." Tanyeli, "Housing and Settlement," 466–467.

38. Kömürcüoğlu, *Ankara Evleri*, 109. Although published in 1950, this dissertation was completed in 1944 and accepted in 1946.

39. Due to a fire at the Faculty of Fine Arts, the first typologies were not published until 1954. Eldem, *Türk Evi Plan Tipleri*. Eldem's complete collection of information and ideas on the Turkish house was not published until 1984. Eldem, *Türk Evi Osmanlı Dönemi*.

40. Tekeli, "The Social Context," 21–23.

41. Eldem had begun with studies of konaks, yalıs, and köşks in Istanbul, but with the increasing populism of the late 1930s he turned his attention to Anatolia. The new national idiom had five major components: (1) It was to be a product of the ground on which it stood: it was to consider local climate, use local materials and local craftsmen. (2) Historical building elements were to be modernized. (3) Modern building materials, when used, were to be covered. (4) Earlier styles of Turkish architecture, civilian and rural, were to be taken as a source of inspiration. (5) The state was to adopt a specific style for all its buildings, and preferably pay for them. Alsaç, "The Second Period," 97. The inspiration for the title of his work, "Toward Local Architecture" ("*Yerli Mimariye Doğru*"), clearly follows Le Corbusier's *Vers une architecture*.

42. However, not all public architecture that is considered Second National Style has a signature of domestic forms. Furthermore, as Bozdoğan points out, the "national" of the National style was contested. There were the modernists who argued that modern architecture was by definition national because it was a rational response to site, climate, context, and so forth ("*Muhitine uygun mimari*"). From Bruno Taut and Ernst Egli to most Turkish architects associated with *Mimar/Arkitekt*, that was the dominant view. These architects advocated learning from the lessons of the vernacular without fixing on one particular "type." Consistent with a national history thesis that appropriated the pre-Ottoman and even pre-Islamic civilizations of Anatolia, the new "national" style thus included revivalist monumental architecture that privileged any pre-Ottoman architecture ever found on Turkish soil. The most famous example is Atatürk's mausoleum, which refers to Hittite structures. The defining aspect of the Second National Style, then, is that it was an Anatolian Turkish rather than an Ottoman historicism that would be suitable to the new republican identity. For a list of representative works in the Second National Style, see Alsaç, "The Second Period," 102–103. Eldem, by moving his research into Anatolia, perhaps felt that he obviated the "Ottoman" associations of the house.

43. The Second National Style was the product of a climate of opinion about the inappropriateness of either modernism or the First National Style. Although officially recognized, it was not officially controlled, and therefore was not "terminated" but was replaced by high modernism due to the changed conditions following World War II. Its program, however, resonates to this day, but without any official associations. See Alsaç, "The Second Period."

44. In 1986, this building won the Aga Khan award for architecture for this sensitivity and for its use of corbels, cantilevers, eaves, and sun shades that recall past architecture in a modern context.

45. Tekeli, "The Social Context," 22.

46. Now demolished. Eldem built other houses in this style, but the Ahmet Ağaoğlu house has been the one most frequently published. The Ağaoğlu house is

discussed and illustrated in Bozdoğan, *Sedad Eldem, Architect in Turkey*, 46–49 and in Aslanoğlu, *Erken Cumhuriyet Dönemi*, 155. For a discussion of Eldem's generation of typologies and their use by him, see Uysal, "'Architectural Type' as a Cultural Schema."

47. Bozdoğan, *Sedad Eldem, Architect in Turkey*, 47.

48. The *"sofa,"* projecting eaves, horizontal window bands, *çıkma/cumbas*, and reinforced concrete were Eldem's signature elements. He was particularly committed to concrete as it could replicate the lightness of timber framing.

49. See her memoirs: *İşittiklerim Gördüklerim Bildiklerim* (What I Heard, Saw and Know, 1973), *Dersaadet* (Gate of Happiness, 1975), *Vaniköy'ünde Fazıl Paşa Yalısı* (The Waterside Residence of Fazıl Paşa in Vaniköy), *Hatırlayabildiklerim* (What I Can Remember), and her novels, *Pertev Bey'in Üç Kızı* (Three Daughters of Pertev Bey, 1968), *Pertev Bey'in İki Kızı* (Two Daughters of Pertev Bey, 1969), *Pertev Bey'in Torunları* (Grandchildren of Pertev Bey, 1969), *Pertev Bey, Üç Kızı, İki Kızı, Torunları* (*Pertev Bey, His Three Daughters, His Two Daughters, His Grandchildren*, three novels published in one volume, 2002).

50. The *Halkevi* or People's Houses were state-sponsored community centers begun in 1932 to spread its ideological principles.

51. Eldem, *"Türk Evi,"* (2), 16.

52. Ibid.

53. Rumeli, as opposed to Anatolia, is the European section of Turkey and the Balkan area of its once Ottoman provinces, such as Albania, Greece, Bosnia, and Bulgaria. It is also the name of my younger daughter. (The older one is Alanya.)

54. Eldem, *"Türk Evi,"* (2) 16.

55. Ley, *Modernism, Post Modernism, and the Struggle for Place*, 8.

56. Koyunoğlu *"Türk Mimari,"* 43.

57. Tekeli, *"The Social Context,"* 21.

58. An important typological characteristic of the Turkish house identified by Eldem was its openness and its connection to nature. I have not addressed his more successful attempts to incorporate these aspects of the Turkish house in his work because their ability to make his new houses visual, recognizable sites of memory is too elusive.

59. Eldem, *"Türk Evi,"* (2).

60. *Ulku* was the voice of the government, as it and the People's Houses were administered by the ruling (and only) party, the Republican People's Party. The People's Houses (*Halkevis*) were an appropriate venue for Eldem, for his ideas fit exactly into their project. These state organizations reached actively and successfully into every level of Turkish society in order to direct and encourage cultural life according to official modernist views. The Halkevis began in 1932. By 1941 there were 379 Halkevis and 131 *Halkodas* (the smaller, People's Room), with more than 500 by the time they closed in 1950. Ertop, "Trends and Characteristics," 153. Their mis-

sion was "to promote love of nation and country, strengthen enthusiasm for reforms, revive the past glory of Turkish history, praise bravery in the War of Liberation, describe the beauties of cities, towns, and villages and each corner of the country in order to create interest in them, focus attention on the ugliness and ridiculousness of bad traditions, stress, with examples, morality in every field, awaken interest in and an inner predisposition for populism" (*Ulku*, March 1934, 76). Thus, the People's Houses were constructed so that the general population could actively participate in the new nationalism. For example, in 1935, *Ulku* announced that 200,000 citizens had cooperated through the Halkevis in pointing out mistakes in or suggesting new words to the Turkish Language Association as they composed their new Turkish vocabulary. Öztürkmen, "The Role of People's Houses."

61. By the end of the 1930s, most authors writing about old houses were writing about the Turkish house. In 1940 Sami Yetik, a student of Hodja Ali Rıza Bey's, wrote about his teacher:

> He was the first to see with the eyes of an artist the beauties of our beloved country that we didn't see; he created with his brush an aesthetic beauty from the condition of the rock, a poem of a thousand colors in the silhouette of a single pistachio tree, a personality in the run down condition of an old Turkish house. (Yetik, *Ressamlarımız*, quoted in Erhan, *Hoca Ali Riza*, 40)

There was also an awareness that Eldem was the repository of information about the Turkish house. Refer to Reşad Ekrem Koçu, below.

62. All of Küçükerman's works discuss this.

63. Originally built as the SATIE (Societé Anonyme Turque d'Installation Electrique) building, it was demolished in 1958.

64. In Amasya in the 1990s, I heard stories of how families would come into town to look at the first apartment buildings with the awe of seeing the first skyscrapers. The urban housing shortage in its most serious aspects has been traced back to 1934. Skidmore, *Construction, Town Planning and Housing in Turkey*, 63–65. Some of this information has been addressed in Bertram, "After the Ottomans Are Gone."

65. Seno, "*Eski Türk Evi*," 13.

66. Alus, "*84 Sene Evvel İstanbul*."

67. This phrase is at the end of each chapter of his 1938–1939 book, *İstanbul Kazan, Ben Kepçe* (Istanbul Is the Cauldron, I Am the Ladle), which describes the characteristics of Istanbul mahalles; this title phrase has entered the vernacular to mean "I've searched all over Istanbul." See "Alus, Sermet Muhtar."

68. Alus, "*Eski Konaklar bize neler anlatıyor? Boğaziçi'nde Kazıklı Yalılar.*"

69. Hisar, *Geçmiş Zaman*, 85.

70. I am not including histories of Istanbul of the classical or pre-classical period that were written at this time, such as Ahmed Refik's famous works *Eski İstanbul*

and *On Altıncı Asırda İstanbul Hayatı*, as these are clearly histories rather than memories.

71. Sometimes referred to as Balıkhane Nazırı Ali Rıza Bey.

72. He published in *Alemdar*, 8 Şubat 1921, and *Peyâm-ı Sabah*, 9 Mayıs 1921–1925— Kanunısani 1922. Some of his papers were bought by Necip Fazıl and published in his *Büyük Doğu* in the mid-1940s. Koz, "Ali Rıza Bey," 200. These newspaper articles were collected and published in newer Turkish as *Bir Zamanlar İstanbul*.

73. However, it was a major opus written in fourteen volumes. These have been condensed, translated into modern Turkish, and annotated. See Abdülaziz entries in the Bibliography.

74. Both include their own observations as well as historical data, although it is difficult to tell these apart. However, their information overlaps to the degree that they are indebted to the works of Esad Efendi (1790?–1848), who wrote in 1870 about the customs of old. Esad-Efendi, *Teşrifat-ı Kadime*.

75. Ahmed Refik held a chair in the History Department of the Literature Faculty of the *İstanbul Darülfünunu* (Istanbul University). It was he and Yahya Kemal who coined the term "Tulip Period" for the early eighteenth century.

76. Eyice, "*Koçu, Reşad Ekrem*," 43.

77. The whole was published in ten volumes, however, between 1958 and 1961.

78. Cesare Biseo had illustrated De Amico's *Constantinopoli*, which Koçu had translated into Turkish in 1936.

79. Ahmet Rasim wrote about the public life of Istanbul in his work *Şehir Mektupları* (Letters from the City), with stories about the public baths "*Hamamcı Ulfet*" (Ulfet of the Public Baths) and bastinado, "*Falaka.*" It was first published in 1900 and republished in 1992. The Library of Congress catalogues it as fiction. Koçu writes that "*Güzel Eleni*" is from Rasim's book called *İki Güzel Günahkâr* (Two Lovely Sinners), which I have been unable to find. His stories were republished in the 1950s, however, as memoirs. See Rasim, "*Eski İstanbul Kış.*"

80. Koçu's encyclopedia was not a catalogue of buildings. For example, it contained information on important historical figures, although whenever possible placing them in their urban context. For a personal discussion of Koçu, houses, and memory, see Pamuk, *Istanbul* (New York: Knopf, 2005).

81. Koçu, "*Ev, Ahşab Evler*," 5402. I estimate that the publication dates of these fascicles occurred ten to twelve years after the information was collected.

82. Ibid.

83. Koçu "*Ahşap Yapı*," 489.

84. This quote by Hamdi Kayalı is taken from Koçu's article on wood construction: "Among us the classic wooden structure was the symbol of the Turk's own spiritual structure, outside it generally had a simple beauty, inside the gleam of a treasury of insight; from the street gate one entered into a treasury of art." Ibid.

85. Seno, "*Eski Türk Evi.*"

86. İA, "*Türkiye Turing ve Otomobil Kurumu*," 316.

87. Terdiman, *Present Past*, 3.

88. The 1920s, 1930s, and 1940s were characterized by a preoccupation with a search for the roots of the Turkish nation and an effort to separate these roots from what were considered later Ottoman and Islamic influences. Even Mehmet Fuat Köprülü, who vigorously rejected the "sun theory of Turkish culture" proposed by extremist nationalist historians, and whose historical method was in many cases more sophisticated than that of his colleagues in the West, dedicated most of his work through the 1940s to a search for origins. For example, he described how Islam had been affected by the indigenous Turkish national spirit (*milli-ruhlarından*). Leiser, in Köprülü, *Some Observations*, i–xi.

89. He does not give an exact location, but he was born in a konak in Beşiktaş in 1875, and "the konak-life that he spent [there] played an important part in his life." İşın, "*Celâl Esad Arseven Üzerine*," 10.

90. According to various legends in Islam, Mt. Kaf (Qaf) is made entirely of emeralds and takes up the space between God and the rest of the sky.

91. Arseven, "*Yoğurtcunun Sesi*," 24.

92. A cotton or wool fluffer used to beat clean such items as the insides of quilts.

93. Arseven, "*Yoğurtcunun Sesi*," 24.

94. Seno, "*Eski Türk Evi*," 16.

95. Salim Şengil's magazine of realistic stories that referred to everyday social and work issues.

96. That a house had seen five generations is a belief that may have been added as a corollary to a memory of heritage and wholeness. Istanbul's history of successive fires meant that very few of its wooden structures lasted longer than 100 years, although the plot it stood on may have been in the family that long or longer. I have mentioned in another chapter that Eldem did not believe that houses were ever conceptualized to last longer than even one generation but were torn down and rebuilt to accommodate the tastes of the new.

97. Akbal, "*Ahşap Ev*," 12.

98. Ibid., 14.

99. Ibid., 14–15.

100. Ibid., 15.

101. I do not use the term "collective unconscious" with Carl Jung's original meaning, which was the part of the mind containing memories and impulses of which the individual is not aware, and common to mankind as a whole rather than to particular social groups.

102. In *Beş Şehir* (Five Cities), he writes, "We're the children of a crisis of mind and identity; we're living the question, 'to be or not to be' more poignantly than Hamlet. As we embrace this dilemma, we will more fully take control of our lives and our work." See also his "The Civilization Shift and the Inner Person" ("*Medeni-*

yet Değiştirme ve İç İnsan") in Tanpınar, *Yaşadığım Gibi*, and see Köroğlu, *Gidenle Gelmeyenin Eşiğinde*, and Atiş, *Structural Analysis*.

103. The figure of the "new man," or *"yeni adam,"* was the figure who met the Kemalist ideal with all of its Western, secular connotations, and all of the implied rejection of the Ottoman viewpoint. The *yeni adam* was a figure in the popular imagination of the Kemalist period; it was the title of a journal begun in 1934 and a type of character in Tanpınar's *Sahnenin Dışındakiler* (as described by Erol Köroğlu in *Gidenle Gelmeyenin Eşiğinde*). Many well-known critics, such as Atilla İlhan, have dealt with the concept of the *yeni adam*. I thank Tracy Lord for calling this trope to my attention.

104. Tanpınar, *Yaşadığım Gibi*, 25. Cited in Koroğlu, *Gidenle Gelmeyenin Eşiğinde*, 35. Translation by Tracy Lord.

105. In 1326, Bursa was established as the first Ottoman capital by Orhan Bey, the son of Gazi Osman, founder of the empire.

106. Including, perhaps, writers who bemoaned the loss of the built environment, such as Yusuf Ziya Ortaç, who wrote, "the skeletons of only one or two [Turkish] houses barely stand in Bursa." Ortaç, *Türk Evleri*.

107. Anderson, *Imagined Communities*, 195–196.

108. The legends of Dede Korkut are orally transmitted myths from the Oghuz tribe of Turks who migrated to Turkey from Central Asia.

109. The idea "sadly but more safely in the past" is taken from Christopher Shaw and Malcolm Chase, who wrote, "Nor does nostalgia necessarily connote despairing rejection of the present. Few admirers of the past would actually choose to return to it. . . . Nostalgia expressed longings for times that remain safely, rather than sadly, beyond recall." *The Imagined Past*, 28.

110. Translated from "Five Cities" in Silay, *An Anthology*, 383.

111. Ibid.

112. Translated in Menemencioğlu, *The Penguin Book of Turkish Verse*, 182–183. I reproduce the poem in its entirety because of its exquisite beauty.

Kandilli'de eski bahçelerde,
Akşam kapanınca perde perde,
Bir hatıra zevki var kederde
Artık ne gelen, ne beklenen var;
Tenha yolun ortasında rüzgâr
Taşrin yapraklariyle oynar.
Gittikçe derinleşir saatler,
Rikkatle, yavaş yavaş ve yer yer
Sessizlik daima ilerler.
Ürperme verir hayâle, sık sık,
Her bir kapıdan giren karanlık

Çok belli ayak sesinden, artık.
Gözlerden azaklaşınca dünya,
Binbir geceden birinde, gûyâ
Başlar rüya içinde rüya.

—Güvemli, *Yahya Kemal ve Şiirleri*, 50

113. Timur, *Geçmiş Günler*, 42.

114. Translated in Menemencioğlu, *The Penguin Book of Turkish Verse*, 182–183.

115. Atiş, *Structural Analysis*, 18.

116. From "Five Cities" (*Beş Şehir*), in Silay, *An Anthology*, 382.

117. Terdiman, *Present Past*, 8.

118. Kuban, *Istanbul, an Urban History*, 422–427.

119. This konak was purchased in 1977 by the Turing (The Turkish Automobile Association) and restored as the Yeşil Ev Hotel, which opened in 1984.

120. Gülersoy, "*Yeşil Ev.*"

121. Topuzlu, *80 Yillik Hatıralarım*, 5.

122. *Ressam Ali Rıza* and *Ressam Üsküdarlı Ali Rıza Bey*.

123. For a complete list with dates, refer to the Cast of Characters.

124. Hisar, "*Resimler Karşısında,*" 184.

125. Ibid., 183.

126. Ibid.

127. Ibid., 282.

128. Hisar, *Geçmiş Zaman Köşkleri*, 7–8.

129. Another modern reference to the old fires and the loss of meaning is a bumper sticker sold in Turkey in the 1990s that read, "*Ne yazık ki beton yanmıyor*" (What a shame that concrete doesn't burn).

130. Havel, "The Need for Transcendence." Havel is a former president of the Czech Republic.

131. The Turkish house is considered here as an image that was created in the past, whether or not what is seen in the present is an original or a replica. Benjamin also suggests that these images of the past come from a past that was "dreaming the present," and when they appear in the present, they appear as dreams of the past, creating a montage that connects the present to the past without teleology, and without a harmonizing whole, yet with a continuity that allows the fragments to cohere as a philosophical representation of history. Buck-Morss, *The Dialectics of Seeing*, 67.

132. Benjamin, "Theses on the Philosophy of History," 681.

133. I am aware, however, that the continuity I am talking about may in part be a continuation of something that was constructed *in* the past.

134. Ortaç, *Üç Katlı Ev*, 6.

135. Ibid., final scene.

136. Akbal, "*Ahşap Ev,*" 15.

137. Thank you to Tracy Lord, who brought this work to my attention. Anayurt Oteli is considered a canon work of Turkish literature but has been very sparsely analyzed. It was made into a movie in the 1980s.

138. Gürbilek has pointed out that the language of the narrative in Anayurt Oteli varies from minimalist and bare when relating the actions of Zebercet in present time to rich and intricate when relating the flashbacks, which are full of family, extended family, and complex social relationships. Gürbilek, "Taşra Sıkıntısı," 87–88. How like the old man in the cartoon of Istanbul, whose "flashback" hallucinations fill the house with warmth and ceremony.

139. From Tanpınar's Beş Şehir, translated by Silay, in An Anthology, 383.

140. Gürbilek analyzes Anayurt Oteli as a comparison between iç and dış, that is, between the konak and what is outside it. Gürbilek, "Taşra Sıkıntısı," 87–88.

141. Gülgeç, "Hikâye-i İstanbul," 118.

142. Altıner, The Konak Book, 7.

143. The Konak Book, "A Study of the Traditional Turkish Urban Dwelling in Its Late Period," clearly refers to Ottoman history. However, in the tradition of a "new republican history" that sought origins in Central Asia, it refers the reader to the origins of the Turkish house in the Central Asian yurt and then to living configurations of the Uygurs. See also Küçükerman for this trope of the Turkish house as a Central Asian tent.

144. "Sedadkent" filters the past through the modernism of Sedad Hakkı Eldem, whose designs they follow.

145. Hisar, Geçmiş Zaman, 7–8.

146. Barthes, "Rhetoric of the Image."

147. See, for example, Çelik, "Urban Preservation as Theme Park."

148. I am grateful to Engin Akarli for this example. I have tried here to examine the rhetorical positions of only the earliest of the different groups that have allied themselves with the image of the Turkish house. Certainly this image is now used in a variety of cultural political contexts, in addition to the fact that all things Ottoman began to become an image industry of their own in the late twentieth century.

149. Cansever, Ben Rûhi Bey Nasılım.

150. It can also be seen as memory disturbances or memory disorders. But this is not merely because these buildings and communities oversimplify memory, limiting it to a single class, a single time, or a single way of life, but because as commodities, "nostalgic architecture" fictionalizes the processes that brought these "authentic" Turkish houses into being. Behind them is no group of local artisans, no real narrative of neighborhood, and the wooden houses are wood-clabbered concrete. At a fundamental level, although they recall to mind memories of values, they may act as the final isolation of the present from the past.

151. Altıner, The Konak Book, 40.

152. Dinçer, "New Owners of Old Quarter," 27.

153. See, for example, Soysal, *Tarihten Günümüze Anadolu'da Konut ve Yerleşmen'in Öyküsü.* The cover of this book, "The Story of Dwellings and Settlement in Anatolia from Historic Times to the Present," is a charming illustration of a little Turkish house with a cumba.

154. James, *The Principles of Psychology,* 425.

155. Ibid.

THE CAST OF CHARACTERS

1. Zürcher, *Turkey, A Modern History.*

bibliography

Abaday, D. *"Boğaz'da Yüz Yıl Önce: Bir Yaşamın Öyküsü." Türkiyemiz* 20 (1990): 34–46.

Abdülaziz, A. *Osmanlı Adet, Merasim ve Tabirleri: İnsanlar, İnanışlar, Eğlence, Dil.* Istanbul: Tarih Vakfı Yayınlar, 1995 (1918).

———. *Osmanlı Adet, Merasim ve Tabirleri: Toplum Hayatı.* Istanbul: Tarih Vakfı Yayınlar, 1995 (1918).

"Abdürrahman Şerefbey Caddesi." In *İstanbul Ansiklopedisi*, edited by R. E. Koçu, 1:164–165. Istanbul: Reşad Ekrem Koçu ve Mehmed Ali Aksoy İstanbul Ansiklopedisi ve Neşriyat Kollektif Şirketi, 1958.

"Afşar Sokağı." In *İstanbul Ansiklopedisi*, edited by R. E. Koçu, 1:229. Istanbul: Reşad Ekrem Koçu ve Mehmed Ali Aksoy İstanbul Ansiklopedisi ve Neşriyat Kollektif Şirketi, 1959.

Ağaoğlu, A. *Üç Medeniyet.* Ankara, 1928.

"Ahşap Yapı." In *İstanbul Ansiklopedisi*, edited by R. E. Koçu, 1:489–493. Istanbul: Reşad Ekrem Koçu ve Mehmed Ali Aksoy İstanbul Ansiklopedisi ve Neşriyat Kollektif Şirketi, 1958.

Akbal, O. "Ahşap Ev." *Seçilmiş Hikâyeler* 12–16 (1947).

Akıncı, U. "Ilhan Tekeli's 'Modernization Project.'" *Turkish Torque Review.* http://tork.blogspot.com/Tekeli_Modernity_Project.html#PAGE%A0TOP (accessed June 25, 2006).

"Aksaray Yangınları." In *İstanbul Ansiklopedisi*, edited by E. E. Koçu, 1:539–542. Istanbul: Reşad Ekrem Koçu ve Mehmed Ali Aksoy İstanbul Ansiklopedisi ve Neşriyat Kollektif Şirketi, 1958.

Aksel, M. *İstanbul'un Ortası.* Ankara: Kültür Bakanlığı, Elif Matbaası, 1977.

al-Attas, S. "The Islamic Worldview: An Outline." In *İslam, Gelenek ve Yenileşme: 1. Uluslararası "Kutlu Doğum" İlmi Toplantısı /Islam / Tradition and Change: The First International "Kutlu Doğum" Symposium*, edited by A. Özcan. Istanbul: ISAM (İslam Araştırmaları Merkezi) (Türkiye Diyanet Vakfı), 1996.

Alić, D., and M. Gusheh. *The Appropriation of the Ottoman Heritage in Socialist Yugoslavia: Bascarsija Project (1948–53)*. Association of the Collegiate Schools of Architecture International Conference, Berlin, 1997.

Ali-Rıza-Bey, *"Bir Zamanlar İstanbul"* (Istanbul in Those Times). Istanbul: *Tercüman Gazetesi*, 1973 (1922).

Alonso, A. M. "The Politics of Space, Time, and Substance: State Formation, Nationalism, and Ethnicity." *Annual Review of Anthropology* 23 (1994): 379–404.

Alsaç, U. "The Second Period of Turkish National Architecture." In *Modern Turkish Architecture*, edited by R. Holod and A. Evin, 94–104. Philadelphia: University of Pennsylvania Press, 1984.

Alsaç, U., E. Madran, et al. *Kültür ve Tabiat Varlıklarının Korunması ve Onarılması Konularında Kaynakça*. Ankara: Kültür ve Tabiat Varlıklarını Koruma Genel Müdürlügü, 1990.

Altıner, A. T., Z. Akay, et al. "Arif Hikmet Koyunoğlu." *Arkitekt* 4 (1991): 34–50.

Altıner, A. T., and C. Budak. *Konak Kitabı/ The Konak Book*. Istanbul: Tepe İnşaat Sanayi, 1997.

Alus, S. M. "*30 Sene Evvel İstanbul.*" *Akşam*, 1930.

———. "*84 Sene Evvel İstanbul.*" *Akşam*, 1932.

———. "*Boğaziçi'nde Kazıklı Yalılar.*" *Tan*, 1 İkinci Teşrin (Kasım), (December) 1936.

———. "Eski Konaklar bize neler anlatıyor?" *Tan*, 21 İkinci Teşrin (Kasım), 1936.

———. *Sermet Muhtar Alus: İstanbul Yazıları*. Istanbul: İstanbul Büyükşehir Belediyesi Kültür İşleri Dairesi Başkanlığı, 1994 (1936).

———. "*40 Yıl Evvelkiler.*" *Akşam*, 1939.

"Alus, Sermet Muhtar." In *İstanbul Ansiklopedisi*, edited by H. Ayhan, 7:232–233. Istanbul: Kültür Bakanlığı ve Tarih Vakfının Ortak Yayınları, 1993.

And, M. *Karagöz: Turkish Shadow Theatre*. Istanbul: Dost, 1975.

———. "Atatürk and the Arts, with Special Reference to Music and Theater." In *Atatürk and the Modernization of Turkey*, edited by J. M. Landau, 215–234. Leiden: E.J. Brill, 1984.

Anderson, B. *Imagined Communities: Reflections on the Origin and Spread of Nationalism*. London: Verso, 1991.

Andrews, W. G. *Poetry's Voice, Society's Song: Ottoman Lyric Poetry*. Seattle: University of Washington Press, 1985.

Andrić, I. *The Vezier's Elephant*. New York: Harcourt, Brace and World, 1962.

Arık, R. *Batılılaşma Dönemi Anadolu Tasvir Sanati*. Ankara: Türkiye İş Bankası, 1976.

———. "Landscapes in Trays." In *Image of Türkiye*, 10–14. Ankara: Tutav and the Promotion Fund of the Turkish Prime Ministry, 1991.

Arseven, C. E. *Constantinople: De Byzance á Stamboul*. Paris: Libraire Renouard, 1909.

———. *"Yoğurtcunun Sesi."* Yedigün 12 (306, 17 İkincikânun 1939): 15.

———. *L'Art Turc: Depuis son origine jusqu'a nos jours.* Istanbul: Devlet Basımevi, 1939.

———. *"Türkiye'de Tanzimat Devrinden Sonra Resim."* In *Türk Sanatı Tarihi: Menşeinden Bugüne Kadar Heykel, Oyma ve Resim*, 3(1): 128–160. Istanbul: Milli Eğitim Basımevi, 1955.

———. *Türk Sanatı Tarihi, Menşeinden Bugüne Kadar.* Istanbul: Istanbul, Milli Eğitim Basımevi, 1961 (1928).

Aslanoğlu, I. *Erken Cumhuriyet Dönemi Mimarlığı.* Ankara: Orta Doğu Teknik Üniversitesi, 1980.

———. "Evaluation of Architectural Developments in Turkey Within the Socio-economic and Cultural Framework of the 1923–1938 Period." *Orta Doğu Teknik Üniversitesi Journal* 7, no. 2 (Spring 1986): 15–41.

———. *Erken Cumhuriyet Dönemi Mimarlığı, 1923–1938.* Ankara: ODTÜ Mimarlik Fakültesi Yayınları, 2001.

Atasoy, N., and J. Raby. *İznik.* Istanbul: Türk Ekonomi Bankası, 1989.

Atay, M. *Tarih İçinde İzmir.* İzmir, Tifset Basım ve Yayın Sanayii, 1978.

Atılgan, Y. *Anayurt Oteli.* Ankara: Bilgi Yayınevi, 1973.

Atiş, S. M. *Structural Analysis of Five Short Stories by the Turkish Author Ahmet Hamdi Tanpınar.* Ann Arbor: University of Michigan Press, 1975.

Aydın, S., and V. Uğurlu. *Hoca Ali Rıza.* Istanbul: Yapı Kredi Yayınları, 1988.

Badgerazart. *Badgerazart Pnashkharhig Pararan* (Illustrated Geographical Dictionary). Venice: St. Lazar Monastery, 1903.

Baker, A., and M. Billinge. *Period and Place: Research Methods in Historical Geography.* London: Cambridge University Press, 1982.

Bakhtin, M. *The Dialogic Imagination*, translated and edited by M. Holquist. Austin: University of Texas Press, 1981.

Balcı, P. *Eski İstanbul Evleri ve Boğaziçi Yalıları.* Istanbul: APA Ofset, 1980.

Balcı, P., ed. *Türk Evi ve Biz.* Istanbul: Türkiye Tarihi Evleri Koruma Derneği Yayınlar, 1993.

Banarlı, N. S. *Resimli Türk Edebiyatı Târihi, Destanlar Devrinden Zamanımıza Kadar.* Istanbul: Devlet Kitapları Milli Eğitiğim Basımevi, 1971.

Barışta, H. *"Özel Müzelerimiz ve Koleksionlarımız Sadberk Hanım Müzesi'ndeki Türk İşlemeleri* / Turkey's Private Museums and Collections: Turkish Needlework in the Sadberk Hanım Museum." *Sanat Dünyamız* 11, no. 33 (1985): 17–26.

Barker, A. *Explorations in Historical Geography: Interpretative Essays.* New York: Cambridge University Press, 1984.

Barthes, R. "Rhetoric of the Image." In *Image, Music, Text*, translated by S. Heath. New York: Hill and Wang, 1977.

Bastea, E. *The Creation of Modern Athens: Planning the Myth.* London: Cambridge University Press, 2000.

———. *Memory and Architecture*. Albuquerque: University of New Mexico Press, 2004.

———. "Storied Cities: Literary Memories of Thessaloniki and Istanbul." In *Memory and Architecture*, 191–210. Albuquerque: University of New Mexico Press, 2004.

Başcı, K. P. "Shadows in the Missionary Garden of Roses: Women of Turkey in American Missionary Texts." In *Deconstructing Images of "the Turkish Woman,"* edited by Z. Arat, 101–123. New York: St. Martin's Press, 1998.

Başkan, S. *Ankara Devlet Resim ve Heykel Müzesi*. Ankara: Ak Yayınları, 1989.

Batur, A. "To be Modern: Search for a Republican Architecture." In *Modern Turkish Architecture*, edited by R. Holod and A. Evin, 68–94. Philadelphia: University of Pennsylvania Press, 1984.

Baudrillard, J. *Simulacra and Simulation*, translated by S. F. Glaser. Ann Arbor: University of Michigan Press, 1995.

Baydar, M. *Hamdullah Suphi Tanrıöver*. Istanbul, Menteş Kitabevi, 1968.

"Bedia." In *İstanbul Ansiklopedisi*, edited by R. E. Koçu, 5:2356–2366. Istanbul: Reşad Ekrem Koçu ve Mehmed Ali Aksoy İstanbul Ansiklopedisi ve Neşriyat Kollektif Şirketi, 1961.

Bedrettin, B. "*Mimarlıkta İnkılap*" (The Revolution in Architecture). *Mimar* 3, no. 8 (1933): 245–247.

———. "*Türk İnkılap*" (The Turkish Revolution). *Mimar* 3, no. 9/10 (1933): 265–266.

Behçet Ünsal, F. *Mimarlık* [special issue on the architecture of 1923–1950], February 1973.

Bejtić, A. *Ulice i Trgovi Sarajeva*. Sarajevo: Muzej Grada Sarajeva, 1973.

Benjamin, W. "Theses on the Philosophy of History." In *Illuminations: Essays and Reflections*, translated and edited by H. Arendt, 253–263. New York: Schocken Books, 1968.

Berger, P., and T. Luckmann. *The Social Construction of Reality: A Treatise in the Sociology of Knowledge*. Garden City, NY: Doubleday, 1966.

Berk, C. *Konya Evleri*. Istanbul, 1951.

Berk, N. *İstanbul Resim ve Heykel Müzesi / The Istanbul Museum of Painting and Culture*. Istanbul: APA Ofset Basımevi, 1972.

———. *Türk ve Yabancı Resimde İstanbul / Istanbul Chez les Peintres Turcs et Etrangers*. Istanbul: Türkiye Turing ve Otomobil Kurumu, 1977.

Berkes, N. *The Development of Secularism in Turkey*. Montreal: McGill University Press, 1964.

Bertram, C. "*Kafana, Konak, Čarşija, Cuprija*: Literary Narrative as an Art-Historical Resource." *The Turkish Studies Association Bulletin* 14, no. 2, 1990.

———. "After the Ottomans Are Gone: Imagining the Turkish Ottoman House." In *The Ottoman House. Proceeds of the International Symposium on The Ottoman*

House, Amasya, Turkey, 1996, edited by S. Ireland and S. Austin. London: Academic Press, 1996.

———. "Restructuring the house, restructuring the self: Gendered meanings of place in the modern Turkish short story." In *Deconstructing Images of "the Turkish Woman,"* edited by Z. Arat, 263–272. New York: St. Martin's Press, 1998.

———. "The Ottoman House in the Turkish Imagination: Monumentalizing the Quotidian / *Türk Tahayyülünde Osmanli Evi: Günlük Hayat ın Anitlaştirilması."* In *Yeni Türkiye Dergisi Project Turk* [a twenty-volume research summary]. Ankara: Ministry of Culture of the Republic of Turkey and the Turkish Historical Society, 2002.

"Beylerbeyinde Bir Yalı." *Arkitekt* 8 (1938): 217.

Bhabha, H. *The Location of Culture.* London: Routledge, 1994.

Birsel, S. *Sergüzeşt-i Nono Bey ve Elmas Boğaziçi.* Istanbul: Türkiye İş Bankası Kültür Yayınları, 1982.

Boschma, C., and J. Perot. *Antoine-Ignace Melling (1763–1831).* Paris: Musée Carnavalet, 1991.

Boyd, M. *The Reflexive Novel: Fiction as Critique.* London: Bucknell University Press, 1983.

Boyer, C. M. *The City of Collective Memory.* Cambridge, MA: MIT Press, 1994.

Bozdoğan, S. "Sedad Hakkı Eldem of Turkey." *Mimar,* 24 June 1987, 44–65.

———. "*Modern Yaşamak: Erken Cumhuriyet Kültüründe Kübik Ev* / To Live Modern: The Cubic House in the Culture of the Early Republic." In *Tarihten Günümüze Anadoldu'da Konut ve Yerleşme /Housing and Settlement in Anatolia, A Historical Perspective,* edited by Y. Sey, 313–328. Istanbul: Türkiye Ekonomik ve Toplumsal Tarih Vakfı, 1996.

———. *Modernism and Nation Building: Turkish Architectural Culture in the Early Republic.* Studies in Modernity and National Identity Series. Seattle: University of Washington Press, 2001.

Bozdoğan, S., and R. Kasaba, eds. *Rethinking Modernity and National Identity in Turkey.* Seattle: University of Washington Press, 1997.

Bozdoğan, S., S. Özkan, et al. *Sedad Eldem, Architect in Turkey.* Singapore: Mimar, Concepts Media, 1987.

Buck-Morss, S. *The Dialectics of Seeing: Walter Benjamin and the Arcades Project.* Cambridge, MA: MIT Press, 1989.

Campo, J. E. *The Other Sides of Paradise: Explorations into the Religious Meanings of Domestic Space in Islam.* Columbia: University of South Carolina Press, 1991.

Cansever, E. *Ben Rûhi Bey Nasılım.* Istanbul: Koza Yayınları, 1976.

Canter, D., M. Krampen, et al. *Environmental Perspectives: Ethnoscapes: Current Challenges in the Environmental Sciences.* Hong Kong: Avebury, 1988.

Cezar, M. *Müzeci ve Ressam Osman Hamdi Bey.* Istanbul: Türk Kültürüne Hazine Vakfı, 1987.

Choay, F. *L'Allégorie du Patrimoine*. Paris: Seuil, 1992.

"*Constantinopoli*." In *İstanbul Ansiklopedisi*, edited by R. E. Koçu, 7:3601–3605. Istanbul: Reşad Ekrem Koçu ve Mehmed Ali Aksoy İstanbul Ansiklopedisi ve Neşriyat Kollektif Şirketi, 1938.

Crane, S. A. "(Not) Writing History: Rethinking the Intersections of Personal History and Collective Memory with Hans von Aufsess." *History and Memory* 8 (Spring/Summer 1996): 5–29.

Craven, Lady E. *A Journey Through the Crimea to Constantinople*. London: G.G.J. and J. Robinson, 1789.

Csepeli, G. *National Identity in Contemporary Hungary*. Boulder, CO, and Highland Lakes, NY: Social Science Monographs, Atlantic Research and Publications, 1997.

Curtis, W. E. *The Turk and His Lost Provinces*. Chicago: Fleming H. Revell, 1903.

Çadırcı, M. "*Anadolu Kentlerinde Mahalle (Osmanlı Dönemi)* / The Neighborhood in Ottoman Towns (Ottoman Period)." In *Tarihden Günümüze Anadoldu'da Konut ve Yerleşme (Housing and Settlement in Anatolia: A Historical Perspective)*, edited by Y. Sey, 257–263. Istanbul: Türkiye Ekonomik ve Toplumsal Tarih Vakfı, 1996.

Çakiroğlu, N. *Kayseri Evleri*. Istanbul: Pulhan Matbaasi, 1952.

Çelik, Z. *The Remaking of Istanbul: Portrait of an Ottoman City in the Nineteenth Century*. Seattle: University of Washington Press, 1986.

———. "Urban Preservation as Theme Park: The Case of Soğukçeşme Street." In *Streets*, edited by Z. Çelik, D. Favro, and R. Ingersoll, 83–94. Berkeley and Los Angeles: University of California Press, 1994.

Cemgil, A. "Makina Medeniyetinden Beklediğimiz Ev." *İnsan* 1–3: 228–232 (1938).

Çeviker, T. *Gelişim Sürecinde Türk Karikatürü II: Meşrütiyet Dönemi (1908–1918)* (Turkish Cartoons during the Developmental Period II: Constitutional Period). Istanbul: Adam Yayınları, 1986.

———. *Nişan G. Berberyan: Terakki Edelim Beyler*. Istanbul: Adam Yayınları, 1986.

Çolak, Y. "Ottomanism vs. Kemalism: Collective Memory and Cultural Pluralism in 1990s Turkey." *Middle Eastern Studies* 42, no. 4 (July 2006): 587–602.

De Amicis, E. *Constantinopoli*. Milan: Fratelli Treves, 1921 (1874).

de Gigord, P. *Images d'Empire: Auz origines de las photographie en Turquie*. Istanbul: Institut d'Etudes Française d'Istanbul, 1996.

Demiray, A. *Resimli Amasya, Tarih, Coğrafya, Salname-Kılavuz ve Kazalar*. Ankara: Güney Matbaacılık ve Gazetecilik T.A.O., 1954.

Demirdirek, A. *Osmanlı Kadınlarının Hayat Hakkı Arayışının Bir Hikayesi*. Ankara: İmge Kitabevi Yayınları, 1993.

———. "In Pursuit of the Ottoman Women's Movement." In *Deconstructing Images of "the Turkish Woman*," edited by Z. Arat, 65–91. New York: St. Martin's Press, 1998.

Denel, S. *Batılılaşma Sürecinde İstanbulda Tasarım ve dış Mekânlarda Değişim ve Nedenleri* (Changes in the Conception and Exterior of Residences in Istanbul during the Westernization Period, and the Causes). Ankara: Orta Doğu Teknik Üniversitesi, 1982.

Dilmen, Güngör. *Aşkımız Aksaray'ın En Büyük Yangını*. Istanbul: Turkiye İş Bankası Kültür Yayınları, 1989.

———. "Our Love Was the Most Devastating Fire of Aksaray / *Aşkımız Aksaray'ın En Büyük Yangını.*" *The Turkish Pen* Summer (1992): 38–48.

Dinçer, I., and Z. M. Enlil. "New Owners of Old Quarter: Migrants and the Reproduction of Historic Urban Spaces." In *Housing Question of the "Others,"* edited by E. M. Komut, 267–280. Ankara: Chamber of Architects, Turkey, 1996.

Duben, A. "Nineteenth and Twentieth Century Ottoman Turkish Family and Household Structure." In *Family in Turkish Society. Sociological and Legal Studies*, edited by T. Erder, 105–126. Ankara: Turkish Social Science Association, 1985.

Duben, A., and Cem Behar. *Istanbul Households, Marriage, Family and Fertility 1880–1940*. Cambridge: Cambridge University Press, 1991.

Durkheim, E. *The Rules of Sociological Method*, translated by W. D. Halls, edited by Steven Lukes. New York: Free Press, 1982 (1895).

Eberts, E. H. *Social and Personality Correlates of Personal Space*. EDRA I. Proceedings of the Ninth Annual Environmental Design Research Association, Tucson, AZ, 1972.

Edib, H. *Shirt of Flame (Ateşten Gömlek)*. New York: Duffield, 1924.

———. *Memoirs of Halide Edip*. New York: Century Co., 1926.

———. *The Clown and His Daughter*. London: Allen and Unwin, 1935.

———. *Conflict of East and West in Turkey*. Lahore: Muhammad Ashraf, 1935.

———. "Arka Sokaktan Görüş: Yuvarlanan Kırklar." *Yedigün* 12 (6 Eylül 1938): 9.

———. "Arka Sokaktan Görüş: Seke Seke Ben Geldim." *Yedigün* 11 (23 Ağustos 1938): 9.

———. "Arka Sokaktan Görüş: Elektra Piyesi, J.Gıraudou'nun eseri." *Yedigün* 11 (261, 8 Şubat 1938): 9.

———. "Arka Sokaktan Görüş: Devika Rani." *Yedigün* 12 (6 Birincikânun 1938): 9.

———. "Arka Sokaktan Görüş: Bayrak İnsan." *Yedigün* 12 (10 Birinci Kânun 1938): 9, 13.

———. *Sinekli Bakkal*. Istanbul: Uycan Matbaası, 1966 (1936).

———. *Sinekli Bakkal*. Istanbul: Atlas Kitabevi, 1984 (1936).

Ekrem, R. M. *Araba Sevdası*. Istanbul: İnkilap Kitabevi, 1996 (1886).

Eldem, S. H. "Yerli Mimariye Doğru." *Arkitekt* 3–4 (1940): 73.

———. "Türk Evi: 1." *Ulku* 2, no. 22 (1942): 10–15.

———. "Türk Evi: 2." *Türkiye Turing ve Otomobil Kurumu Belleteni*, Augustos 1942.

———. *Türk Evi Plan Tipleri*, 3 vols. Istanbul: İstanbul Teknik Üniversitesi-Mimarlık Fakültesi, 1954.

———. "Birgi'deki Çakırağa Konağı." *Türkiyemiz* 1 (Haziran 1970): 11–15.

————. *Köşkler ve Kasırlar/Kiosks and Pavillions.* Istanbul: Devlet Güzel Sanatlar Akademisi Yüksek Mimarlık Bölümü Kürsüsü, 198?.

————. *Türk Evi Osmanlı Dönemi / Turkish Houses in the Ottoman Period.* Istanbul, 1984.

Emin, M. Untitled. *Hayat* II, 66 (1928): 261.

Enginün, I. *Halide Edip Adıvar'ın Eserlerinde Doğu ve Batı Meselesi.* Istanbul: Milli Eğitim Bakanlığı Yayınları, 1993.

Ergenç, O. "Osmanlı Şehrindeki Mahalle'nin İşlev ve Nitelikleri Üzerine" (The Function and Characteristics of the "Neighborhood" in the Ottoman City). *Osmanlı Araştırmaları / The Journal of Ottoman studies* 4 (1984): 69–78.

Ergin, O. *Muallim Cevdet'in Hayatı, Eserleri ve Kütüphanesi* Istanbul: Bozkurt Basımevi, 1937.

Erginbaş, D. *Diyarbakir Evleri.* Istanbul: İstanbul Matbaacılık, 1954.

Erhan, K. *Hoca Ali Rıza.* Ankara: Türkiye İş Bankası Kültür Yayınları, 1980.

Ertop, K. "Trends and Characteristics of Contemporary Turkish Literature." In *The Transformation of Turkish Culture: The Atatürk Legacy,* edited by G. Renda and C. M. Kortepeter, 145–164. Princeton, NJ: Kingston Press, 1986.

Esad-Efendi. *Teşrifat-ı Kadime.* Istanbul: Matbaa-i Amire, 1870.

Esen, N. *Türk Romanında Aile Kuruma.* Istanbul: Boğaziçi Üniversitesi, 1997.

Eser, L. *Kütahya Evleri.* Istanbul: Pulhan Matbaası, 1955.

"Ev, Ahşab Evler." In *İstanbul Ansiklopedisi,* edited by R. E. Koçu, 10:5400. İstanbul, Reşad Ekrem Koçu ve Mehmed Ali Aksoy İstanbul Ansiklopedisi ve Neşriyat Kollektif Şirketi, 1961.

Evin, A. *Origins and Development of the Turkish Novel.* Minneapolis: Bibliotheca Islamica, 1983.

Eyice, S. "Koçu, Reşad Ekrem." In *İstanbul Ansiklopedisi,* edited by H. Ayhan, 41–43. Istanbul: Kültür Bakanlığı ve Tarih Vakfı'nın Ortak Yayınları, 1993.

Faroqhi, S. *Men of Modest Substance: House Owners and House Property in Seventeenth-Century Ankara and Kayseri.* London: Cambridge University Press, 1987.

Findley, C. V. *Bureaucratic Reform in the Ottoman Empire.* Princeton, NJ: Princeton University Press, 1980.

Finn, R. P. *The Early Turkish Novel 1872–1900.* Istanbul: Isis Yayımcılık, İstanbul Matbaası, 1984.

Friedman, J. "The Past in the Future: History and the Politics of Identity." *American Anthropologist* 94, no. 4 (1992): 837–857.

Galip, M. "Ankara Evleri" (Ankara Houses, in Ottoman Turkish). *Muallimler Birliği Mecmuası* 8 (1926): 354–359.

Garnett, L. M. J. *Turkish Life in Town and Country.* London: George Newnes, 1891.

Geertz, C. *The Interpretation of Cultures: Selected Essays.* New York: Basic Books, 1973.

Geertz, H. "The View from Within." In *Architecture as Symbol and Self Identity: Form: A Vocabulary and Grammar of Symbols*, 63–68. Seminar Four in the series Architectural Transformations in the Islamic World, 1979.

Georgiadis, S. Review of *The Creation of Modern Athens: Planning the Myth. Journal of the Society of Architectural Historians* 60, no. 3 (2001): 361–362.

Gladstone, W. E. *The Bulgarian Horrors and the Question of the East*. London, 1876.

Glassberg, D. "Public History and the Study of Memory." *The Public Historian* 18 (Spring 1996): 7–23.

Goleman, D. *Emotional Intelligence*. New York: Bantam Books, 1997.

Göçek, F. M. *Rise of the Bourgeoisie, Demise of the Empire: Ottoman Westernization and Social Change*. New York: Oxford University Press, 1996.

Göçek, F. M., ed. *Social Constructions of Nationalism in the Middle East*. SUNY Series in Middle Eastern Studies. Ithaca: State University of New York Press, 2002.

Göktaş, U. "Karagöz Shadow Shows." *Image of Turkey* 7: 26–29, 1987.

Grabar, O. "Pictures or Commentaries: The Illustrations of the Maqamat of al Hariri." In *Studies in Art and Literature of the Near East in Honor of Richard Ettinghausen*, edited by P. Chelkowski, 84–104. Middle East Center, University of Utah, Salt Lake City, 1974.

Gregory, D. *Ideology, Science, and Human Geography*. New York: St. Martin's Press, 1978.

———. *Geographical Imaginations*. London: Blackwell, 1995.

Gülersoy, Ç. "Yeşil Ev." In *İstanbul Ansiklopedisi*, edited by H. Ayhan, 7:508–509. Istanbul: Kültür Bakanlığı ve Tarih Vakfı'nın Ortak Yayınları, 1993.

Gülgeç, İ. "Hikâye-i İstanbul" (An Istanbul Romance) (cartoon). *Istanbul Magazine / İstanbul Dergisi* 17 (1996): 117–120. Istanbul Tarih Vakfı.

Güntekin, R. N. *Yaprak dökümü, İnkilap ve Aka Kitabevleri*. Istanbul: Milli Egitim Basimexi, 1971.

Gürbilek, N. "Taşra Sıkıntısı." *Defter* 7, no. 22 (1994): 74–92.

Gürpınar, H. R. *Şık*. Istanbul: Pınar Yayınevi, 1964 (1889).

———. *Kadın Erkekleşince*. Istanbul: 1974 (1916).

Güvemli, Z. *Yahya Kemal ve Şiirleri*. Istanbul: Yeni Mecmua Yayını, Şaka Matbaası, 1948.

Hafiz. *The Divan-i Hafiz*. Bethesda, MD: Iranbooks, 1997.

Hakkı, İ. "Yeni Mimari Değişikleri." *Yeni Adam*, 15 Kanunu Sani 1934.

Halbwachs, M. *On Collective Memory*. Chicago: University of Chicago Press, 1992.

Harvey, D. *The Condition of Postmodernity*. London: Blackwell, 1989.

Havel, V. "The Need for Transcendence in the Postmodern World." *The Futurist*, July–August 1995. http://dieoff.org/page38.htm (accessed January 19, 2007).

Hisar, A. *Geçmiş Zaman Fıkraları (ve) Ali Nizamı Beyin Alafrangalığı ve Şeyhliği*. Istanbul: Ötüken Neşriyat, 1977 (1952).

———. "Resimler Karşısında Duygular." In Boğaziçi Yalıları (ve) Geçmiş Zaman Köşkleri, 4:180–187. Istanbul: Ötüken Neşriyat, Abdülhak Şinasi Hisar Bütün Eserleri, 1978.

Hisar, A. Ş, İstanbul ve Pierre Loti. Istanbul: Baha Matbaası, 1958.

———. Geçmiş Zaman Köşkleri: Boğaziçi Yalıları. Istanbul, Varlık Yayınevi, 1968 (1954).

Hobsbawm, E., and H. Trevor-Ranger, eds. The Invention of Tradition. Cambridge: Cambridge University Press, 1983.

Holub, R. C. Reception Theory. A Critical Introduction. London: Methuen, 1984.

Hüsameddin, H. Amasya Tarihi. Amasya Belediyesi Kültür Yayınları (1986).

İstanbul Belediyesi. İstanbul Şehri Rehberi. Istanbul: Matbaacılık ve Neşriyat Türk Anonim Şirketi ve Alâeddin Klişehane ve Matbaası, 1934.

"İş ve Eserde Her Telakkiden 75 Türk Meşuru Arasında Nefs Muhasebesi." Büyük Doğu (2 Kasım-Cuma 1945): 6.

Işın, E. "Celâl Esad Arseven Üzerinem." Celâl Esad Arseven: Eski Galata ve Binaları, edited by Ç. Gülersoy. Istanbul: Çelik Gülersoy Vakfı İstanbul Kütüphanesi Yayınları, 1989.

Jackson, P. Maps of Meaning: An Introduction to Cultural Geography. London: Unwin Hyman, 1989.

James, W. "Conception." In The Principles of Psychology, chap. 12, n. 17, 1890. http://psychclassics.yorku.ca/James/Principles/prin12.htm (accessed January 2007).

James, W. "The Principles of Psychology." In Great Books of the Western World: The Great Ideas, edited by R. M. Hutchins, M. J. Adler, and W. Gorman. Chicago: Wm. Benton, Encyclopaedia Britannica, 53, 1952 (1890). http://psychclassics .yorku.ca/James/Principles/index.htm (accessed January 2007).

James, W. "Memory." In The Principles of Psychology, chap. 16, 1890. http://psychclassics.asu.edu/James/Principles/prin16.htm (accessed January 2007).

Johnston, R. J. Philosophy and Human Geography: An Introduction to Contemporary Approaches. London: Edward Arnold, 1983.

Jones, R. A. "Durkheim's 'The Rules of Sociological Method.'" In Emile Durkheim: An Introduction to Four Major Works, edited by R. A. Jones, 60–81. Beverly Hills, CA: Sage, 1895.

Kandioti, D. "Gendering the Modern: On Missing Dimensions in the Study of Turkish Modernity." In Rethinking Modernity and National Identity in Turkey, edited by Sibel Bozdoğan and Reşat Kasaba, chap. 8. Seattle: University of Washington Press, 1997.

Kansu, A. The Revolution of 1908 in Turkey. Leiden: E. J. Brill, 1997.

Karaosmanoğlu, Y. K. Excerpts from "Mansion for Rent." In An Anthology of Turkish Literature, edited by K. Silay, 106–108. Bloomington: Indiana University Press, 1996 (1922).

———. Kiralık Konak. Istanbul: İletişim, 1996 (1922).

———. *Sodom ve Gomore.* Istanbul: Remzi Kitabevi, 1928.

Karpat, K. *Ottoman Population 1830–1914, Demographic and Social Characteristics.* Madison: University of Wisconsin Press, 1985.

Kelly, J. D., and M. Kaplan. "History, Structure, and Ritual." *Annual Review of Anthropology* 19 (1990): 119–150.

Kemal, N. "Aile." *İbret* 56 (Teşrinisani 1288, Nov. 19, 1872): 7.

———. *Zavallı Çocuk—Üç fasıldan ibaret tiyatro oyunu* (Poor Child—A Play in Three Acts). Istanbul: Kenan Basımevi ve Klişe Fabrikası, 1940 (1873).

———. *İntibah: Sergüzeşt-i Ali Bey (İntibah: Ali Bey'in Sergüzeşt).* Istanbul: Inkilap Kitabevi, 1960 (1876).

Kemal, O. *Baba Evi.* Istanbul: Varlık Yayınları, 1963 (1949).

Keyman, F. *Kemalism, Modernity and Tradition: The Question of Democracy in Turkey.* Paper presented at the Middle East Studies Association annual meeting, San Francisco, 1997.

Khan, S. "Memory Work: The Reciprocal Framing of Self and Place in Émigré Autobiographies." In *Memory and Architecture*, edited by Eleni Bastea. Albuquerque: University of New Mexico Press, 2004.

Kılıç, A. *50 Yıllık Yaşantımız:1923–1933.* Istanbul: Milliyet Gazetesi Yayınları, 1975.

Kısakürek, N. F. *Ahşap Konak.* Istanbul: Bedir Yayınevi, 1964.

Koloğlu, O. "Hüseyin Cahit Yalçın." In *İstanbul Ansiklopedisi*, edited by H. Ayhan, 7:414. Istanbul: Kültür Bakanlığı ve Tarih Vakfı'nın Ortak Yayınları, 1993.

Kömürcüoğlu, E. *Ankara Evleri.* Istanbul: İstanbul Matbaacılık, 1950 (1944).

Kongar, E. "Turkey's Cultural Transformation." In *The Transformation of Turkish Culture: The Atatürk Legacy*, edited by G. Renda and C. M. Kortepeter, 19–68. Princeton, NJ: Kingston Press, 1986.

Kostof, S. "Cities and Turfs." *Design Book Review* Fall (1986): 35–39.

Kostof, S. *America By Design.* New York: Oxford University Press, 1987.

Koyunoğlu, M. H. "Türk Mimari" (in Ottoman Turkish). *Türk Yurdu* 3, no. 16 (1928): 42–44, 197–199.

———. "Ankara Evleri." *Türk Yurdu* 3, no. 23 (1929): 46–47.

Koz, M. S. "Ali Rıza Bey." In *İstanbul Ansiklopedisi*, edited by H. Ayhan, 1:200. Istanbul: Kültür Bakanlığı ve Tarih Vakfı'nın Ortak Yayınları, 1993.

Köprülü, M. F. "Naima." *Encyclopedia of Islam*, new ed., edited by C. E. Bosworth, 4:952. Leiden: E.J. Brill, 1996.

———. *Some Observations on the Influence of Byzantine Institutions on Ottoman Institutions*, translated by Gary Leiser. Ankara: Türk Tarih Kurumu, 1999.

Köroğlu, E. *Gidenle Gelmeyenin Eşiğinde: A. H. Tanpınar'ın Romanlarında Zaman Kavramı.* Istanbul: Boğaziçi Üniversitesi, Sosyal Bilimler Enstitüsü, Türk Dili ve Edebiyatı Bölümü, 1996.

Kuban, D. "Anadolu-Türk Şehri: Tarihi Gelişmesi, Sosyal ve Fizikıkı Özellikleri Üzerine Bazi Gelişmeler." *Vakıflar Dergisi* 7 (1968): 53–73.

———. "Celâl Esad Arseven ve Kürt Sanatı Kavramı." Mimarlık 7 (72 Ekim 1969): 18.

———. The Turkish Hayat House. Istanbul: Eren Yayıncılık ve Kitapcilik Ltd., 1995.

———. Istanbul, an Urban History. Istanbul: The Economic and Social History Foundation of Turkey, 1996.

Kurdakul, S. Şairler yazarlar sözlüğu. Istanbul: Bilgi Yayınevi, 1971.

Küçükerman, Ö. Anadolu'daki Geleneksel Türk Evinde Mekân Organizasiyonu Açısından Odalar. Istanbul, 1973.

———. Kişi-çevre ilişkilerinde çağdaş gelişimler. Istanbul: Istanbul Devlet Güzel Sanat Akademisi, 1978.

———. Turkish House in Search of Spatial Identity. Istanbul: Türkiye Turing ve Otomobil Kurumu, 1978.

Lachmann, Renate. Memory and Literature: Intertextuality in Russian Modernism. Minneapolis: University of Minnesota Press, 1997.

Lara, A. "The Stories We're All In Together." San Francisco Chronicle, 1997, B12.

Le Corbusier. The Modulor: A Harmonious Measure to the Human Scale, Universally Applicable to Architecture and Mechanics. London: Faber and Faber, 1954.

———. Vers une architecture. Paris: Arthaud, 1977.

Lefebvre, H. The Production of Space. Oxford: Blackwell, 1991.

Leiser, G. "A Brief History of Ankara. Part II." In History of Ankara, with T. Cross. Vacaville, CA: Indian Ford Press, 1998.

LeVine, M. Re-imagining the Development of Jaffa and Tel Aviv. Paper presented at the Middle East Studies Association annual meeting, Providence, RI, 1996.

Lewis, B. The Emergence of Modern Turkey. London: Oxford University Press, 1968.

Lewis, P. W. "Three Related Problems in the Formulation of Laws in Geography." The Professional Geographer 17, no. 5 (1965): 24–27.

Ley, D. "Modernism, Post Modernism, and the Struggle for Place. Seminar on the Power of Place." Post Modern Topics in Architecture and Urban Planning. Syracuse University, New York, 1986.

Lowenthal, D. The Past Is a Foreign Country. Cambridge: Cambridge University Press, 1985.

Lowenthal, D., and M. J. Bowden, eds. Geographies of the Mind. Oxford: Oxford University Press, 1976.

Lynch, K. The Image of the City. Cambridge, MA: MIT Press, 1960.

Mahfouz, N. Palace Walk. New York: Anchor Books/Doubleday, 1956.

Mardin, Ş. The Genesis of Young Ottoman Thought. Princeton, NJ: Princeton University Press, 1962.

———. "Super Westernization in Urban Life in the Ottoman Empire in the Last Quarter of the Nineteenth Century." In Turkey, Geographic and Social Perspectives, edited by P. Benedict, E. Tümertekin, and F. Mansur, 403–446. Leiden: E. J. Brill, 1974.

———. *Religion and Social Change in Modern Turkey: The Case of Beiüzzaman Said Nursi*. Albany: SUNY Press, 1989.

———. "Cultural Change and the Intellectual: A Study of the Effects of Secularization in Modern Turkey: Necip Fazil and the Nakşibendi." In *Cultural Transitions in the Middle East*, edited by S. E. Mardin. Leiden: E.J. Brill, 1994.

McGarty, C., S. A. Haslam, et al. "The Effects of Salient Group Memberships on Persuasion." *Small Group Research* 25 (1994): 267–293.

McMurtry, L. *Walter Benjamin at the Dairy Queen: Reflections on Sixty and Beyond*. New York: Simon & Schuster, 2001.

"Memory and Imagination." In *Great Books of the Western World: The Great Ideas*, edited by R. Hutchins, J. Adler, et al. Chicago: Wm. Benton, Encyclopaedia Britannica, 1952.

Menemencioğlu, N., ed. *The Penguin Book of Turkish Verse*. New York: Penguin Books, 1978.

Midhat, A. *Felâtun ile Râkim Efendi*. Istanbul: Kırkanbar Matbaası, 1875.

———. *Henüz On Yedi Yaşında*. Istanbul: Vakit Matbaası, 1943 (1881).

Mills, A. "Boundaries of the Nation in the Space of the Urban: Landscape and Social Memory in Istanbul." *Cultural Geographies* 13, no. 3 (2000): 367–394.

Mitchell, T. *Colonising Egypt*. Berkeley and Los Angeles: University of California Press, 1991.

Mithat, A. *Jön Türk*. Istanbul: İtimat Kütüphanesi, 1910.

———. *Avrupa Adab-ı Muaşereti yahud Alafranga* (European, or *Alafranga*, Etiquette). Istanbul: Akçağ Yayınlar, 2001 (1894).

Moravanszky, A. *Competing Visions: Aesthetic Invention and Social Imagination in Central European Architecture, 1867–1918*. Cambridge, MA: MIT Press, 1998.

Mortaş, A. "*Evlerimiz*." *Arkitekt* 6, no. 1 (1936): 24.

Murad, M. M. *Turfanda mı, yoksa turfa mı?* Istanbul: Kultur Bakanlığı, 1980 (1891).

Mutluay, R. *100 Soruda Çağdaş Türk Edebiyatı "1908–1972."* Istanbul: Gerçek Yayınevi, 1973.

———. *Elli Yılın Türk Edebiyatı* (Turkish Literature of the Past Fifty Years). Istanbul: Baha Matbaası, 1973.

Muzaffer, M. "*Memuriyet Sizin Olsun! Yeni Kavuştuğum Evim Bana Yeter*." *Muhit* (Surroundings) 4, no. 46 (1932): 36–37.

Münir, H. "*Yakup Kadri ile bir Saat*." *Yedigün* 11 (8 Şubat, 1928): 14–16.

———. "*Büyük Elçimiz Hamdullah Suphi Dinlerken*." *Yedigün* 12 (4 Birinciteşrin 1928): 14–17.

Nalbantoğlu, G. "The Birth of an Aesthetic Discourse in Ottoman Architecture." *METU Journal of the Faculty of Architecture* 8, no. 2 (1988): 115–122.

———. "Architects, Style, and Power: The Turkish Case in the 1930s." *Twenty-One* 1, no. 2 (Spring 1990): 38–53.

———. "Between Civilization and Culture: Appropriation of Traditional Dwelling Forms in Early Republican Turkey." *Journal of Architectural Education* 47, no. 2 (1993): 66–74.

Nalbantoğlu, U. *An Architectural and Historical Survey of the Development of the "Apartment Building" in Ankara: 1923–1950.* Ankara, 1981.

Nayır, Z. "Arnavutköy." MET U *Journal of the Faculty of Architecture* 4, no. 2 (1978).

Nazim, N. *Zehra.* Ankara: Dün-Bugün Yayınevi, 1960 (1890?).

Necatigil, B. *Çevre.* Istanbul: Varlık, 1951.

Necipoğlu, G. *Architecture, Ceremonial, and Power: The Topkapi Palace in the Fifteenth and Sixteenth Centuries.* Cambridge, MA: MIT Press, 1991.

Nirven, S. "*Cumba.*" In *İstanbul Ansiklopedisi,* edited by R. E. Koçu, 7:3621–3623. Istanbul: Reşad Ekrem Koçu ve Mehmed Ali Aksoy İstanbul Ansiklopedisi ve Neşriyat Kollektif Şirketi, 1961.

Nisari, A. *Metinli Türk Edebiyatı, Liselerin Dördüncü Sınıfları için. Millî Eğitim Vekilliğince ders Kitabı Olarak Kabul Edilmiştir.* Ankara: Inkilâp Kitabevi, 1953.

Nora, P., ed. *Realms of Memory: The Construction of the French Past.* European Perspectives Series. New York: Columbia University Press, 1996.

Nutku, Ö. "A Panorama of Turkish Theater under the Leadership of Atatürk." In *The Transformation of Turkish Culture: The Atatürk Legacy,* edited by G. N. Renda and C. M. Kortepeter, 165–178. Princeton, NJ: Kingston Press, 1986.

Nürettin, İ. "*Eski Türk Evleri.*" *Fikirler* 1/20 (1928): 6ff.

Ödekan, A. *Türkiye'de 50 yılda yayınlanmış Arkeoloji, Sanat Tarihi ve Mimarlık Tarihi ile ilgili yayınlar bibliografyası (1923–1973).* Istanbul: İstanbul Teknik Üniversitesi Mamarlık Fakultesi Yayınları, 1974.

Okay, O. *Batı Medeniyet Karşısında Ahmed Midhat Efendi.* Ankara: Baylan Matbaası, 1975.

Önöl, H. S. "*Cumbadan Rumbaya.*" In *İstanbul Ansiklopedisi,* 7:3623–3624. Istanbul: Reşad Ekrem Koçu ve Mehmed Ali Aksoy İstanbul Ansiklopedisi ve Neşriyat Kollektif Şirketi, 1961.

Orga, I. *Portrait of a Turkish Family.* New York: Macmillan, 1950.

Orleans, P., and S. Schmidt. *Mapping the City: Environmental Cognition of Urban Residents.* EDRA I. Proceedings of the Ninth Annual Environmental Design Research Association, Tucson, AZ, 1970.

Ortaç, Y. Z. "*Türk Evleri*" (Turkish Houses). *Çinaraltı* 1 (1941): 3.

———. *Üç Katlı Ev.* Istanbul: Aydabir Yayınları, 1953.

Ortaylı, İ. "The Family in Ottoman Society." In *Family in Turkish Society,* edited by T. Erder, 93–104. Ankara: Turkish Social Science Association, 1985.

———. *İstanbul'dan Sayfalar.* Istanbul: Hil Yayın, 1987.

Osman, R. *Edirne Rehnuması.* Vilayet Matbaası, 1920 (1337 AH).

Özal, M. *Cephelerden Kurtuluş Savaşı'na: İmparatorluktan Cumhuriyet'e.* Erdine: Türk Cumhuriyet Kültür Bakanlığı, 1992.

Ozankaya, Ö. "Reflections of Şemseddin Sami on Women in the Period Before the Advent of Secularism." In *Family in Turkish Society*, edited by T. Erder, 127–145. Ankara: Turkish Social Science Association, 1985.

Özcan, A. "*Açılış Konuşması.*" In *İslam, Gelenek ve Yenileşme: 1. Uluslararası "Kutlu Doğum" İlmi Toplantısı /Islam, Tradition and Change: The First International "Kutlu Doğum" Symposium*, edited by A. Özcan, 1–3. Istanbul: ısam:İslam Araştırmaları Merkezi (Türkiye Diyanet Vakfı), 1996.

Özcan, N. "*Darülelhan.*" In *İslam Ansiklopedisi*, edited by H. Ayhan, 8:518–520. Istanbul: Türkiye Diyanet Vakfı İslam Ansiklopedisi Genel Müdürlüğü, 1986.

Özturk, Serdar. "Karagoz Co-Opted: Turkish Shadow Theatre of the Early Republic (1923–1945)." *Asian Theatre Journal* 23, no. 2 (Fall 2006): 292–313.

Öztürkmen, A. "The Role of People's Houses in the Making of National Culture in Turkey." *New Perspectives on Turkey* 11 (1994): 159–181.

Paçacı, G. "*Darü'l-elhân.*" In *İstanbul Ansiklopedisi*, edited by H. Ayhan, 2:556–558. Istanbul: Kültür Bakanlığı ve Tarih Vakfı'nın Ortak Yayınları, 1993.

Paksoy, H. B. "Nationality and Religion: Three Observations from Ömer Seyfettin." In *Central Asian Survey* (Oxford), 3, no. 3 (1984): 109–115. http://vlib.iue.it/carrie/texts/carrie_books/paksoy-6/cae20.html (accessed Jan. 6, 2007).

Pamuk, Orhan. *Istanbul: Memories and the City.* New York: Knopf, 2005.

Parla, Jale. *Babalar ve Oğullar.* Istanbul: İletişim Yayınları, 1990.

Parmenter, B. M. *Giving Voice to Stones: Place and Identity in Palestinian Literature.* Austin: University of Texas Press, 1994.

Patrick, M. M. *Under Five Sultans.* New York: Century Co., 1929.

Pavlides, E. "Architectural Change in a Vernacular Environment, A Case Study of Eressos, Greece." EDRA: *Environmental Design Research Association Journal* 16 (1985): 57–65.

Pekean, I. *Te Inchpes Hruandanin Aghjike Berdakaghak hars Tarin* (How the Girl from Hruandanin Was Taken as a Bride to Berdakaghak). Filatelfia: Tparan "Krunk"-I, 1958.

Petkov, K. *Infidels, Turks, and Women: The South Slavs in the German Mind, ca. 1400–1600.* New York: Peter Lang, 1997.

Preziosi, D. "Introduction: Power, Structure, and Architectural Function." In *The Ottoman City and Its Parts: Urban Structure and Social Order (Subsidia Balcanica, Islamica et Turcica, 3)*, edited by I. A. Bierman, R. A. Abou-El-Haj, and D. Preziosi. New York: Aristide D. Caratzas, 1991.

Prokić, D. "*Muslimani u Bosni i Hercegovini*" (Muslims in Bosnia and Hercegovina). In *Savremena Bosna i Hercegovina* (Contemporary Bosnia and Hercegovina), edited by M. V. Knežević, 30. Subotica, 1928.

Rasim, Ü. "*Eski İstanbul Kış.*" *Resimli Tarih Mecmua* 3 (1952): 1288–1290.

Razi, F. "*Ay Hanımefendi.*" *Resimli Şark* 25 (1931): 19–21.

Refik, A. *Eski İstanbul.* Istanbul: Kanaat Kütphanesi, 1931.

———. *On Altıncı Asırda İstanbul Hayatı (1553–1591)*, 2nd ed. Istanbul: Maarif Vekaleti, 1935.

Renda, G. "Wall Paintings in Turkish Houses." In *Fifth International Congress of Turkish Art*, edited by G. Feher, 711–735. Budapest: Akademiai Kiado (Hungarian Academy of the Sciences), 1978.

———. *A History of Turkish Painting*. Geneva: Palasar, 1988.

———. "Resimde Çağdaşlaşma / Modernization in Painting." In *İstanbul: Dünya Kenti/World City*, edited by T. Vakfı, 176–183. Istanbul: Türkiye Ekonomik Toplumsal Tarih Vakfı, 1996.

Safa, P. *Cumbadan Rumbaya*. Istanbul: Kanaat Kitabevi, 1936.

———. "Modern Türk Kızı." In *Modern Türkiye Mecmuası* 1 (1938): 1–3.

———. "Utanmaya Dair." *Yedigün* 12 (8 İkincitesrin. 1938): 14–16.

———. *Fatih-Harbiye*. Istanbul: Ötüken Yayınevi, 1976 (1931).

Sahir, C. "Altıncı Resim Sergisi." *Hayat* (1929): 9–15.

Said, E. W. *Orientalism*. New York: Pantheon Books, 1978.

———. *Culture and Imperialism*. New York: Knopf/Random House, 1993.

Sakaoğlu, N. "İstanbulin." In *İstanbul Ansiklopedisi*, edited by H. Ayhan, 4:253. Istanbul: Kültür Bakanlığı ve Tarih Vakfı'nın Ortak Yayınları, 1993.

———. "Yangınlar: Osmanlı Dönemi." In *İstanbul Ansiklopedisi*, edited by H. Ayhan, 7:427–438. Istanbul: Kültür Bakanlığı ve Tarih Vakfı'nın Ortak Yayınları, 1993.

Sami, Ş. *Taaşuk-i Talât ve Fitnat* (The Romance of Talât and Fitnat). Ankara: Ankara Üniversitesi Dil ve Tarih-Coğrafya Fakültesi, 1978 (1872).

Sayar, A. G. *A. Süheyl Ünver: Hayatı, Şahsiyeti ve Eserleri: 1898–1986*. Istanbul: Eren, 1994.

Sayı. "Ali Rıza'nın Hayatı ve Eserleri." *Osmanlı Ressamlar Cemiyeti Gazetesi* 18 (1912): 100 (1330AH).

Scarparo, S. "An Analysis of the Video *One Way Street* and of Walter Benjamin's Dialectical Thinking." *Deep South* 1, no. 20 (May 1995). http://www.otago.ac.nz/ DeepSouth/vol1no2/scarparo_issue2html (accessed August 1997).

Schick, I. C. "The Women of Turkey as Sexual Personae: Images from Western Literature." In *Deconstructing Images of "the Turkish Woman,"* edited by Z. Arat, 83–100. New York, St. Martin's Press, 1998.

Schimmel, A. *Deciphering the Signs of God*. New York: SUNY Press, 1994.

Sedadkent "Klasik Sedadkent—Çağdaş Sedadkent." *İstanbul* 17 (1996): 4–5.

Seno, C. "Eski Türk Evi." In *Türkiye Turing ve Otomobil Kurumu Belleteni* Kasim-Aralık (1945): 15–17.

Şenyer, E. "Traditional Turkish Puppet Shadow Play, Hacivat and Karagöz" and additional titles. In Turkish and English. http://www.karagoz.net/ (accessed February 2007).

Şerifoğlu, Ömer Faruk. *Hoca Ali Rıza*. TBMM Milli Saraylar. İstanbul: Yapı Kredi Yayınları, 2005.

Sevengil, R. A. *İstanbul Nasıl Eğleniyordu? 1453–1927'ye kadar*. İstanbul, İletişim Yayınları. (1985) (1927)

Sey, Y. "To House the New Citizens: Housing Polices and Mass Housing." In *Modern Turkish Architecture*, edited by R. Holod and A. Evin, 153–177. Philadelphia: University of Pennsylvania Press, 1984.

Seyfeddin, Ö. "*Ashab-ı Kehfimiz: İctimaî Roman*." Istanbul: Kanaat Kitaphanesi, 1918.

———. "*İlk Düşen Ak*." Istanbul: Rafet Zaimler Yayınevi, 1962, 67–68 (1918).

———. "The Secret Temple (*Gizli Mabet*)." In *An Anthology of Turkish Literature*, edited by K. Silay, 270–273. Bloomington: Indiana University Press, 1996 (1923).

———. "*Harem*." *Harem: Ömer Seyfettin Bütün Eserleri*, vol. 2. Istanbul, Dergâh Yayınlari, 2000.

Sezai, S. *Sergüzeşt: Bir Esir Kızın Romanı*. Istanbul: Milli Eğitim Basımevı, 1972 (1899).

Shaw, C., and M. Chase, eds. *The Imagined Past: History and Nostalgia*. Manchester: Manchester University Press, 1989.

Shaw, S. J., and E. K. Shaw. *History of the Ottoman Empire and Modern Turkey: Reform, Revolution, and Republic. The Rise of Modern Turkey 1808–1975*. Cambridge: Cambridge University Press, 1977.

"Sign and Symbol." In *Great Books of the Western World: The Great Ideas*, edited by R. Hutchins, J. Adler, et al. Chicago: Wm. Benton, Encyclopaedia Britannica, 1952.

Silay, K. *Nedim and the Poetics of the Ottoman Court: Medieval Inheritance and the Need for Change*. Indiana University Turkish Studies Series. Bloomington, IN, 1994.

Silay, K., ed. *An Anthology of Turkish Literature*. Indiana University Turkish Studies Series. Bloomington, IN, 1996.

Simavi, S. *Hürriyet Apartmanı: Dört Perdelik Piyes*. Istanbul: Yedigün Neşriyatı, 1940.

"*Şişli*." In *İstanbul Ansiklopedisi*, edited by H. Ayhan, 7:184–185. Istanbul: Kültür Bakanlığı ve Tarih Vakfı'nın Ortak Yayınları, 1993.

Siyavuşgil, S. *Karagöz: Its History, Its Characters, Its Mystical Spirit*. Istanbul: Milli Eğitim Basımevi, 1961.

Skeates, R. "What Can the Annaliste Approach Offer the Archaeologist?" *Papers from the Institute of Archaeology* I (1990): 56–61.

Skidmore, Owings, and Merrill, Architects. *Construction, Town Planning and Housing in Turkey*. New York: Skidmore, Owings and Merrill, Architects, 1951.

Soja, E. W. *Postmodern Geographies: The Reassertion of Space in Critical Social Theory*. London: Verso, 1989.

———. Postmodern Urbanization. In *Postmodern Cities and Spaces*, edited by S. Walker and K. Gibson. Cambridge, MA: Blackwell, 1995.

————. *Thirdspace: Journeys to Los Angeles and Other Real and Imagined Places.* Oxford: Blackwell, 1996.

Sönmez, E. "Turkish Women in Turkish Literature of the Nineteenth Century." *Die Welt des Islams* 12, no. 1–2 (1973): 1–73.

Soysal, M. *Tarihten Günümüze Anadolu'da Konut ve Yerleşmen'in Öyküsü.* Istanbul Türkiye Ekonomik ve Toplumsal Tarih Vakfı, 1996.

Spasojević, B. *Arhitektura stambenish palata austrougarskog period a u sarajevu.* Sarajevo: "Svjetlost" OOUR Zavod za Udžbenike i Nastavna Sredstva, 1988.

Stea, D. "Architectural Cognition and the Architecture of Human Settlement: An Interdisciplinary Approach." EDRA 9. Proceedings of the Ninth Annual Environmental Design Research Association, Tucson, AZ, 1978.

Stephens, J. G. *Incidents of Travel in Greece, Turkey, Russia and Poland.* New York: Cosimo Classics, 2007 (1839).

Suphi, H. *"Eski Türk Evleri."* *Türk Yurdu* 5 (1912): 1216–1221.

————. *"Eski Türk Evleri."* *Türk Yurdu* 6 (1912): 2063–2069.

Suphi, H. *"Türk Ocakları Merkez Binasının Açılma Nutku."* *Türk Yurdu* 4–24 (29–223 Mayıs 1930): 77ff.

Tagliaventi, G. *Urban Renaissance: A Vision of Europe.* Bologne: Triennale II Exhibition of Architecture and Urbanism, Istanbul Habitat II, 1996.

Tanpınar, A. H. *Beş Şehir.* Ankara: Ulku, 1946.

————. *"Türk Edebiyatında Cereyanlar."* In *Edebiyat Üzerine Makalelerm,* edited by A. H. Tanpınar. Istanbul: M.E.B. Devlet Kitapları, 1969.

————. *Sahnenin Dışındakiler.* Istanbul: Büyük Kitaplık, 1973 (1950).

————. *Yaşadığım Gibi.* Istanbul: Dergah Yayınları, 1977.

Tansuğ, S. *Çağdaş Türk Sanatı.* Istanbul: Remzi Kitabevi, 1986.

Tanyeli, U. *"Anadolu'da Bizans, Osmanlı Öncesi ve Osmanli Dönemlerinde Yerleşme ve Barınma Düzeni* / Housing and Settlement Patterns in the Byzantine, Pre-Ottoman and Ottoman Periods in Anatolia." In *Tarihden Günümüze Anadoldu'da Konut ve Yerleşme (Housing and Settlement in Anatolia, A Historical Perspective),* edited by Y. Sey, 405–471. Istanbul: Türkiye Ekonomik ve Toplumsal Tarih Vakfı, 1996.

————. *"Osmanlı Barınma Kültüründe Batılılaşma-Modernleşme: yeni bir simegeler dizgesinin oluşumu* / Westernization-Modernization in the Ottoman Wohnkultur: The Evolution of a New Set of Symbols." *Tarihden Günümüze Anadoldu'da Konut ve Yerleşme (Housing and Settlement in Anatolia, A Historical Perspective),* edited by Y. Sey, 284–297. Istanbul: Türkiye Ekonomik ve Toplumsal Tarih Vakfı, 1996.

Taragchean, A. S. *Marzuani hay awetaranakan zhoghovurde (Patmagirk Marzuani hay awetaranakanutean).* Pruklin: Tparan Mshak, 1960.

Tayla, H. *"Türk Evi."* *Sanat* 6 (June 1977): 68–76.

Taylor, R. "On the Shores of the Bosphorus." *Hali* 9 (1987): 50–52.

Tekeli, I. "The Social Context of the Development of Architecture in Turkey." In *Modern Turkish Architecture*, edited by R. Holod and A. Evin, 9–33. Philadelphia: University of Pennsylvania Press, 1984.

———. "Nineteenth Century Transformation of Istanbul Metropolitan Area." In *Villes Ottomanes à la Fin De L'Empire*, edited by P. Dumont and F. Georgeon, 22–36. Paris: L'Harmattan, 1992.

———. "*Türkiye'de Siyasal Düşüncenin Gelişimi Konusunda Bir Ust Anlatı*" (A Meta Narrative on the Development of Political Thought in Turkey), in *Modern Türkiye'de Siyasi Düsünce*, Cilt 3, *Modernlesme ve Batıcılık*. *İletısim* 19–42, 2002.

TEM. "*Hidiv Köşkleri*" (advertisement). *Skylife, Turkish Airlines Magazine*, 1996, 33.

Terdiman, R. *Present Past: Modernity and the Memory Crisis*. Ithaca, NY: Cornell University Press, 1993.

Thomas, L. V. *A Study of Naima*. New York: New York University Press, 1972.

Thompson, M. P. "Reception Theory and the Interpretation of Historical Meaning." *History and Theory* 32, no. 3 (October 1993): 248–272.

Timur, S. "*Geçmiş Günler*." *Seçilmiş Hikâyeler Dergisi* 6 (1952): 37–42, 54.

Tolman, E. C. "Cognitive Maps in Rats and Men." *Psychology Review* 55 (1948): 189–208.

Topuzlu, C. *Yarınki İstanbul*. Istanbul: Kenan Basımevi, 1937.

———. *80 Yıllık Hatıralarım*. Istanbul: Güven, 1951.

Tuan, Y. *Topophilia, a study of environmental perception, attitudes and values*. Englewood Cliffs, NJ: Prentice Hall, 1974.

"*Türk Ocakları Merkez Binası*." *Türk-Yurdu* 4–24 (Mart–Nisan 1930): 79–81.

"*Türkiye Turing ve Otomobil Kurumu* (TTOK)." In *İstanbul Ansiklopedisi*, edited by H. Ayhan, 7:316–319. Istanbul: Kültür Bakanlığı ve Tarih Vakfı'nın Ortak Yayınları, 1993.

Turner, V. *From Ritual to Theatre: The Human Seriousness of Play*. New York: PAJ Publications, 1982.

Unat, F. *Osmanlı Sefirleri ve Sefaretnâmeleri*. Ankara: Türk Tarih Kurumu Basımevi, 1968.

UNICEF. *The Environment and Youth (Çevre ve Biz Gençler)*: Youth Painting and Literature Competition (Gençlerarası Resim ve Yazın Yarışması). Ankara: ISKI, 1992.

Ünver, A. S. "*Edirne Evleri*." *Yeni Mecmua* 41, no. 85–86 (1923) (1339).

———. "*Şark Odası*" (The Oriental Room, in Ottoman Turkish). *Milli Mecmua* 25–48 (38, 1923): 626–627.

———. "*Türk Evi*" (in Ottoman Turkish). *Milli Mecmua* 41 (10 Haziran 1923): 668–670.

———. "*Eski Türk Evinde Ocak*" (The Hearth in the Old Turkish House, in Ottoman Turkish). *Milli Mecmua* 6, no. 68 (1926): 1098–1011.

———. "*İzmit Hatıraları*" (Memories of İzmit, in Ottoman Turkish). *Milli Mecmua* 47 (72 Teşrini Evvel 1926): 1163–1165.

————. *Ressam Ali Rıza*. Istanbul, 1949.

————. *Ressam Üsküdarlı Ali Rıza Bey: Hayatı ve Eserleri. 1858–1930*. Istanbul, 1949.

————. *Dr. Rıfat Osman: Edirne Sarayı*. Istanbul: Türk Tarih Kurumu Yayınları, 1957.

————. "Ali Riza Bey (Üsküdarlı)." In *İstanbul Ansiklopedisi*, 2:703–704. Istanbul: Reşad Ekrem Koçu ve Mehmed Ali Aksoy İstanbul Ansiklopedisi ve Neşriyat Kollektif Şirketi, 1959.

————. *Ressam Ali Rıza Bey'e Göre Yarım Asır Önce Kahvehanelerimiz ve Eşyası*. Istanbul, 1967.

————. *Dr. Rıfat Osman'a göre Edirne Evleri ve Konakları*. Istanbul: Türkiye Turing ve Otomobil Kurumu, 1983 (1979).

Üstünkök, O. "Ten Years with Seventeen-ten: A Decade in the Conservation of Traditional Vernacular Houses." M.E.T.U. *Journal of the Faculty of Architecture, Ankara, Orta Doğu Teknik Üniversitesi. Mimarlık Fakültesi* 9, no. 2 (1989): 117–124.

Uşaklıgil, H. Z. *Aşk-i Memnun*. Istanbul: Hilmi Kitabevi, 1962 (1898).

Uysal, Zeynep Ciğdem. "'Architectural Type' as a Cultural Schema and Its Synectic Use in Architectural Design: Sedat Hakki Eldem's Typological Architecture in the Pursuit of Cultural Identity; Final Research Proposal." http://ncsudesign. org/content/baran/ddn701/uysal_ddn701_final.pdf (accessed Feb. 4, 2007).

Uzluk, S. "Ustad Ali Rıza Bey." *Servet-i Fünün* 1469 (1337), 1919.

Vecih, H. "Ankara Resim Sergisi Münasebetiyle." *Hayat* 31, 1927.

Vedad, H. "San'at'ta İnkilap" (The Revolution in Art)(in Ottoman Turkish). *Hayat*, 9–12, 1927.

Vervliet, R., ed. *Methods for the Study of Literature as Cultural Memory*. Proceedings of the XXth Congress of the International Comparative Literature Association, vol. 6. Amsterdam: Rodopi Bv Editions, 2000.

Volkan, V., and N. Itzkowitz. *Turks and Greeks: Neighbors in Conflict*. Huntingon: Eothen Press, 1994.

White, C. *Three Years in Constantinople*. London: H. Colburn, 1845.

Winfield, M., M. Q. Smith, S. Balance, and A. Powell, "The Yakapoğlu Konak: An Old Turkish House at Sürmene Kastil." *Anatolian Studies* 10 (1960): 197–203.

Witoszek, N. "Collective Memory and National Identity: The Case of Sweden, Germany and Italy." http://www2.hu-berlin.de/gemenskap/inhalt/publikationen/arbeitspapiere/ahe_1c.html (accessed January 2007).

Yalçın, H. "Ev Sevgisi." *Yedigün* 5 (119): 5 (1935).

————. *Edebî Hatıralar* (Literary Reminiscences). Istanbul: Akşam Kitaphanesi, 1935.

————. "Değişen Kadın." *Yedigün* 7 (158): 5 (1936).

————. "Ev ve Apartman." *Yedigün* 11 (265): (5 Nisan): 5 (1938).

Yaman, Z. Y. "*Osmanlı Ressamlar Cemiyeti.*" In *İstanbul Ansiklopedisi*, edited by H. Ayhan, 6:176–177. Istanbul: Kültür Bakanlığı ve Tarih Vakfı'nın Ortak Yayınları, 1993.

Yavuz, H. *Felsefe ve Ulusal Kültür.* Istanbul: Çağdaş Yayınları, 1975.

Yavuz, Y., and S. Özkan. "Finding a National Idiom: The First National Style." In *Modern Turkish Architecture*, edited by R. Holod and A. Evin, 51–57. Philadelphia: Univeristy of Pennsylvania Press, 1984.

"*Yeni Kamus*" (New Dictionary). *Kalem* 6 (1930): 5.

"*Yeni Resim Sergisi Münasebetiyle.*" *Akşam Gazetesi*, 25 Mayıs 1922.

Yetik, M. S. *Ressamlarımız.* Güzel Sanatlar Birliği Resim Neşriyatı, 1940.

Yurdu, T. "*Bir Aylık-Ocak Haberleri: Türk Ocakları Merkez Binasının Açılması.*" *Türk-Yurdu* 4–24 (Mayıs-Nisan 1930): 77–89.

Yurtbaşı, M. *A Dictionary of Turkish Proverbs.* Ankara: Turkish Daily News, 1993.

Yücel, A. "Pluralism Takes Command: The Turkish Architectural Scene Today." In *Modern Turkish Architecture*, edited by R. Holod and A. Evin, 119–152. Philadelphia: University of Pennsylvania Press, 1984.

Zeki, S. "Babamın Evi." *Hayat.* 4:17 (1928).

Zıya, A. "*Binanın İçinde Mimar.*" *Mimar* 1, no. 1 (1931): 14ff.

Ziya, C. "*Ev Döşemesi ve Bugünkü Ev Kültürü.*" *Resimli Şark* 10 (1931): 46–48.

Zürcher, E. J. *Political Opposition in the Early Turkish Republic: The Progressive Republican Party, 1924–1925.* Leiden: E.J. Brill, 1991.

———. *Turkey: A Modern History.* London: Taurus, 1997.

index